Eugène Atget: *Unknown Paris*

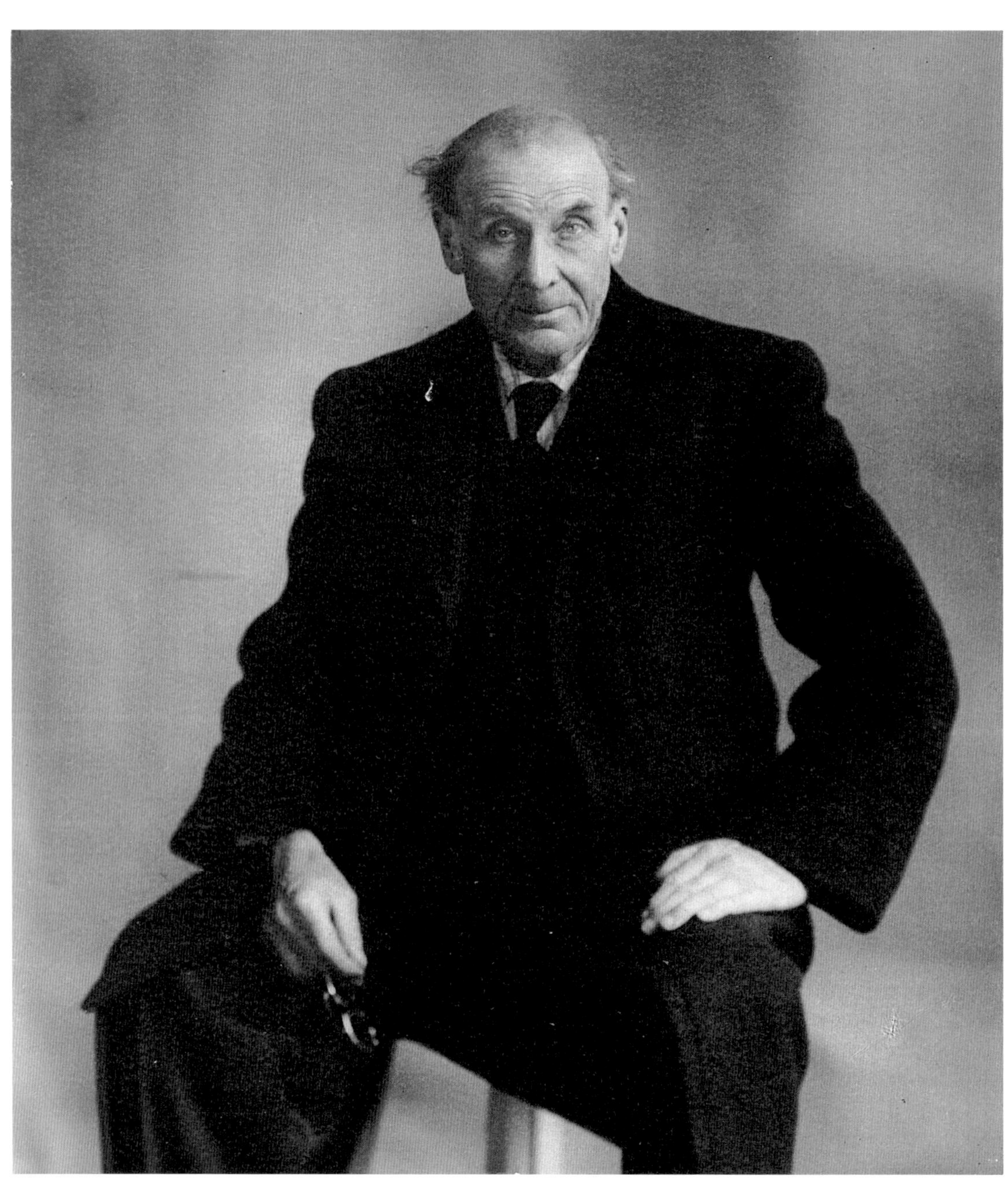

Ill. 1 Berenice Abbott, *Portrait of Eugène Atget*, 1927

Eugène Atget
Unknown Paris

David Harris

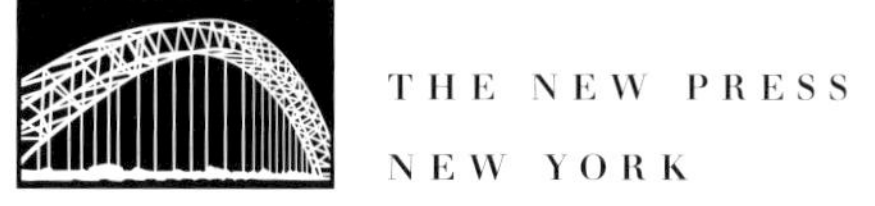

THE NEW PRESS
NEW YORK

Originally published in France as *Eugène Atget: Itinéraires parisiens*
by Editions des musées de la Ville de Paris/Editions du patrimoine
Published in the United States by The New Press, New York, 2003
Distributed by W.W. Norton & Company, Inc., New York

Page 199 constitutes an extension of this copyright page.

LIBRARY OF CONGRESS CATALOGING-IN-PUBLICATION DATA
Harris, David, 1950-
Eugène Atget: unknown Paris / David Harris.
p. cm.
Includes bibliographical references and index.
ISBN 1-56584-868-3 (hc.)—ISBN 1-56584-854-3 (pbk.)
1. Photography, Artistic. 2. Atget, Eugène, 1857–1927. 3. Paris (France)—Pictorial works.
I. Title.
TR653.H35 2003
779'.092—dc21
2003050961

The New Press was established in 1990 as a not-for-profit alternative to the large, commercial publishing houses currently dominating the book publishing industry. The New Press operates in the public interest rather than for private gain, and is committed to publishing, in innovative ways, works of educational, cultural, and community value that are often deemed insufficiently profitable.

The New Press
38 Greene Street, 4th floor
New York, NY 10013
www.thenewpress.com

In the United Kingdom:
6 Salem Road
London W2 4BU

Book design by Lovedog Studio

Printed in Canada

10 9 8 7 6 5 4 3 2 1

Contents

Preface and Acknowledgments

Eugène Atget: Unknown Paris is an English-language version of *Eugène Atget: Itinéraires parisiens* (Paris Musées and Éditions du patrimonine, 1999). The French-language publication constituted the catalogue for an exhibition of the same title, which was commissioned by Paris Musées and shown at the Musée Carnavalet in Paris from October 13, 1999, to January 16, 2000. The exhibition was circulated to the Museum of the City of New York, where it was shown from November 4, 2000, to February 4, 2001, and to the Art Gallery of Ontario in Toronto, where it was exhibited from February 28 to May 27, 2001.

Originally, *Eugène Atget: Itinéraires parisiens* was conceived as a complementary exhibition to one devoted to Berenice Abbott's massive project *Changing New York*, shown concurrently at the Musée Carnavalet. In addition to acknowledging Abbott's seminal role in championing Atget's work, *Itinéraires parisiens* was concerned with revealing how differently Atget approached the conceptual and practical aspects of photographing a city: While Abbott worked toward single and definitive images that would distill the essence of New York City, Atget constructed sequences and series of photographs that, in their cumulative effect, would describe the intimate character of Paris's historical spaces.

At the Musée Carnavalet, I am grateful to its director, Jean-Marc Léri, for his support of this project and providing me with the opportunity to present this new interpretation of Atget's architectural and urban photography. Françoise Reynaud, curator of photography, generously shared her intimate knowledge of Atget's work and arranged for me to have extended access to the museum's Atget collection. Through many conversations, she also contributed immeasurably to the development of my ideas, and dealt with many of the logistical aspects of both the exhibition and the publication. Danielle Chadych and Catherine Tambrun offered advice and expertise. I was admirably aided by four interns, Carol Bergami, Christophe Bouquet, Fannie Escoulen, and Valérie-Anne Lemeure, who carried out the initial cataloguing and contributed in various ways to the field research. Finally, Christiane Dole helped in innumerable ways with the realization of both the exhibition and the publication, and I am grateful for her meticulous work.

At the Caisse nationale des monuments historiques et des sites, Pascal Gauthier kindly made his invaluable Atget database, developed over several years, available to me. I am also grateful to Liza Daum, at the Bibliothèque historique de la Ville de Paris, to Sylvie Aubenas and Catherine Fournier, at the Bibliothèque nationale de France for facilitating my research in their respective institutions, and to Father Jérôme Beau, the abbot of the Church of Saint-Séverin, who allowed me access to the church's roof. At Paris Musées, I would like to express my gratitude to Denis Caget and Sophie Lecat, for administrating the exhibition, and to Arnauld Pontier and Florence Jakubowicz, for skillfully overseeing the French publication.

The photographers Geoffrey James, Jürgen Nefzger, Mark Ruwedel, Bob Thall, and especially Robert Burley helped me to understand more concretely the problems facing Atget as an architectural photographer. Rod Slemmons helped refine my initial ideas. For my stays in Paris, I would like to thank Élizabeth Reynaud, Alain and Françoise Paviot, and Martine d'Arc for their various kindnesses.

At The New Press, I am extremely grateful to André Schiffrin for undertaking this project, and allowing me the time to review and prepare the manuscript. I took this opportunity to correct a few minor mistakes and oversights in the original French edition and to clarify some of my ideas, but the text, in all other respects, remains identical. I am also grateful to production editor Sarah Fan, copyeditor Suzanne Lander, and designer Brian Mulligan for their work in the realization of this publication.

Finally, in this as in all my work, I remain indebted to Linda Eerme, and offer this book to her in gratitude for her love and unfailing encouragement over many years.

David Harris

Eugène Atget: *Unknown Paris*

Chapter 1

Observing Eugène Atget

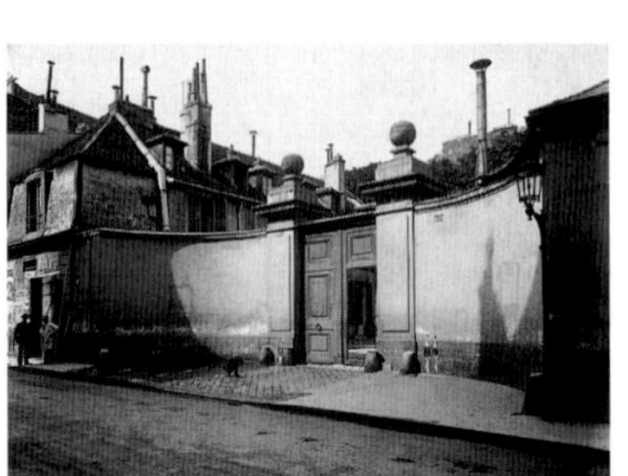

Ill. 2 Stables, Hôtel de Croy, 6 rue du Regard, 6th, 1902

During the first quarter of the twentieth century, the relatively short, stocky figure of photographer Eugène Atget became a familiar sight in Paris. Since he took approximately five thousand negatives in the city between 1898 and a few months before his death in 1927, the majority of which were made in the middle part of the day, Parisians had frequent opportunities to observe Atget transporting his photographic equipment through the streets, setting up his camera on its tripod, and making views along the streets, in the public gardens, within the city's famous churches, and in the courtyards of elegant town houses.

There are no recorded accounts by his contemporaries of Atget actually engaged in photographing, and he left only a few brief references as to his motives and concerns as a photographer. However, traces of his presence as an urban figure remain preserved within the images he produced. As a result of lengthy exposures, most passersby appear only as an indistinct ghostly blurs (ill. 30–34 and cat. 4.7), but many curious and interested Parisians stopped to watch the photographer at work: shopkeepers hover on the pavement in front of their displays (cat. 3.15, 6.1, and 7.6), occupants of the buildings pose before their doorways (ill. 11, cat. 2.1), while cyclists and schoolchildren pause in the midst of their daily routines (cat. 7.15 and 4.10). Whether the two men, who stand deferentially at the extreme left of Atget's 1911 photograph of the stables of the Hôtel de Croy (ill. 2), thinking themselves out of range of the camera's coverage, engaged Atget in conversation seems entirely likely, but what the substance of that conversation would have been and how Atget would have explained his reasons for photographing this particular entrance remain unknown.

While Atget generally composed his photographs to exclude his own reflection, his camera and his entire figure were, on occasion, unavoidably included. The camera, shrouded by its dark cloth, appears reflected in the mirrors set into two of the fireplaces of the lavishly decorated eighteenth-century salon of the Hôtel Matignon at 57 rue de Varenne,[1] and his equipment and uncertain features are dimly captured in the shimmering glass of various bistro and cabaret entrance doors.[2] However, in his 1902 photograph of the shop window at 21 rue Faubourg-Saint-Honoré, Atget is clearly visible, reflected in

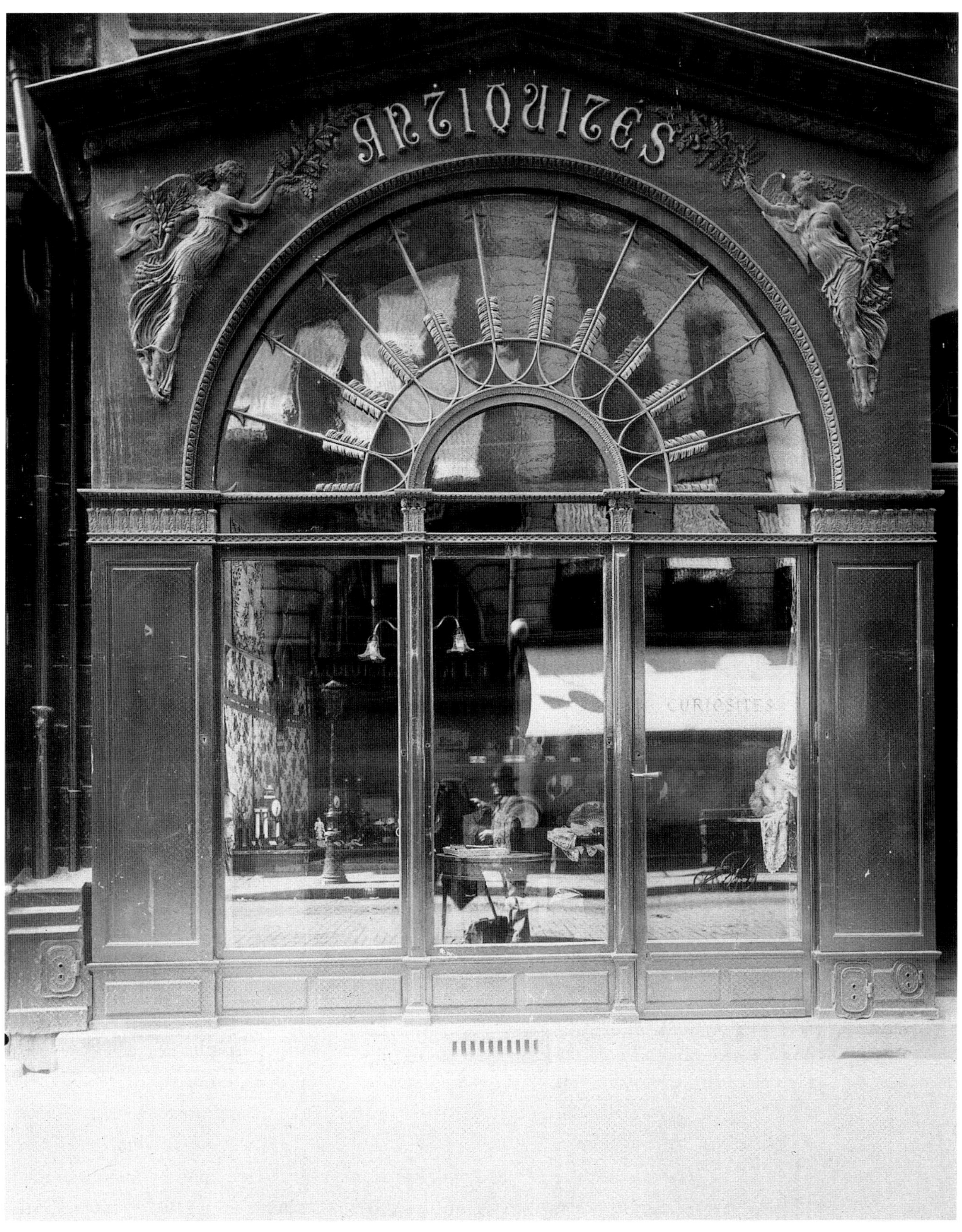

Ill. 3 Empire-style store, 21 rue Faubourg-Saint-Honoré, 8th, 1902

the central vertical glass pane (ill. 3). Neatly dressed in a jacket and tie with a hat to shade his eyes from the fierce midday sun, and with his bag of photographic materials at his feet, he stands patiently in profile with his camera on its tripod at the edge of the sidewalk; his left hand rests on the back of the camera, perhaps to steady it, while he holds the lens cover in his right hand.

More than any other single photograph, this image epitomizes the photographic process, catching the photographer in the midst of his daily work as the exposure is being made. The structure of the image permits us to see simultaneously the subject—the facade of an early nineteenth-century shop window—and to grasp how Atget constructed his photograph. We are invited to imaginatively enter into the process of its making and, on a more general level, to consider how Atget carried out his profession as an architectural and urban photographer in Paris.

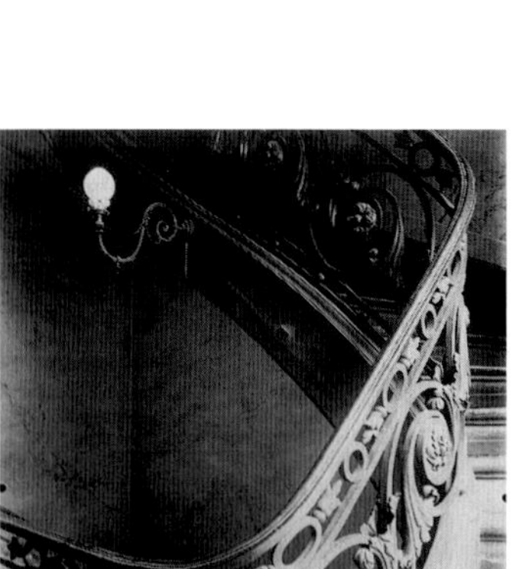

Ill. 4 Staircase, Hôtel Sully-Charost, 11 rue du Cherche-Midi, 6th, 1904–1905

While a single photograph can illuminate certain aspects of Atget's practice, it is through the examination of pairs and, as this publication will describe, sequences of consecutively made images that we are able to delve into his creative process and to observe the results of his mind at work on a more profound level. In taking two contiguous views on the staircase of the Hôtel Sully-Charost in 1904–05, to consider one example (ill. 4 and 5), Atget chose this particular vantage point in order to take advantage of the light from an unseen window that illuminates the darkened space.[3] In the first photograph, Atget positioned his camera on the landing so that the iron balustrade was viewed from slightly above. In framing this view, he deliberately used the sinuous form of this balustrade to sculpt the space of the stairwell and, together with the ornate lamp fixture and the far wall, to suggest how the stair rises through a succession of floors. In the second photograph, Atget moved his camera perhaps as little as half a meter along the landing and lowered it so that a portion of the balustrade is now silhouetted against a dark ground, and the details of its design are brought into clear relief.

In making such seemingly minor adjustments between the first and second views, the subject of the photographs and the purposes they serve have altered. While the first is concerned with articulating an interior space, the second image has sacrificed all sense of an architectural context in favor of providing information about the decorative ironwork. In both photographs, Atget was addressing an audience of architects, historians, and antiquarians who shared an interest in this particular building and in the form of eighteenth-century staircases, but in the second image, he was specifically creating a document that would serve as source material for architects and craftsmen. The two

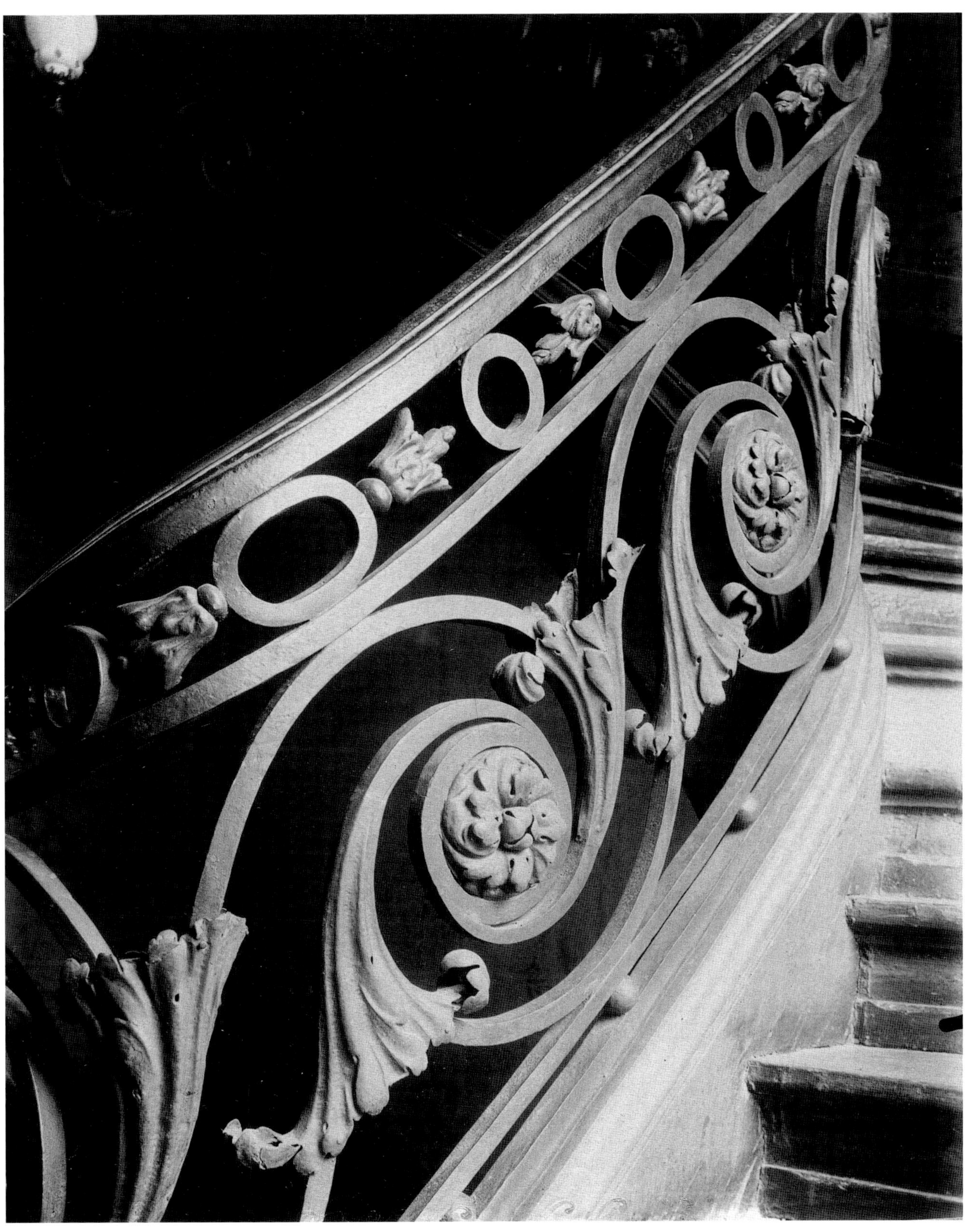

Ill. 5 Detail of banister, Hôtel Sully-Charost, 11 rue du Cherche-Midi, 6th, 1904–1905

photographs reveal Atget's commercial mind at work, responding to the different needs of his clients.

On an overcast day in 1914, Atget made two photographs in the garden of the former convent of the Carmes Déchaux (now the Institut catholique de Paris; ill. 6 and 7).[4] Unlike the two images of the staircase in the Hôtel Sully-Charost, it is impossible to determine the exact order in which he took them, although it seems plausible that he took the more descriptive horizontal view first, followed by the more poetic vertical photograph. While both views were made within a few meters of one another, Atget has altered the visual relationship between the three principal forms—the circular stone pond and stone benches in the foreground, the mass of shrubs and trees in the middle ground, and the prominent clock tower of Saint-Joseph des Carmes in the background. The horizontal image describes how the central pathway bisects the space of the garden and connects it with the convent building, glimpsed beyond the gate at the end of the path, while the vertical allows the visual conjunction of the pond and the church's spire to capture the tranquil, slightly melancholic atmosphere of the place. That Atget preserved and printed both photographs when, in terms of purely documentary value, one would have served his purposes adequately enough, indicates that he considered both to be successful as images. In contemplating these views, one realizes that, for Atget, the process of making photographs could yield unpredictable and even unanticipated results.

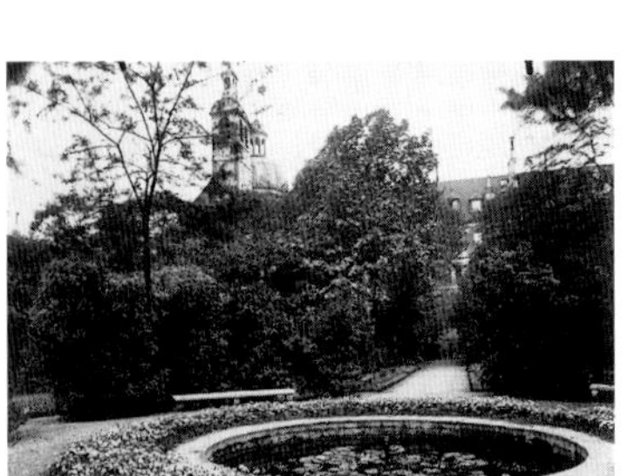

Ill. 6 Garden of the former convent of the Carmes Déchaux (now the Institut catholique de Paris), 70 rue de Vaugirard, 6th, 1914

Since he left so little evidence of his concerns as a photographer, our knowledge of Atget derives almost entirely from the evidence found in his photographs. In considering the differences between consecutively made images, we encounter Atget's mind actively moving, making decisions concerning how subjects were to be defined, and assessing the effect that slight adjustments concerning distance, camera angle, framing, and the orientation of the negative would have on the final image. In treating Atget's photographs as the distillation of his thoughts and as the blending of commercial and creative considerations, our sense of Atget separates itself from any lingering romantic and nostalgic currents still enveloping his work. The figure of Atget *as a photographer,* whose form is dimly reflected in bistro windows and more clearly in the shop along the rue Faubourg-Saint-Honoré, assumes a less enigmatic and far more defined presence.

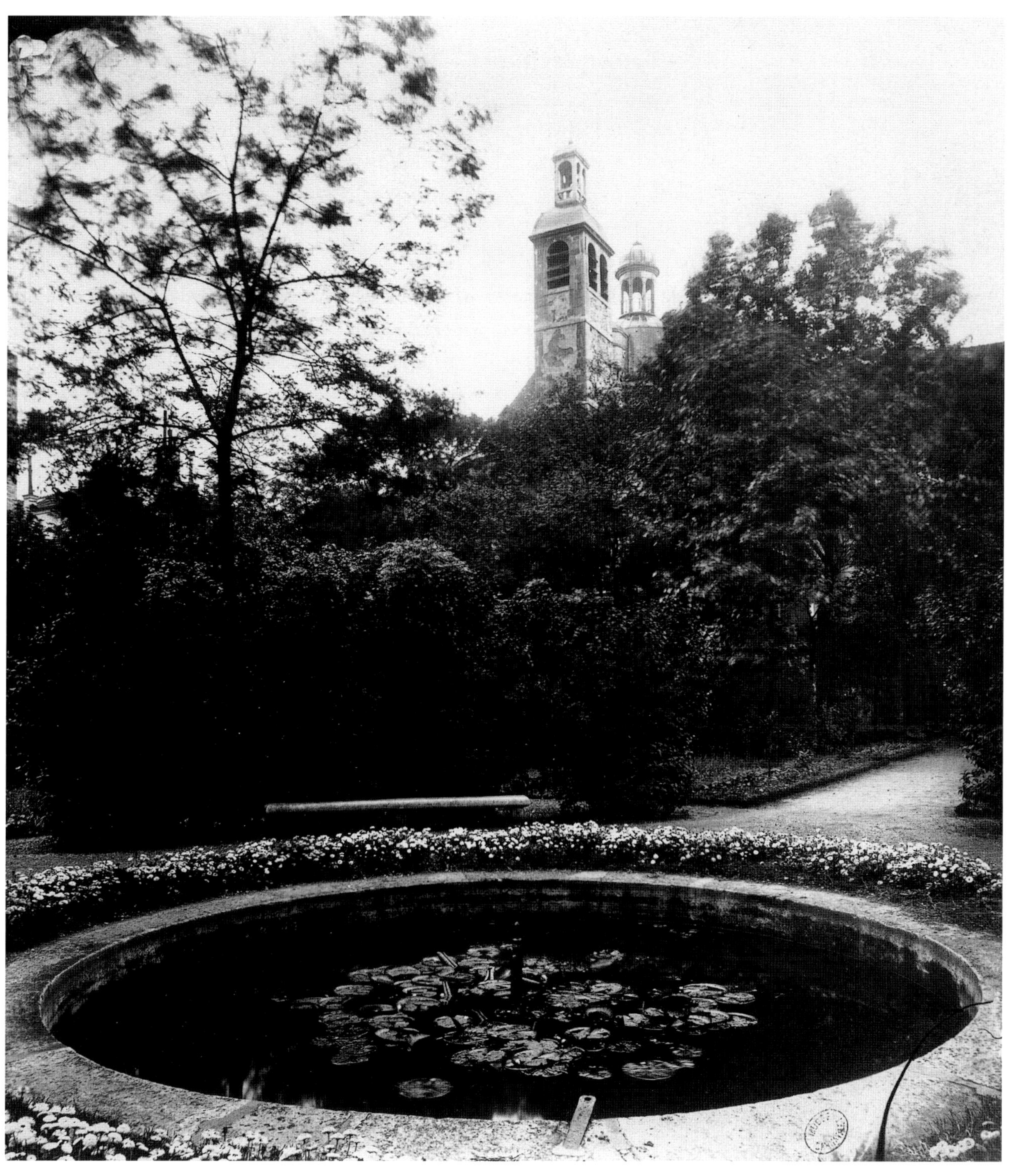

Ill. 7 Garden of the former convent of the Carmes Déchaux (now the Institut catholique de Paris), 70 rue de Vaugirard, 6th, 1914

Chapter 2

Atget's Life As a Commercial Photographer

When the young American photographer Berenice Abbott purchased the considerable residue of Atget's photographic estate from André Calmettes in late June 1928,[1] she knew virtually nothing of the substance of Atget's career or the circumstances of his life, and asked Calmettes if he would provide her with some information. In the resulting brief memoir, which took the form of an eloquent elegy, Calmettes movingly blended anecdotal details with a summation of a life's achievement as a photographer and, in few deft strokes, sketched the outlines of a proud and eccentric personality.[2] In Calmettes' estimation, Atget's ambition was "to create a collection of all that which both in Paris and its surroundings was artistic and picturesque." In pursuit of this daunting subject, Calmettes wrote that "every morning, getting up at dawn, he went everywhere, entered everywhere... Paris and her old churches, her monuments, her miseries and her treasures were photographed by Atget." His artistic vision, as well as the frugal regime of his life, were driven by a uncompromising will:... "in art and in hygiene he was absolute. He had very personal ideas on everything which he imposed with extraordinary violence. He applied this intransigence of taste, of vision, of methods, to the art of photography and miracles resulted." Calmettes concluded his reminiscence with a final indelible image: "Paris will no longer see that strange silhouette, the face with its expression of energy, this Balzacian personage, always enveloped in the immense worn overcoat, an old round hat on his head, hands eaten by the acids necessary to his profession."

Calmettes' brief letter provides the point of departure for subsequent interpretations of Atget and studies of his work, since it drew upon a long and intimate friendship, dating from the early to mid-1880s after both had left the Conservatoire nationale de musique et de déclaration. He described Atget's project much as the photographer himself had characterized it in his letters (discussed later in this chapter) to Paul Léon, directeur des Beaux-Arts, in November 1920. From the late 1920s through the 1960s, Abbott was instrumental in preserving Atget's reputation and promoting his work through articles and books, by organizing and lending to exhibitions, by printing his negatives, and by selling prints of his photographs.[3] Beginning in the late 1950s and intensifying in the late 1970s and early 1980s, a number of researchers have methodically verified each of the facts in Calmettes' biographical sketch, and have established a firm chronology for his life and clarified many details surrounding his practice as a photographer.[4] This information has been augmented by the publication of documents relating to Atget's professional relationship with various public institutions who constituted his clientele, and through interviews with a number of people who had known him late in his life.[5] While certain of Calmettes' assertions, such as Atget's early years at sea, have remained unconfirmed, and while others appear to reflect the photographer's practice only in his later life, such as his predilection for photographing early in the morning, Calmettes' characterization of Atget's single-minded and passionate commitment to documenting the architectural fabric of pre-Revolutionary Paris and his stubbornly independent and dogmatic personality have remained at the core of interpretations of his work.

As a result of this extensive and meticulous research, much more is now known of Atget's personal life and of his career as a commercial photographer.[6] Jean-Eugène Atget was born on February 12, 1857, in Libourne (near Bordeaux), probably received some formal education, and may have spent some time at sea. By 1878, he was living in Paris, where over the next four years he completed his military service while briefly attending the Conservatoire nationale de musique et de déclaration as a drama student for three terms. His life between 1882 and 1892 is undocumented but, according to Calmettes, Atget made a modest living as a character actor, touring with small repertory-theater companies in the provinces and on the outskirts of Paris, before retiring from the stage and eventually establishing himself, in his early forties, as a commercial photographer in Paris itself. By 1892, he was furnishing academic painters with photographs for preliminary studies and, while he continued to develop this market (encompassing a wide range of artists, from book illustrators to avant-garde painters) throughout his life,[7] he had begun by 1897 to concentrate his photography upon the surviving architecture and the picturesque streets in the historical center of the city.

By the late 1890s, concern over preserving the architectural integrity as well as the character of *le vieux Paris* (a term corresponding roughly to the architecture and decorative arts that predated the 1789 revolution) had intensified in reaction to Georges-Eugène Haussmann's vast program of urban renewal and modernization. Beginning in the mid-1850s, the city's urban fabric of intimate, although often overcrowded and unhealthy, neighborhoods was systematically demolished and replaced by a vast network of grand boulevards, interspersed with prominently sited historical monuments and civic parks, and served by efficient transportation and sanitation facilities. With the loss of the earlier city arose both a nostalgia for earlier times and the desire to preserve what remained against future destruction.[8] The founding of the Commission municipale du vieux Paris in 1898 (the official civic organization responsible for guarding and documenting the architectural heritage of the city), and of local historical and preservationist societies, as well as the appointments of such influential historians as Georges Cain as curator at the Musée Carnavalet in 1898 and Marcel Poëte as chief librarian at the Bibliothèque historique de la Ville de Paris in 1903, provided Atget with a core of institutional clients whose personal referrals led to the establishment of an informal network of private clients. While Atget never worked directly for the Commission, his datable photographs certainly indicate that he had access to information concerning particularly vulnerable buildings and threatened areas in the city, most probably through his friendships with the playwright Victorien Sardou and one of his clients, the painter Édouard Detaille, both of whom were prominent members of the Commission.[9]

Atget quickly realized the necessity and practical advantages of organizing his work into discrete categories.[10] By May 1898, he had split his earliest photographs of *le vieux Paris* into two major series, each with independent numbering systems. The first was *L'Art dans le vieux Paris* (Art in Old Paris); initially, this was devoted to famous monuments and picturesque street scenes, but after 1900, Atget increasingly concentrated upon residential, ecclesiastical, and, to a lesser extent, institutional architecture in the 1st to the 7th arrondissements.[11] His photographs treated structures in considerable detail but usually in isolation from their urban context. In documenting *hôtels* (lavish town houses), Atget only concentrated upon the historically and architecturally significant portions of these buildings—the facades, entrance portals, courtyards, vestibules, interior staircases, and formal reception rooms—and created coherent and self-contained descriptions of these spaces and their decoration. Within churches, he documented the interior spaces with their sculptural ensembles, choir stalls, and elaborate ironwork. The second series, *Paris pittoresque* (Picturesque Paris), was originally created to accommodate his photographs of street trades, the *petits métiers* but, once completed in 1900, Atget suspended work on the series.[12] He subsequently revived it between 1910 and 1915, and again after 1920 in order to include more marginal areas of the city such as the quays and the area lying immediately outside of the city's then fortified walls known as the *zone militaire*. Also included were aspects of urban life not treated elsewhere, such as antiquated transportation vehicles, kiosks, boutiques, window displays, and street circuses. To these two series, Atget added a third in 1906, *Topographie du vieux Paris* (Topography of Old Paris).[13] This originated as a commission from Marcel Poëte of the Bibliothèque historique de la Ville de Paris to carry out a detailed topographical survey of the historical center of Paris, which would update Charles Marville's earlier extensive photographic documentation, made between 1865 and 1868 and completed in 1877.[14] Between 1906 and 1912, Atget systematically photographed the streets, *passages* (passageways), and public squares in the 1st to the 7th arrondissements. After a break in 1912, he continued until 1915, but far less comprehensively, concentrating upon specific streets rather than entire neighborhoods, and even following the course of demolition, particularly along the Left Bank. While all three Parisian series covered the same area within the city, each series was concerned with different aspects of urban form and experience.

Atget's working year was divided into overlapping phases of activity. In general, he appears to have photographed from March through October, often working on several series concurrently.[15] He developed his negatives in relatively small groups soon after taking them (perhaps even on the same day), and assigned to each negative the next available number in the relevant series. Atget, and in all likelihood his companion, Valentine Compagnon, printed the photographs throughout the year, concentrating in the summer when conditions were optimum for contact printing.[16] In the late autumn he began his institutional visits, typically offering for sale the current year's work. The majority of institutional sales were made between January and June, although sales to the Musée Carnavalet and the Bibliothèque historique de la Ville de Paris continued throughout the year.[17]

As a fiercely independent small-businessman working mostly on speculation, Atget developed a simple method for organizing and classifying his work so as to maintain control over each series as it developed, and thereby easily segregating and offering only those portions that he felt would be of potential interest and particular relevance to his varied clientele. To begin with, he maintained a series of paperbound reference albums for each of his principal series and subseries. In these albums, he filed copies of the prints in numerical order, and annotated each page with the title, negative number, and occasionally the date of the image. While all of his clients shared a common interest in *le vieux Paris,* each had specialized needs that determined why they acquired the photographs and how they, in turn, used them. In order to best serve his customers, Atget would select a group of images from his reference albums and, presenting them in specially prepared albums, would encourage his clients either to make a selection or to acquire the contents of the album in its entirety.[18] Finished prints were delivered either unmounted or mounted on heavy card, or as albums, again depending upon the particular requirements of the institution or the individual client.[19] In 1910, Atget also began regularly offering complete albums, intended to be kept intact, to institutions. This marketing scheme began with the Musée Carnavalet's purchase of the album *Intérieurs Parisiens,*[20] and continued with the sale of ten further albums over the next four years. The Bibliothèque nationale purchased six specially produced leather-bound albums between 1911 and 1915.[21]

Once established, the rhythm and pattern of Atget's working year seems to have remained relatively stable until 1914. He made his first institutional sales in 1898, a relatively modest total of 175 prints to the Musée de Sculpture comparée du Trocadéro and to the Musée Carnavalet.[22] By 1901, Atget had produced over 1,000 negatives of *le vieux Paris* (as well as 450 non-Parisian views and approximately 385 studies of plants and landscapes), and during that year alone, sold more than 1,800 photographs to the Musée de Sculpture comparée, the Musée Carnavalet, the Bibliothèque historique de la Ville de Paris, the Bibliothèque nationale, the École des beaux-arts, and the Musée des Arts decoratifs. Between 1898 and 1914, he sold in excess of 15,000 photographs to these major institutions and libraries. Although the evidence is far less complete than that for institutions, Atget was simultaneously engaged in selling hundreds of photographs to a variety of private clients.[23] He furnished architects, interior decorators, and artisans engaged in the building trades with photographs which would serve as visual models for designing and fabricating historically accurate architectural ensembles and decorative elements, such as iron balustrades and elaborate wood panelling. He supplied painters, engravers, illustrators, and set designers with photographs as study and source material, and provided both antiquarians and amateur historians with photographic documentation of individual buildings and entire neighborhoods.[24]

With the advent of World War I, Atget's institutional sales fell off dramatically; in 1915, he sold only two albums to the Bibliothèque nationale, and made no further institutional sales until 1919. Similarly his own photographic output slowed down, and from 1916 through 1918 he appears to have made no photographs in Paris. Out of concern for the safety of his glass-plate negatives, Atget transferred them from his fifth-floor apartment to the basement at 17 *bis* rue Compagne-Première. On February 4, 1918, he drew up his will.[25]

With the restoration of peace, interest in le vieux Paris had lessened to such a degree that, sensing the diminishing commercial worth of his negatives—he had already sold prints of these same negatives to the major institutions—although still convinced of their intrinsic and permanent historical value, in November 1920, Atget approached Paul Léon, directeur des beaux-arts, who was responsible for the Commission des monuments historiques, the state's collection of historical negatives. After a brief negotiation, he sold 2,621 negatives (comprising 1,053 from the series *L'Art dans le vieux Paris* and 1,568 from the two series *Topographie du vieux Paris* and *Paris pittoresque*) to the government in December for the substantial sum of 10,000 francs.

Atget's three letters to Paul Léon are significant documents in themselves since they constitute his clearest and most sustained statement concerning his work.[26] In describing his photographs, he stressed the comprehensiveness of his documentation:

> For more than twenty years by my own work and personal initiative, I have gathered from all the old streets of Vieux Paris photographic plates, 18 x 24 format, artistic documents of the beautiful civil architecture of the 16th to the 19th century: the old *hôtels*, historic or curious houses, beautiful facades, beautiful doors, beautiful woodwork, door knockers, old fountains, stairways *de style* (wood and wrought iron); the interiors of all the

> churches of Paris (comprehensive views and artistic details: Notre-Dame, Saint-Gervais-et-Protais, Saint-Séverin, Saint-Julien-le-Pauvre, Saint-Étienne-du-Mont, Saint-Roch, Saint-Nicolas-du-Chardonnet, etc. etc.). This vast artistic and documentary collection is today complete. I could say that I possess all of Vieux Paris.

Equally, he emphasised the historical significance of these negatives, depicting much that by 1920 had "completely disappeared: for example, the neighborhood of Saint-Séverin has completely changed. I have the entire neighborhood, over twenty years, until 1914, demolitions included." In reading these letters, it becomes evident that Atget considered his photographs as constituting a single body of work, rather than merely an accumulation of disparate views.

When Atget began to photograph Paris again in 1919, his approach was far less ambitious and comprehensive than it had been before the war. He carried out more limited surveys, such as a new series of *hôtels*, and continued to explore specific urban forms, such as courtyards, whose earlier negatives he had deliberately excluded from the 1920 sale.[27] He worked in areas that he had largely abandoned early in his career, notably Montmartre and Passy, and in 1923 embarked upon a new series of Parisian parks. As his work became increasingly personal, Atget revisited and rephotographed many of the earlier sites; he became attracted to working at different times of the day, often photographing at dawn, and responding to transient seasonal conditions, such as the luminescent fogs of winter mornings. His album sales to the Musée Carnavalet, which resumed in 1921 and continued until after his death in 1928, reveal how he adapted to postwar attitudes. He sold work that either concentrated upon areas of the city which had disappeared, such as the 1913 photographs of the demolition around the Church of Saint-Séverin and the 1914 series of the parc Delessert (a large private garden in Passy), or emphasized the picturesque aspects of Montmartre and elsewhere. Probably over the winter of 1924–25, still apprehensive about the future of his life's work, he approached the Bibliothèque nationale, proposing that it become the repository for 2,150 negatives, comprising aspects of Paris not included in his 1920 sale, and covering the small villages and royal gardens of the Ile-de-France region. The sale was unsuccessful.[28]

On June 20, 1926, Valentine Compagnon, his companion of over forty years, died. After her death, Atget photographed very little and, slightly more than a year later, died on August 4, 1927. André Calmettes, the executor of Atget's estate, disposed of a further 2,000 negatives to the Commission des monuments historiques in 1927,[29] then sold the remainder of the estate to Berenice Abbott in June 1928.

Chapter 3

Atget at Work

In his photograph of the shop at 21 rue Faubourg-Saint-Honoré (ill. 2), Atget constructed an elaborate portrait of himself as an architectural and urban photographer, showing not only his equipment but the conditions under which he carried out his trade.[1] While this view was made in 1902, it could easily stand as a self-portrait of Atget at almost any point in his career since he neither changed his equipment nor altered his technique. Unfortunately, his camera, its square form largely obscured by its dark cloth, has not survived; when Berenice Abbott inquired about the equipment after his death, she learned that it had been discarded.[2] From an analysis of his surviving prints, it is thought that Atget purchased a large-format-view camera at the beginning of his career and continued to use it throughout his life. Such a camera would have consisted of a wooden box with a ground glass for examining the potential image at the rear and with adjustable bellows and lens at its front.[3]

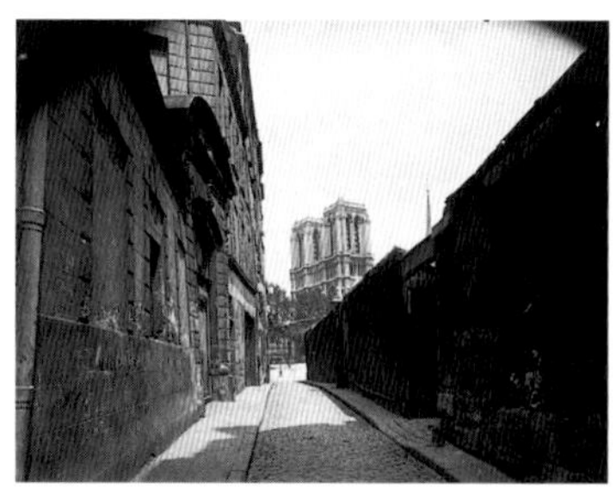

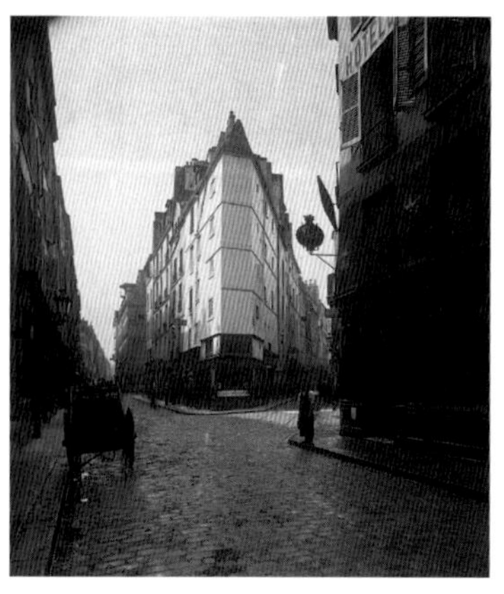

Ill. 29 Rue Saint-Julien-le-Pauvre, toward the quai de Montebello and Notre-Dame, 5th, June 1923

Ill. 30 Corner of the rue de Seine and the rue de l'Échaudé, 6th, 1905

Once Atget had identified a subject and established the appropriate viewing distance from it, he would unpack his camera from its satchel, carefully mount it on its wooden tripod, and adjust the orientation of the panel at the rear of camera, depending upon whether he was making a horizontal or vertical negative. In composing his view, Atget would drape a dark cloth over himself and the camera in order to study the image, which appeared on the ground glass in color, but laterally reversed, upside down, relatively dim, and with darkened edges. He would make any necessary adjustments to the camera's position, shifting it slightly backward, forward, or sideways so as to include either more or less of the subject, and to frame it precisely. He would gradually extend and retract the bellows until finally reaching the exact point where the camera's lens had brought the subject into sharp focus. According to Abbott, Atget used a "trousse-objectif," a convertible lens that, by simply removing or adding different components, allowed him to alter the lens's coverage from a normal angle to that of a wide-angle view without changing the camera's position.[4] In addition, Atget also had the option of raising the camera's front panel, which held the lens, in order to reduce the amount of immediate foreground visible.

While this simple camera movement allowed him to include the upper portions of buildings and tree branches in his photographs, it also produced the characteristic darkened curves at the upper edges of his images, an effect referred to as "vignetting,"[5] and a slight softening of the image's definition toward the edges of the photograph (see for example, ill. 29 and 30).

Once Atget was satisfied with the composition, he would extract a wooden negative holder from his traveling bag (visible at his feet in the photograph), which probably held two negatives, and carefully position the holder in the vertical groove at the rear of the camera. Before leaving his darkroom, he would have inserted the commercially prepared unexposed glass-plate negatives into the holder. Having estimated the approximate exposure time based upon past experience of photographing under similar conditions,[6] he would close the lens, and wait for tree branches to settle or passersby in the immediate vicinity to move along, before carefully removing the protective panel from the inner side of negative holder and uncovering the lens in order to expose the negative.[7] Following the exposure, he would replace the lens cover and reinsert the protective panel. He would then either move his camera, on its tripod, to a nearby position, or dismantle and pack up all of his equipment if he were moving any distance, where he would repeat the same procedures for each successive exposure.

To photograph with a large-format-view camera on a tripod in Paris was not only a physically arduous activity, but a slow and exacting process, one in which each view had to be carefully selected and considered, and each exposure methodically made. As a descriptive and interpretative process, it required an intimate understanding of how a particular format of camera and lens would render the overall space and articulate the relationships within it. Practical decisions of where to stand, how best to frame a view, and when to make an exposure were shaped as much as by the specific architectural and lighting conditions encountered at a site, as by Atget's awareness of the distinctive needs of the various markets he served, and by his cumulative experience and vision as a photographer accrued over many years of professional practice.

Except during his first two years of work in Paris,[8] Atget does not appear to have considered representing a site by a single definitive photograph, but consistently produced sequences and clusters of topographically related images that would provide a cumulative portrait of the site, and that could later be

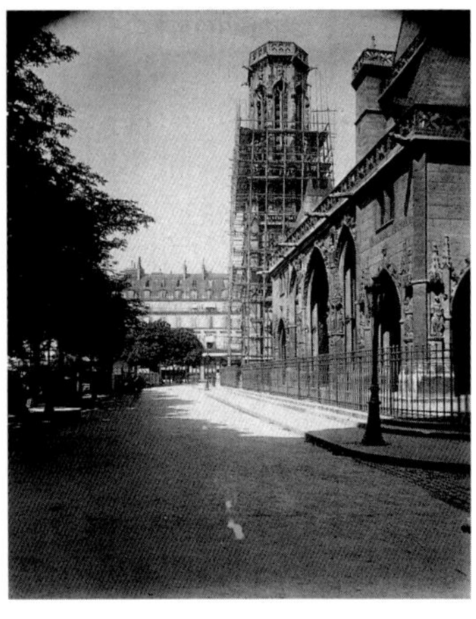

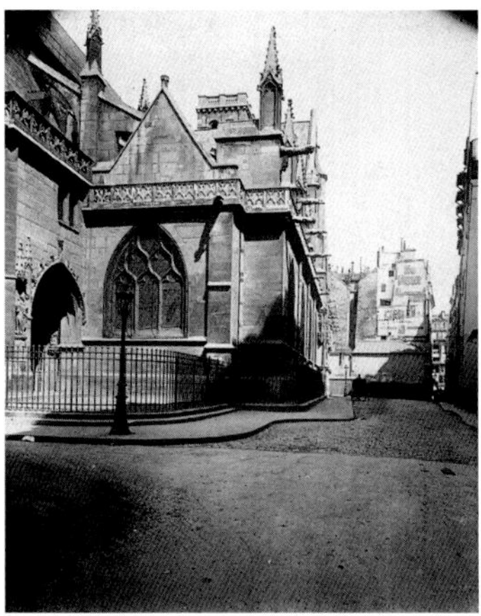

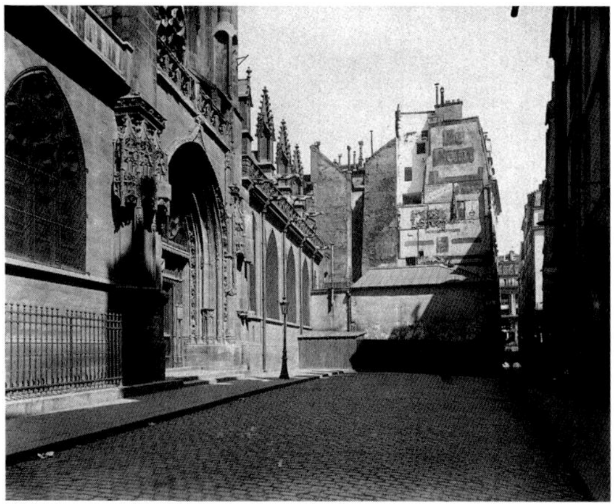

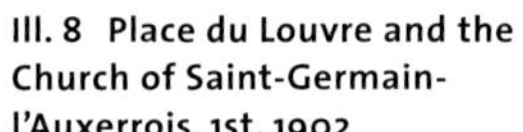

Ill. 8 Place du Louvre and the Church of Saint-Germain-l'Auxerrois, 1st, 1902

Ill. 9 Rue des Prêtres-Saint-Germain-l'Auxerrois, from place du Louvre, 1st, 1902

Ill. 10 Rue des Prêtres-Saint-Germain-l'Auxerrois, 1st, 1902

offered, either in part or in their entirety, to his clients. By examining particular sequences, one begins to recognize both the characteristic ways in which Atget composed his individual photographs and the recurring patterns that underlay his coverage of different kinds of urban spaces.

When Atget photographed the place du Louvre and its intersection with the rue des Prêtres-Saint-Germain-L'Auxerrois in 1902, to consider one example, he specifically chose an afternoon when the strong raking light illuminated both the western and southern facades of the Church of Saint-Germain-L'Auxerrois (ill. 8–10). In the morning, the principal facade is entirely cast in shadow. Atget chose his first camera position so that he could survey the church's western facade, a vantage point that then allowed him, by only shifting his camera a few meters, to establish a second position from which to look into the rue des Prêtres-Saint-Germain-L'Auxerrois. By incorporating the same lamp post into both images, Atget provided the viewer with a point of orientation with which to grasp the topographical relationship of the two views. When seen together, the two photographs encompass a ninety-degree sweep that describes the juncture of two public spaces. While the photographs do not provide a continuous representation of these spaces—in fact, only in his two 1923 images of the intersection of the rue des Ursins and the rue des Chantres did Atget create an almost seamless two-part panorama[9]—they are symptomatic of Atget's practice of making two views from closely related camera positions.[10] In addition to allowing Atget to conserve his energy and work more efficiently, such a strategy had a commercial advantage: Since the two photographs were conceived of as independent images, they could be sold separately or marketed as a pair. Atget made his third image from a position farther along the rue des Prêtres-Saint-Germain-L'Auxerrois. This camera position allowed him to present the illuminated side of the church and to indicate how the street itself contracts into a narrow lane, which in 1902 ended at the rue de Pont-Neuf.[11]

The succession of the three interlocking views treats the church as inseparable from its immediate urban environment. Unlike earlier photographs by Édouard Baldus (1813–1889), which were made from the elevated colonnade of the palais du Louvre and which, in conformity with Hausmann's urban ideas, presented the church as an isolated architectural monument seen from an ideal viewpoint,[12] Atget was concerned with describing how it was normally encountered by pedestrians and perceived from street level. This approach permeates all of his Parisian work.

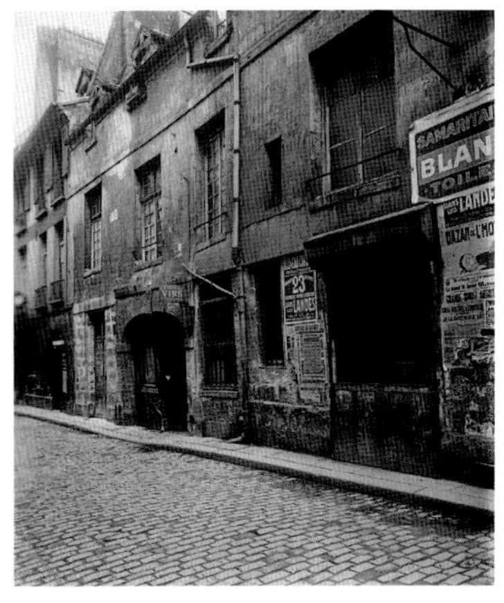

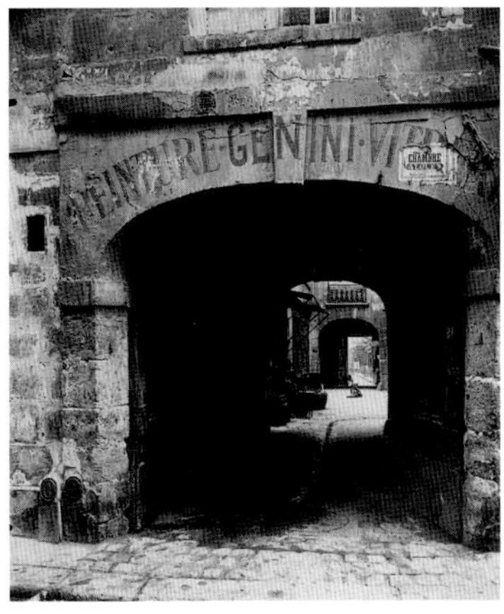

Ill. 11 6 rue des Guillemites, 4th, 1911

Ill. 12 Entrance, passage des Singes, 6 rue des Guillemites, 4th, 1911

More complex urban spaces required greater numbers of images to describe their characters and configurations. While Atget appears to have followed regular and recurring patterns in constructing these sequences, he did not always number the resulting negatives in the exact order in which he took them. In 1911, to take one instance, Atget made seven photographs of the passage des Singes, a thirty-five-meter-long partially covered passageway connecting the rue des Guillemites with the rue Vielle-du-Temple.[13] If the images are arranged strictly following their negative numbers, they result in a seemingly aimless, almost random method of working (ill. 14, 11, 17, 13, 12 and, as unrelated numbers, 16 and 15). As a record of how Atget produced this group of images, this order seems unlikely, considering that he frequently photographed this and similar types of spaces, such as courtyards, throughout his career. As a specialist in urban photography, it was essential that Atget clearly and coherently describe architectural forms and spaces and, as a commercial photographer, carry out his work economically and efficiently while ensuring that his coverage included all aspects of interest to his prospective clients. Assuming that Atget worked in a logical way, two recurring patterns can be proposed: first, that he began with the distant and overall view before proceeding to the more detailed ones; and, second, that he moved progressively forward through spaces, rather than walking awkwardly backward and forward with his heavy camera and tripod. As a result, Atget's description of a site in the form of a sequence of linked views arose directly from his method of photographing it.

With this in mind, the seven images of the rue des Guillemites and the passage des Singes can be sequenced into an orderly description of the successive

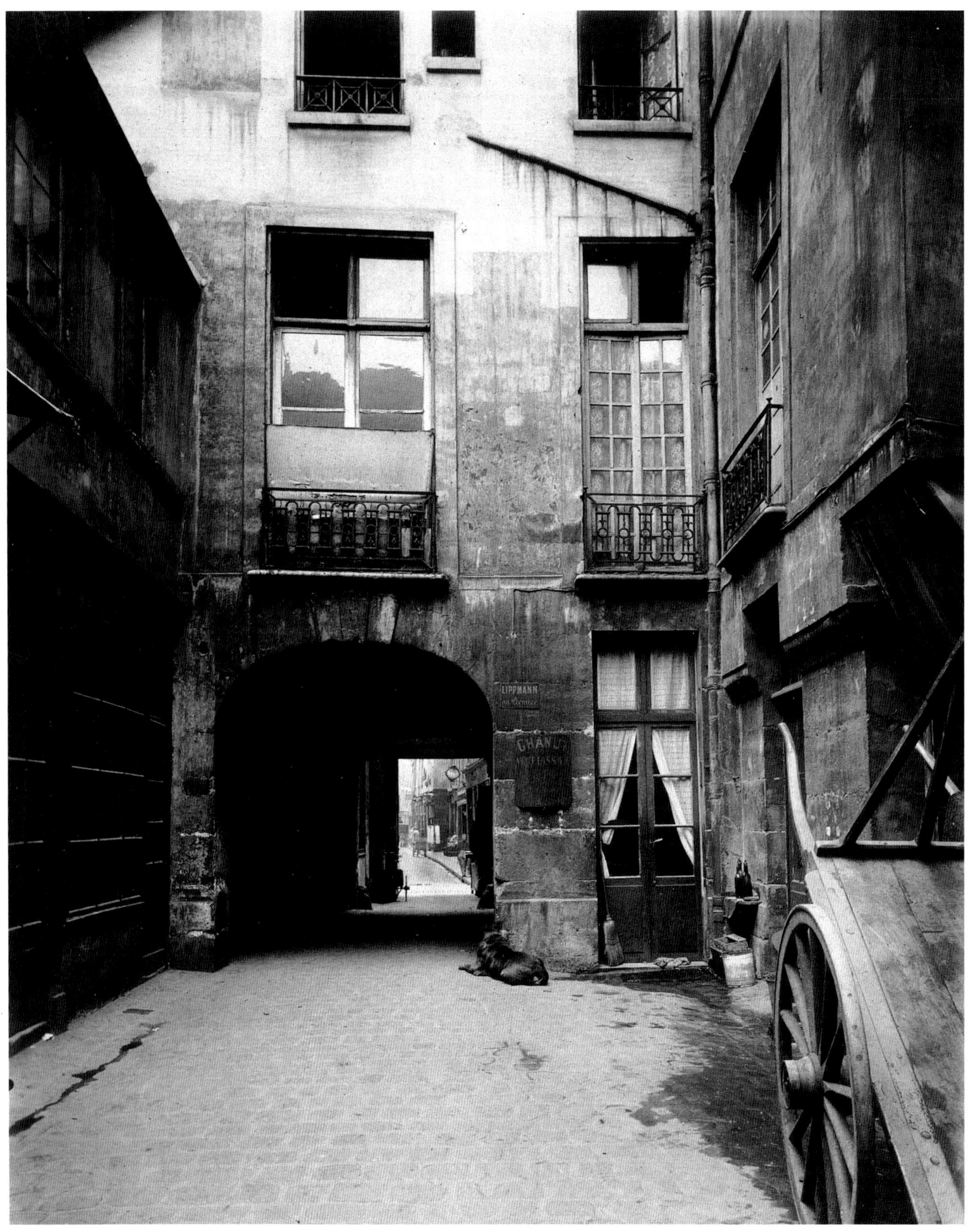

Ill. 13 Passage des Singes, toward the rue Vieille-du-Temple, 4th, 1911

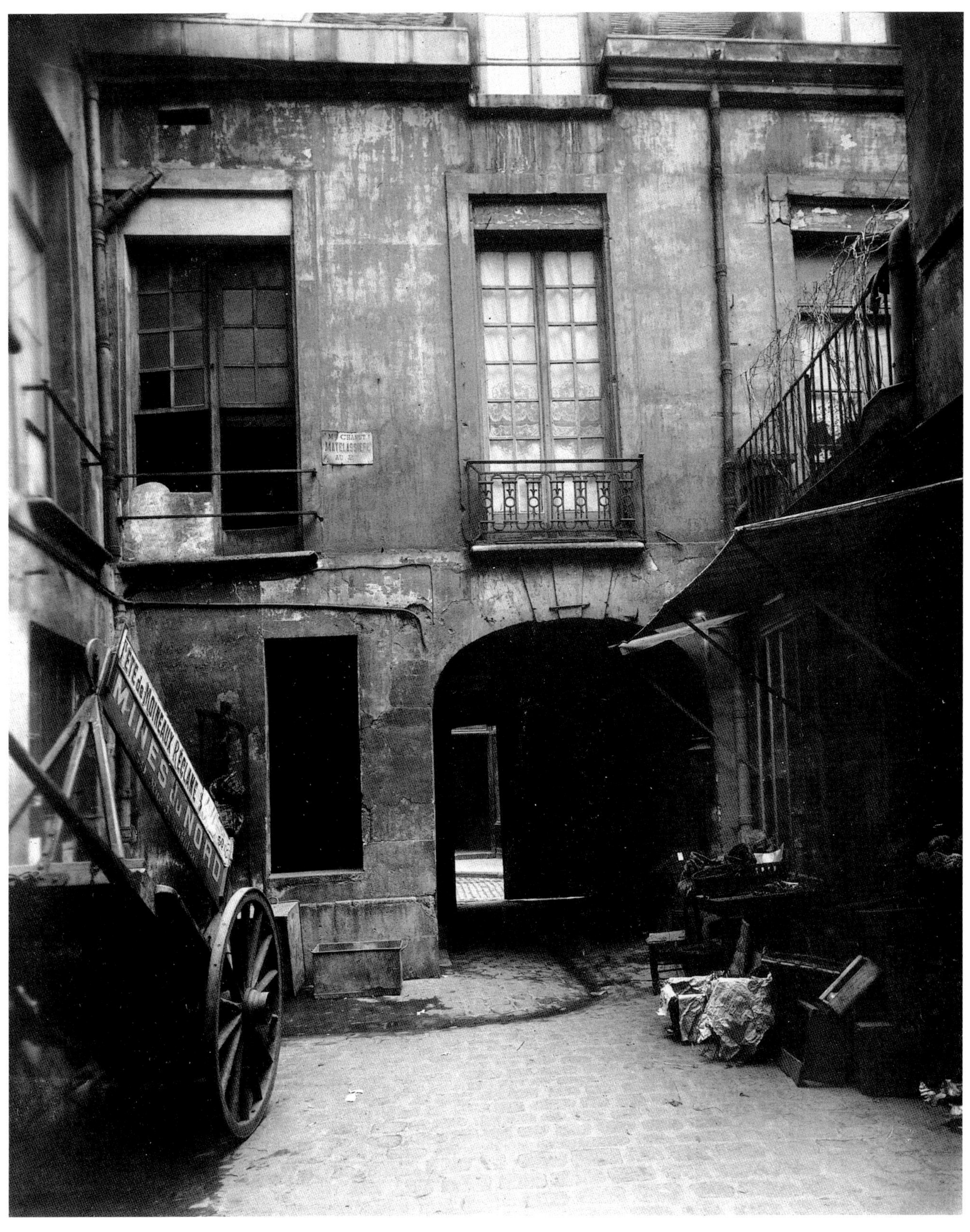

Ill. 14 Passage des Singes, toward the rue des Guillemites, 4th, 1911

architectural spaces (ill. 11–17). Each image reveals the next camera position, a procedure which imaginatively simulates the physical experience of walking along the street, stopping to look into the *passage*, entering and exploring it, before re-emerging and continuing along the rue des Guillemites.[14] In composing the individual images, Atget avoided strictly axial views, and consistently positioned his camera slightly to one side, in order to enhance rather than diminish the sensation of looking through a succession of spaces. In moving his camera forward from the exterior view on rue des Guillemites to the next camera position within the courtyard, Atget maintained the same sight line in order to convey a sense of the linking function of the *passage* (ill. 12 and 13). In addition, he frequently used a prominent element in the immediate foreground, such as a cart or vegetable stand, to establish a sense of scale, and to begin guiding the viewer through the fictive space of the photograph. Once assembled, the entire sequence provides a clear architectural description of the *passage*, its relationship to the two streets and, in his photographs of the vegetable stand and the well head, how it functioned as a communal space for those living and working in the immediate vicinity.

If this is a convincing reconstruction of how Atget worked as a commercial architectural photographer, then it is evident that he did not necessarily number his negatives in the order in which he exposed them but probably in the order in which they were developed and processed. Atget incorporated the seven photographs into three separate series: five of the images became part of *Topographie du vieux Paris* (ill. 11–14 and 17), the general view of the vegetable stand was included in *L'Art dans le vieux Paris* (ill. 15), and the detailed view formed part of *Paris pittoresque* (ill. 16). Whether Atget made these classification decisions as he was selecting and composing his views or later as he was numbering them is impossible to determine, and this practice may well have varied throughout his life. Regardless of the actual circumstances surrounding his decisions, these views reveal how Atget worked on several series concurrently. In addition to creating a coherent description of the site, and assembling images of potential value to his varied clientele, he was simultaneously pursuing his own interests. At this time, he was collecting examples of how goods were displayed in shops and kiosks, and he would later include the closer view of the vegetable stand (ill. 16) in his 1912 album, *Métiers, boutiques et étages de Paris*.[15]

If, to take an example of an interior space, the seven views Atget took in the stairwell of the Hôtel Dodun at 21 rue Richelieu in 1904–1905 are arranged into their probable sequence, they also reveal a sustained progression through the space. Using the ample natural illumination provided by the entrance door and the pairs of windows on each of the two landings, Atget began his work on the ground floor with both a general and a detailed view of the elaborate iron balustrade (ill. 18–19). He then proceeded to the first-floor landing, where he made three closely related views (ill. 20–22), before moving partway up the staircase to photograph the allegorical sculpture in its niche (ill. 23), and finally to the second-floor landing where he made his last view (ill. 24).

These photographs reveal how Atget's approach to documenting indoor space closely paralleled his outdoor practice. He moves systematically through the entire space, beginning at the entrance and ending with the furthest interior point. He also moves from overall to detailed views. The seven photographs form a cohesive group that concisely describes the overall interior space: Atget uses the form of the iron balustrade as it rises through two floors to focus and unite the sequence, and includes two detailed views of the ornate ironwork and one of the statue to complete his description. While the overall sequence can be convincingly reconstructed, it is not always possible to be certain about the order in which Atget made particular images, such as the two variant views he took on the first-floor landing (ill. 20 and 21). While the actual order itself can be variously argued, having developed the negatives, Atget evidently felt that both were worth preserving and printing. The more inclusive view provides a clearer sense of the space of the staircase as it ascends through different levels; the closer view produces a more visceral effect, created by the proximity of the balustrade and the more insistent presence of the sculpture.

In photographing Paris, Atget was limited to what he could reasonably carry, and, in examining topographically and numerically related clusters of photographs, one can identify sequences of between six and eight, very occasionally nine, images that appear to have been made on the same day. In some instances, these are groups taken within the same interior space, as with Atget's seven views in the interior of the Hôtel Dodun (ill. 18–24), his seven images of the vestibule of the Hôtel de Beauvais (cat. 1.11–1.17), or the eight views of the Church of Saint-Séverin (cat. 7.21–7.28). In other instances, the photographs share similar weather or lighting conditions, such as the seven views in the passage des Singes (ill. 11–17), the six views made after a rainfall at the corner of the rue de Sévigné and the rue de Jarente (cat. 3.9–3.14), or the nine photographs made in late morning and midday along the rue des Prêtres-Saint-Séverin and the rue Boutebrie in 1912 (cat. 7.56–7.64). In those relatively infrequent instances when Atget dated his work, the numbers of the negatives

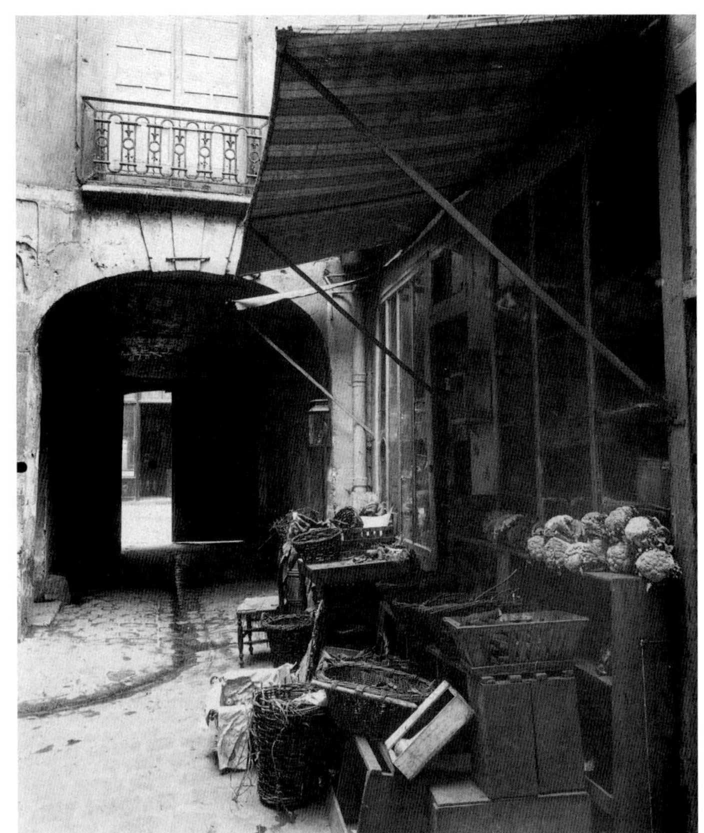

Ill. 15 Vegetable stand, passage des Singes, 4th, 1911

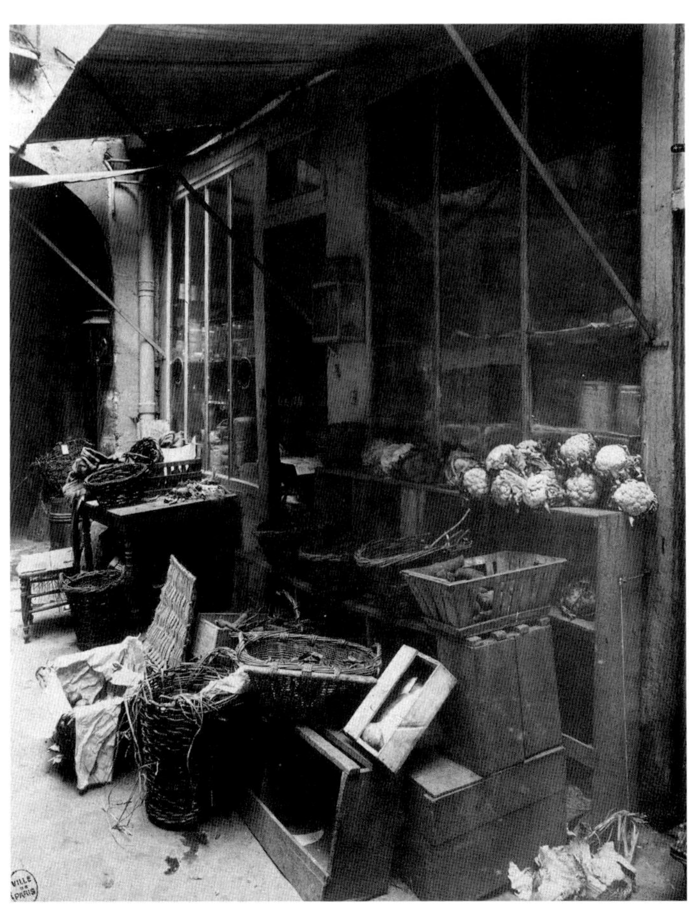

Ill. 16 Detail of vegetable stand, passage des Singes, 4th, 1911

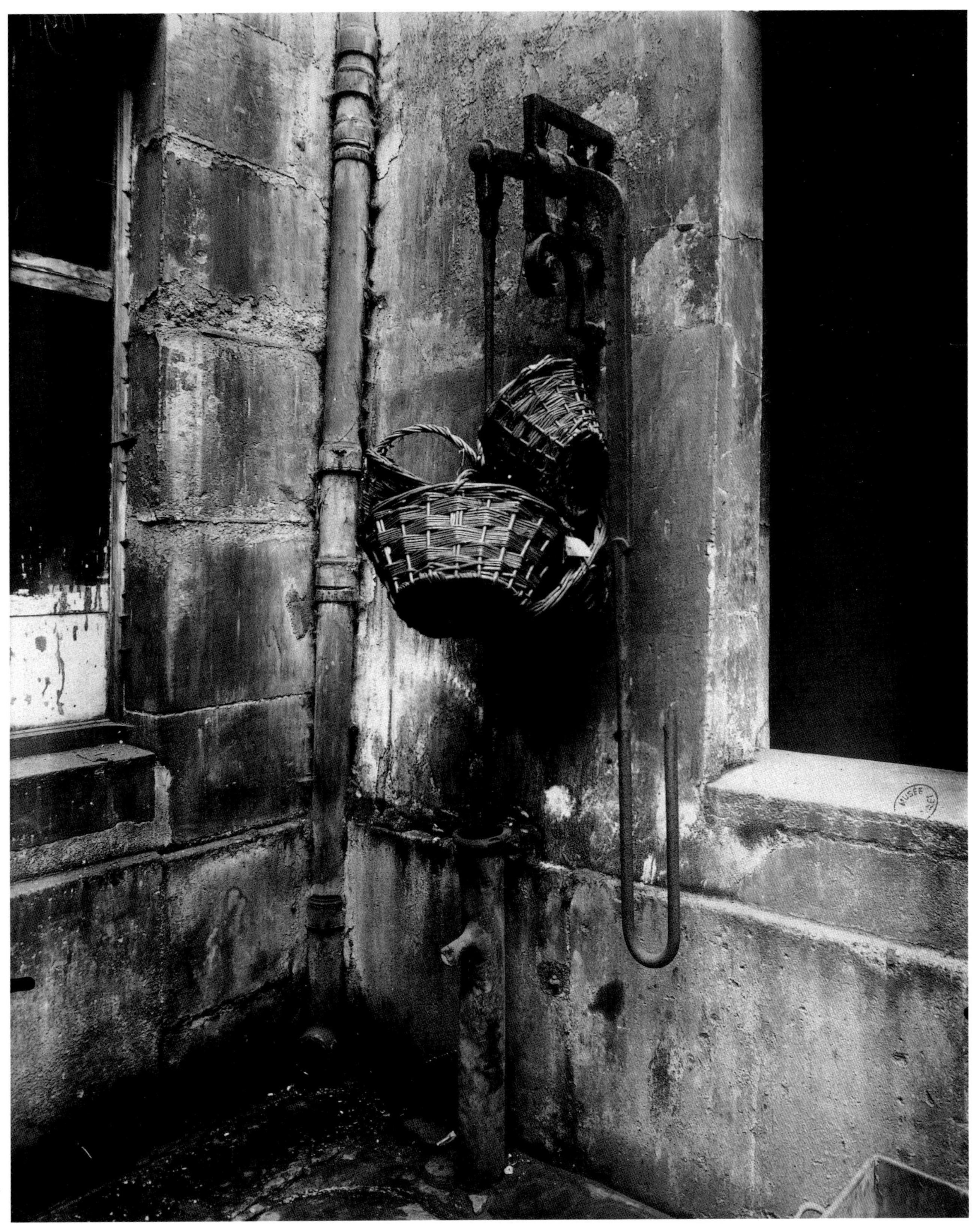

Ill. 17 Well, passage des Singes, 4th, 1911

also fall within this range, such as the eight views he made on March 15, 1913, of the demolition of the rue de la Parcheminerie (cat. 7.67–7.74). However, Atget's daily rate of exposed negatives must remain indeterminate and conjectural, as the total may have varied for a number of reasons, including the subject itself, atmospheric conditions, the distance which he would have had to travel, and other sites he may have also photographed on the same day.[16] This output may also have varied over the course of his career.

Having completed his documentation of most sites, such as the Hôtel Dodun and the passage des Singes, Atget saw little, if any, commercial advantage in returning to take further views and rarely did so. On the occasions when he did, a comparison between the images (sometimes made decades apart) provides further insight into his way of working. After he sold the 2,621 negatives to the Commission des monuments historiques in December 1920, he returned to a number of the sites over the following six years, presumably to replenish his stock of images. When, for example, Atget revisited the rue Berton in Passy in 1922 and photographed the house Balzac had occupied between 1840 and 1847, he stood close to the same spot where he had placed his camera nine years earlier in 1913 (ill. 25 and 26). Since it seems unlikely that Atget would have seen any commercial incentive in replicating the earlier view so precisely, one must conclude that the similarities between the two images spring from Atget's characteristic and habitual response to photographing in this type of environment. In turn, the subtle differences between the two images are only partly attributable to different lighting conditions, with the earlier image having been made on an overcast day and the later one on a sunny morning. In the second view, the positioning of his camera, both closer to Balzac's house and to the retaining wall, enabled Atget to reveal slightly more of the exterior wall of the house and thus enhance the sense of space along this stretch of the road and its contraction into a narrow lane in the distance. The years of photographic experience informed his approach and ultimately contributed to this refinement of his vision.

From the standpoint of an architectural and urban photographer, Atget's principal reason for rephotographing a site normally sprang from urban changes, requiring him to replace a now outdated view. His 1912 photograph of the rue Saint-Julien-le-Pauvre, to take one instance, superseded his 1899 image, as the demolition of the annex of the Hôtel Dieu in 1908–09 created a vista opening directly onto Notre-Dame Cathedral (ill. 27 and 28). In remaking this view for a third time in 1923 (ill. 29), he may have been partially motivated to replace the

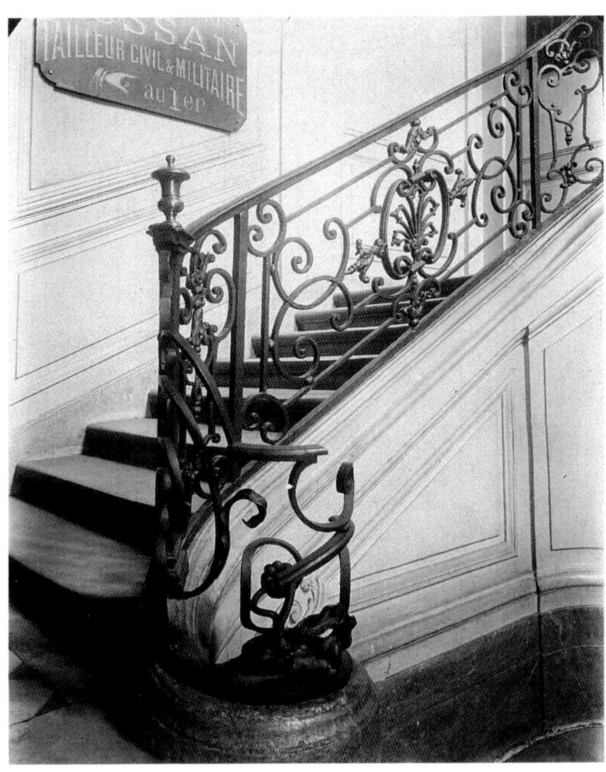

Ill. 18 Staircase, ground floor, Hôtel Dodun, 21 rue de Richelieu, 1st, 1904–1905

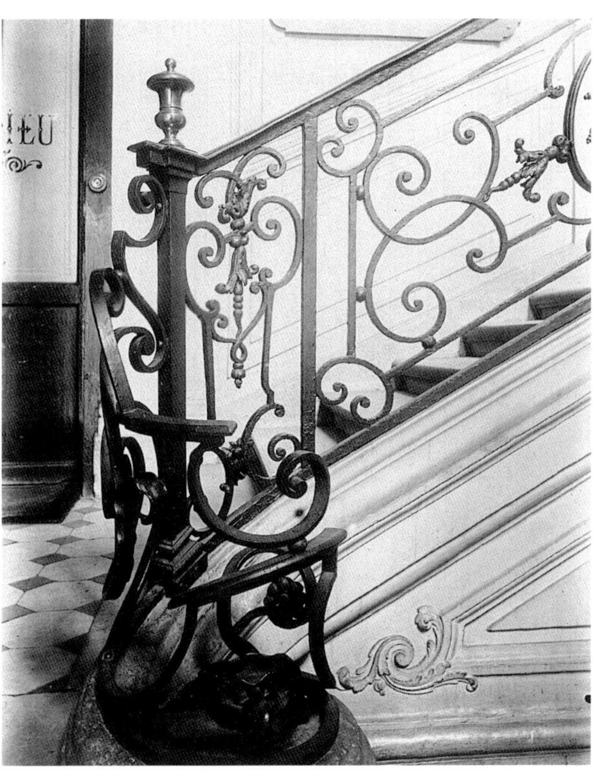

Ill. 19 Detail of staircase, ground floor, Hôtel Dodun, 21 rue de Richelieu, 1st, 1904–1905

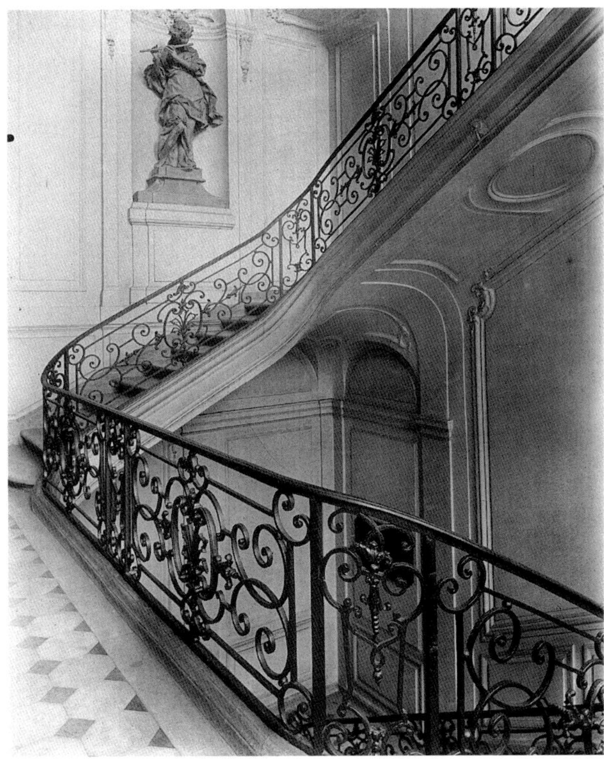

Ill. 20 Staircase, first-floor landing, Hôtel Dodun, 21 rue de Richelieu, 1st, 1904–1905

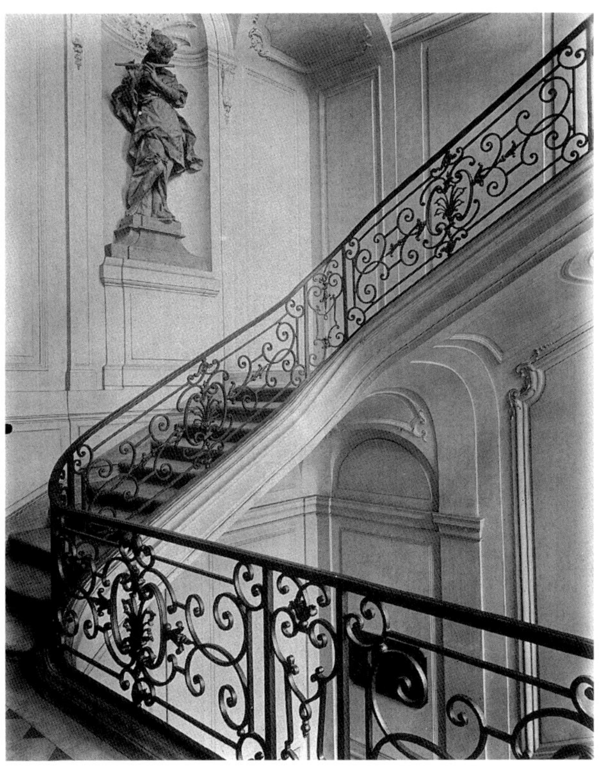

Ill. 21 Staircase, first-floor landing, Hôtel Dodun, 21 rue de Richelieu, 1st, 1904–1905

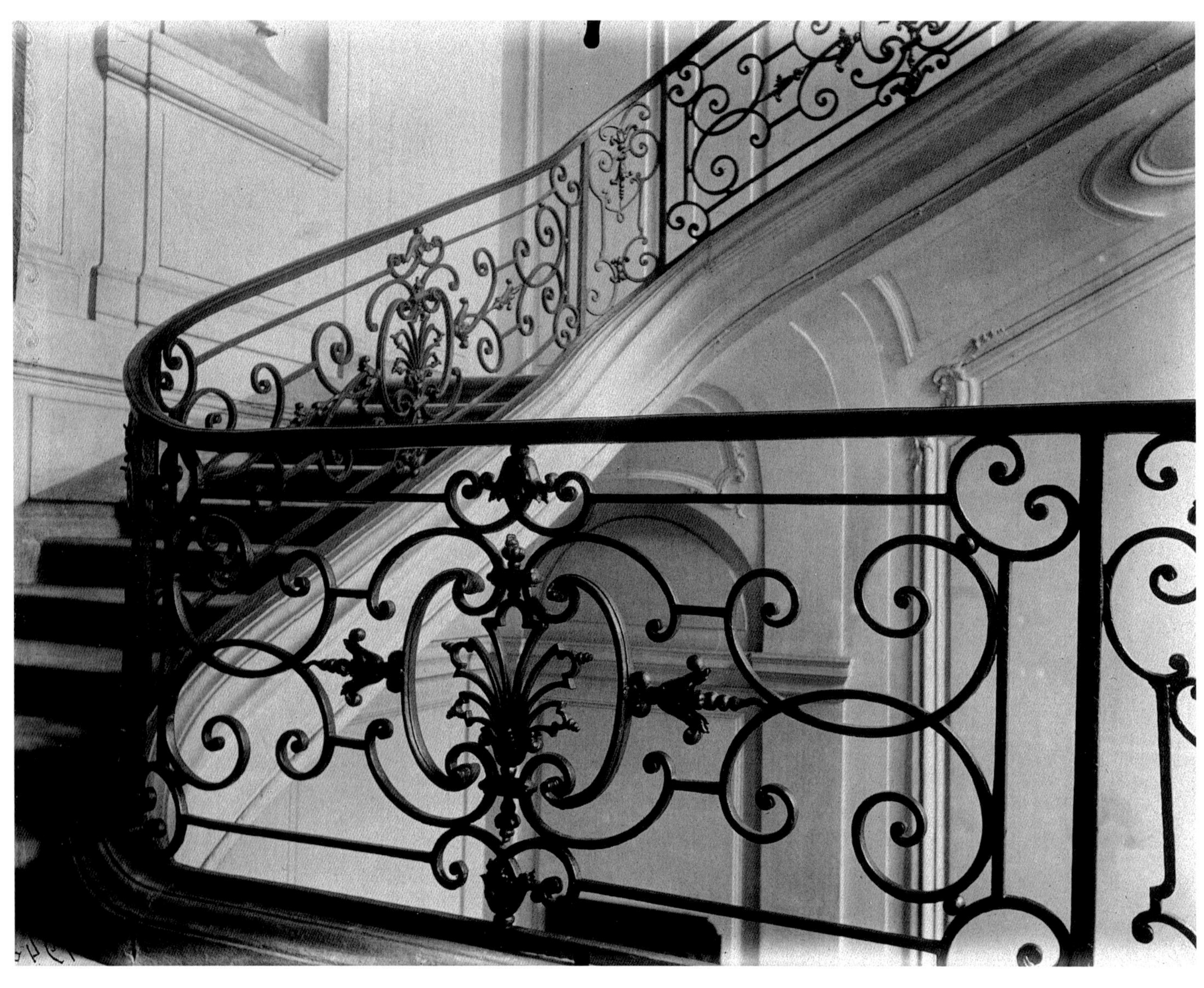

Ill. 22 Detail of banister, first-floor landing, Hôtel Dodun, 21 rue de Richelieu, 1st, 1904–1905

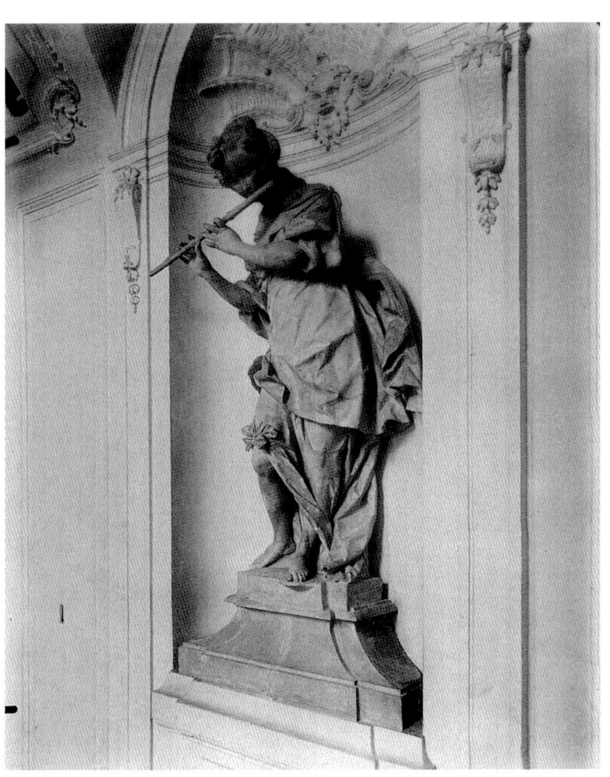

Ill. 23 Statue in niche between first and second floors, Hôtel Dodun, 21 rue de Richelieu, 1st, 1904–1905

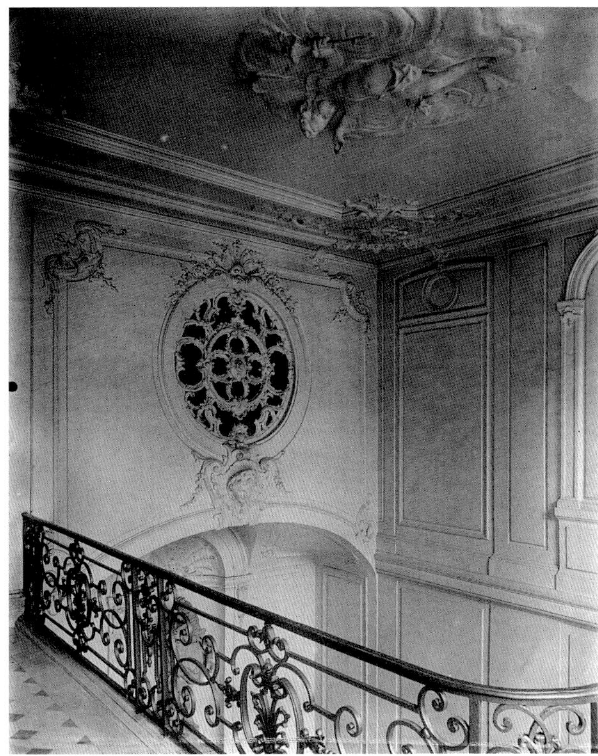

Ill. 24 Staircase, second-floor landing, Hôtel Dodun, 21 rue de Richelieu, 1st, 1904–1905

earlier two negatives, both sold in 1920, but his decision to adopt a horizontal format is more surprising. The vertical format had sympathetically echoed the tall, narrow constraints of the street itself, and had effectively masked the spatial distortions created by the use of a wide-angle lens. In the 1923 view, Atget again took up a position close to that he adopted in 1899, but now employed the wide-angle lens to create an image in which the pronounced spatial recession of the walls and buildings bordering the street was neutralized by the more symmetrical presentation and the stabilizing effect of the horizontal format.

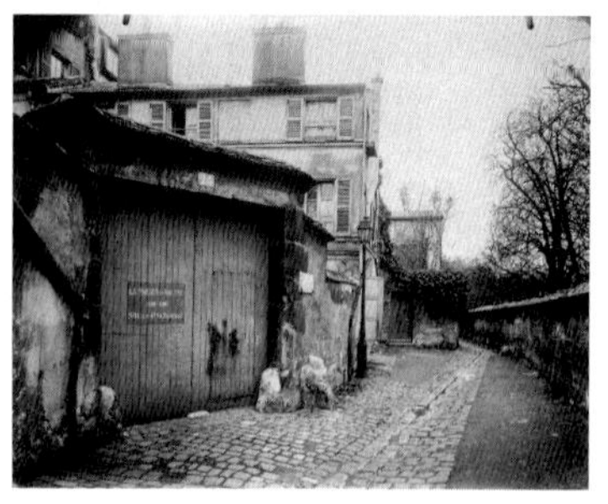

Ill. 25 Balzac's house, 24 rue Berton, 16th, 1913

The five photographs that Atget made in 1905, 1911, and 1924 of the block of buildings at the point where the rue de l'Échaudé converges with the rue de Seine serve to illustrate the process of photographing a site over an extended period of time (ill. 30–34). The reasons for his returning may lie with a lingering dissatisfaction with his earlier treatment of this complex urban form, and the sense that he had not yet found the ideal balance between scale and mass, between the space of the streets and the triangular wedge of the buildings. Under varying climatic conditions, at different times of day, and from various camera positions, Atget repeatedly photographed this site until, on an early morning in May 1924, he produced two images that may have finally satisfied him. While the camera positions of these last two views both lie within a few meters of his two 1911 images (compare ill. 31 with 33, and 32 with 34), the slight shifts in angle of vision and framing, coupled with the soft, enveloping early-morning light, created a delicate equilibrium between the volume of the buildings and the receding perspectives of the two streets.

The patterns of how Atget pursued the daily business of photographing become apparent as one assembles and studies entire groups of photographs taken at specific sites. The succession of views made in the passage des Singes or the suite of images taken of the stairwell of the Hôtel Dodun allows one to follow his progress through the spaces and, at the same time, to observe his mind at work. Atget interpreted the purpose of architectural and urban photography as creating a progressively unfolding description. A single vantage point could never adequately encompass a site; rather, several viewpoints and a sequence of related images were necessary to elucidate fully the particularities of the spatial configuration. Moreover, Atget's photographs were directly related to the urban forms they described, and he modified his method to accommodate the particularities of a *passage*, a staircase, or an intersection of two streets. In examining all of the photographs Atget took at a single location, one can readily see how he addressed and proceeded through the space, and, on those occasions when he revisited and rephotographed such sites, how he subtlety refined his approach.

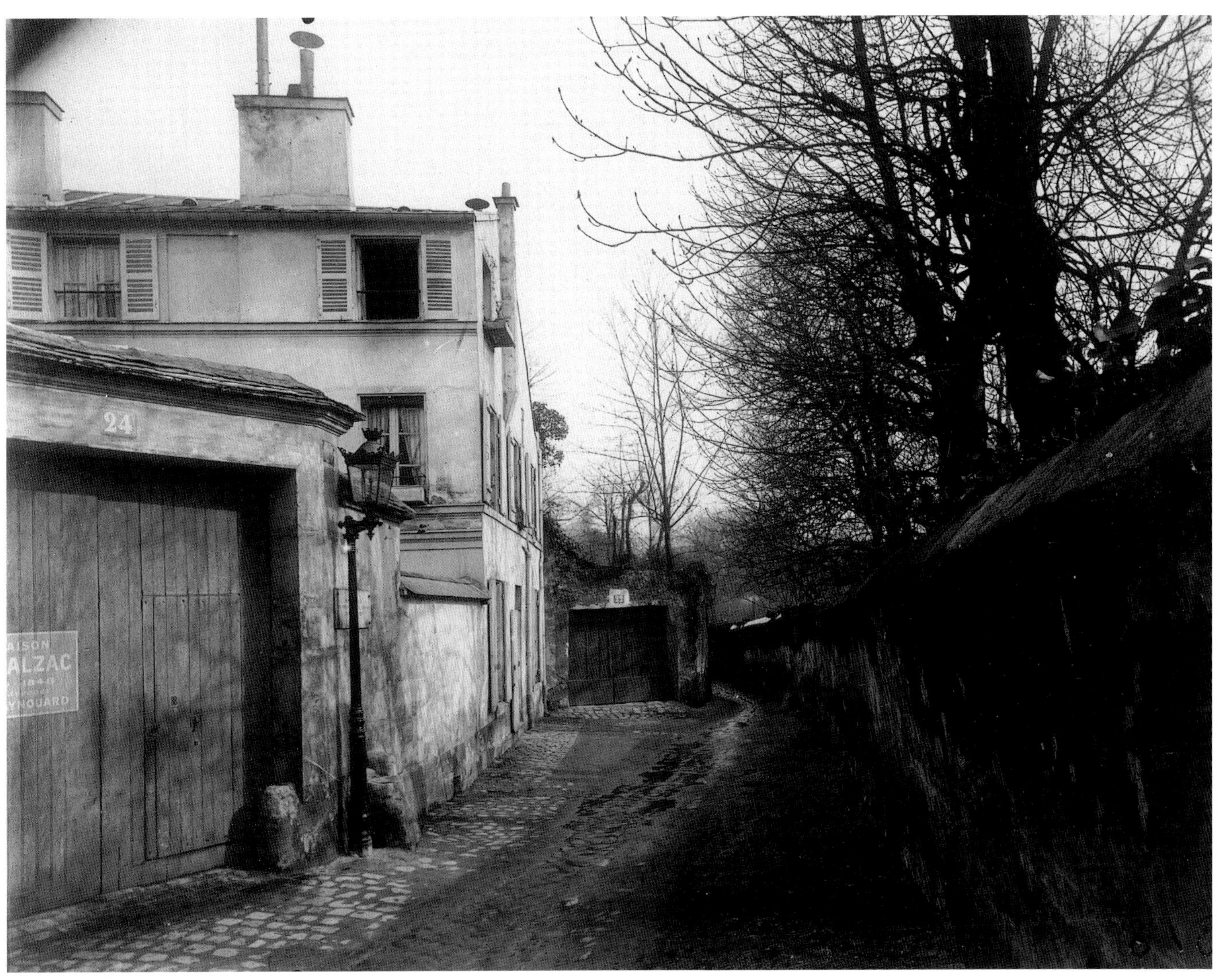

Ill. 26 Balzac's house, 24 rue Berton, 16th, March 1922

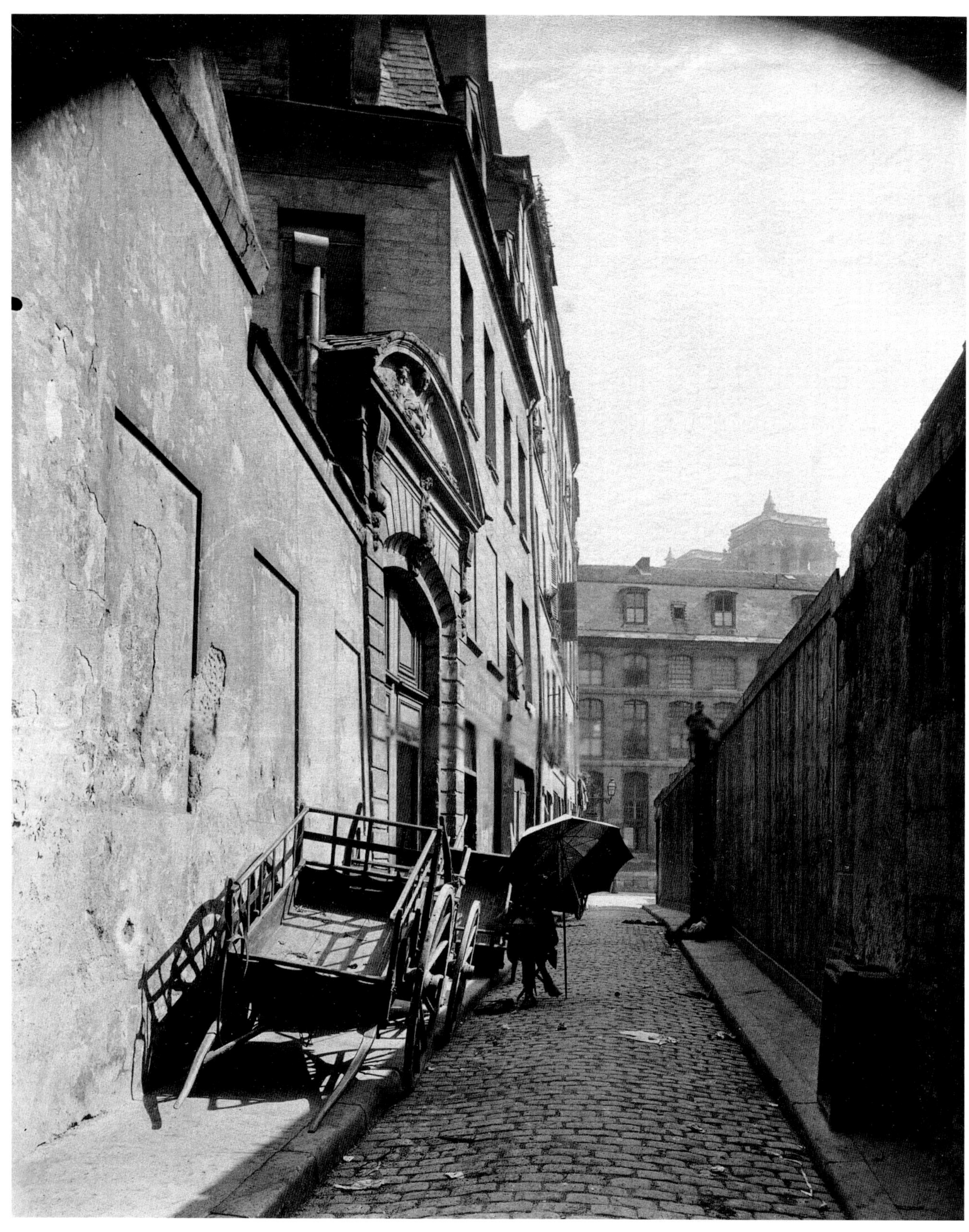

Ill. 27 Rue Saint-Julien-le-Pauvre, toward the rue de la Bûcherie and the former annex of the Hôtel-Dieu, 5th, August 1899

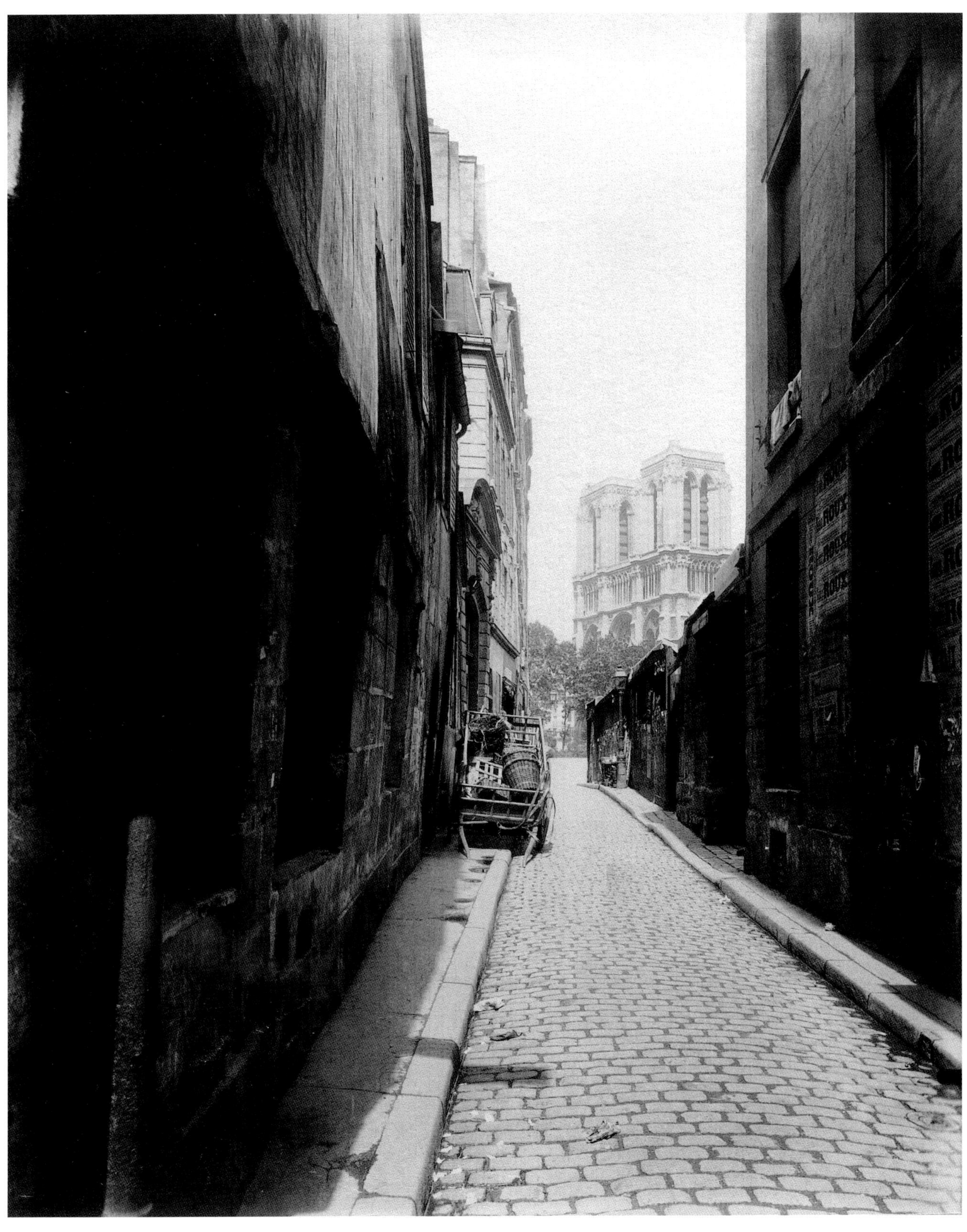

Ill. 28 Rue Saint-Julien-le-Pauvre, toward the quai de Montebello and Notre-Dame, 5th, 1912

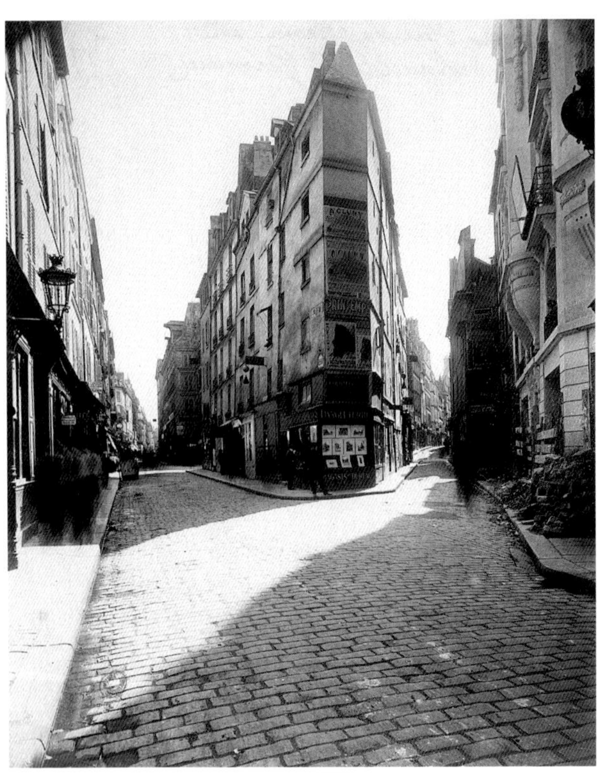

Ill. 31 Corner of the rue de Seine and the rue de l'Échaudé, 6th, 1910–1911

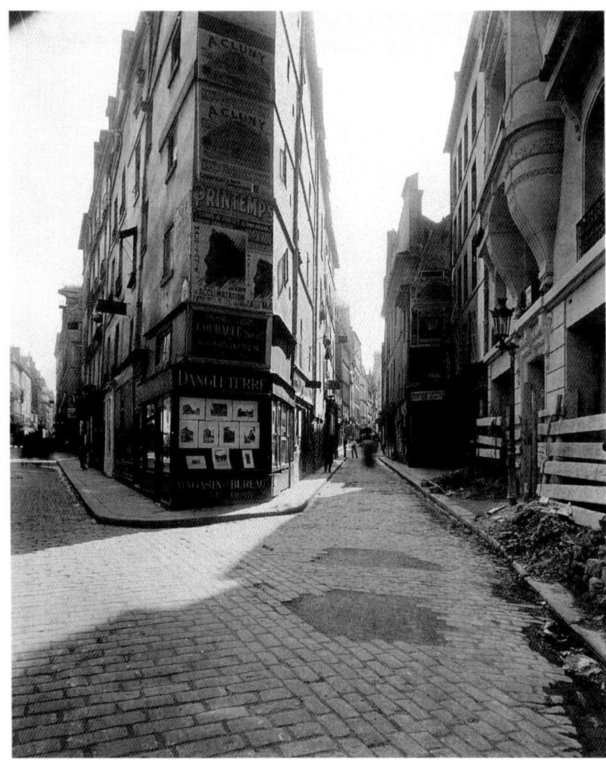

Ill. 32 Corner of the rue de Seine and the rue de l'Échaudé, 6th, 1910–1911

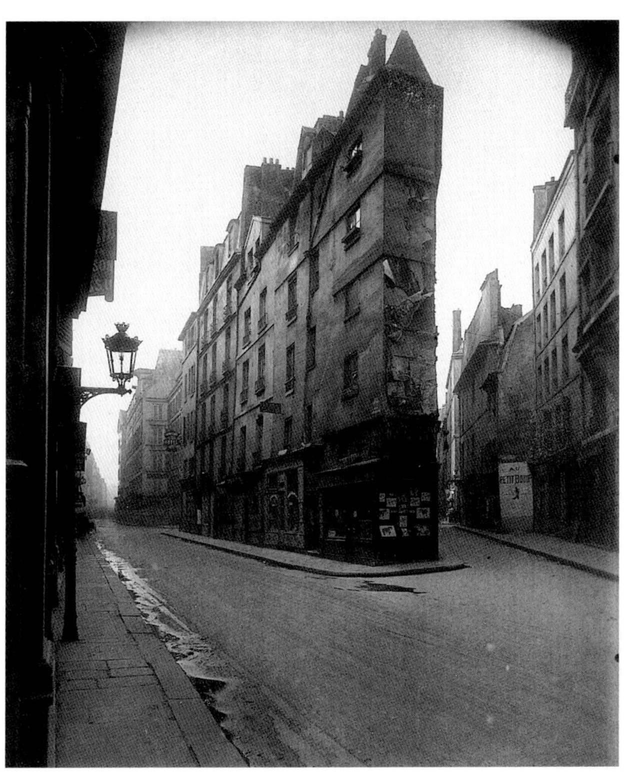

Ill. 33 Corner of the rue de Seine and the rue de l'Échaudé, 6th, May 1924

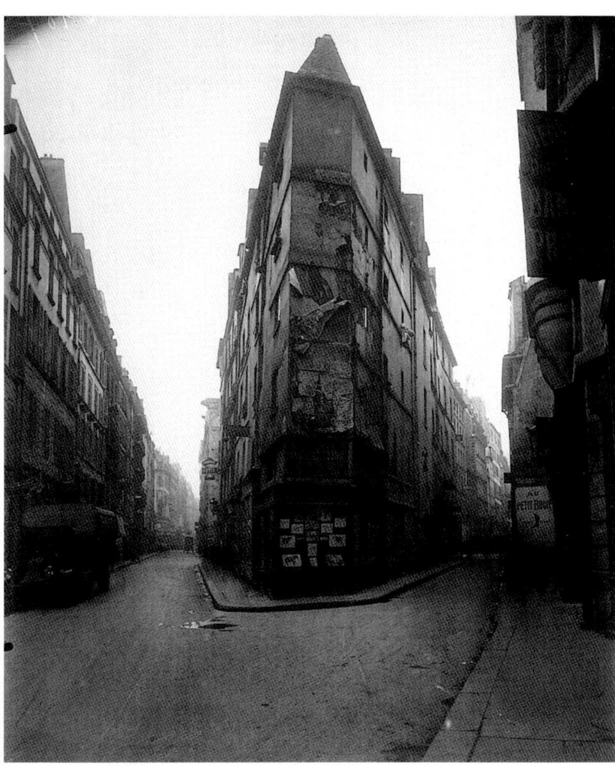

Ill. 34 Corner of the rue de Seine and the rue de l'Échaudé, 6th, May 1924

Chapter 4 Seven Parisian Sites

This chapter presents seven case studies. Since this publication derives from the vast holdings of the Musée Carnavalet, the selection of sites is confined to those within the city limits, and excludes the surrounding picturesque villages and royal gardens in the Ile-de-France region. The choice also reflects the nature of the museum's current holdings. The Musée Carnavalet purchased approximately 2,750 photographs (including ones from outside Paris) directly from Atget between 1898 and 1927.[1] The majority of these images were from negatives made before 1914, and only 170 images date from the 1920s. In 1952, the museum acquired an additional topographical collection of 3,594 Atget photographs, all of whose negatives date from the prewar period. As a result, five of the studies presented here are drawn exclusively from photographs taken before 1914, while the final two include images spanning Atget's entire working life.

Each study has been selected to represent a distinctive urban typology: these include a town house (the Hôtel de Beauvais and the Hôtel de Ranes); a contiguous group of streets (those of the rue du Parc-Royal, the rue de Sévigné, and the rue de Jarente); an intersection (the point at which the rue de l'Abbaye, the rue Cardinale, the rue de l'Échaudé, the passage de la Petite-Boucherie, and the rue de Bourbon-le-Château all converge); a public square (place Bernard Halpern); the quays (those surrounding the Pont-Neuf); and lastly, an important building within its neighborhood (the Church of Saint-Séverin and the cluster of streets bordering it). Each site has also been chosen to reveal, upon close examination, a different aspect of Atget's method of photographing architectural and urban spaces. Each represents a place where the photographer worked intensively for a limited time, or one to which he returned periodically (place Halpern) or even regularly over a period of many years (Saint-Séverin). For each of the case studies, all known photographs from a single or multiple photographic excursions have been reassembled and sequenced in their probable order. Finally, in order to provide a basis of comparison between Atget's photographs and the site itself, all of the sites, with the exception of portions of only two, remain largely unchanged today.[2]

In this chapter, only a selection of images are reproduced. For each site, the entire sequence is illustrated in the catalogue, beginning on page 169.

1. Hôtel de Beauvais, 68 rue François-Miron, 4th arrondissement, 1900 and 1902

Atget made seventeen photographs of the Hôtel de Beauvais, an unusual example of residential architecture with significant historical associations. In 1654, Pierre de Beauvais and his wife, Catherine-Henriette Bellier, *femme de chambre* of Anne d'Autriche, purchased three buildings along rue François-Miron (formerly rue Saint-Antoine) and commissioned Antoine Le Pautre, architect of Louis XIII, to design a sumptuous town house upon an irregularly shaped piece of land. Construction was completed by August 26, 1660, when Queen Anne d'Autriche, together with Mazarin and Turenne witnessed from its balconies the procession of her son Louis XIV after his marriage to Marie Thérèse, *l'infante d'Espagne*.[3] The *hôtel* later became the residence of a number of celebrated diplomats and financiers, before finally being acquired by the city of Paris in 1943. It is presently under restoration.

On his first visit to the Hôtel de Beauvais in August 1900, Atget photographed the building, which still retained the vestiges of commercial shops along its ground floor, as part of the street facade, and made an axial view of its original doorway (cat. 1.1 and 1.2). Two years later, in a closely related group of fifteen photographs, made over a period of at least two days, he extensively documented the entrance door, the courtyard, and the vestibule.[4] He made a sequence of six views in which, continuing from his 1900 axial view and maintaining the same sight line, he proceeded into the courtyard, turned around, and worked back toward the entrance (cat. 1.5–1.10). The camera positions of catalogue entries 1.7 and 1.8 are very close to one another and mark the point at which the photographer pivoted his camera. Within the entrance vestibule with its elegant stone staircase, decorated with pairs of Corinthian columns and a sculptural relief by Martin Desjardins, Atget positioned his camera on the far side and, by progressively shifting it laterally, produced four successive views that dealt with the formal architectural vocabulary (cat. 1.11 and 1.14) and the experience of the interior space (cat. 1.12 and 1.13). He made his final three views by moving in stages up the staircase (1.15–1.17).

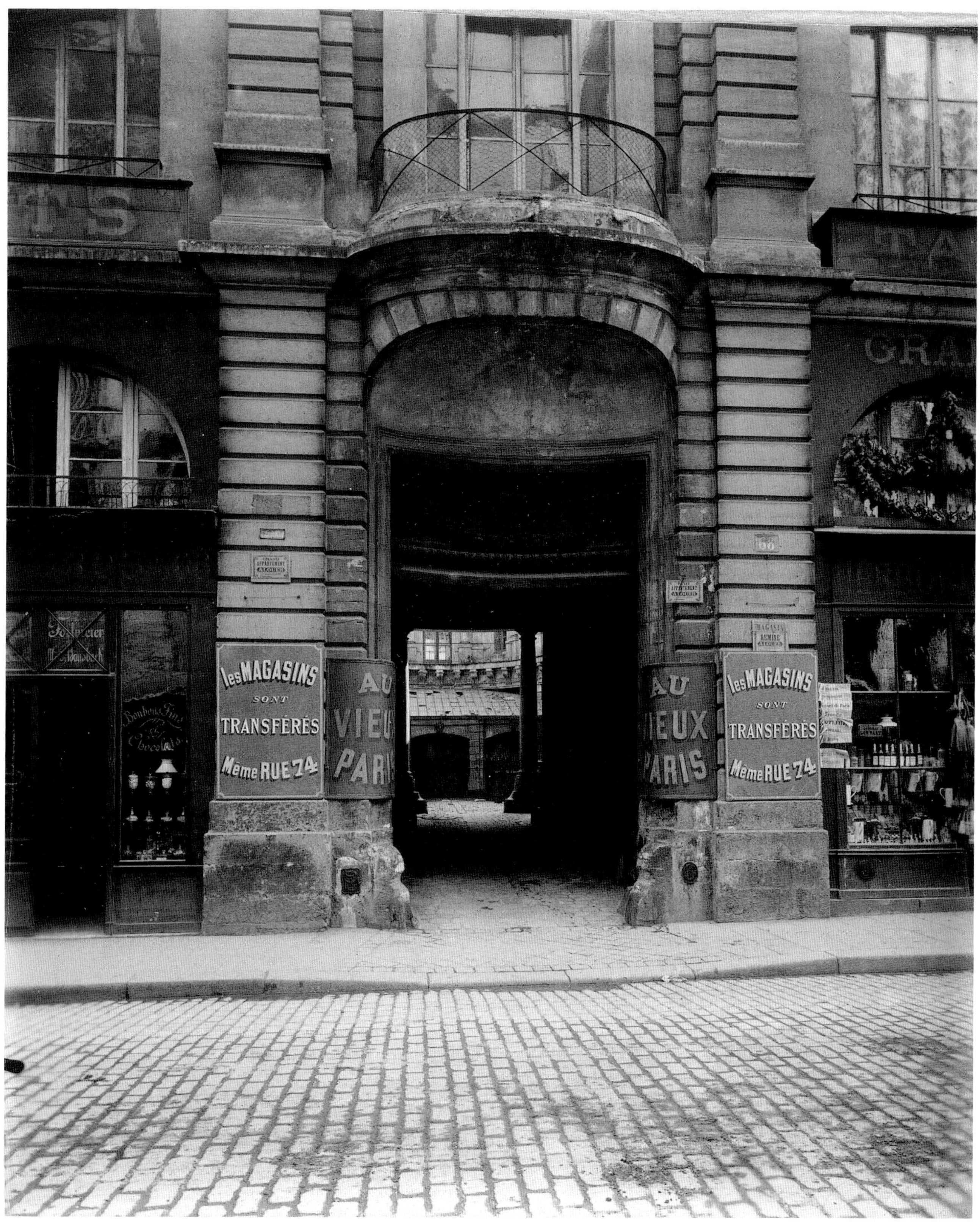

1.2 Entrance portal, Hôtel de Beauvais, August 1900

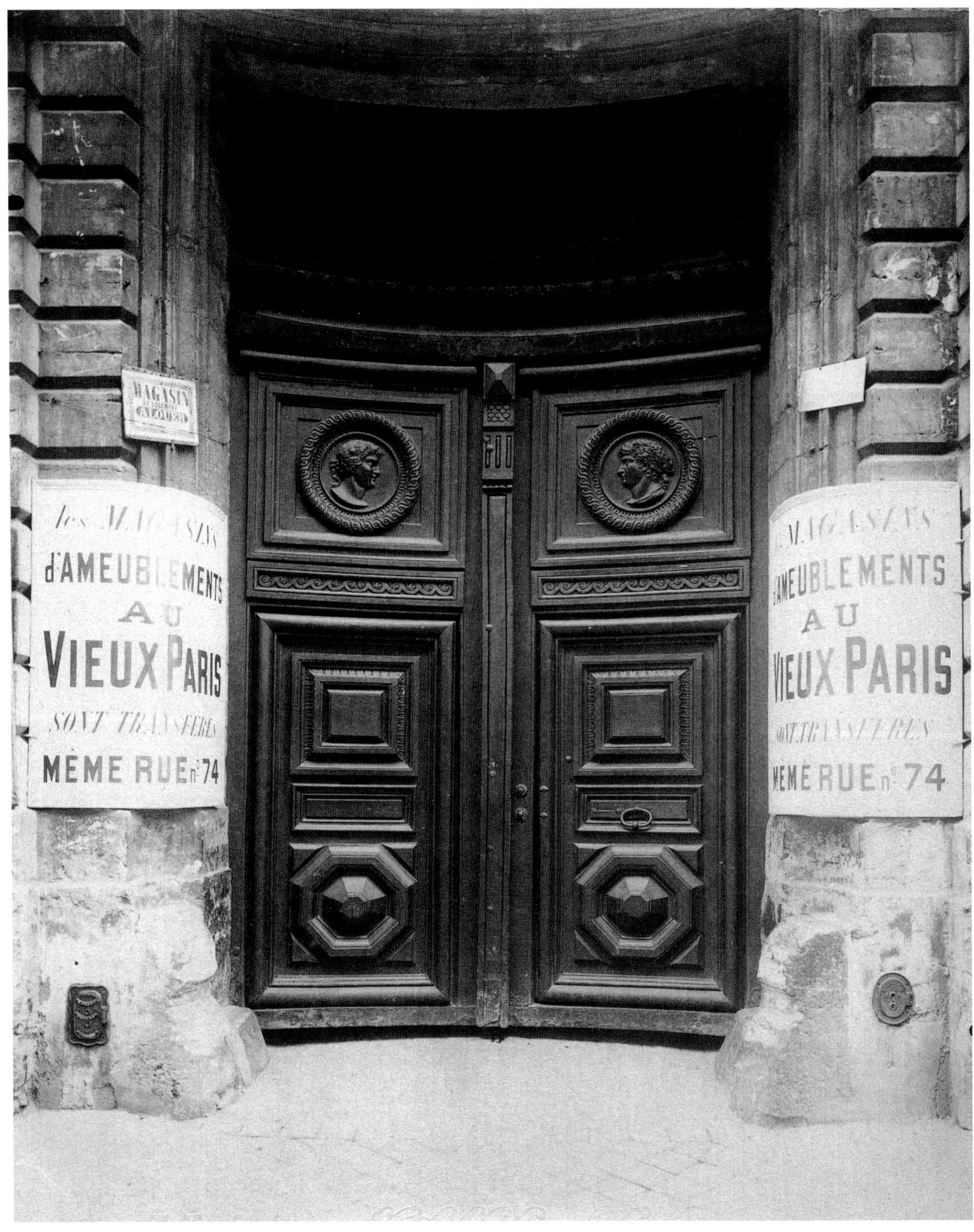

1.3 Entrance door, Hôtel de Beauvais, 1902

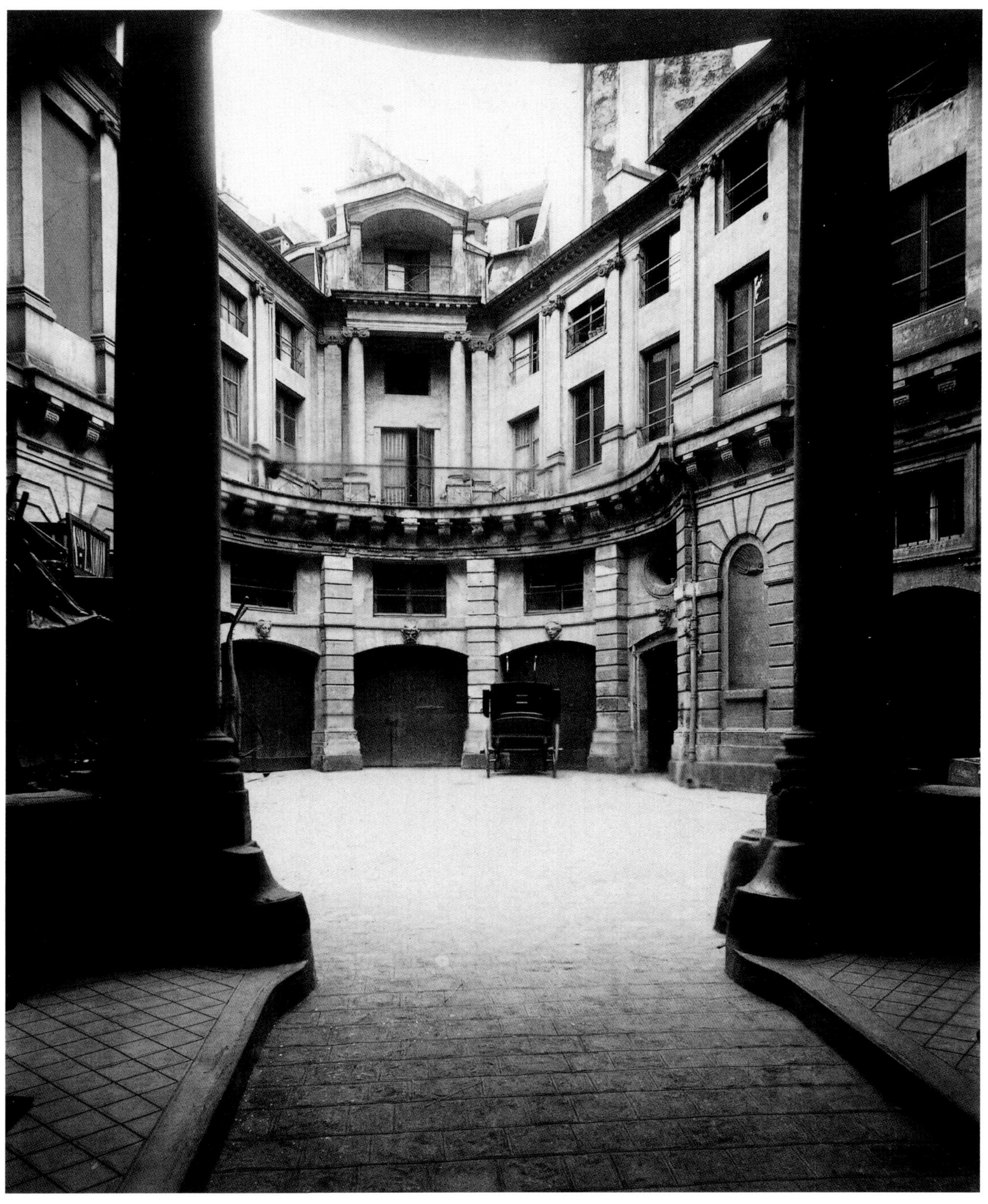

1.5 View from the entrance portal into courtyard, Hôtel de Beauvais, 1902

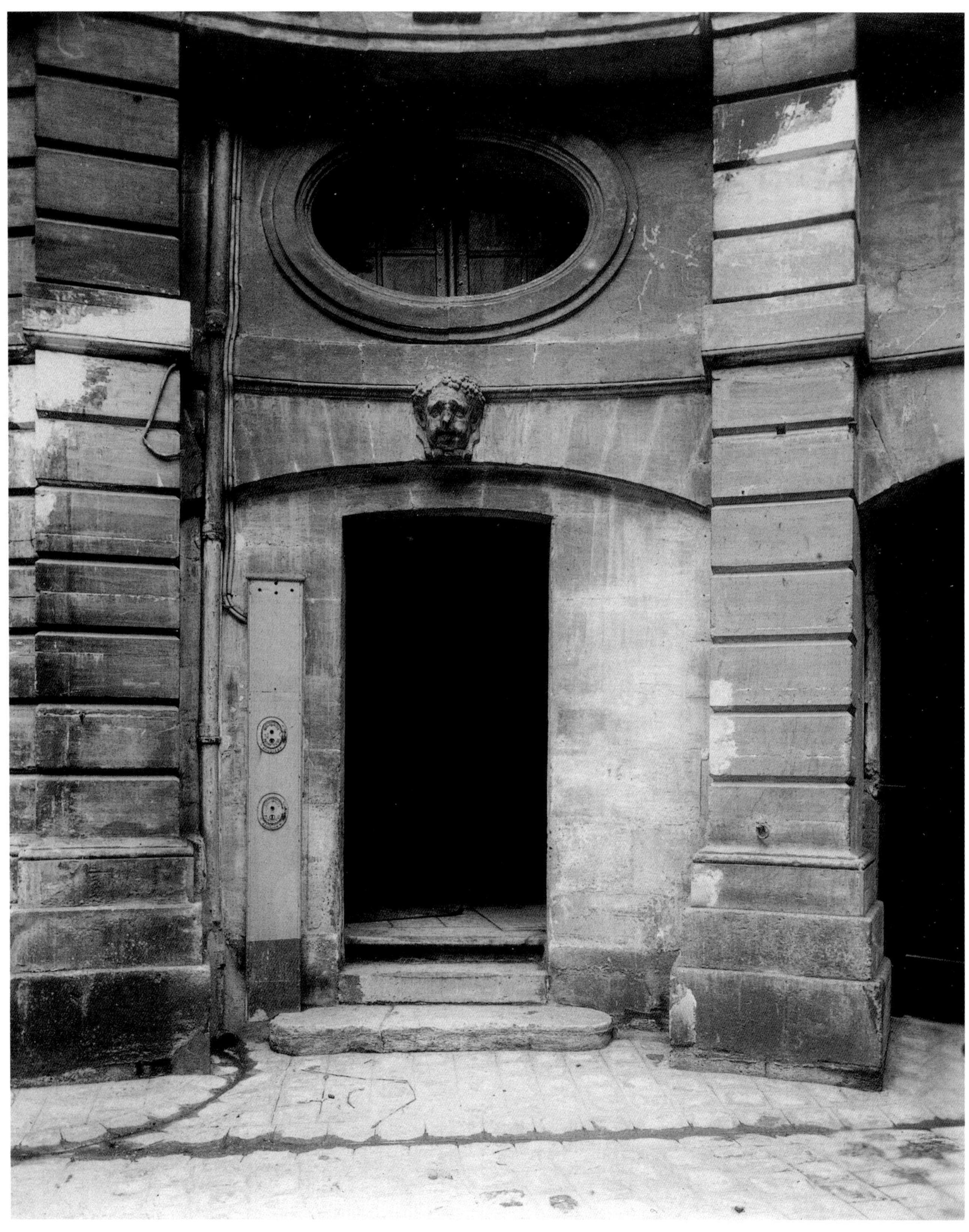

1.7 Courtyard, entrance to back-staircase, Hôtel de Beauvais, 1902

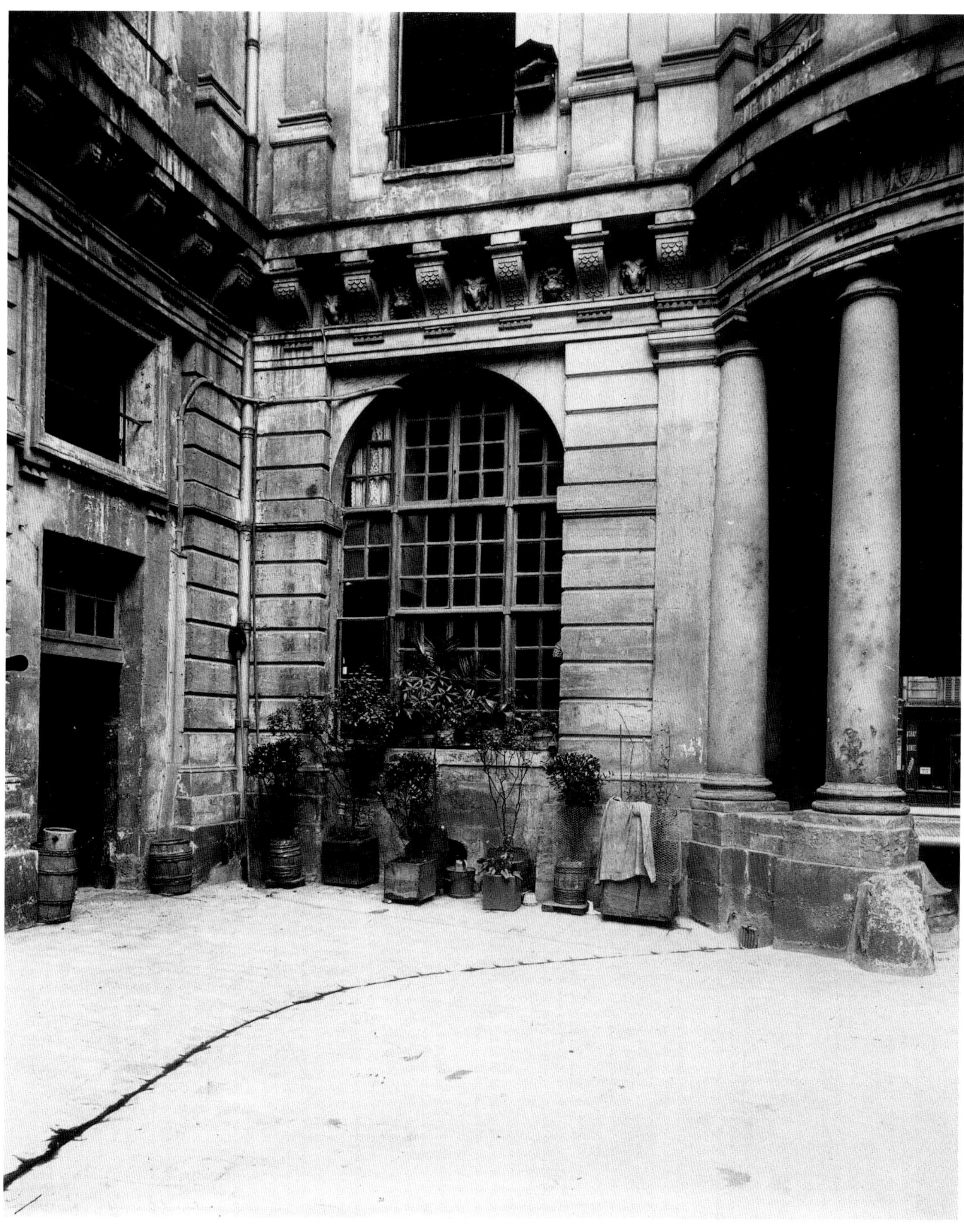

1.9 Corner of courtyard to the left of entrance portal, Hôtel de Beauvais, 1902

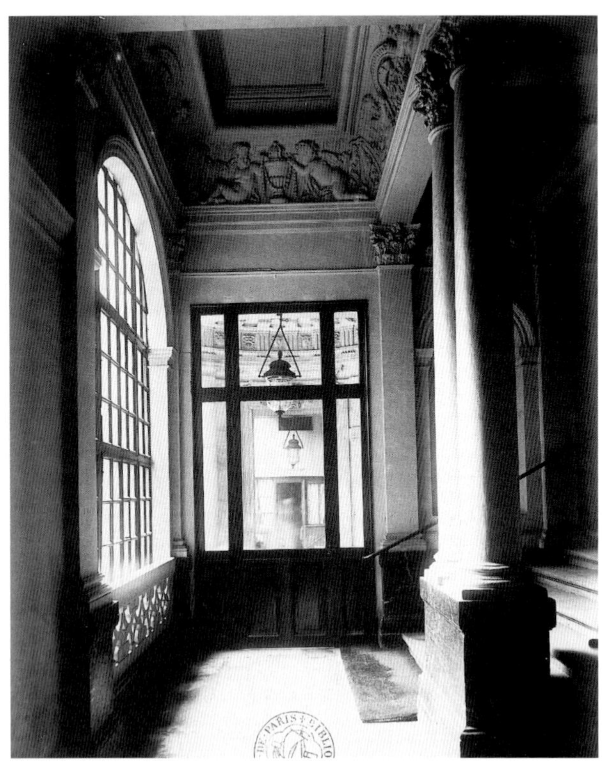

1.11 Vestibule of the grand staircase, Hôtel de Beauvais, 1902

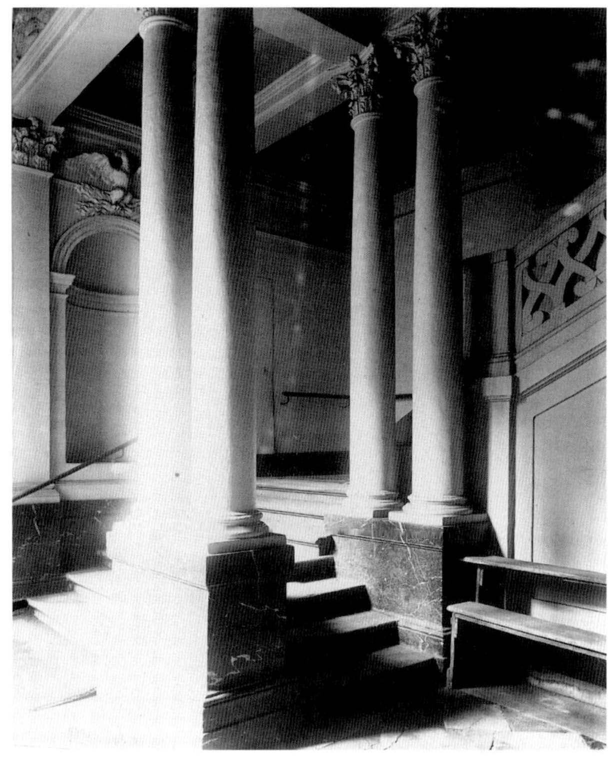

1.12 Vestibule and grand staircase, Hôtel de Beauvais, 1902

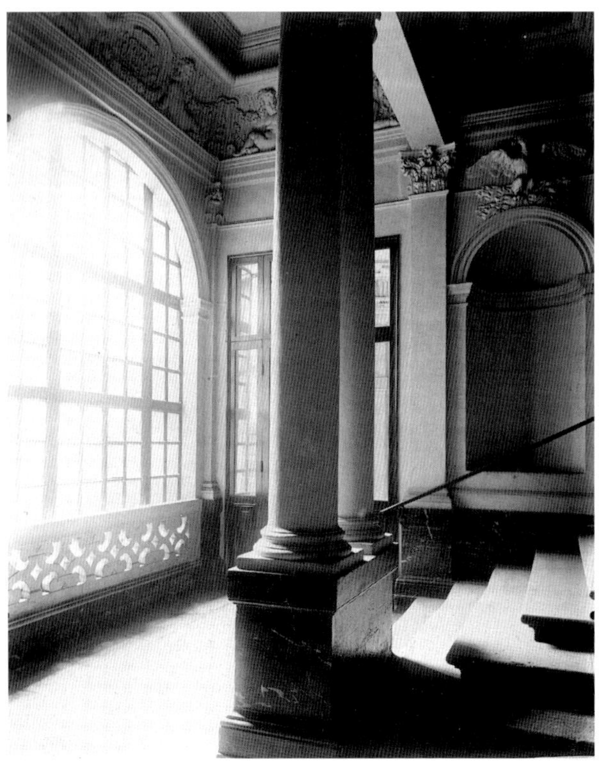

1.13 Vestibule and grand staircase, Hôtel de Beauvais, 1902

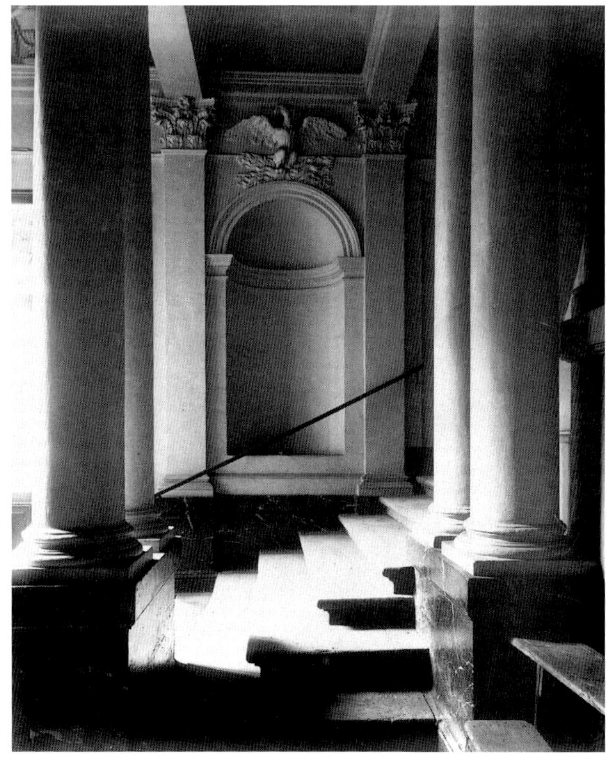

1.14 Vestibule, grand staircase with niche, Hôtel de Beauvais, 1902

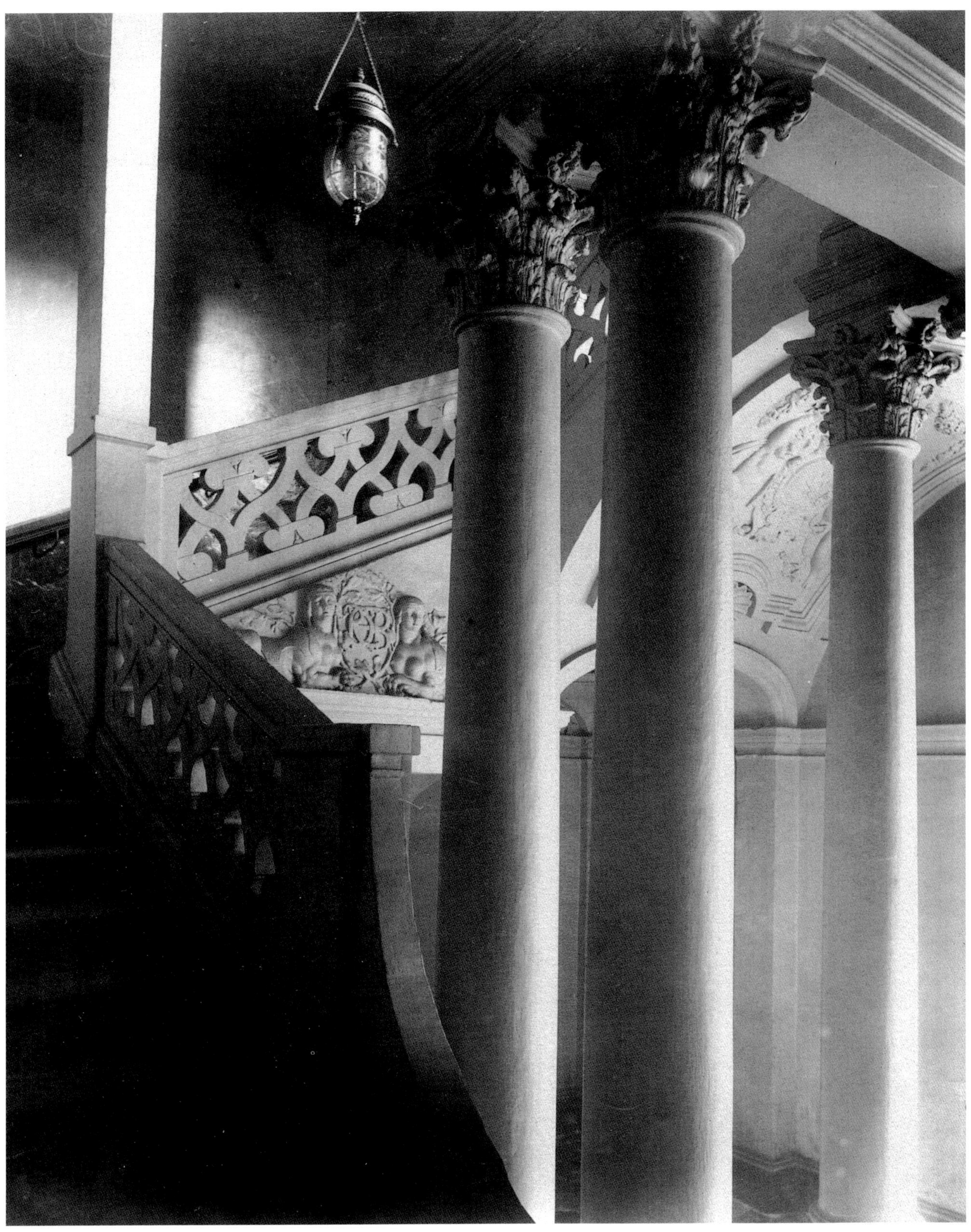

1.15 Grand staircase, first flight, Hôtel de Beauvais, 1902

2. Hôtel de Ranes and the rue Visconti, 6th arrondissement, 1910

In 1910, as part of his evolving series *Topographie du vieux Paris*, Atget took at least twenty-eight photographs along the rue Visconti, a relatively short and narrow street running between the rue de Seine and the rue Bonaparte.[5] Unlike his documentation of the Hôtel de Beauvais, where he treated the building largely in isolation from its relationship with the street, Atget integrated the quiet courtyard of the Hôtel de Ranes, where Jean Racine was thought to have died,[6] into his coverage of the street.

Atget documented the courtyard in a sequence of five photographs, following his regular method of creating linked views that systematically describe the courtyard (cat. 2.1–2.5), and also made three related views around the entrance portal itself (cat. 2.6–2.8). Two of the former views reveal how the archway signals the *hôtel*'s formal entrance from the street (cat. 2.1–2.2). The latter three views describe the street as seen from the covered portal. Atget made the first photograph looking diagonally across the narrow street toward the courtyard at number 24 (cat. 2.6), and then, by shifting his camera's position and framing only slightly, made the second view looking down the street toward the rue Bonaparte (cat. 2.7). After moving his camera a few meters beyond the portal, Atget took the third view, looking along the length of the street toward the rue de Seine (cat. 2.8). The resulting three views form a kind of panoramic sweep of the street.

In this group of eight photographs, Atget adopted two different viewpoints—corresponding to the perspectives of the owner of the property and the pedestrian—in order to examine how private and public spheres meet within the transitional space of the *hôtel*'s entrance.

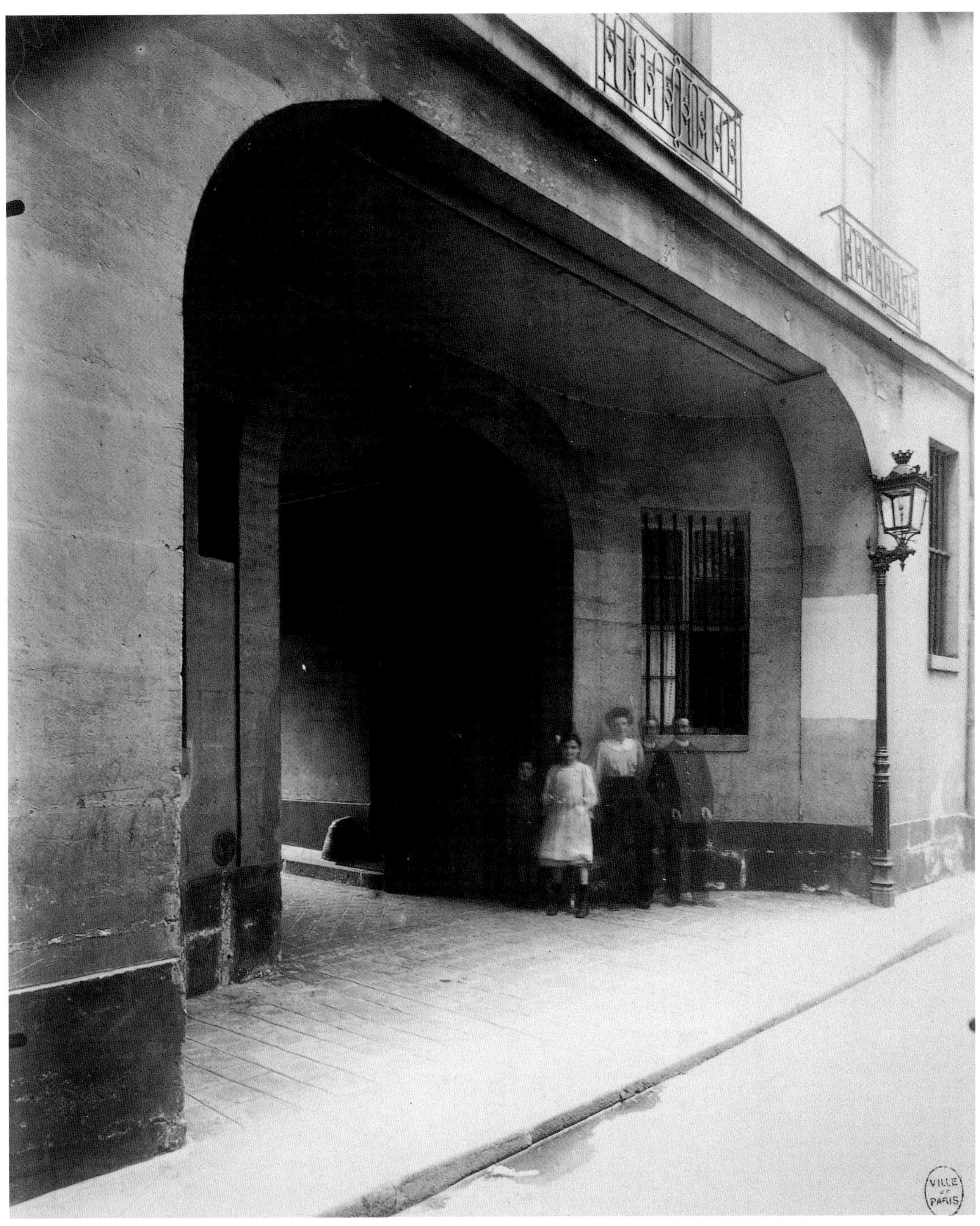

2.1 Entrance portal, Hôtel de Ranes, 21 rue Visconti, 1910

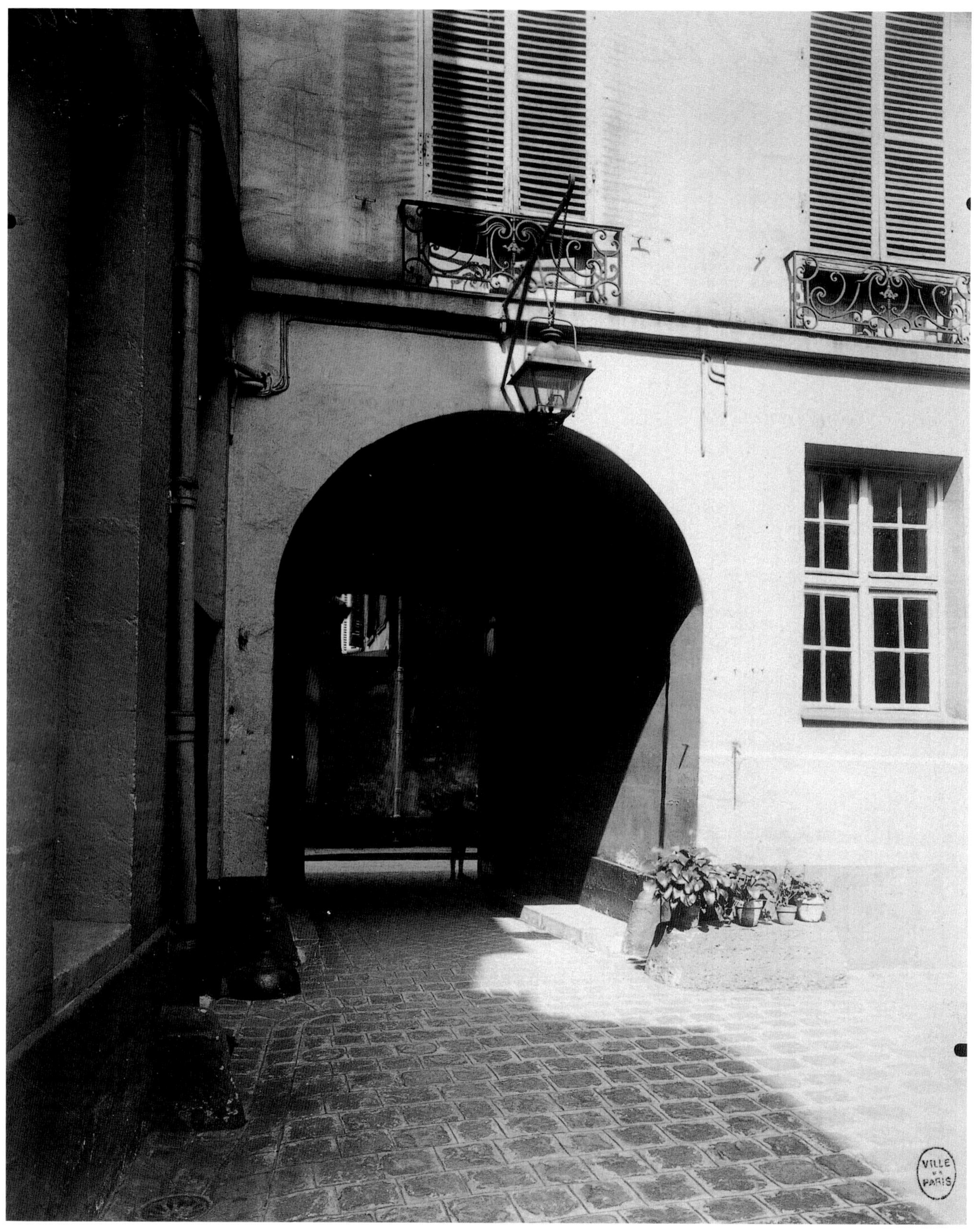

2.4 Courtyard, toward entrance portal and street, Hôtel de Ranes, 21 rue Visconti, 1910

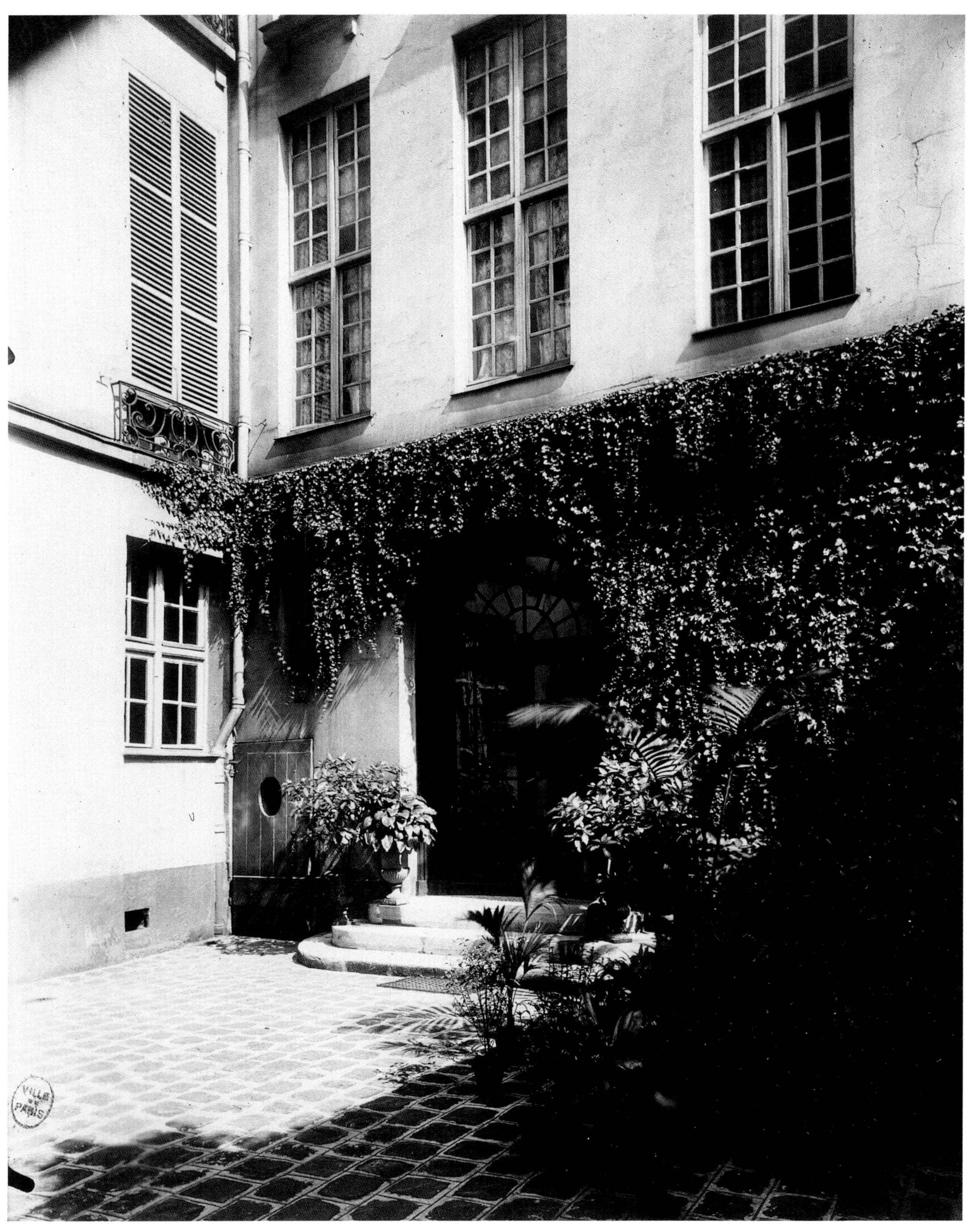

2.5 Courtyard entrance, Hôtel de Ranes, 21 rue Visconti, 1910

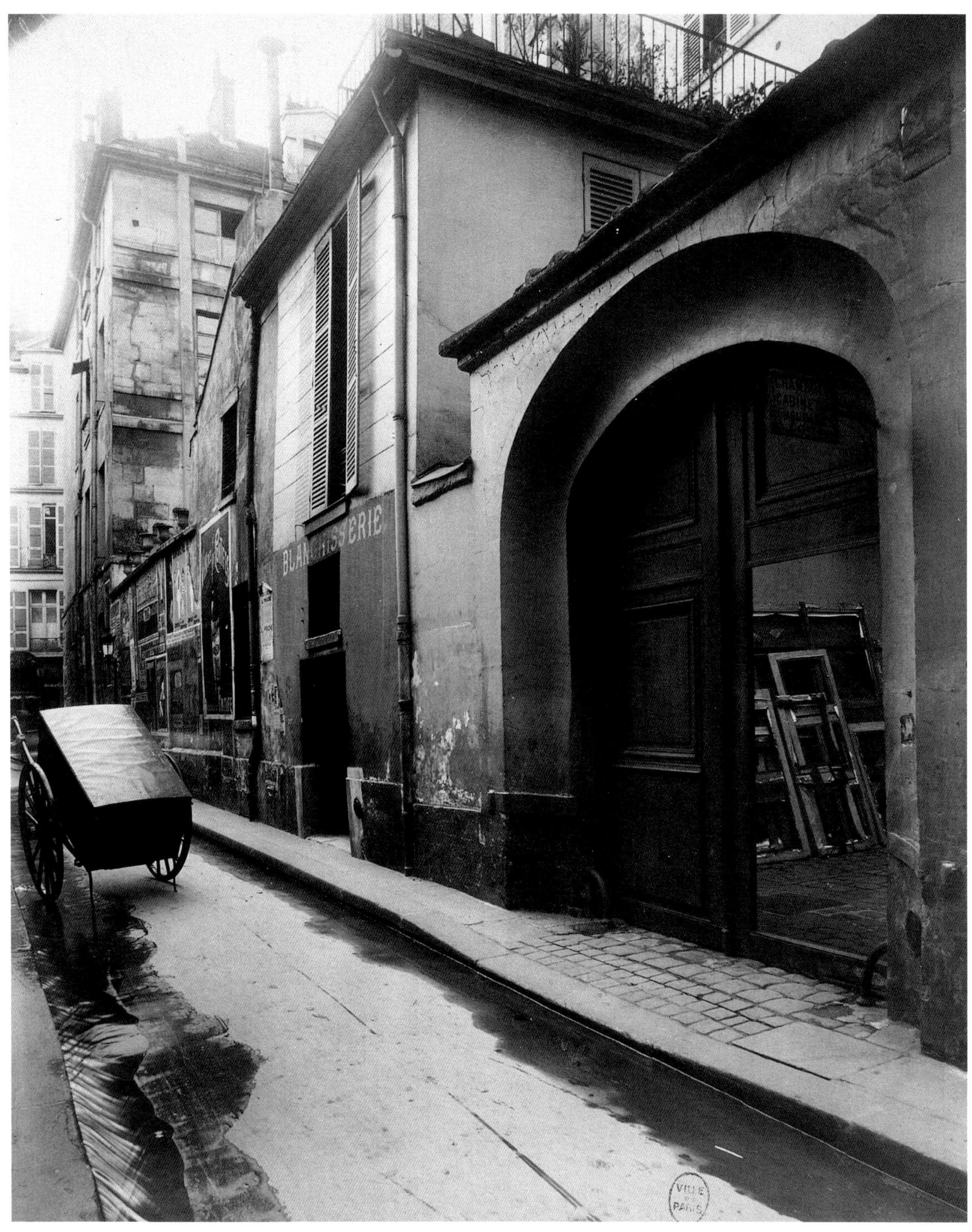

2.7 24 rue Visconti and view toward the rue Bonaparte, 1910

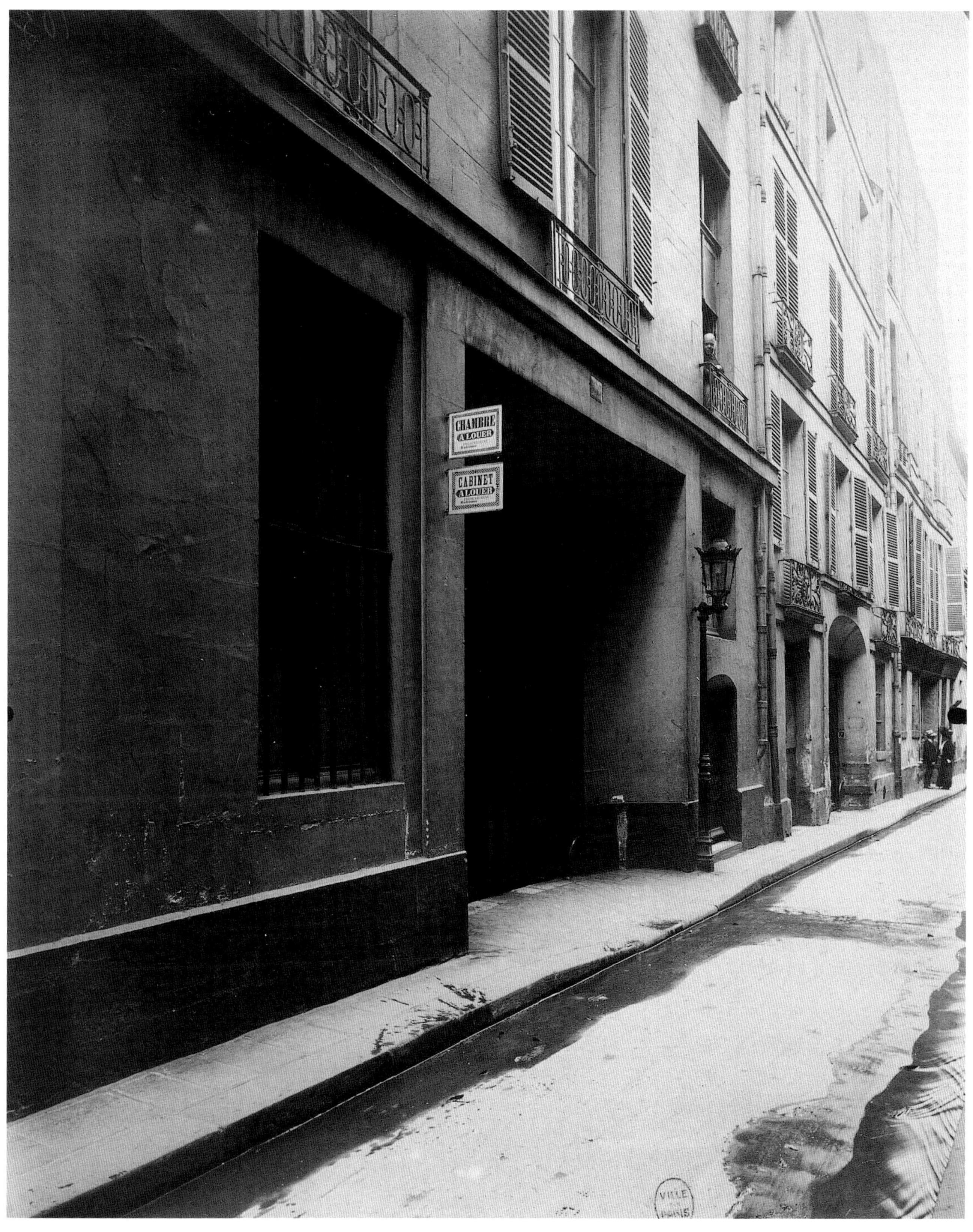

2.8 22 rue Visconti and view toward the rue de Seine, 1910

3. The rue du Parc-Royal, the rue de Sévigné, and the rue de Jarente, 3rd and 4th arrondissements, 1911

In the course of carrying out his massive survey *Topographie du vieux Paris*, Atget normally confined himself to working within a relatively small cluster of streets, adding to the cumulative documentation in small increments. He adopted a flexible working method, allowing climatic and lighting conditions to influence his approach to, and even the content of, this survey.

During 1911, for example, he concentrated upon the streets in the vicinity of the Bibliothèque historique de la Ville de Paris and the Musée Carnavalet, located respectively at 29 and 23 rue de Sévigné. On one sunny afternoon, he photographed along the illuminated northern side of the rue Parc-Royal and the eastern side of the rue de Sévigné but entirely omitted from his coverage the structures on the opposite (shaded) sides of these two streets (cat. 3.1–3.8).[7] He stopped his work at the point where the rue de Sévigné shifts in its alignment and the sunlight would have fallen directly into his camera lens (cat. 3.8). When he next returned, the sun was no longer a factor. Whether he deliberately waited for such overcast conditions to continue his documentation or simply accepted them is conjectural, but he entirely altered his way of working. On this visit, he confined himself to the intersection where the rue Jarente meets the rue de Sévigné and, from three separate camera positions, made six views. Two of the views record buildings with historical associations along the western side of the rue de Sévigné, which would have been extremely difficult to photograph on a sunny afternoon (cat. 3.9 and 3.10). Three views form an overlapping ninety-degree sweep, looking east along the rue de Jarente and south down the rue de Sévigné toward the rue Saint-Antoine (cat. 3.11–3.13). The final view concentrates upon a doorway (cat. 3.14). When he subsequently resumed his work on another sunny afternoon, he continued from exactly the point where he had previously stopped and worked systematically along the rue de Jarente, but only photographing on the north side of the street (cat. 3.15–3.20).[8]

While it is impossible to determine whether this sequence of twenty views[9] represents three successive days or simply different weather and lighting conditions over a shorter or even longer period of time, it nevertheless demonstrates the extent to which Atget's documentation responded to external conditions.

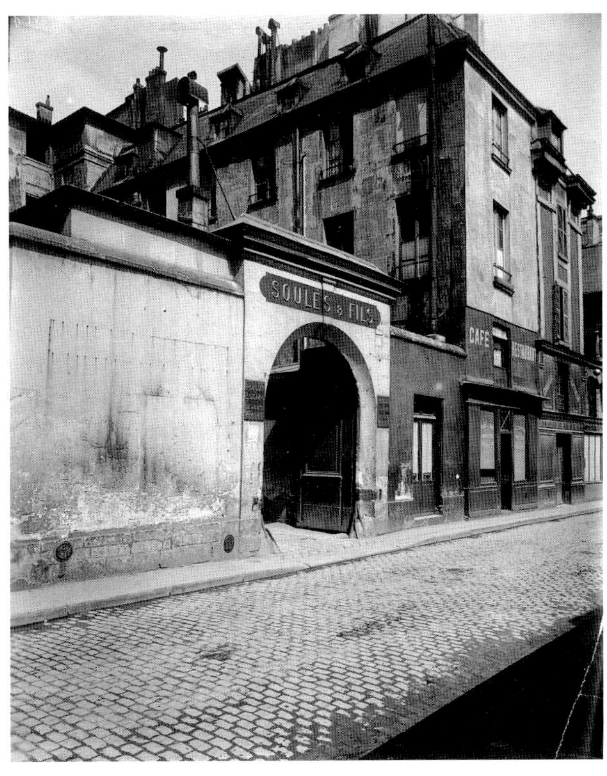

3.1 Hôtel de Vigny, 10 rue du Parc-Royal, 3rd, 1911

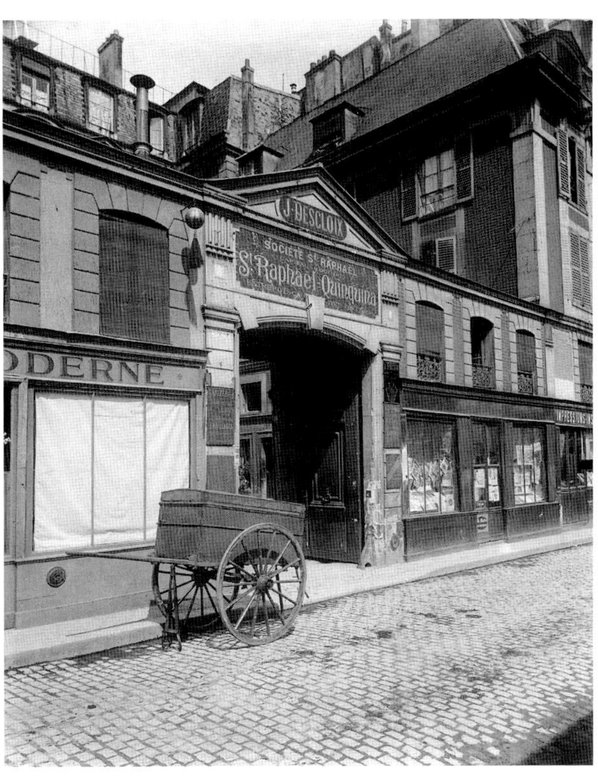

3.2 Hôtel Graux Marly, 8 rue du Parc-Royal, 3rd, 1911

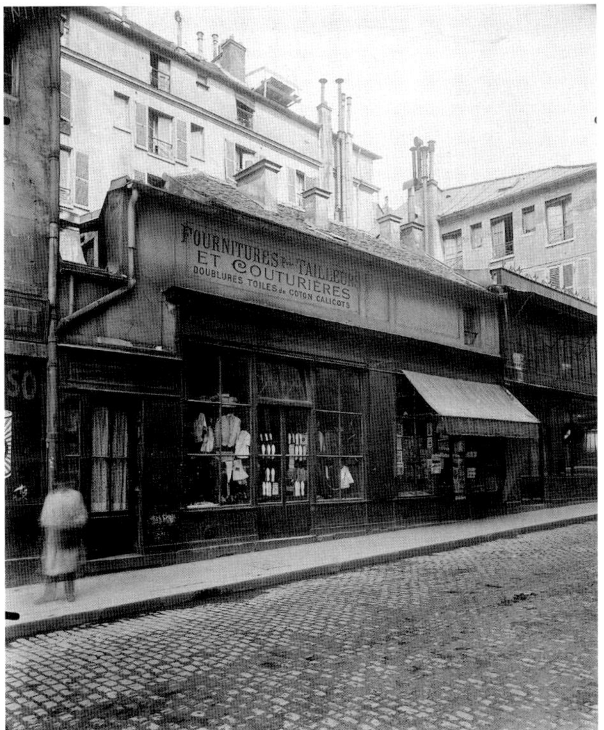

3.3 Old house and shops, 2 rue du Parc-Royal, 3rd, 1911

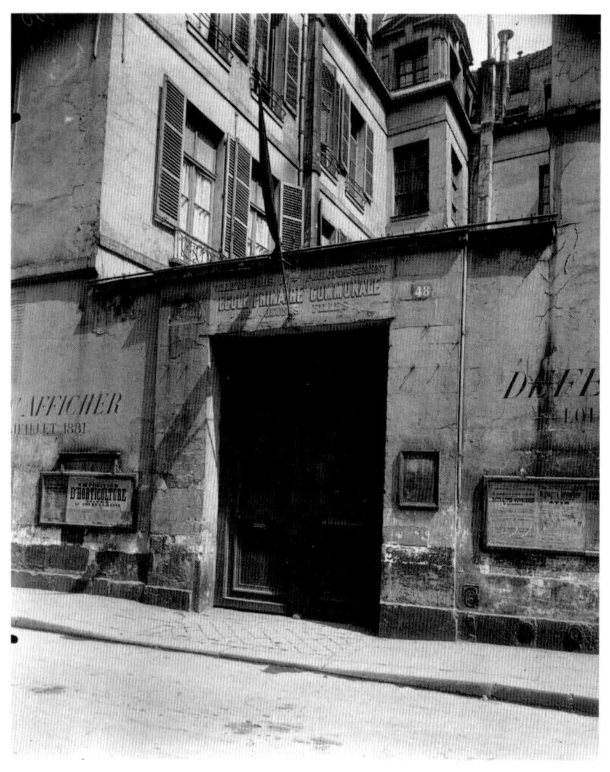

3.4 Hôtel de Joncquières, 48 rue de Sévigné, 3rd, 1911

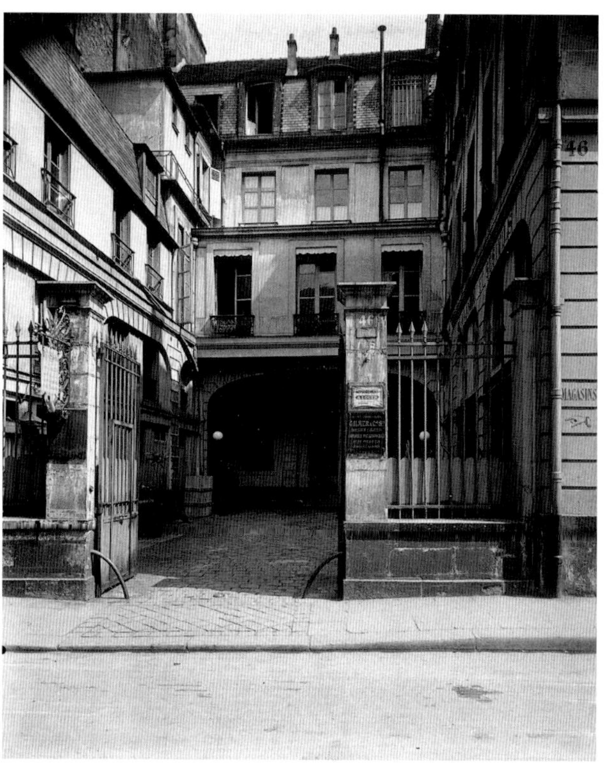

3.5 Hôtel de Joncquières, 46 rue de Sévigné, 3rd, 1911

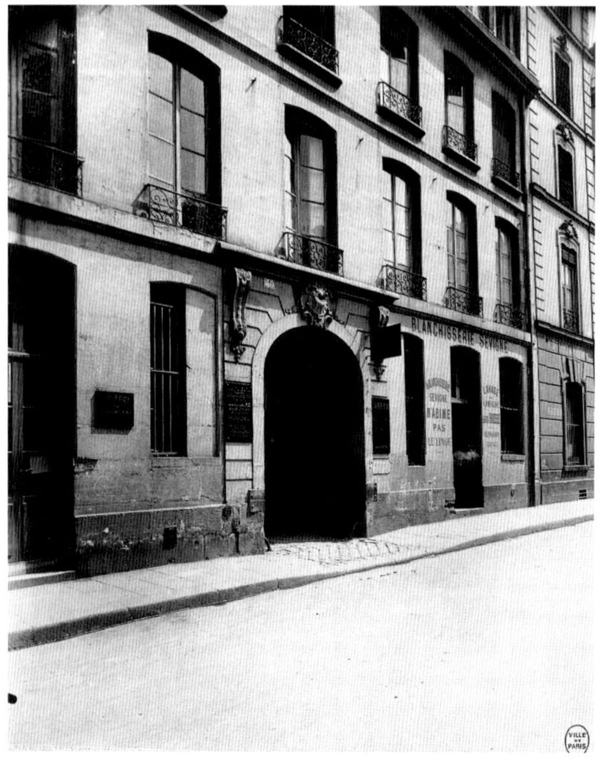

3.6 Hôtel, 40 rue de Sévigné, 3rd, 1911

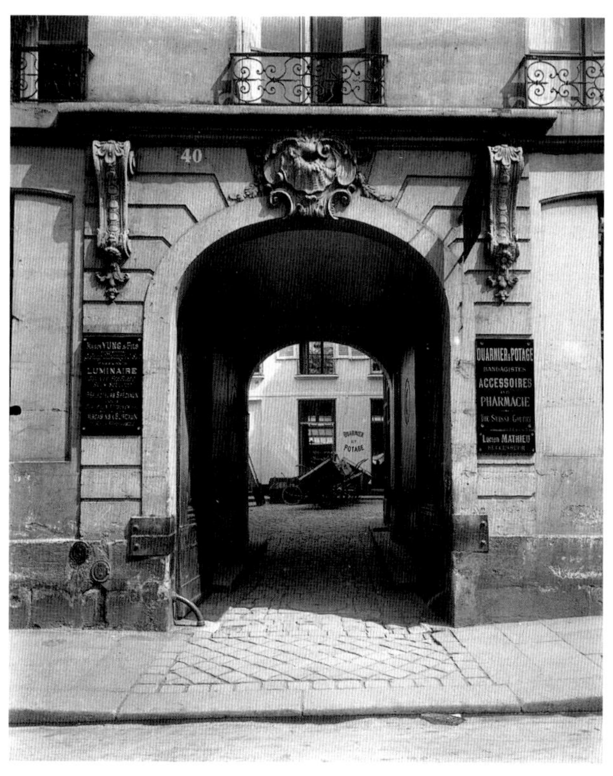

3.7 Entrance portal, 40 rue de Sévigné, 3rd, 1911

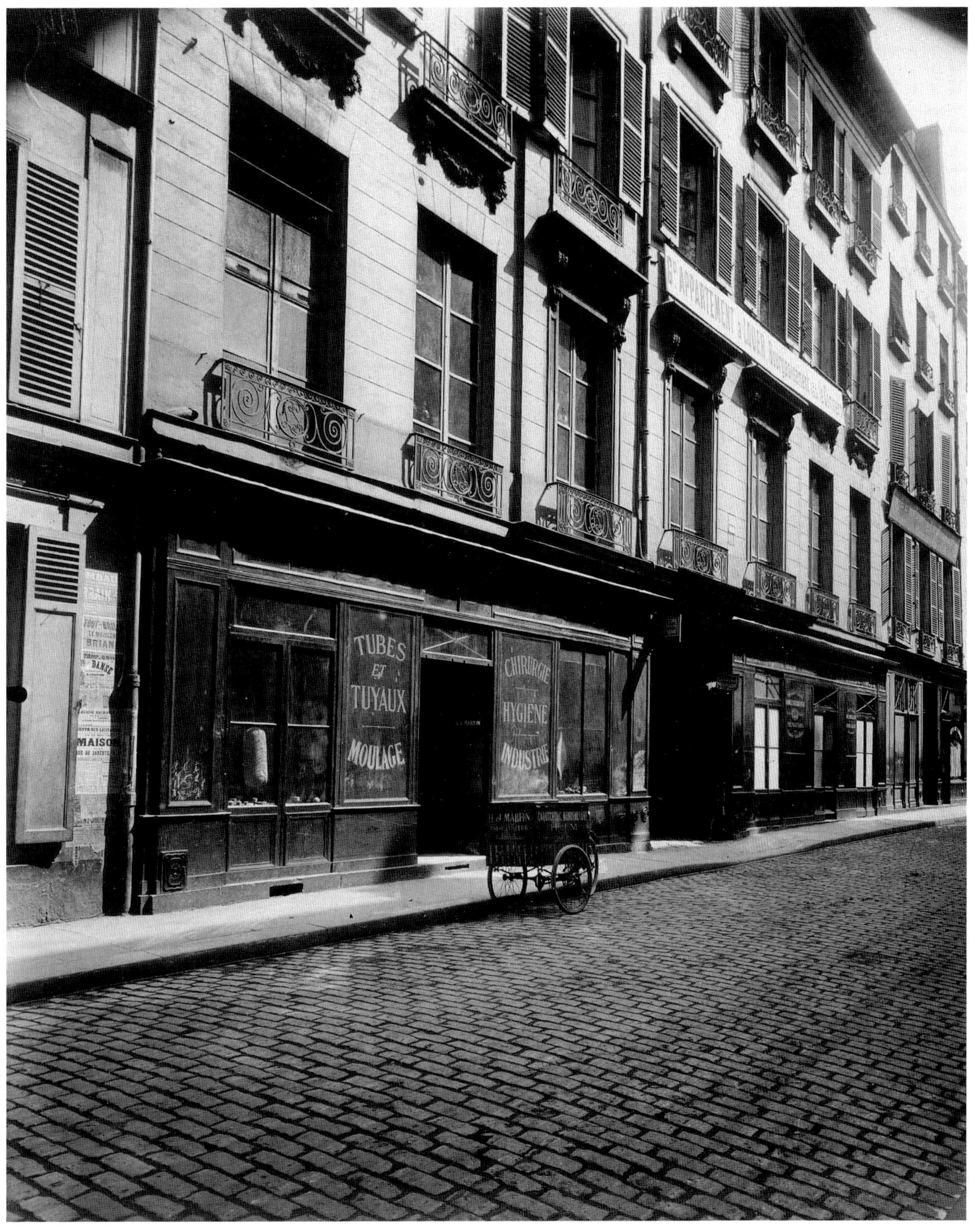

3.8 22–28 rue de Sévigné, 4th, 1911

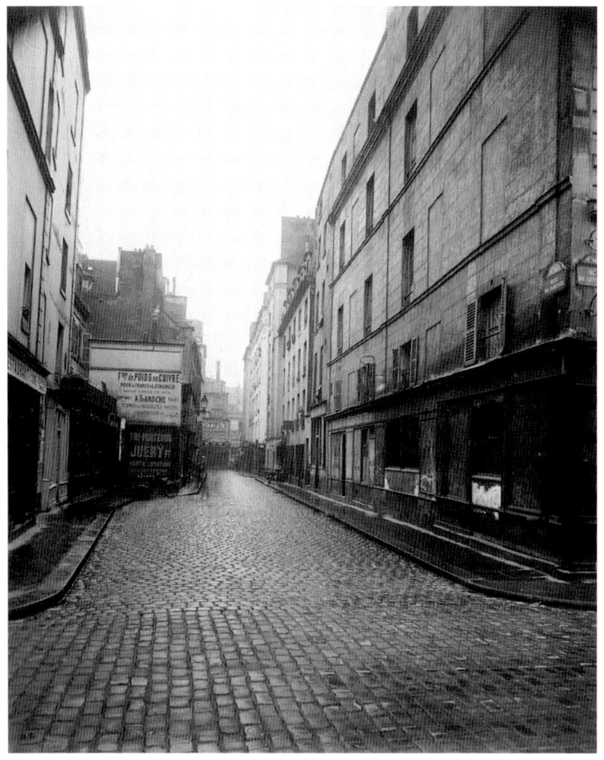

3.11 Rue de Jarente, from the corner of the rue de Sévigné toward the rue de Turenne, 4th, 1911

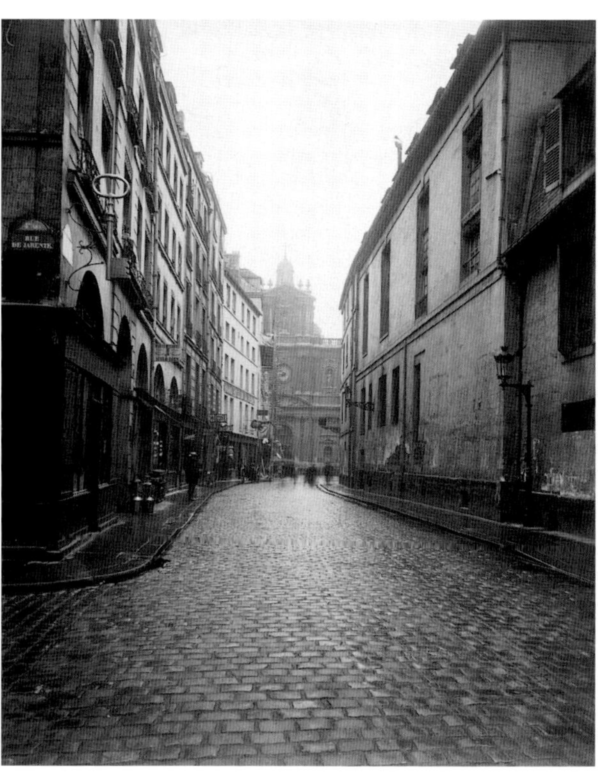

3.12 Rue de Sévigné, from the corner of the rue de Jarente toward the Church of Saint-Paul-Saint-Louis, 4th, 1911

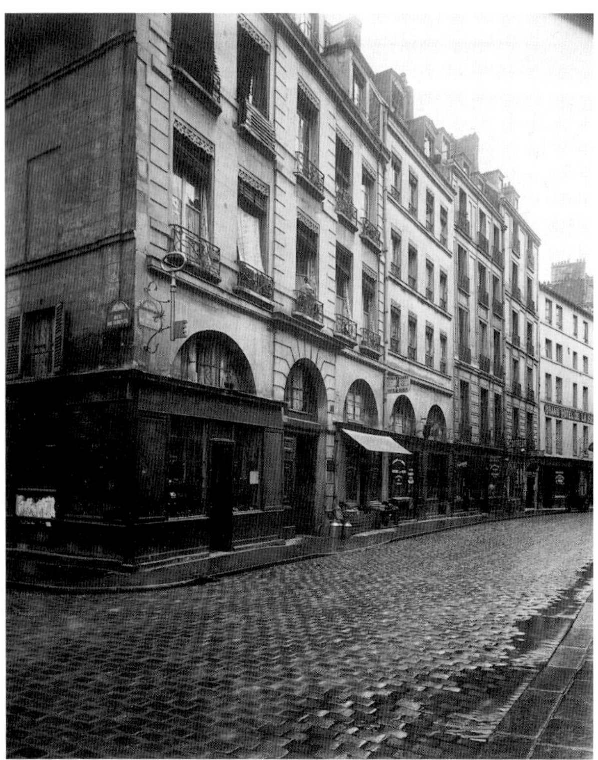

3.13 Rue de Sévigné, even-numbered side of the street, from the corner of the rue de Jarente toward the rue Saint-Antoine, 4th, 1911

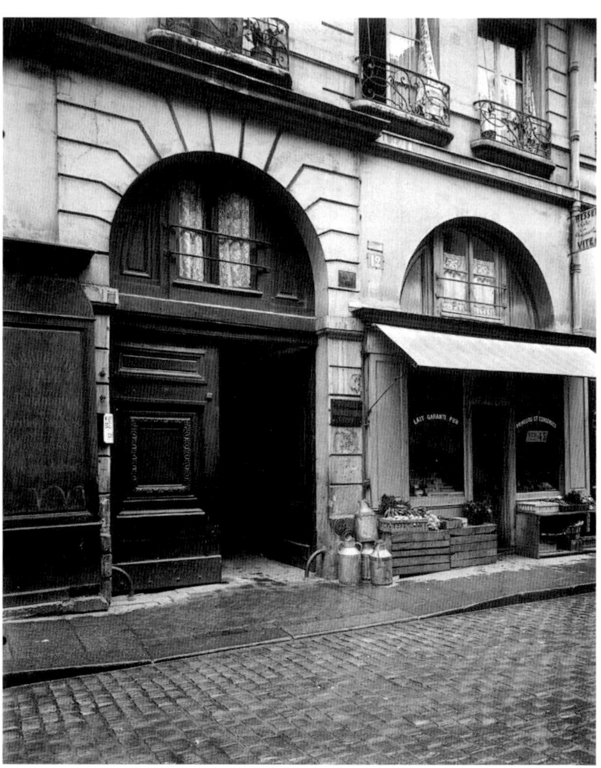

3.14 Hôtel, 12 rue de Sévigné, 4th, 1911

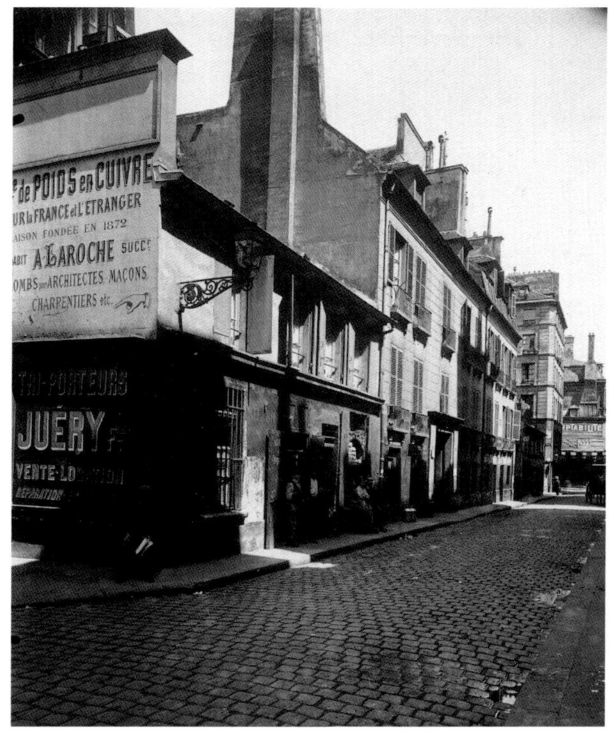

3.15 Buildings along the north side of the rue de Jarente, toward the rue de Turenne, 4th, 1911

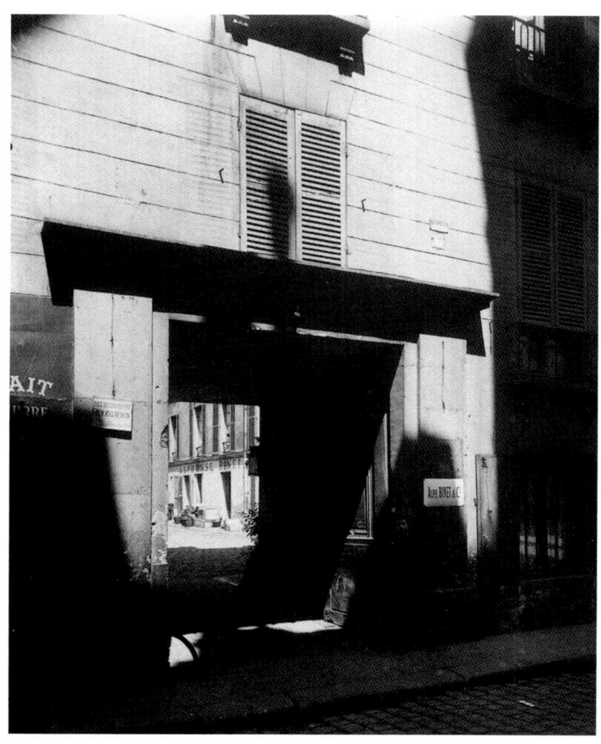

3.16 Old house, 6 rue de Jarente, 4th, 1911

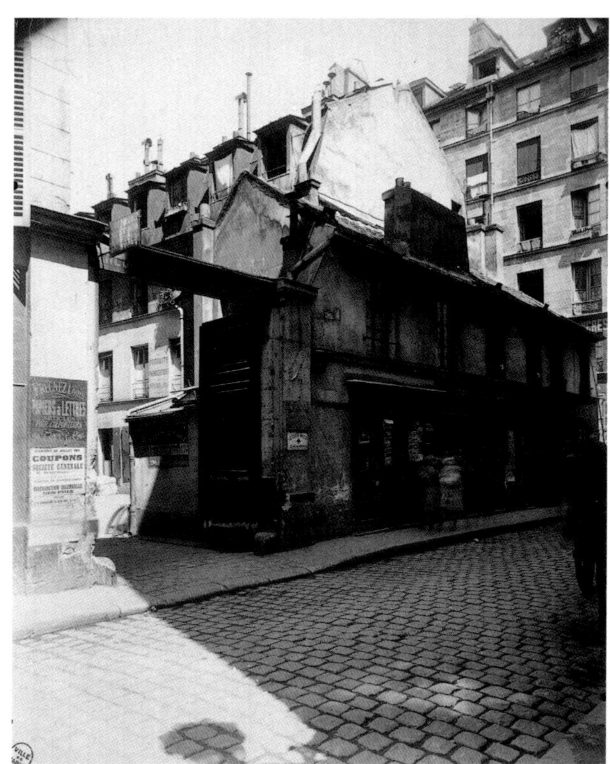

3.17 4 rue de Jarente, from the rue Caron, 4th, 1911

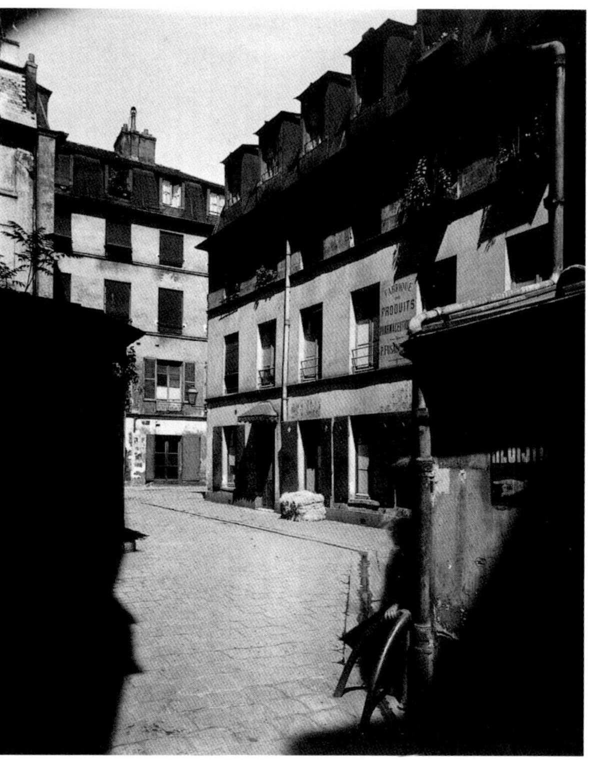

3.18 Courtyard, 4 rue de Jarente, 4th, 1911

4. Intersection of the rue de l'Abbaye, the rue Cardinale, the rue de l'Échaudé, the passage de la Petite-Boucherie, and the rue Bourbon-le-Château, 6th arrondissement, 1910

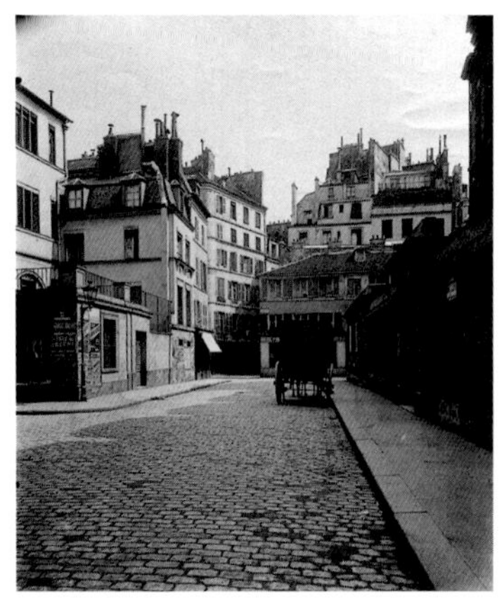

4.1 Rue de l'Abbaye, toward the passage de la Petite-Boucherie with the intersection of the rue de Furstenberg on the left, 1910

In 1910, as part of *Topographie du vieux Paris*, Atget adopted a particular strategy to photograph the complex urban space created by the intersection of five streets behind the Church of Saint-Germain-des-Prés. He used the Épicerie de l'Abbaye, which occupied the corner bounded by the rue Cardinale, the rue de l'Échaudé, and the rue de l'Abbaye as the central point, and constructed a set of ten related images around this grocery store. Some images were taken along the converging streets and situate the shop as a point of orientation (cat 4.1, 4.2, and 4.4–4.8), while others were made from the vantage point of the shop itself, and form reverse views of several of these same streets (cat. 4.3 and 4.9–4.10). In photographing this intersection, Atget renders it as a transitional space, where the pedestrian's orientation shifts and his direction changes. He made two pairs of views at the edges of the intersection which, separated by only a few yards from one another, suggest the dynamic and mutable character of this space (cat. 4.7 and 4.8; 4.9 and 4.10).

While it is difficult to reconstruct the sequence of views with absolute certainty, it would appear that Atget carried out this work on two separate occasions.[10] He took the photographs along the rue de l'Abbaye, the rue Cardinale, and the passage de la Petite-Boucherie on a sunny afternoon (cat. 4.1–4.5), and those along the rue de l'Échaudé, the rue Bourbon-le-Château, as well as the two views from the grocery store on an overcast day (cat. 4.6–4.10).

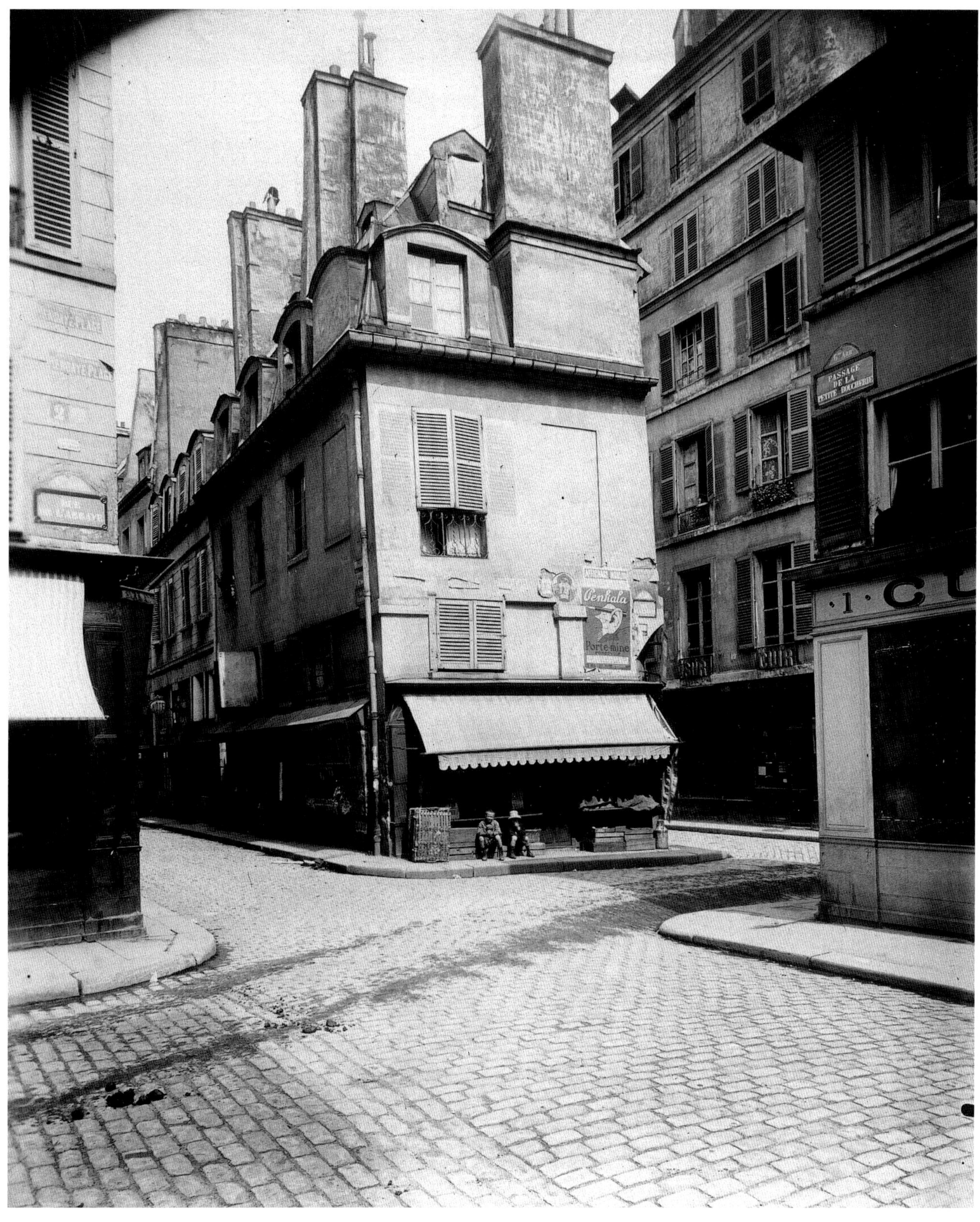

4.2 Épicerie de l'Abbaye, at the intersection of the rue de l'Abbaye, the rue Cardinale, the rue de l'Échaudé, and the passage de la Petite-Boucherie, 1910

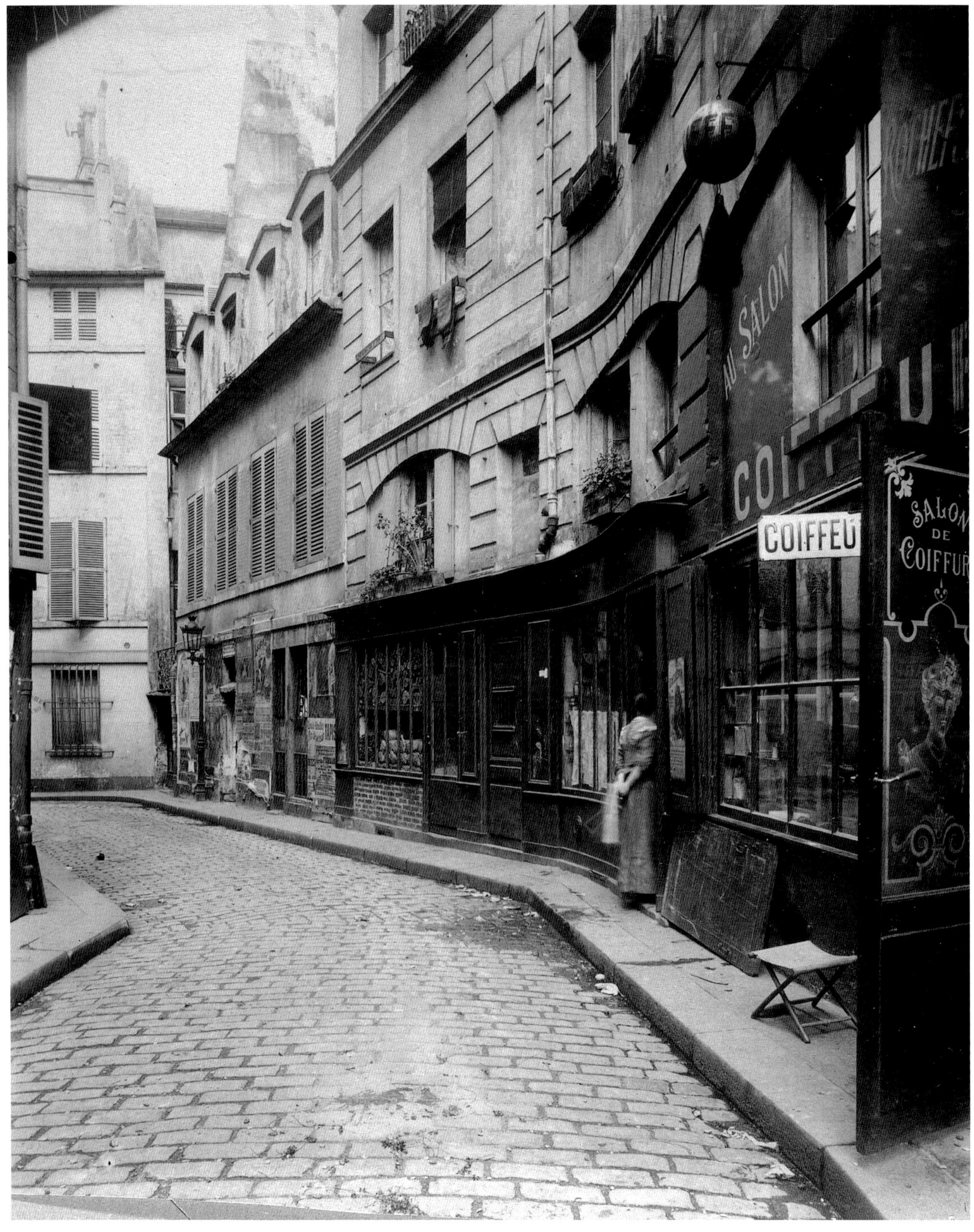

4.3 Rue Cardinale, 1910

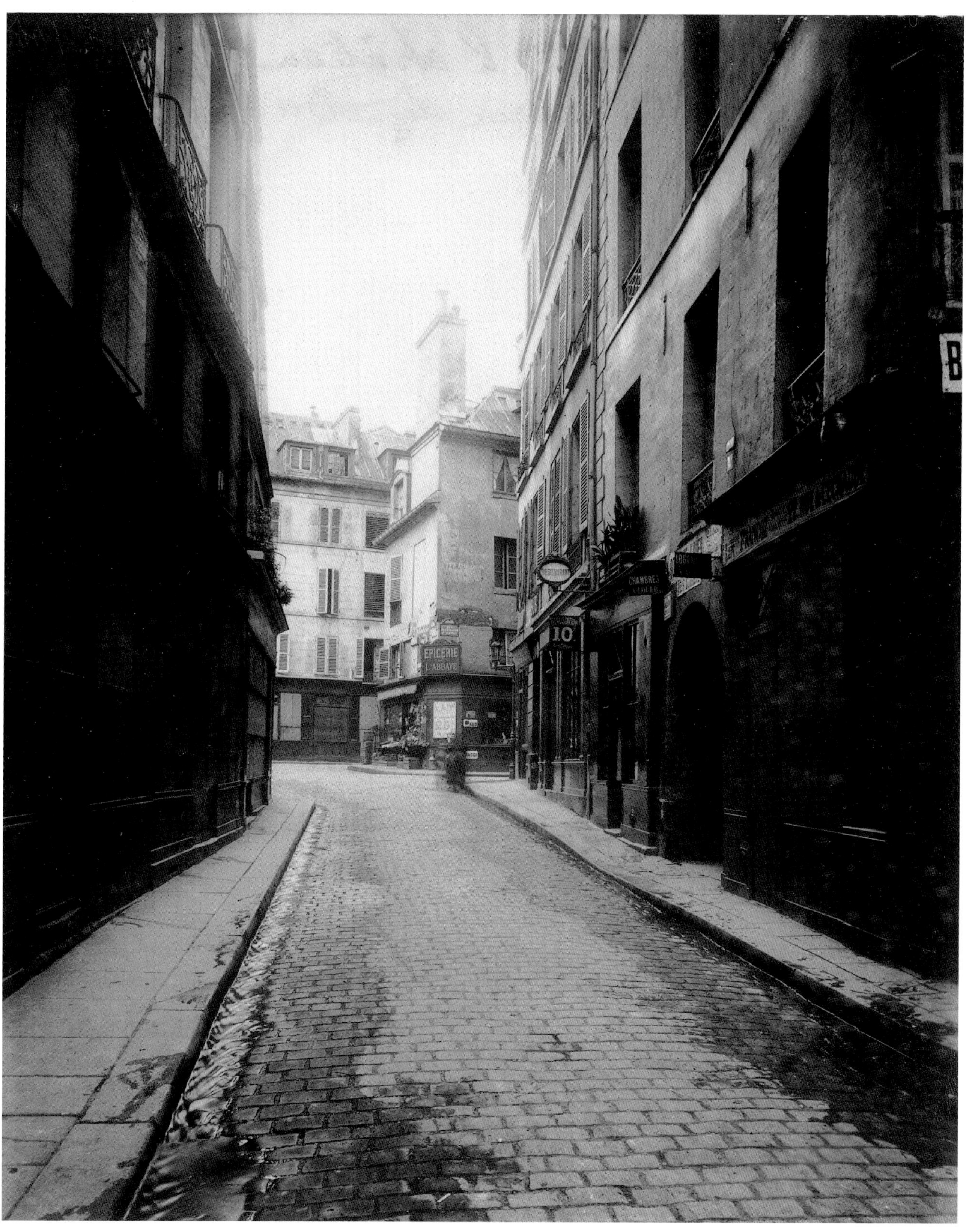

4.6 Rue Bourbon-le-Château, from the rue de Buci toward the rue de l'Échaudé and the rue Cardinale, 1910

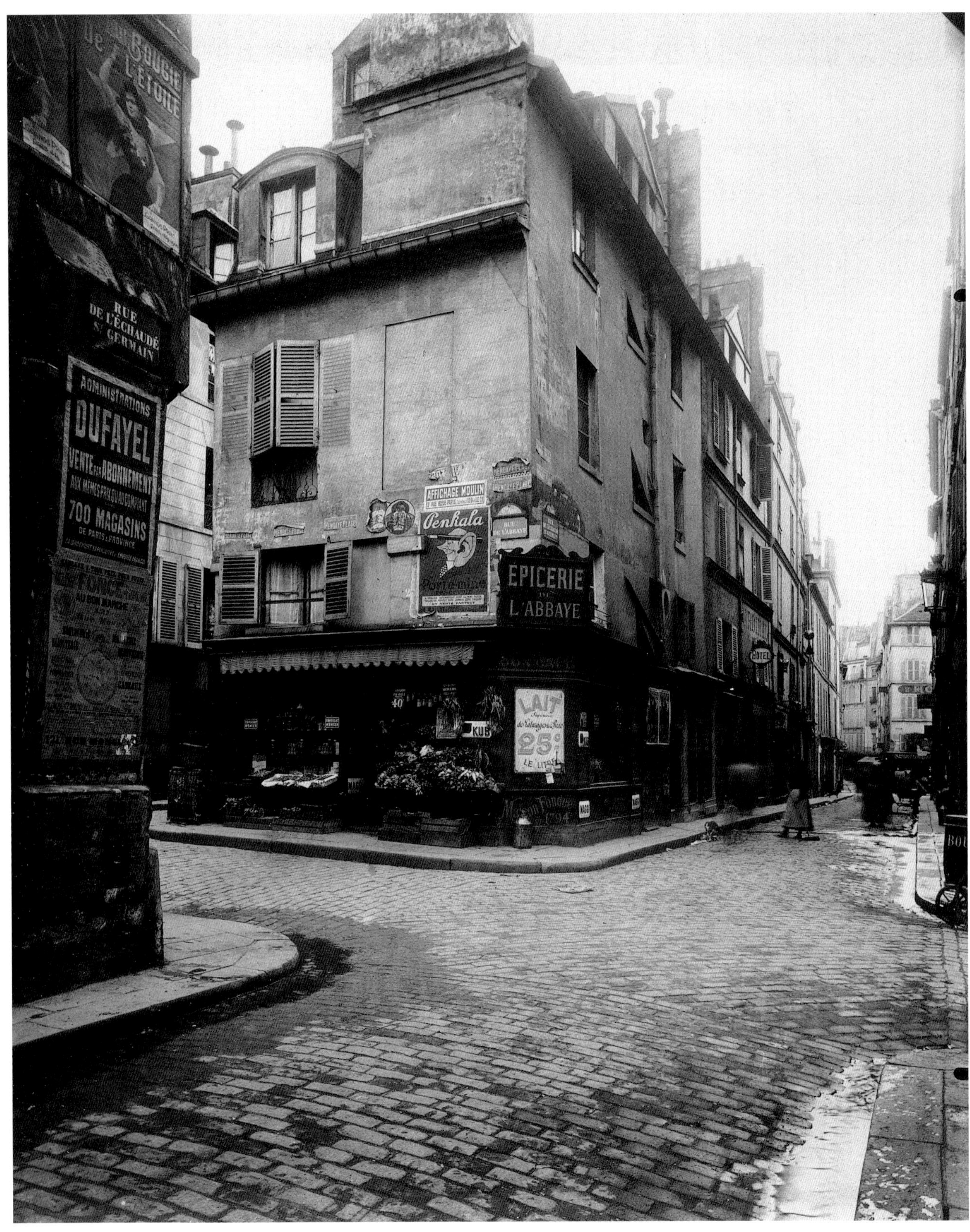

4.7 Épicerie de l'Abbaye, corner of the rue de l'Abbaye and the rue de l'Échaudé, 1910

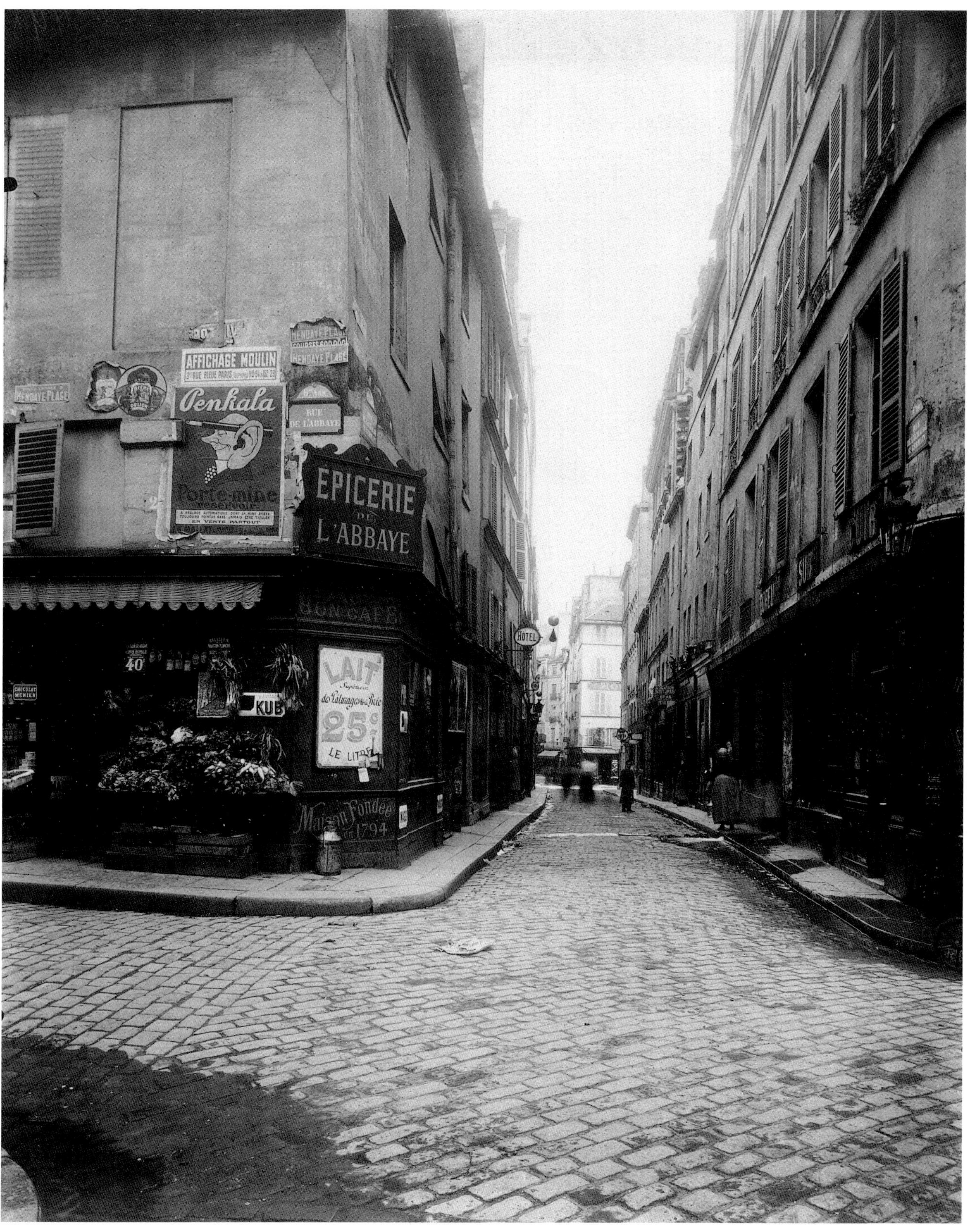

4.8 Rue de l'Échaudé, from the intersection of the rue de l'Abbaye and the rue Bourbon-le-Château, 1910

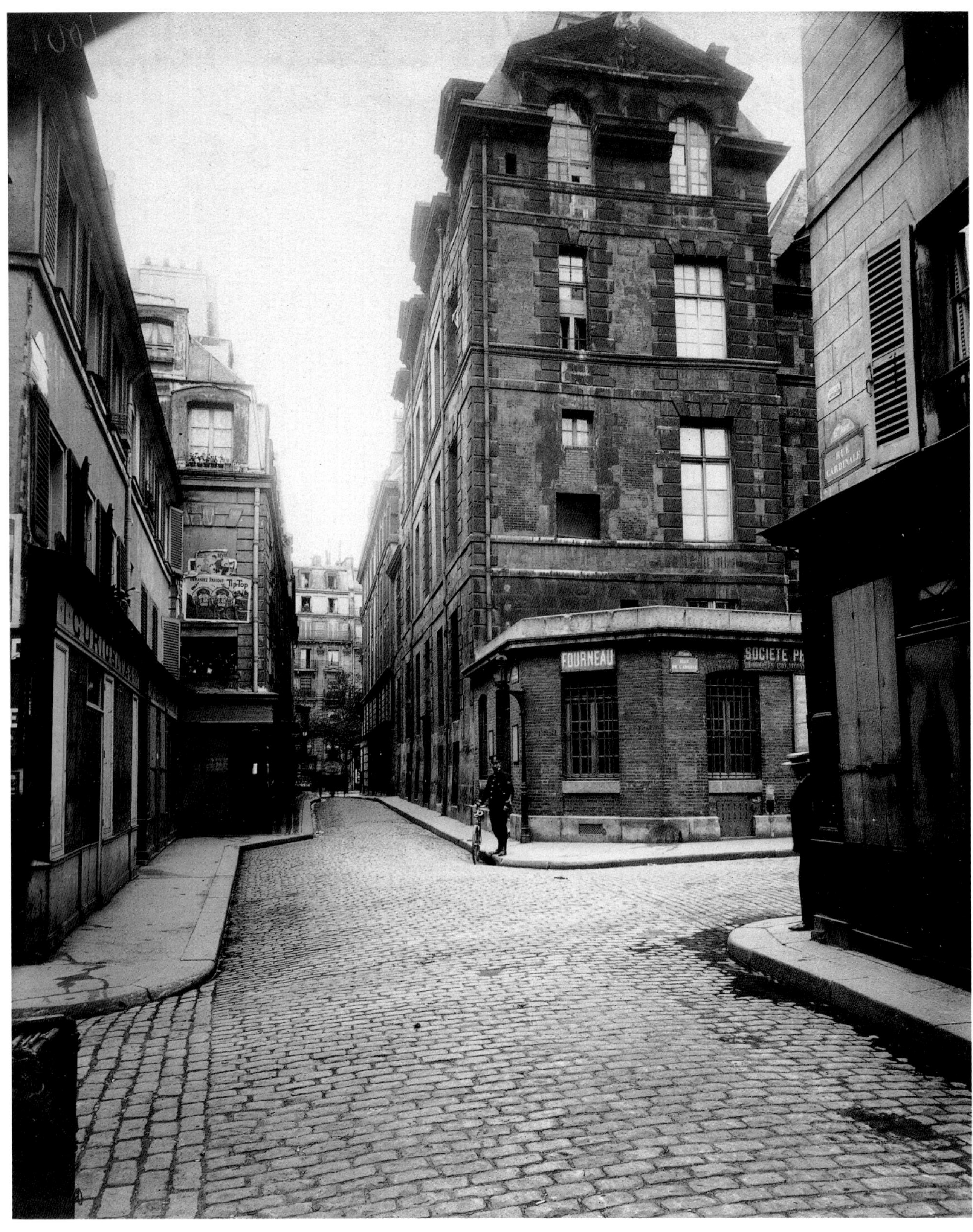

4.9 Passage de la Petite-Boucherie, from the corner of the rue de l'Abbaye and the rue Cardinale, 1910

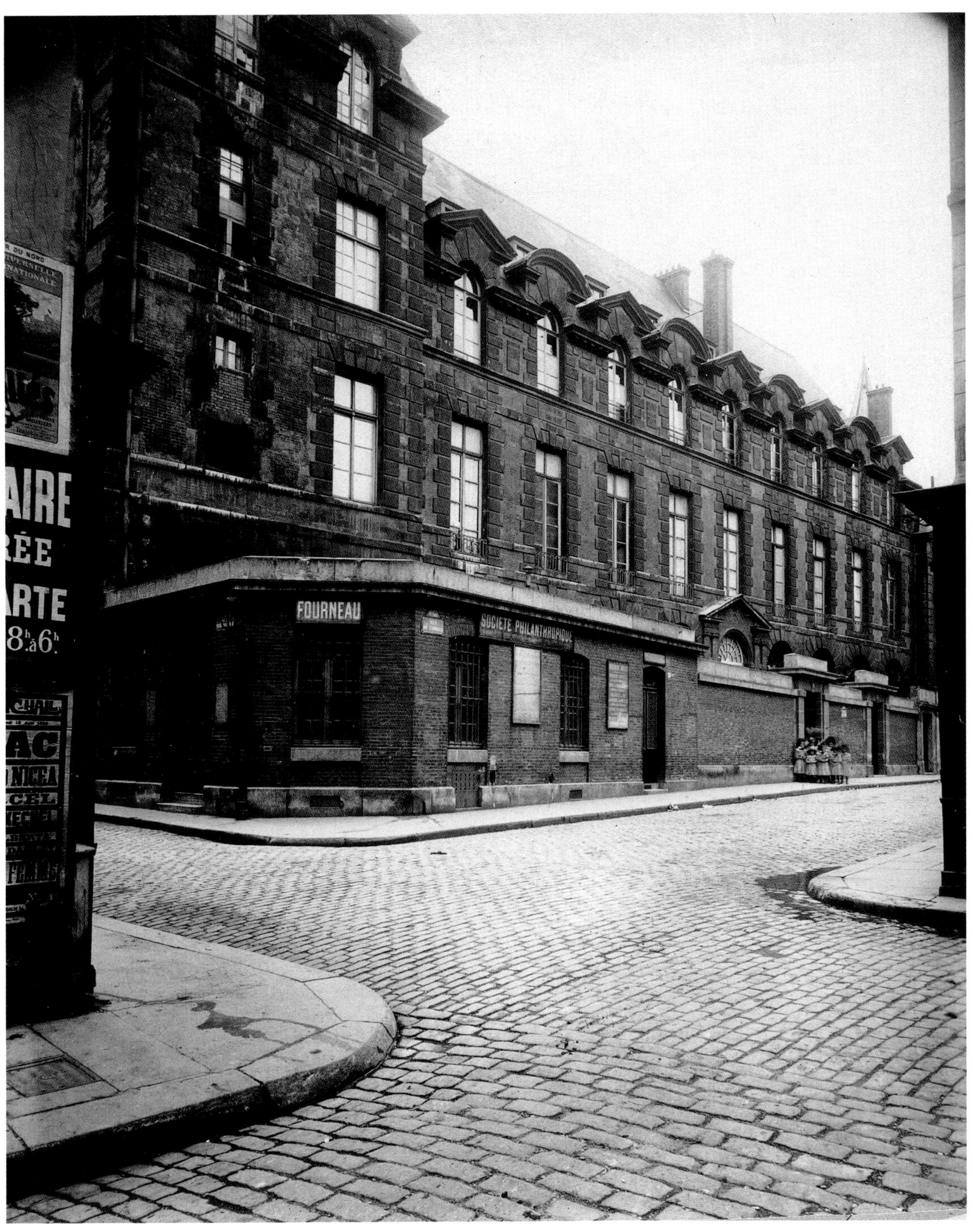

4.10 Former Abbey Palace of Saint-Germain-des-Prés, 3 rue de l'Abbaye, seen from the Épicerie de l'Abbaye, 1910

5. The quays surrounding the Pont-Neuf, 1st and 6th arrondissements, 1911

Unlike the previous studies, which considered groups of photographs made either on a single day or within a few days of one another, Atget's twenty-two photographs of the quays around the Pont-Neuf were made over the summer and autumn of 1911 as part of an extended survey of this section of the river Seine.[11]

His earliest two images center upon a scenic painter standing on the Écluse de la Monnaie below the Pont-Neuf (cat. 5.1 and 5.2). Atget consciously selected this vantage point because it allowed him to evoke the multiplicity of activities simultaneously occurring on the river, the quays, and across the Pont-Neuf. In his succeeding views, Atget adapted many of the strategies he had developed in *Topographie du vieux Paris* to describe the space along the quays: He took corresponding views that, from opposite sides of the river, survey the same space (cat. 5.2 and 5.3); he constructed a sequence of five interconnected views that systematically progress around the quai du Vert-Galant (cat. 5.4–5.6 and 5.8–5.9);[12] and he took two views from beneath the Pont-Neuf that survey the reach of the quays in opposite directions and situate the bridge in relationship to the pont des Arts and the pont au Change (cat. 5.10 and 5.11).

When Atget worked along the Right Bank, he favored the afternoon sun that, falling through the overhanging branches, created a dappled effect along the stone pavement. In photographing the Pont-Neuf, he began with two images made along the quai de la Mégisserie (cat. 5.12–5.13). In a later sequence of four views, Atget began from a position west of pont des Arts, passed under this bridge, and approached the Pont-Neuf, but ended his coverage at the point at which the dense planting of trees rendered this area too dark to photograph (cat. 5.14–5.17). He returned to the neglected area in the autumn when the more open conditions of the vegetation allowed him to make four interlocking views (cat. 5.18–5.21). As part of this same day's work, he rephotographed his two earlier views along the quai de la Mégisserie from similar vantage points (compare cat. 5.12 and 5.23, and 5.13 and 5.22).

While Atget was principally concerned with describing the quays as discrete working spaces between the upper street level (repeatedly signaled by stone ramps and steps) and the river, he would also have been conscious of the mythic dimensions that the river and this bridge occupied at the heart of the city.

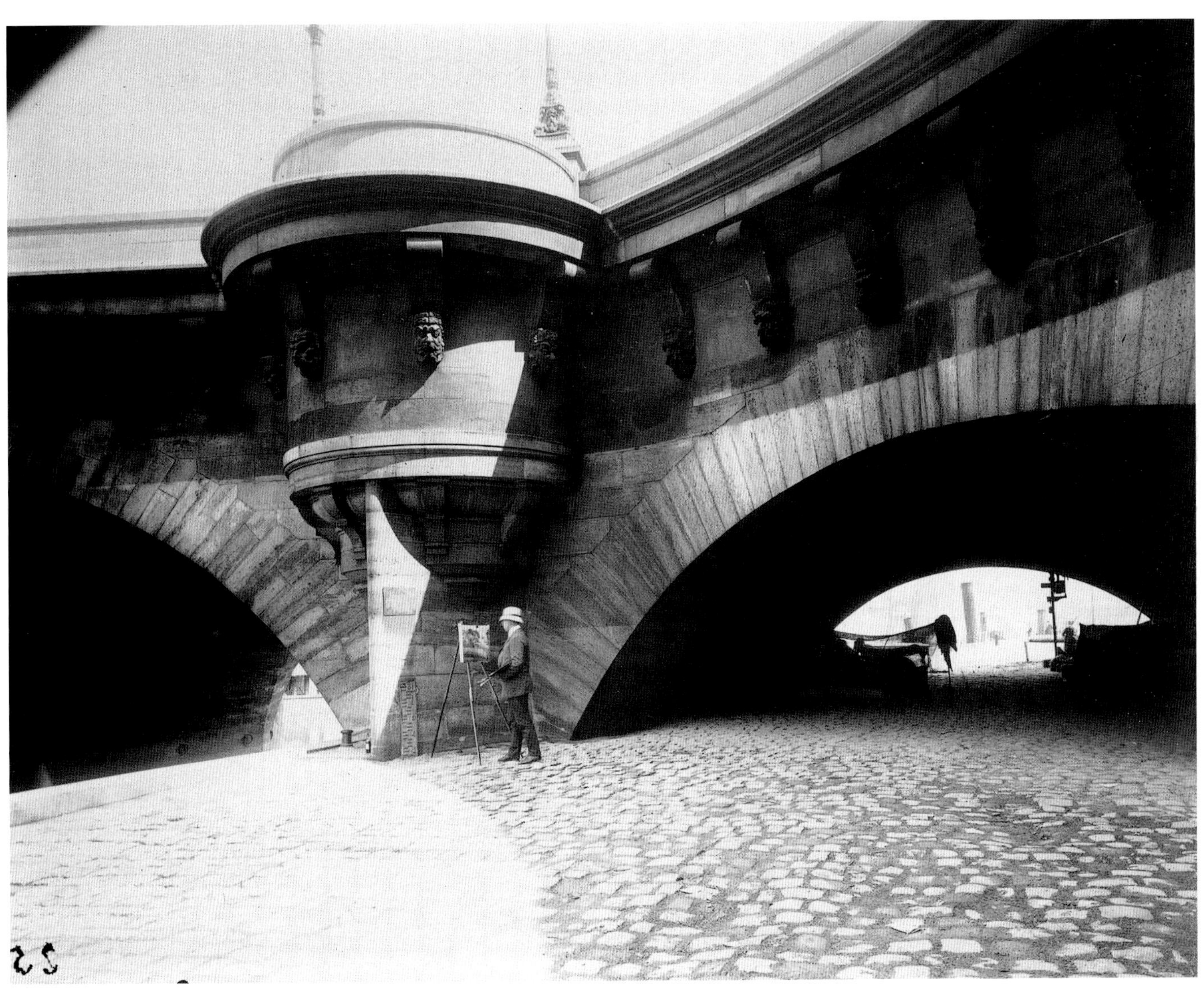

5.1 **Pont-Neuf, from the écluse de la Monnaie, 6th, 1911**

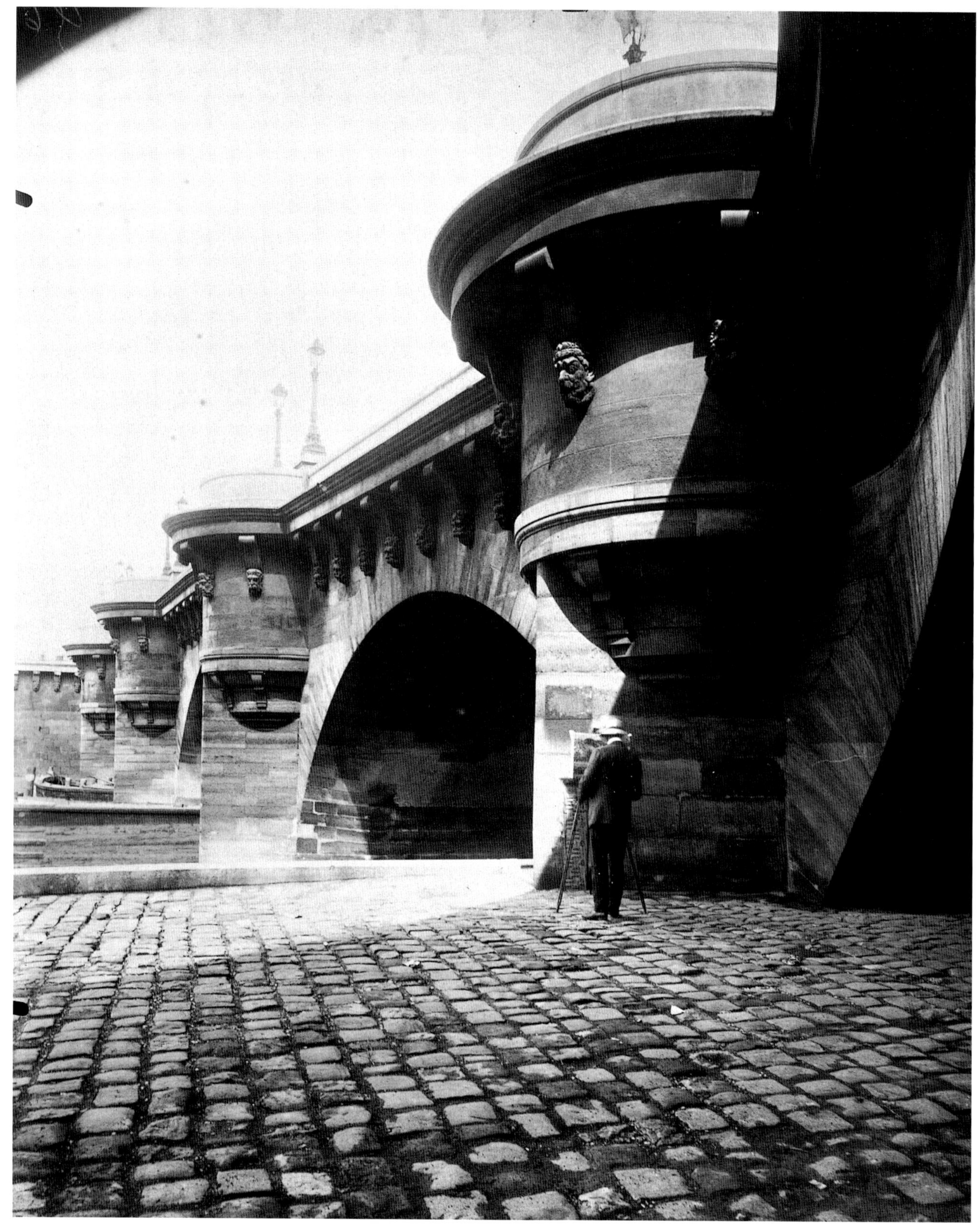

5.2 Pont-Neuf, from the écluse de la Monnaie, 6th, 1911

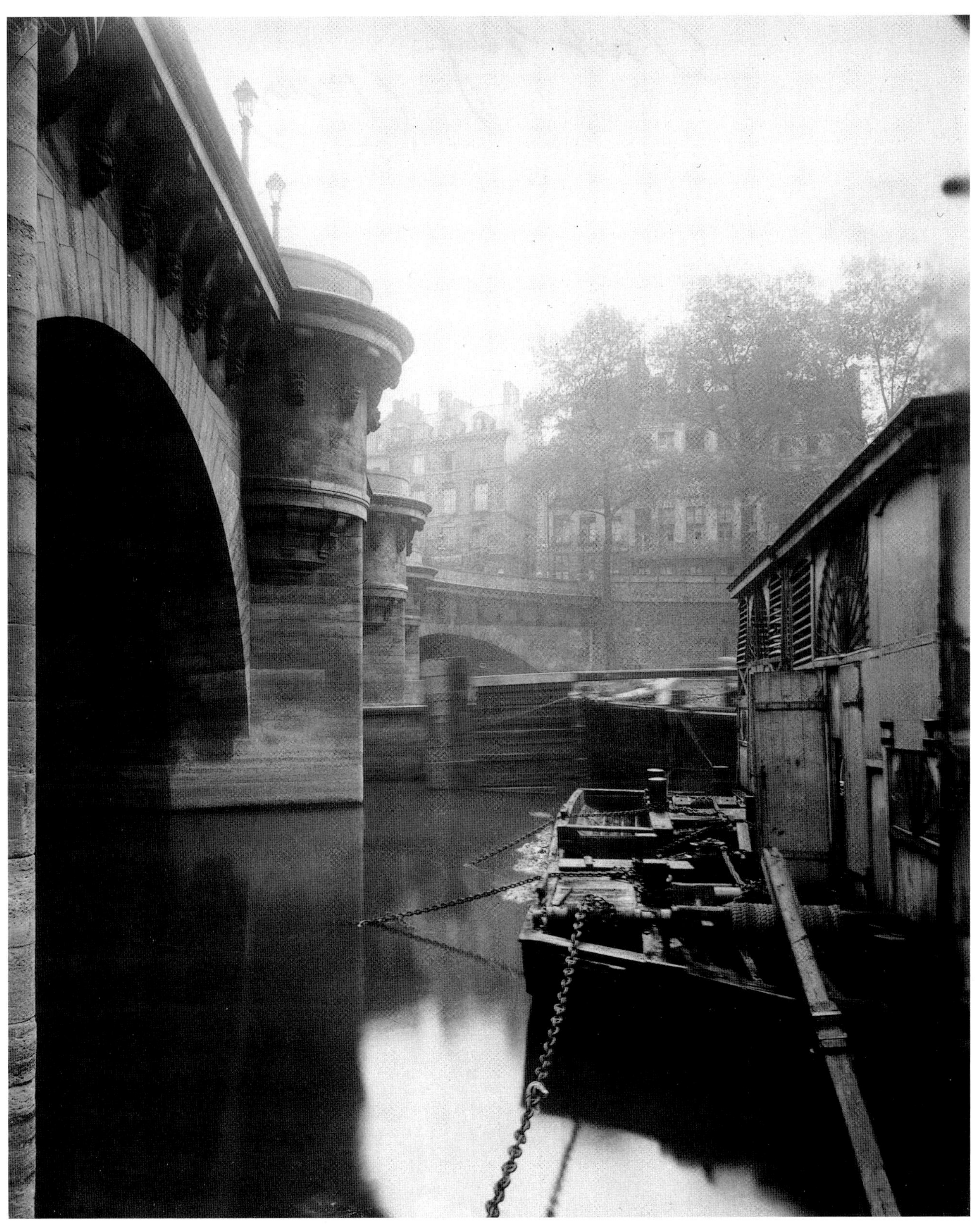

5.3 Pont-Neuf, from the banks of the Vert-Galant, south side, toward the quai de Conti, 1st, 1911

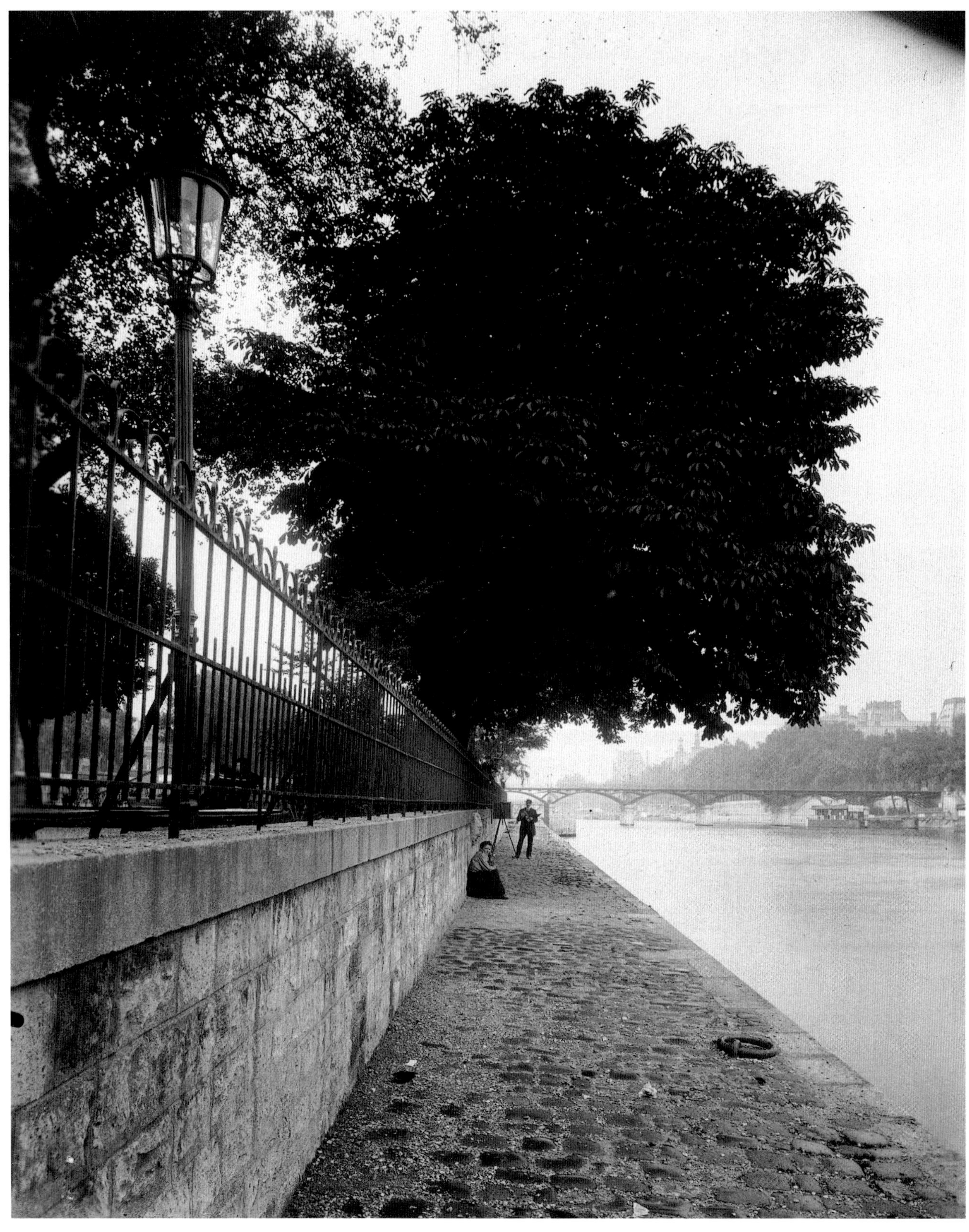

5.4 Banks of the Vert-Galant, north side, toward the pont des Arts, 1st, 1911

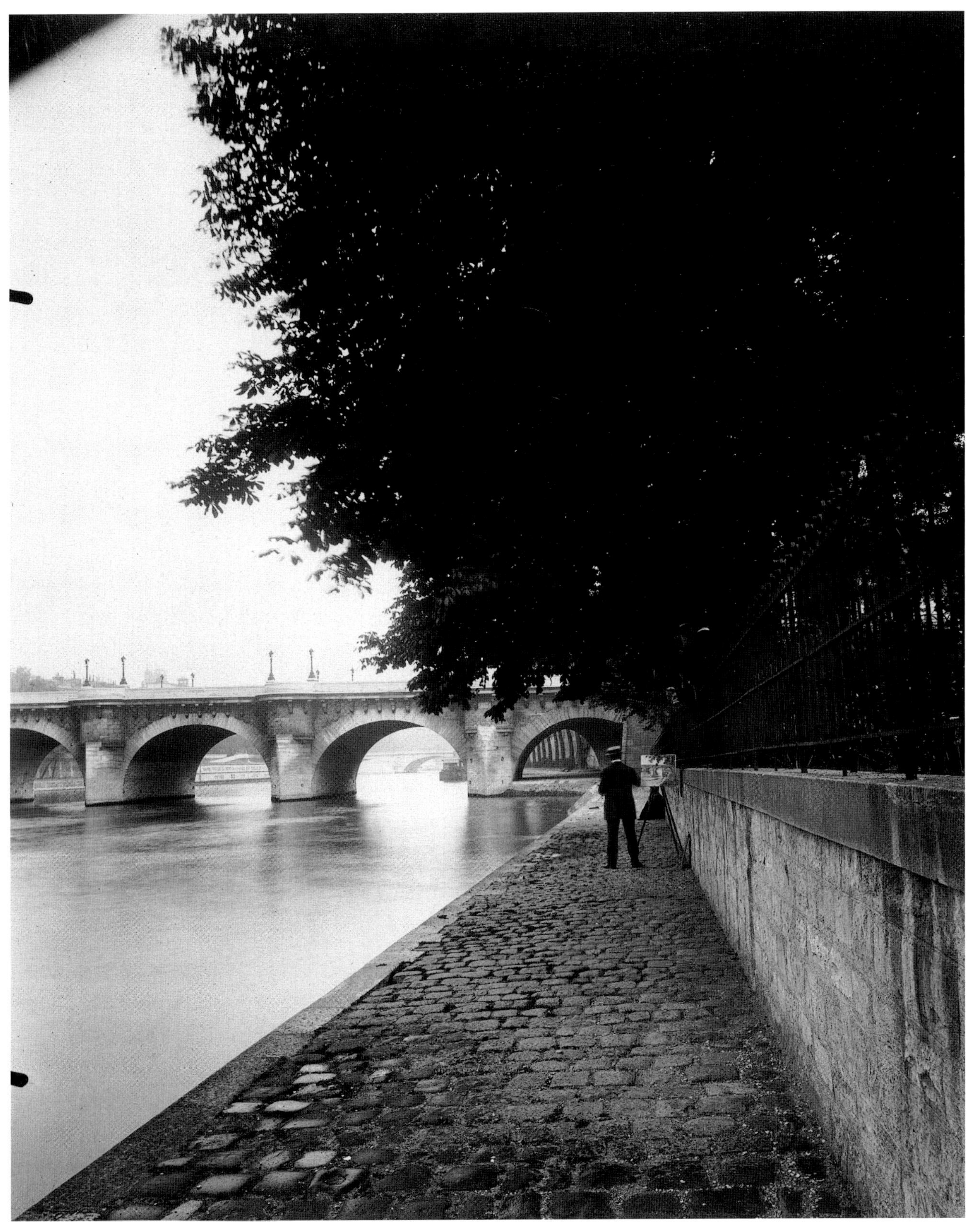

5.5 **Banks of the Vert-Galant, north side, toward the Pont-Neuf, 1st, 1911**

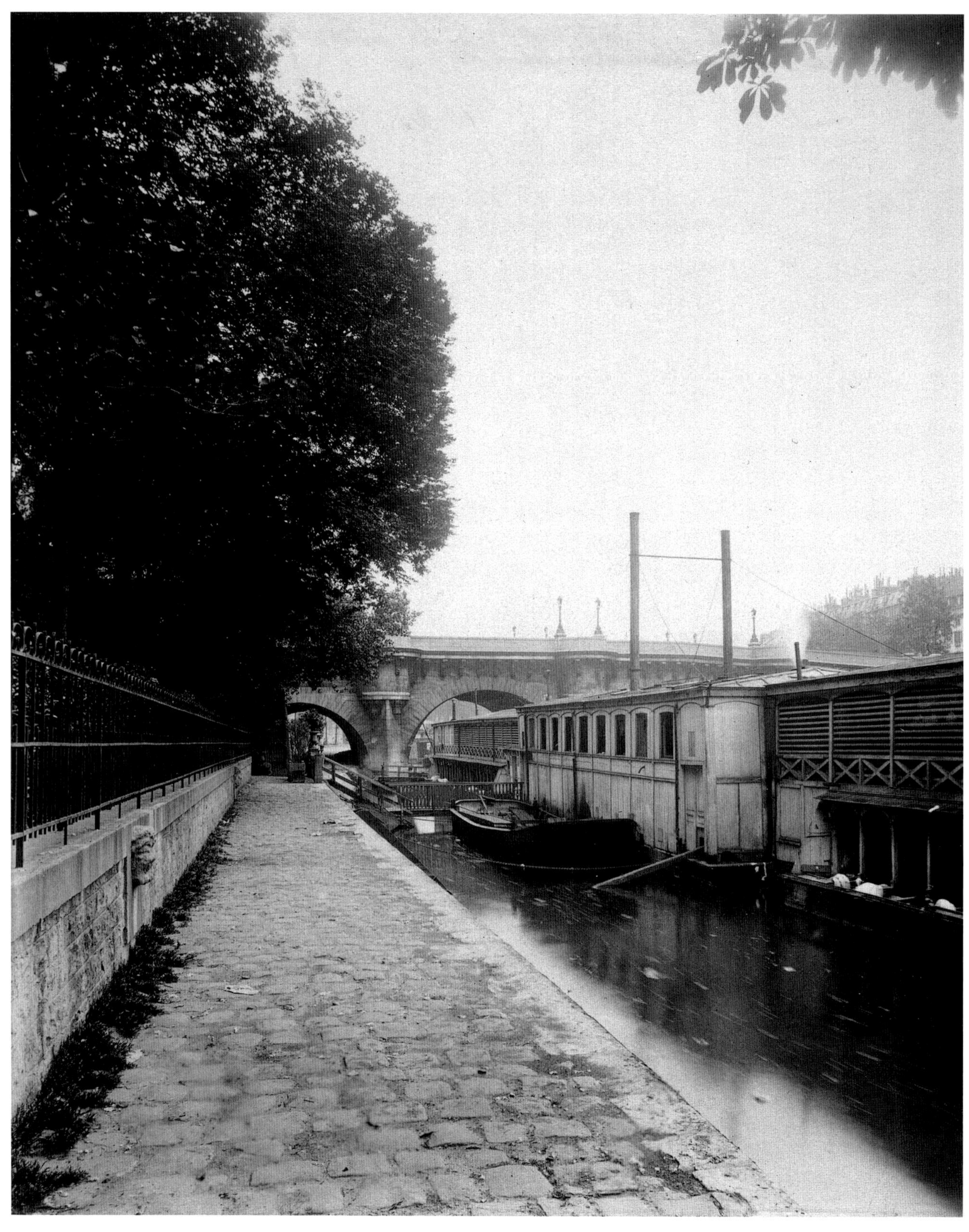

5.6 Banks of the Vert-Galant, south side, toward the Pont-Neuf, 1st, 1911

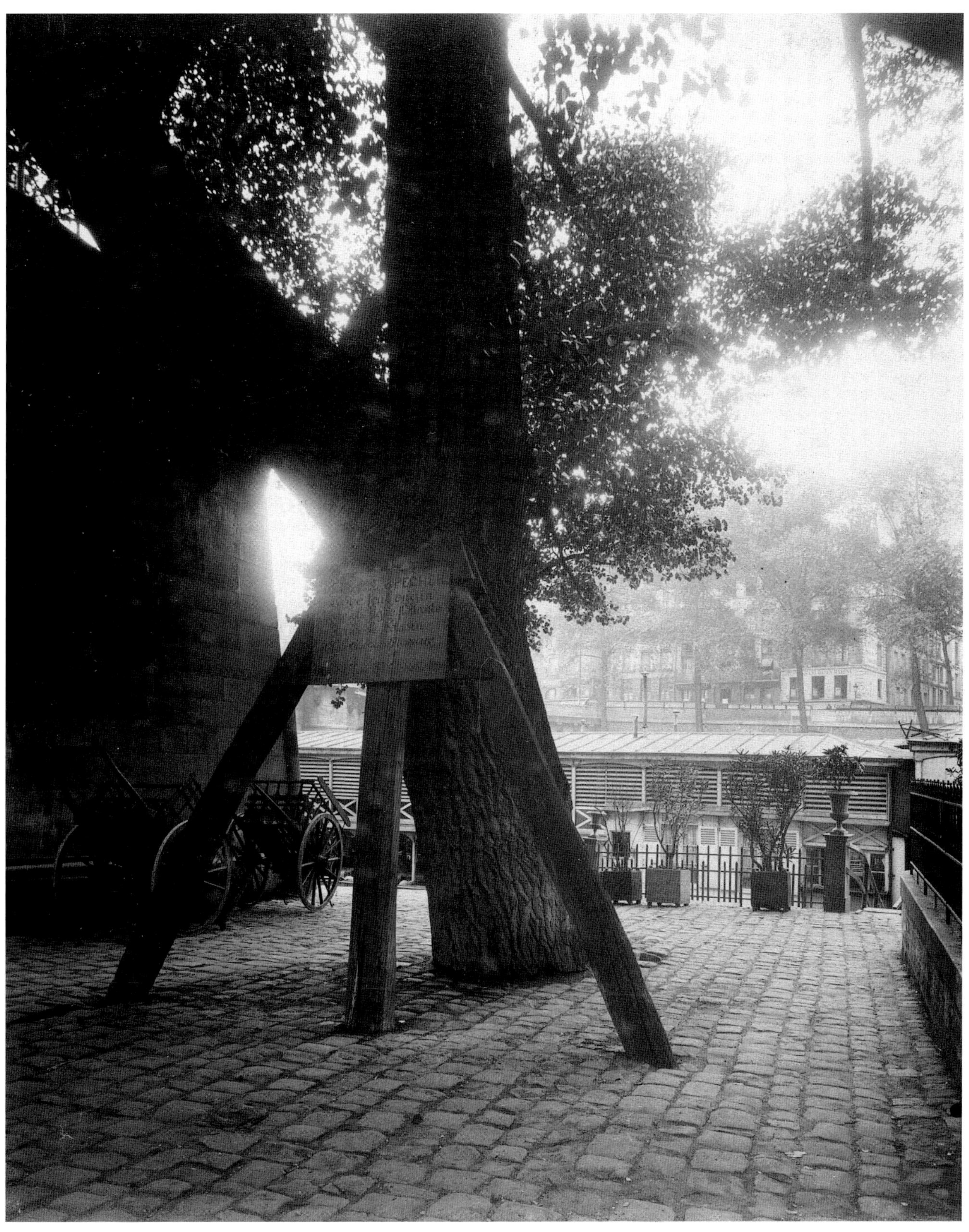

5.7 Near the entrance of the garden of the Vert-Galant, toward the quai de Conti, 1st, 1911

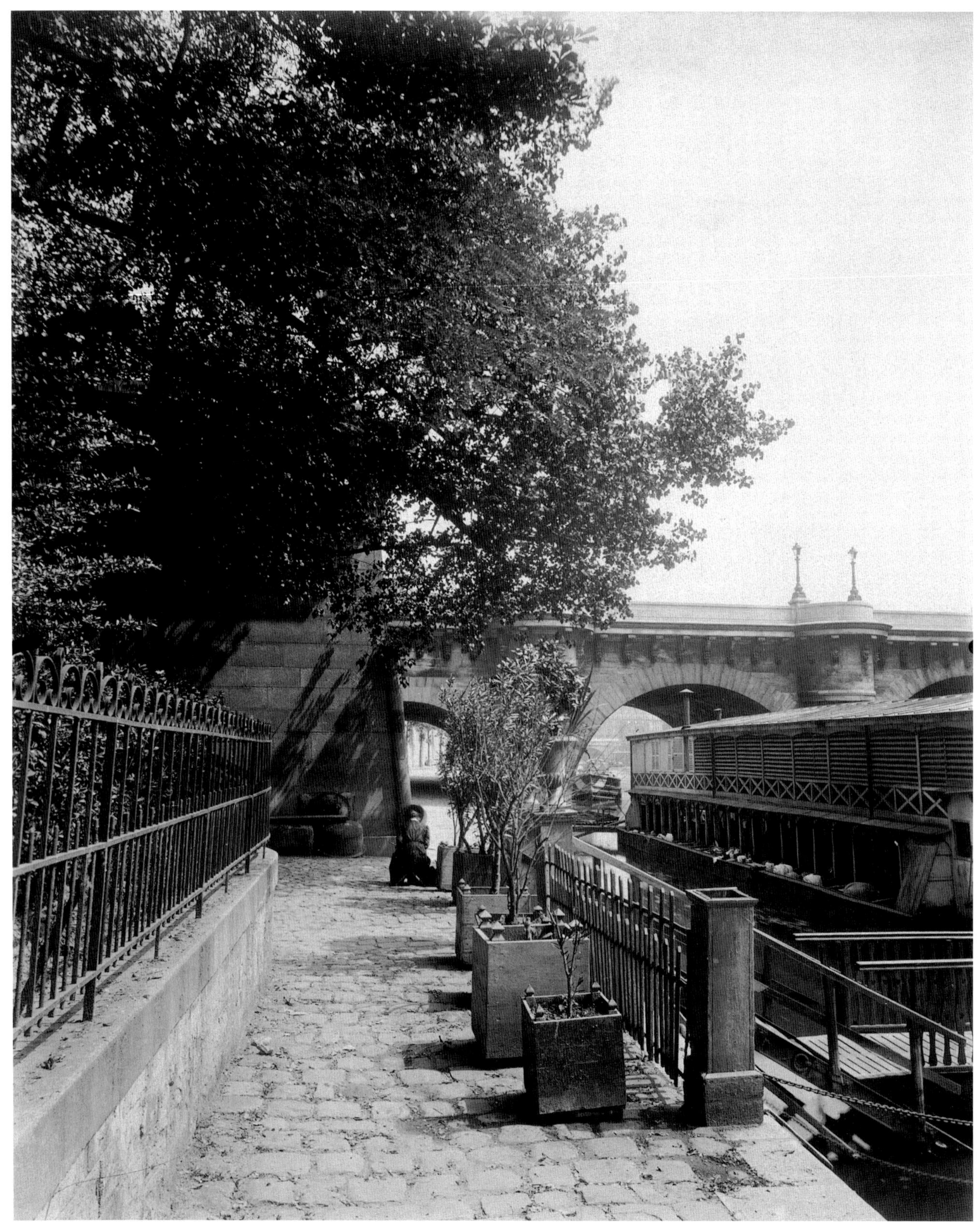

5.8 Banks of the Vert-Galant, south side, toward the Pont-Neuf, 1st, 1911

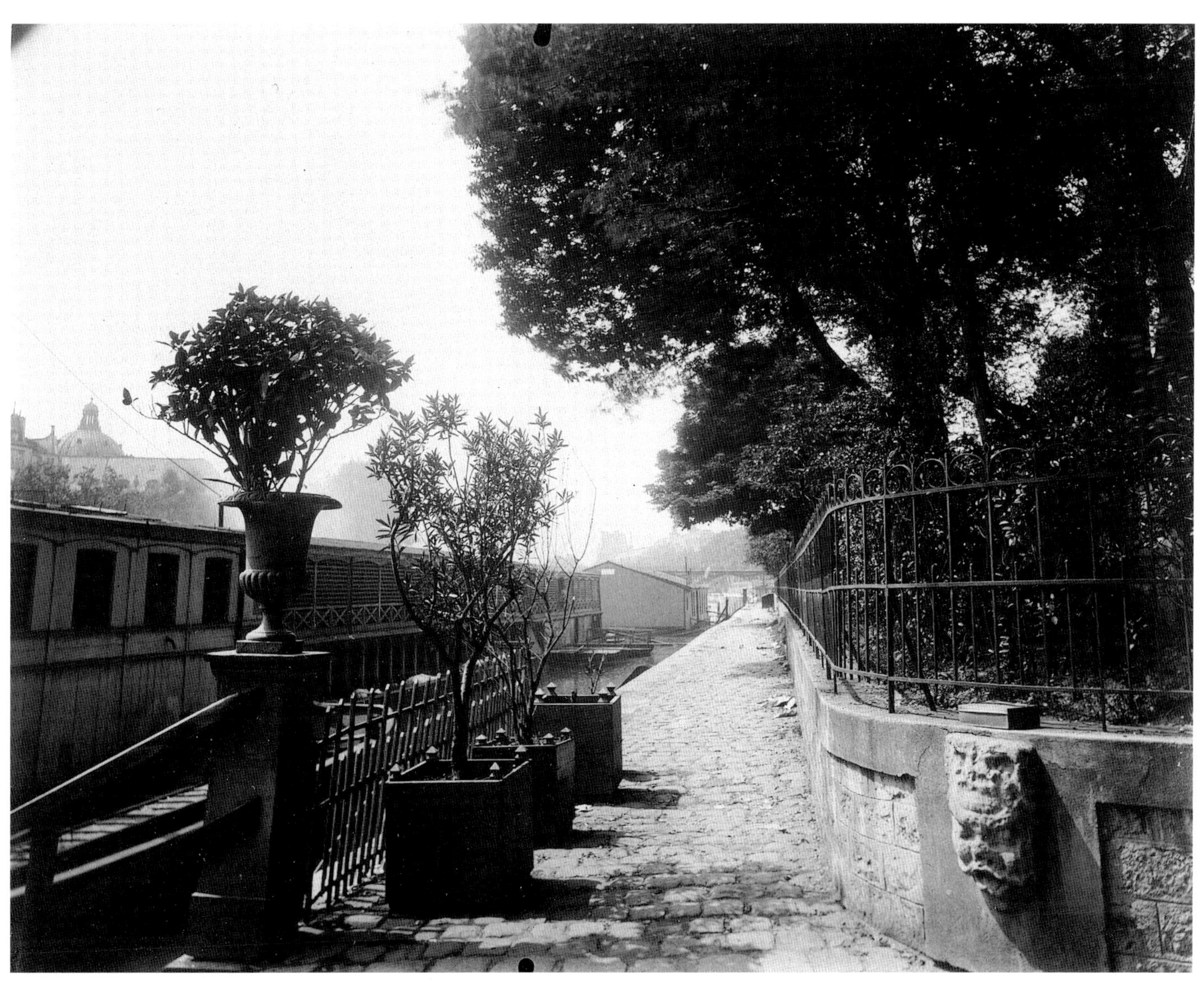

5.9 Banks of the Vert-Galant, south side, toward the pont des Arts, 1st, 1911

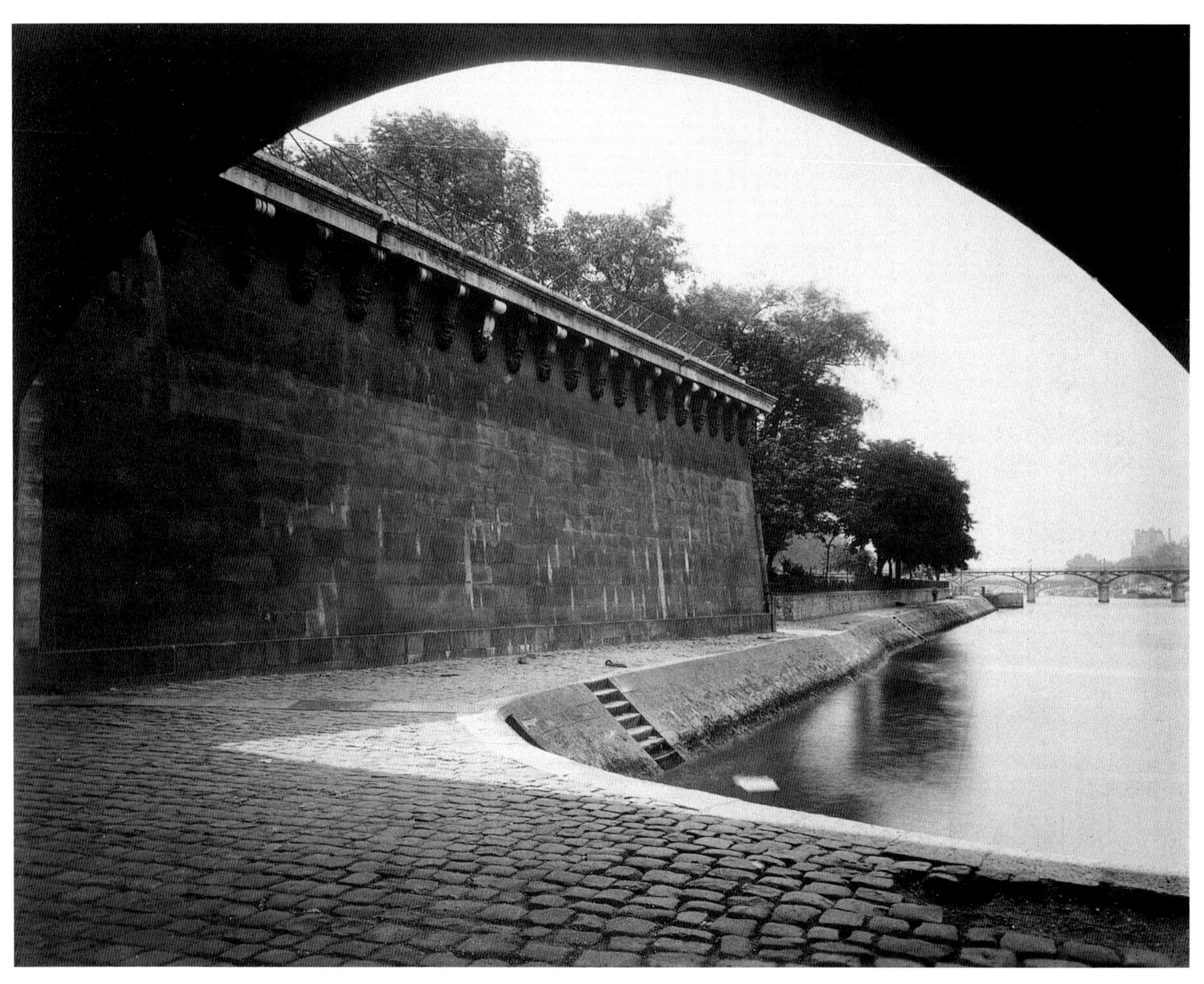

5.10 **Beneath the Pont-Neuf, north side, toward the Vert-Galant and the pont des Arts, 1st, 1911**

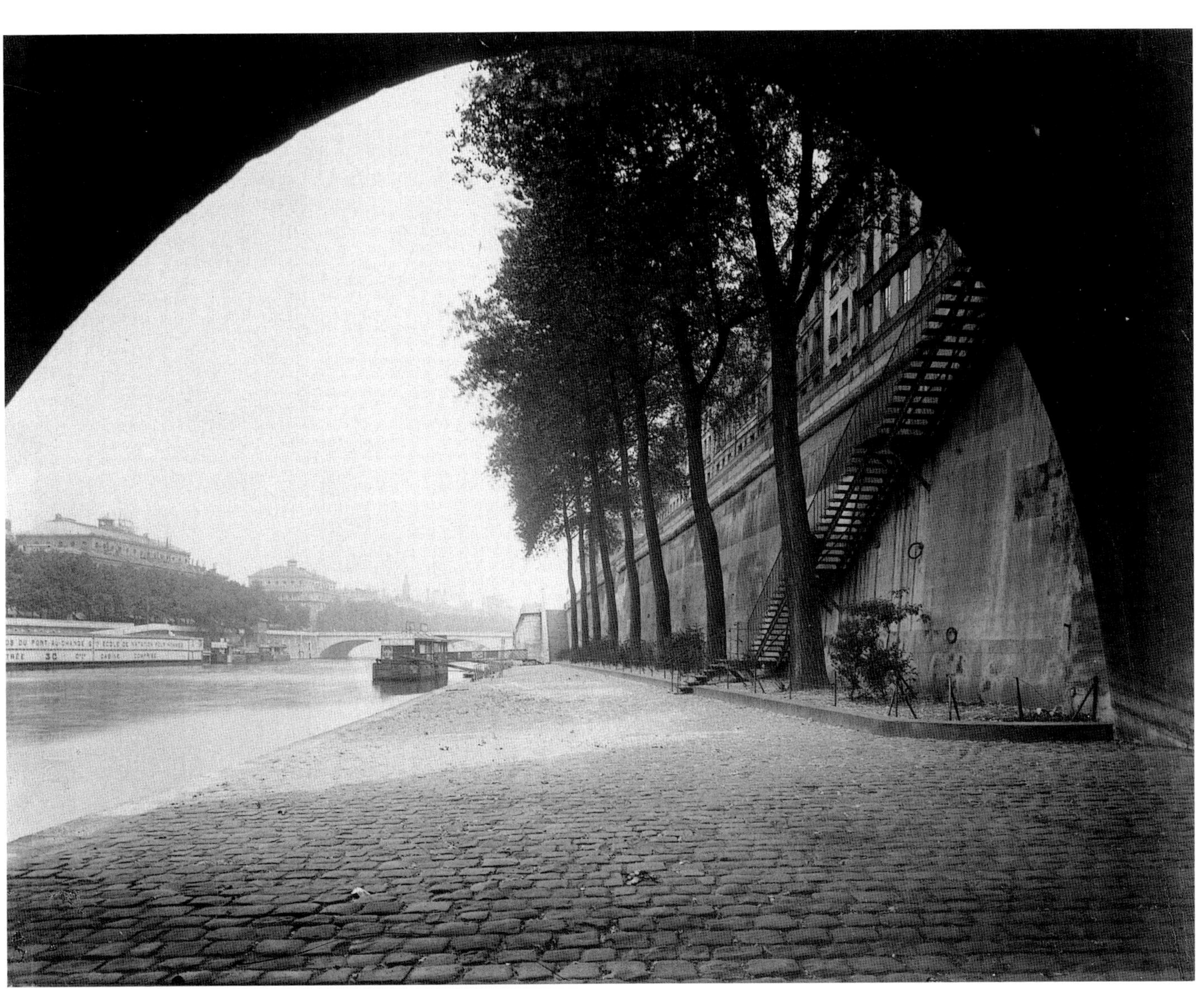

5.11 Beneath the Pont-Neuf, north side, toward the quai de l'Horloge and the pont au Change, 1st, 1911

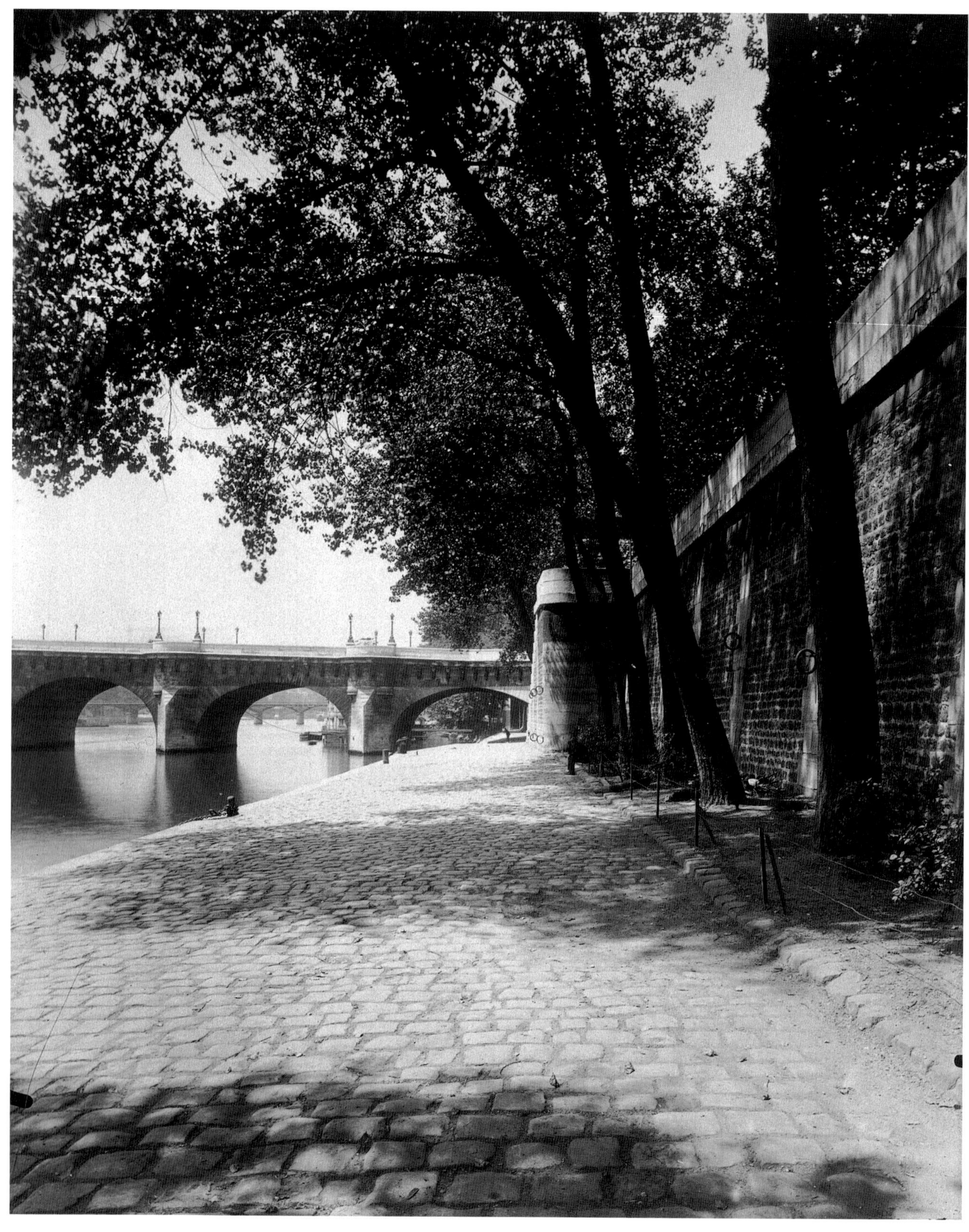

5.12 Port de la Mégisserie, toward the Pont-Neuf, 1st, 1911

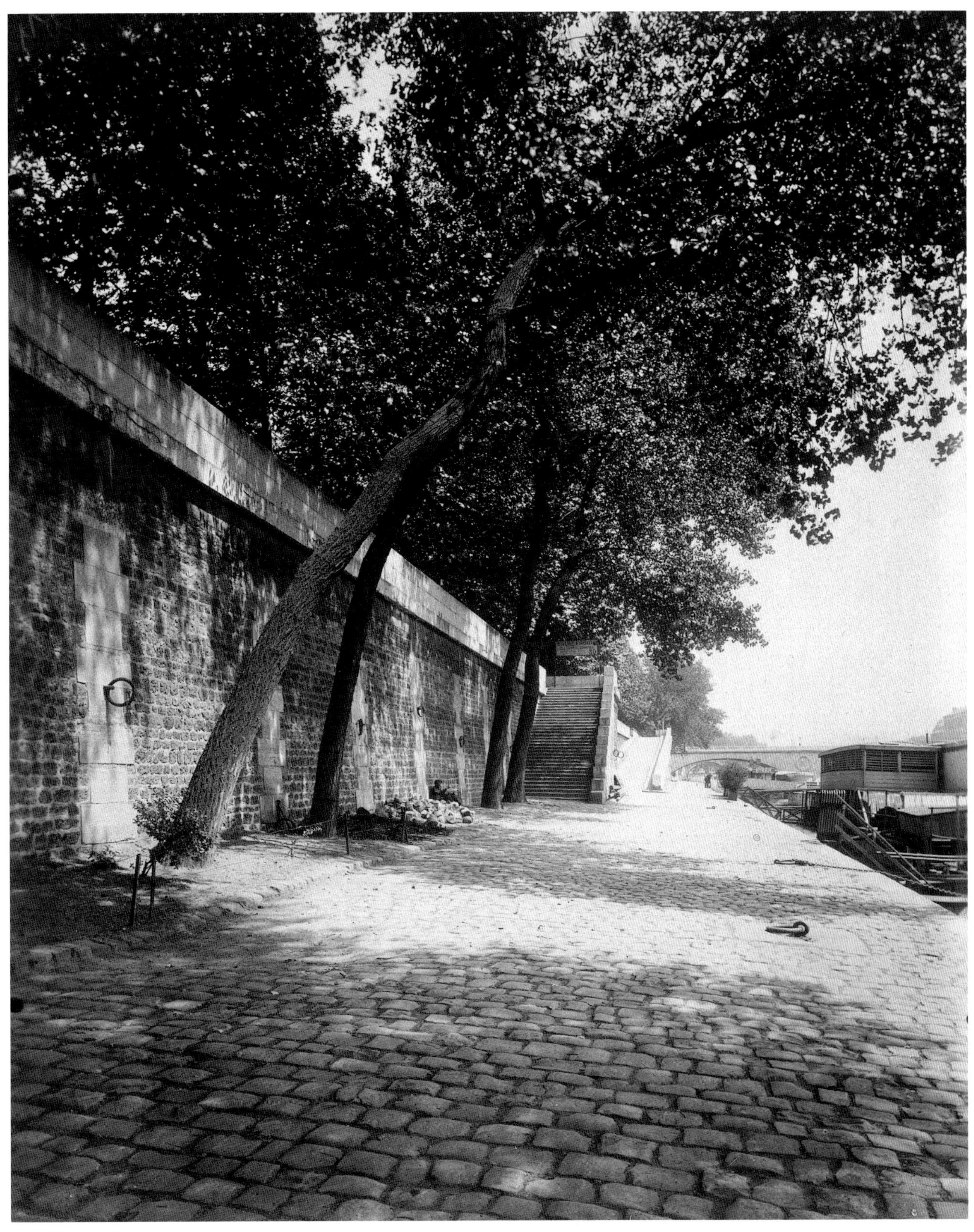

5.13 Port de la Mégisserie, toward the pont au Change, 1st, 1911

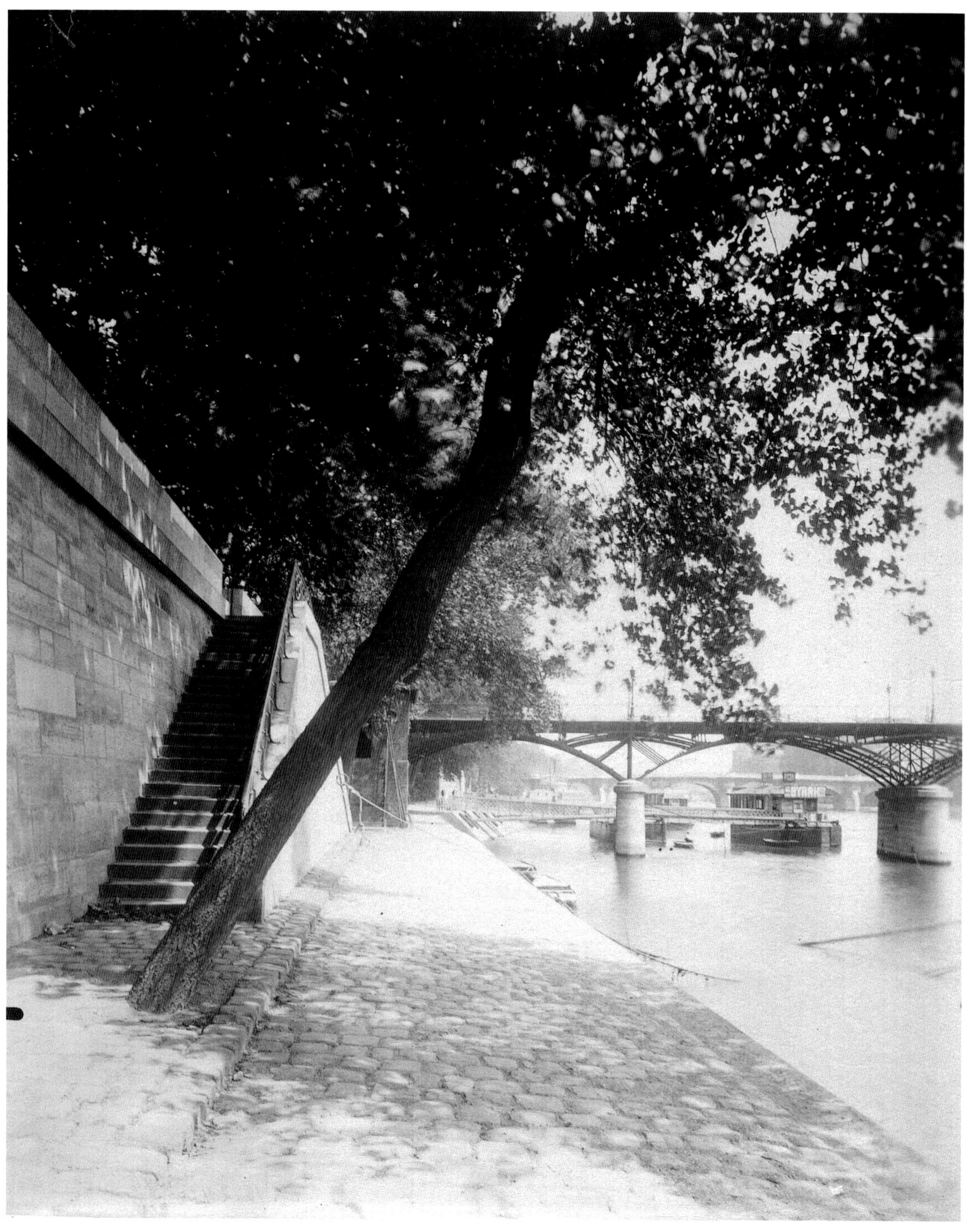

5.14 Port du Louvre, toward the pont des Arts, 1st, 1911

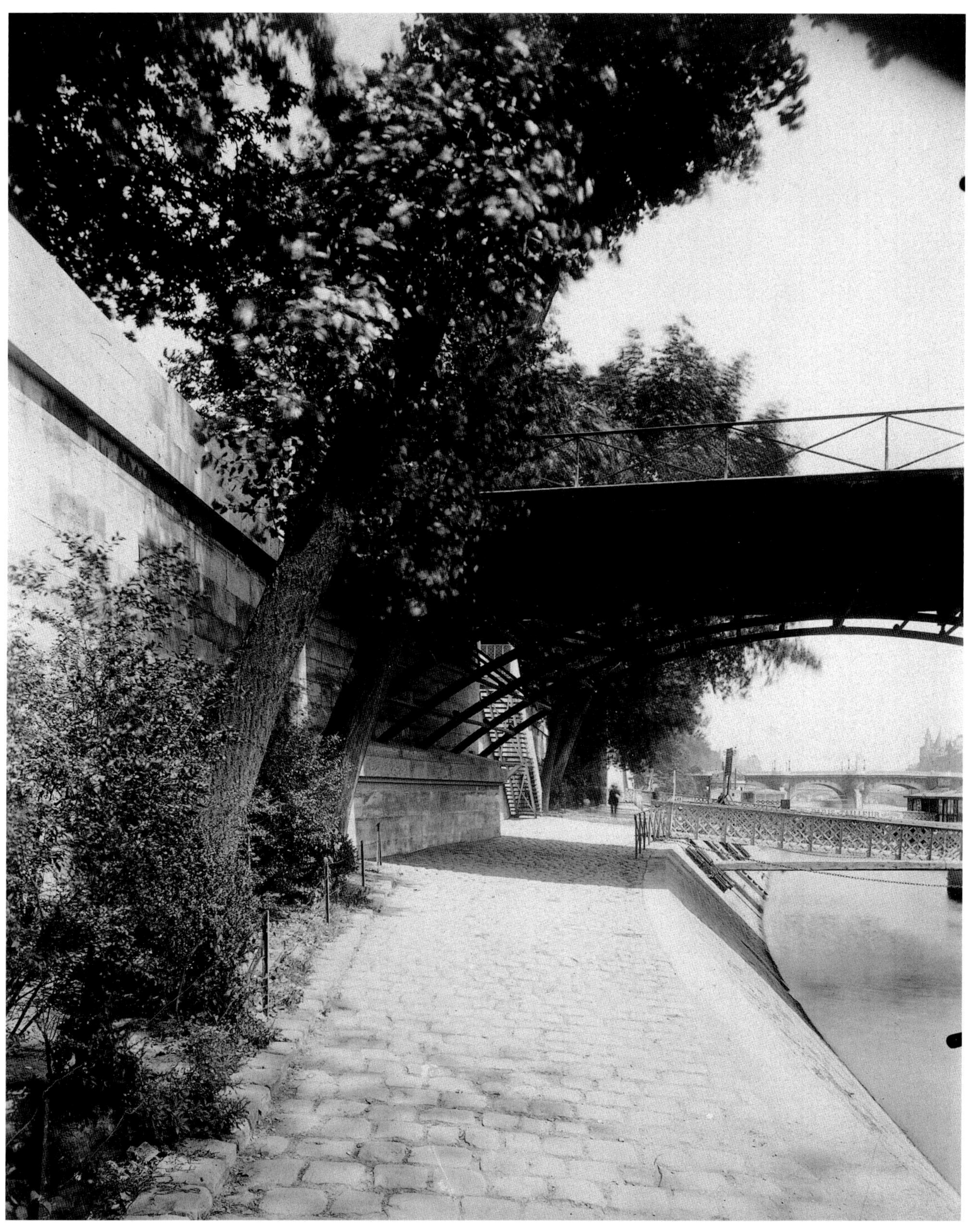

5.15 Port du Louvre, toward the pont des Arts and the Pont-Neuf, 1st, 1911

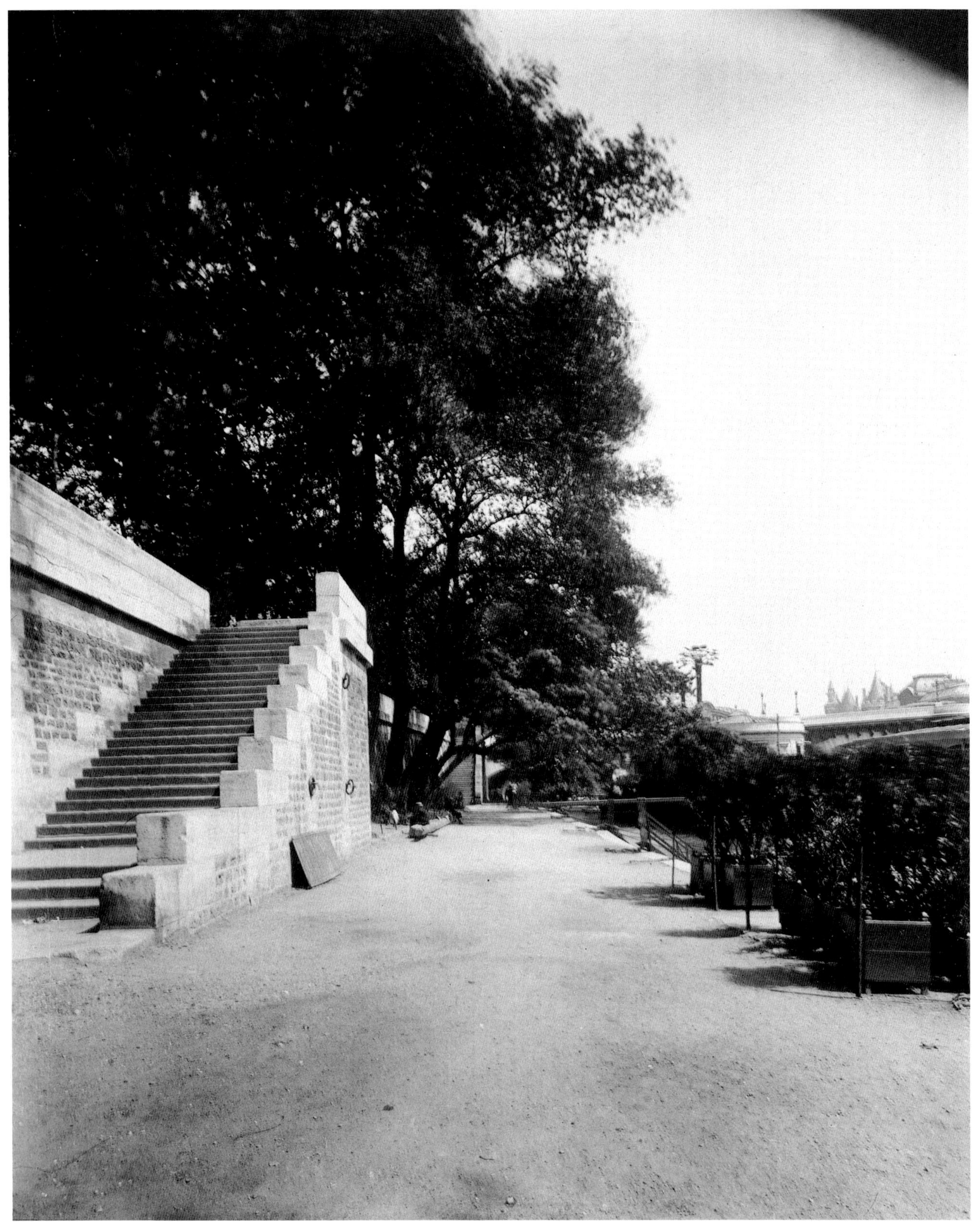

5.16 Port du Louvre, toward the Pont-Neuf, 1st, 1911

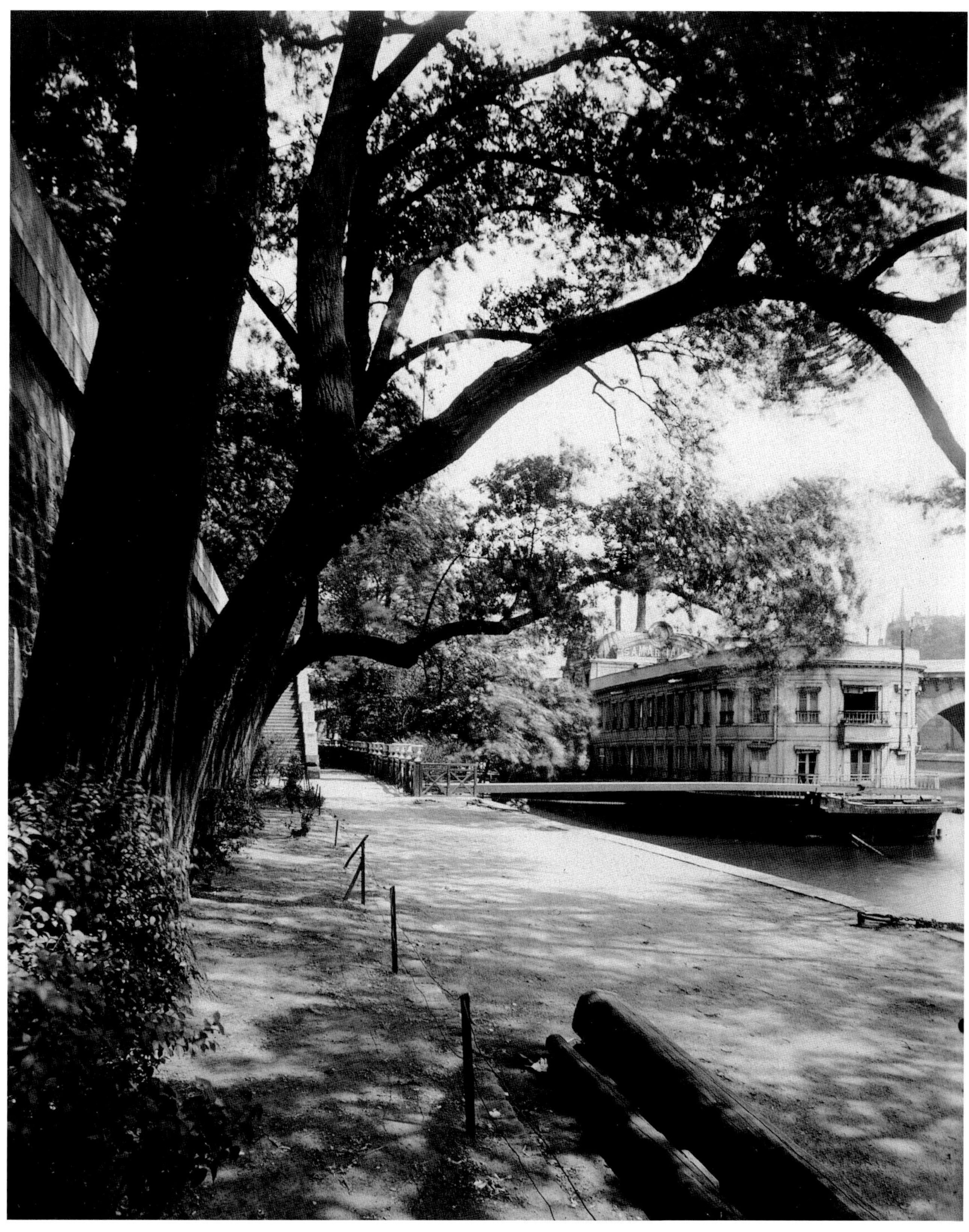

5.17 Port du Louvre, toward the Pont-Neuf, 1st, 1911

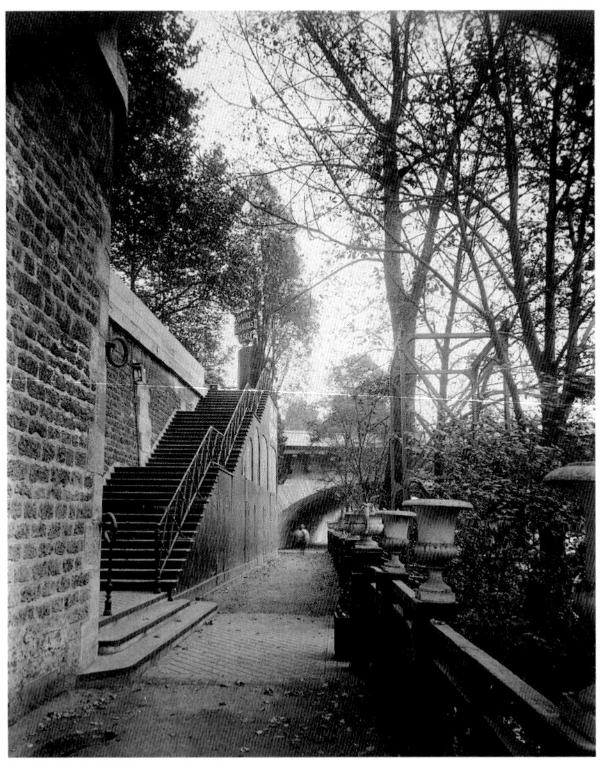

5.18 Port du Louvre, toward the Pont-Neuf, 1st, 1911

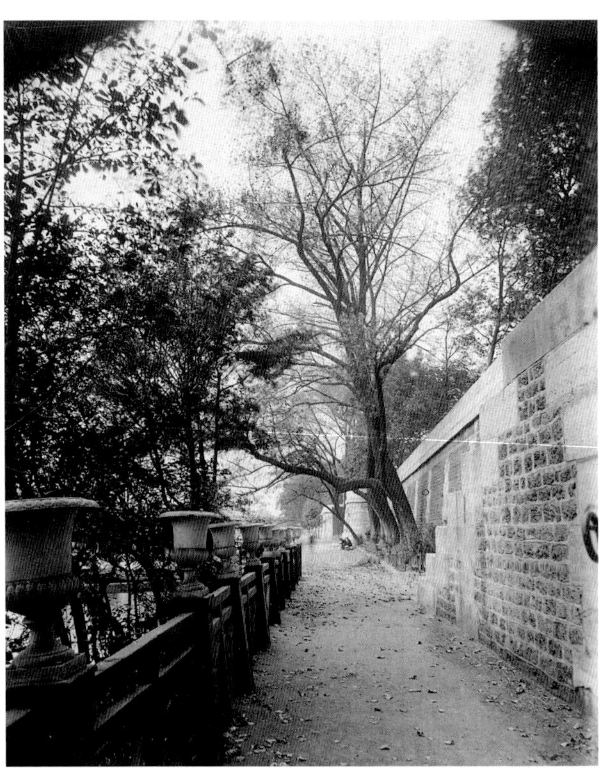

5.19 Port du Louvre, toward the pont des Arts, 1st, 1911

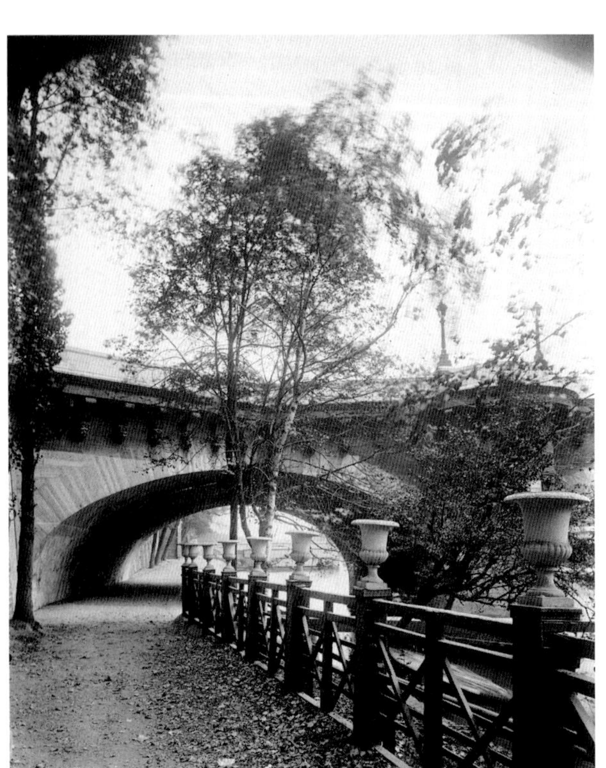

5.20 Port du Louvre, near the Pont-Neuf, toward the quai de la Mégisserie, 1st, 1911

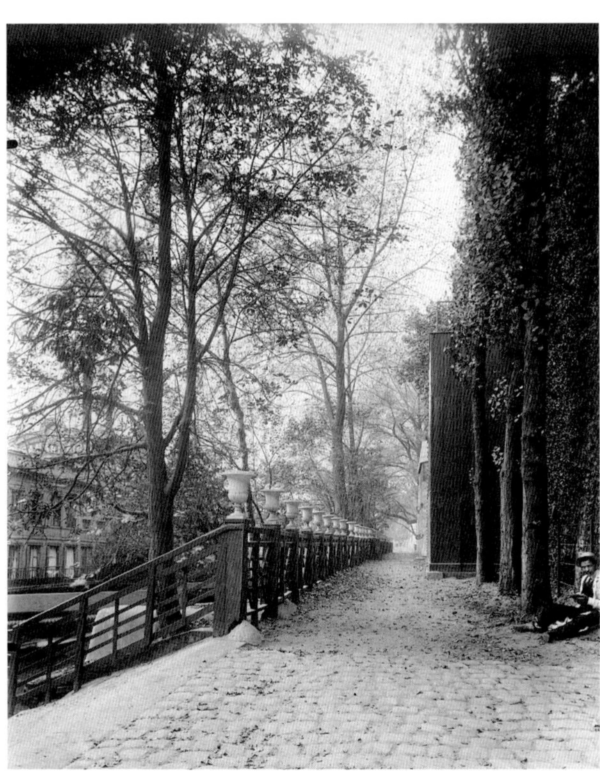

5.21 Port du Louvre, near the Pont-Neuf, toward the pont des Arts, 1st, 1911

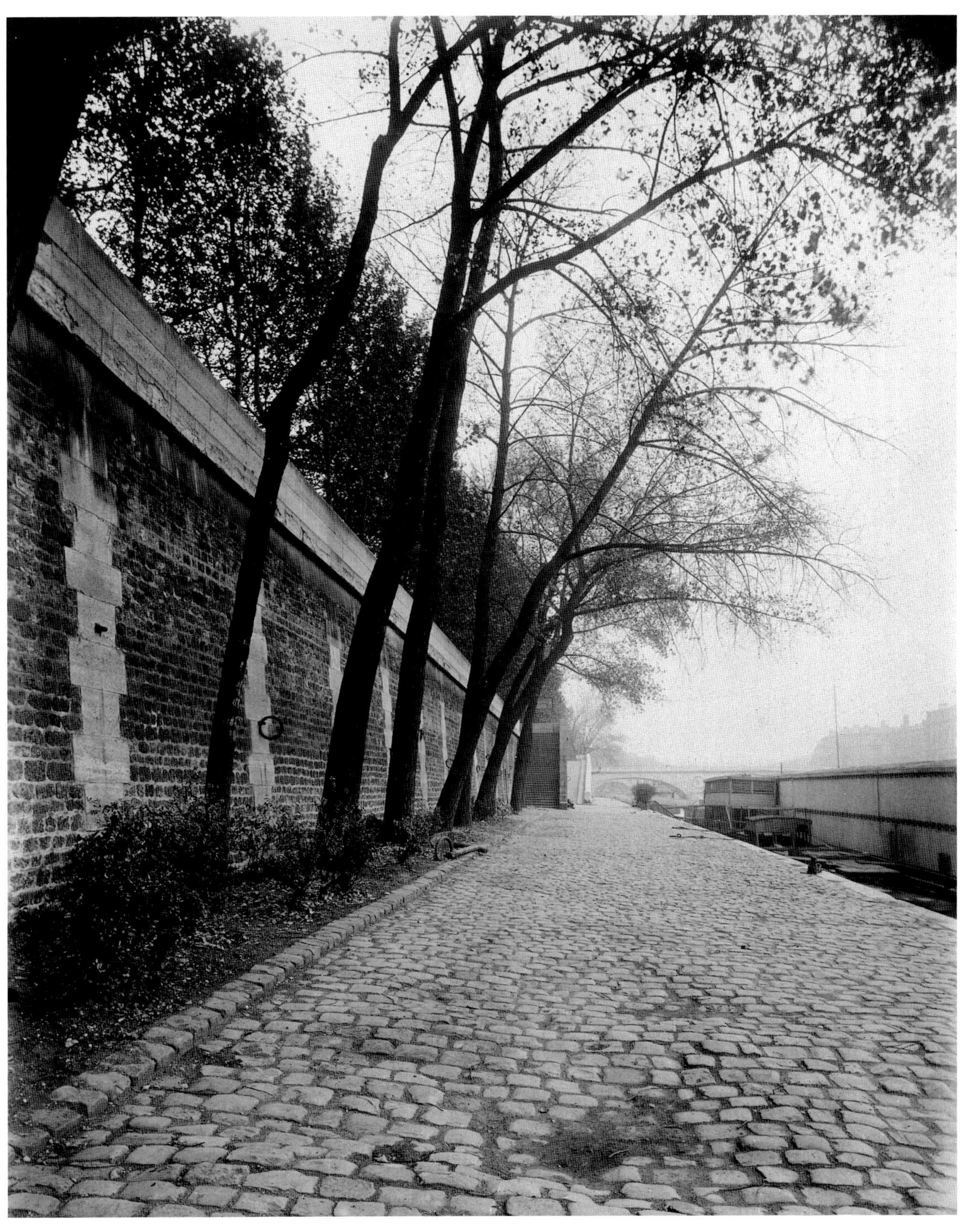

5.22 Port de la Mégisserie, toward the pont au Change, 1st, 1911

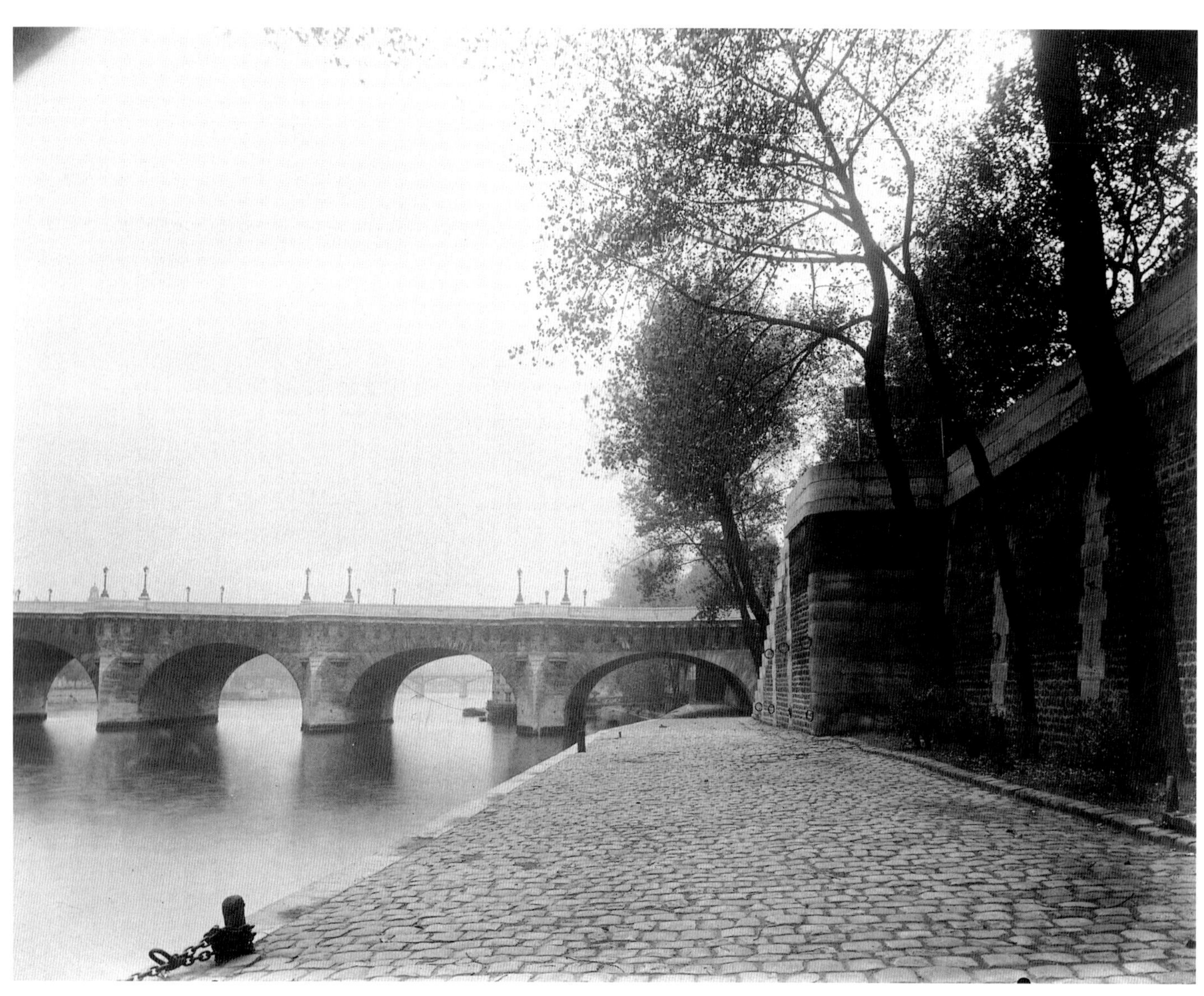

5.23 Port de la Mégisserie, toward the Pont-Neuf, 1st, 1911

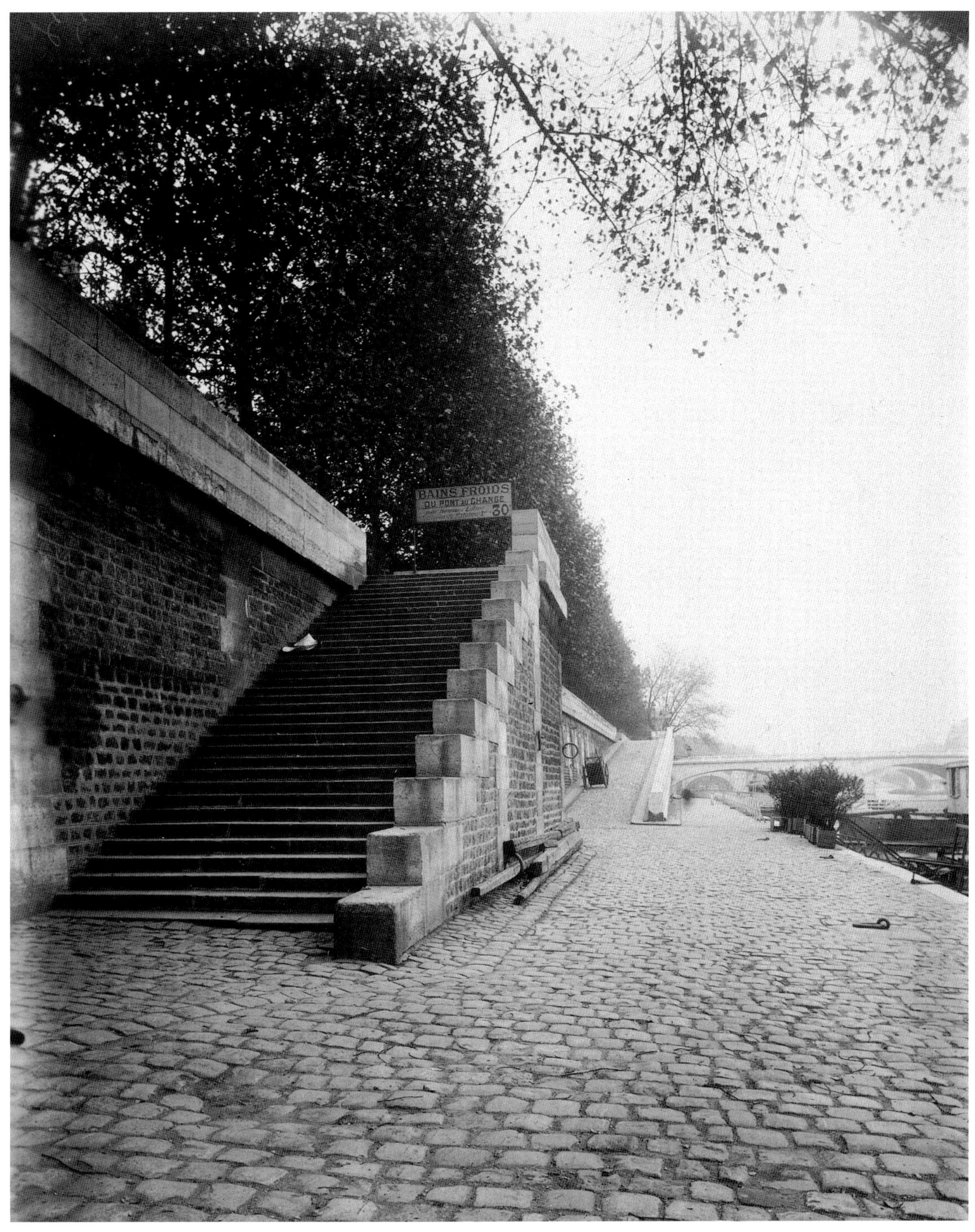

5.24 Port de la Mégisserie, toward the pont au Change, 1st, 1911

6. Place Bernard Halpern, 5th arrondissement, 1898, 1923, and 1924

On a rainy day in May 1898, Atget photographed the clock tower of the Church of Saint-Médard from the quiet square formed by the intersection of the rue des Patriarches, the rue Daubenton, and the rue du Marché des Patriarches (cat. 6.1). In this image from his series *Paris pittoresque*, Atget positioned his camera and used the wide-angle lens to describe the space of this public square and to produce an evocative image in which the church's tower functions as an essential landmark and point of orientation within the neighborhood. While Atget returned to this square at various times throughout his career—for example, he documented the surrounding streets in 1909 and 1914 as part of his series *Topographie du vieux Paris*—he specifically revisited this view twenty-five years later in the late autumn of 1923, and again in the summer of 1924. The spindly young tree, seen in the center of his 1898 view, had now attained its maturity. In his two 1923 views, he used the darkened silhouettes of the lamp standard and the trees in the square to structure the pictorial space and cradle the distantly seen clock tower (cat. 6.2 and 6.3). In his 1924 view, the single tree with its canopy of overhanging leaves, coupled with the vignetting effect of the lens, emphasized the secluded character of this quiet square (cat. 6.4). In positioning his camera so that the clock tower was consistently framed by the foreground trees, Atget constructed four images which, in quite different ways, emphasized the picturesque nature of this site.

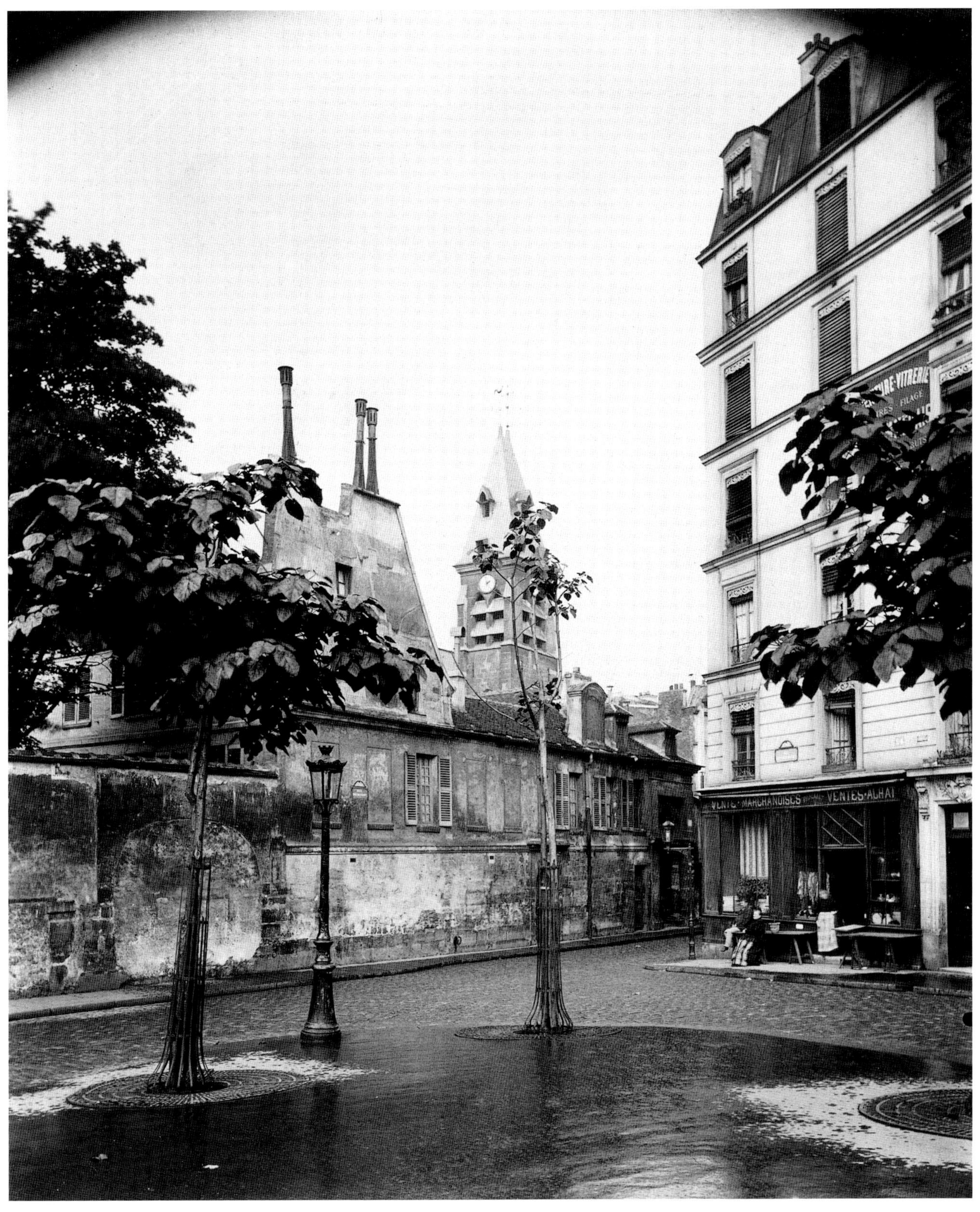

6.1 Place Bernard Halpern, toward the rue Daubenton and the Church of Saint-Médard, May 1898

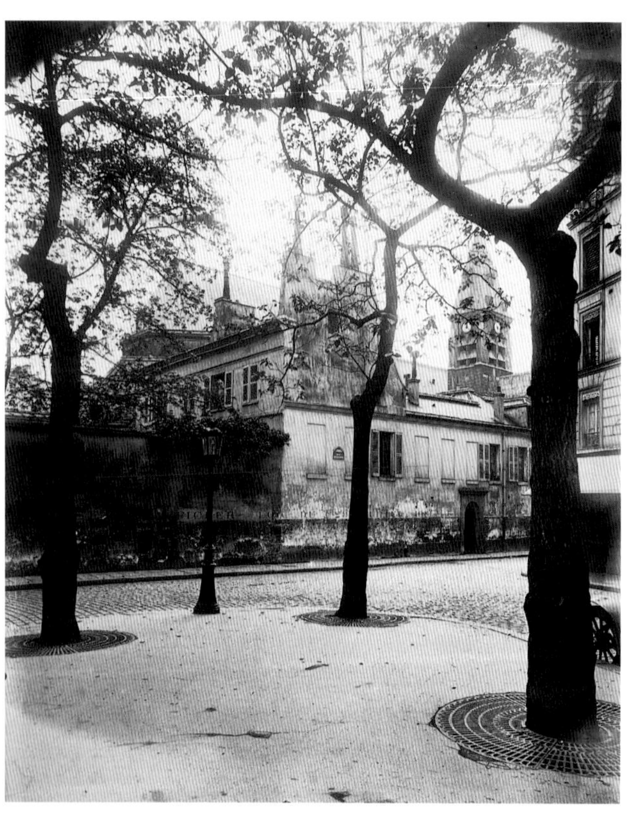

6.2 Place Bernard Halpern, toward the rue Daubenton and the Church of Saint-Médard, 1923

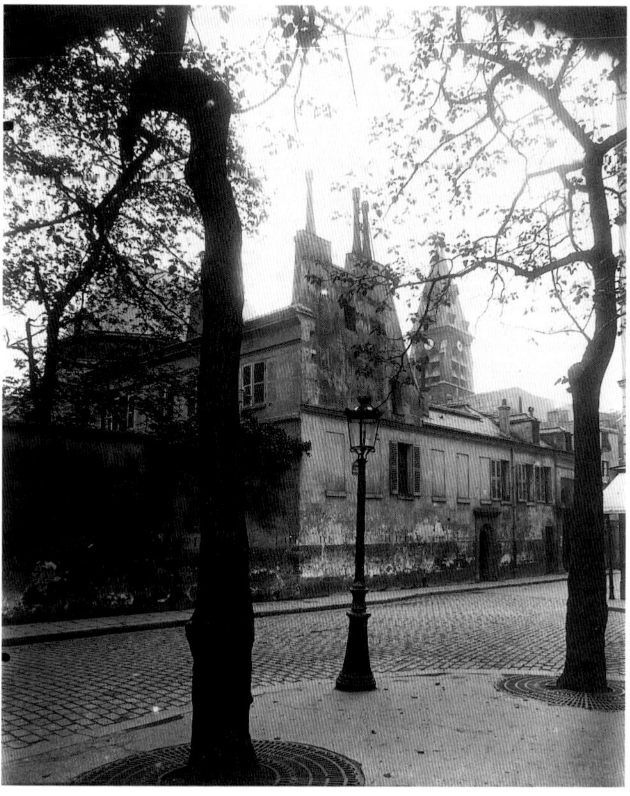

6.3 Place Bernard Halpern, toward the rue Daubenton and the Church of Saint-Médard, 1923

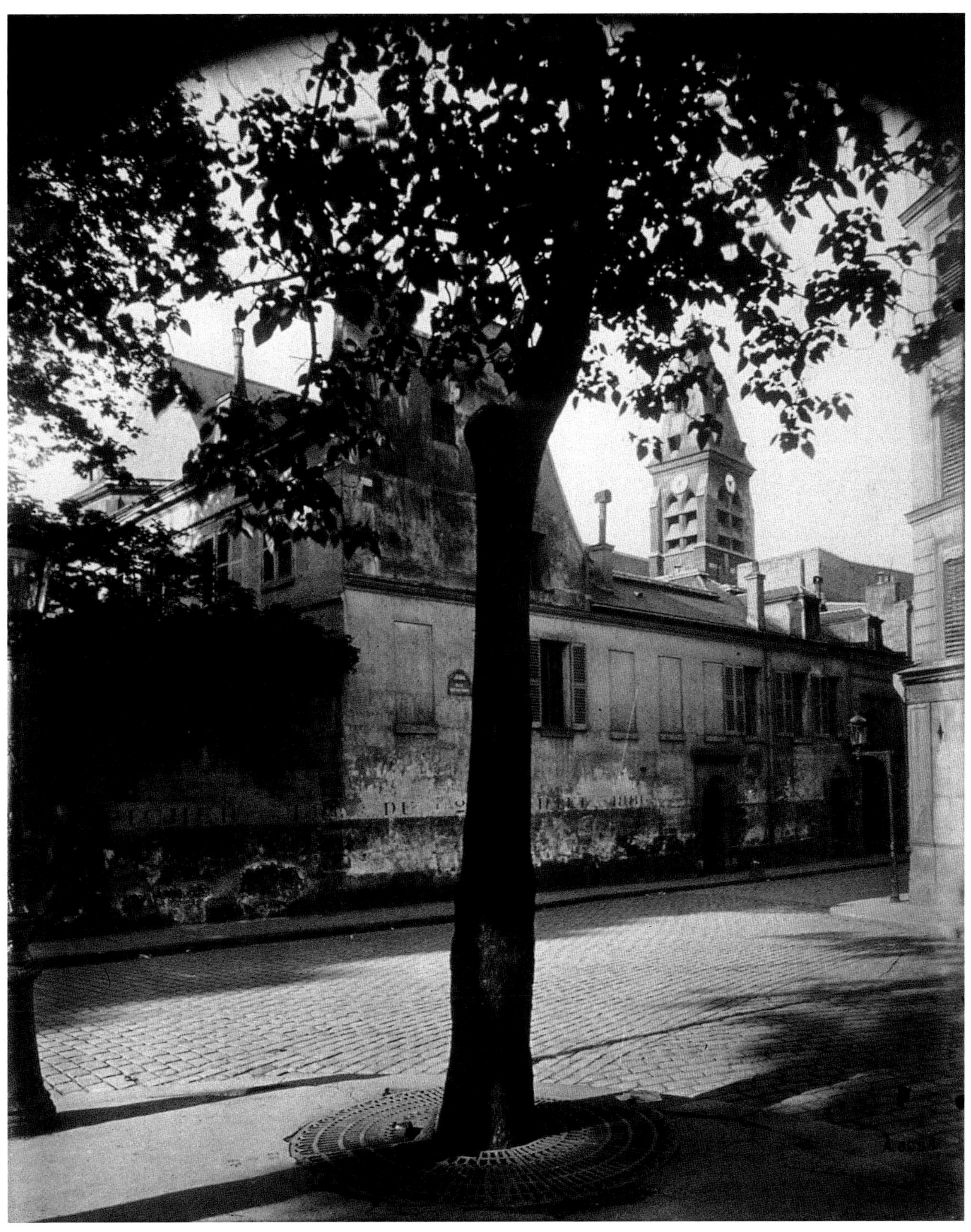

6.4 Place Bernard Halpern, toward the rue Daubenton and the Church of Saint-Médard, 1924

7. The Church of Saint-Séverin, 5th arrondissement, 1898–1923

Beginning as a modest parish church, Saint-Séverin was rebuilt in the thirteenth century and subsequently enlarged in the middle of the fourteenth century. After a severe fire around 1448, it was largely rebuilt in its present form during the second half of the fifteenth century, with only portions of the facade, the clock tower, and the first three spans of the central nave surviving from the earlier structure. The seemingly vast interior (50 meters in length and 34 meters wide) consists of five naves with a row of outside chapels and a double ambulatory surrounded by nine radial chapels. To the south of the church lay the presbytery garden, surrounded by a cloister that contained the church's former charnel house. The unusual structure of the cloister, the only surviving example in Paris, was virtually rebuilt during its restoration in the 1920s. The church is bound by the rue des Prêtres-Saint-Séverin to the west, the rue Saint-Séverin to the north, the rue Saint-Jacques to the east, and the rue de la Parcheminerie to the south.

Atget made ninety-four photographs of the church and the surrounding streets between 1898 and 1923.[13] He extensively photographed not only the church itself—its exterior, interior, roof, and garden—but thoroughly documented its immediate surroundings, and repeatedly returned, over the period of twenty-five years, to record the razing of the buildings and the widening of the narrow streets adjacent to Saint-Séverin. In contrast to the previously discussed case studies, wherein Atget's documentation of a particular site was limited to a relatively small number of images, his far more comprehensive treatment of Saint-Séverin demonstrates a broader and more profound engagement with the urban character of this neighborhood.

If Atget's subject had simply been the church and the neighboring streets, he would have completed his documentation by 1903. Instead, his interest lay in the intimate and integral relationship between the forms of architecture and urban space. By 1902, when the newsstand immediately adjacent to the east end of the church along rue Saint-Jacques was demolished, Atget must have sensed that while the church itself would remain unchanged, its surroundings would be gradually and irrevocably altered. In examining the succession of photographs he produced, and in noting the perseverance with which he followed and documented the course of urban renewal, one can see how Atget developed particular strategies, including that of repeating earlier views, in order to create a permanent and comparative record of the transformation of this area over time.

In both 1899 and 1923, Atget made views of the west front of the Church of Saint-Séverin from similar camera positions (compare cat. 7.11 and 7.96). These two photographs bracket his coverage and poignantly articulate the scope of his project. In the earlier image, the buildings along the narrow and twisting street picturesquely frame the church's facade within an almost medieval urban context. In the later view, Atget used the camera's horizontal format to reveal how the demolition of the buildings and the straightening of the street, as part of Hausmann's program, had now isolated the church.

Considering the extent of Atget's commitment and the thoroughness of his documentation, it is not surprising that he singled out Saint-Séverin in his letters to Paul Léon in 1920 as an example of the comprehensiveness and historical value of his photography. He included seventy-six negatives of the church and its neighborhood in the 1920 purchase, to which an additional six were added in 1928.

This study has been subdivided into seven sections.

i. Earliest views of the Church of Saint-Séverin and environs, 1898–1903

When Atget first photographed the church in 1898, he was confronted with the challenge of producing architectural photographs of this ecclesiastic structure. The narrow streets and encroaching buildings prevented Atget from establishing a single viewpoint from which to survey the entire structure. As a result, he adopted an alternative strategy, one more consistent with his approach to photographing the city. By moving around the church's periphery, Atget produced four views emphasizing Saint-Séverin's position within a picturesque urban context (cat. 7.1–7.4).

Over the following five years, he returned on ten separate occasions to Saint-Séverin and added to his coverage in single or small clusters of views. He included the church's main portal (cat. 7.5) and the presbytery garden (cat. 7.8–7.10), and, although in a seemingly haphazard way, gradually documented other aspects of the neighborhood, including views made from opposite ends of the same street, as seen in his photographs of the rue de la Parcheminerie (cat. 7.6 and 7.18) and the rue Saint-Jacques (cat. 7.16 and 7.17).

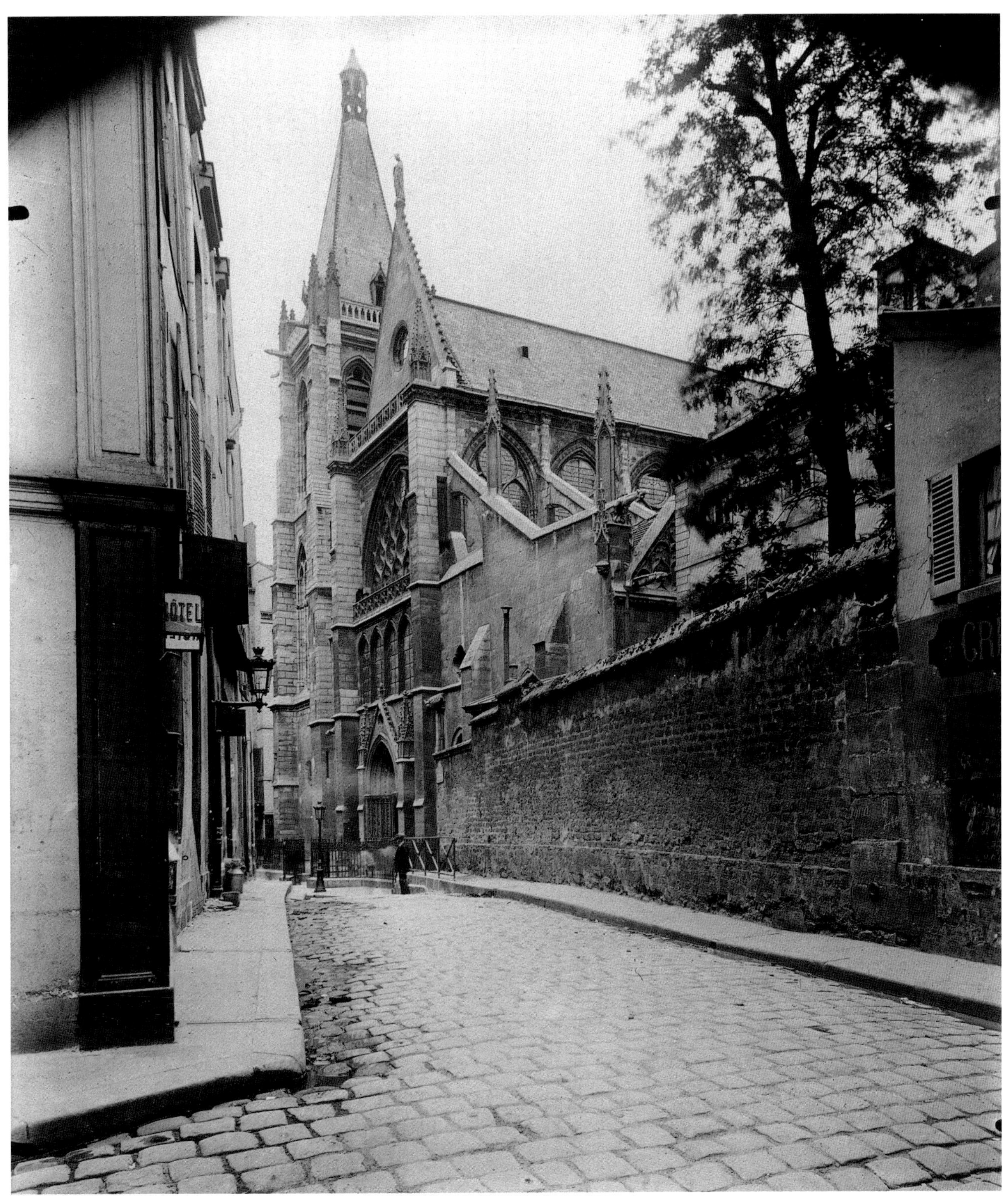

7.1 Rue des Prêtres-Saint-Séverin, toward the church, 1898

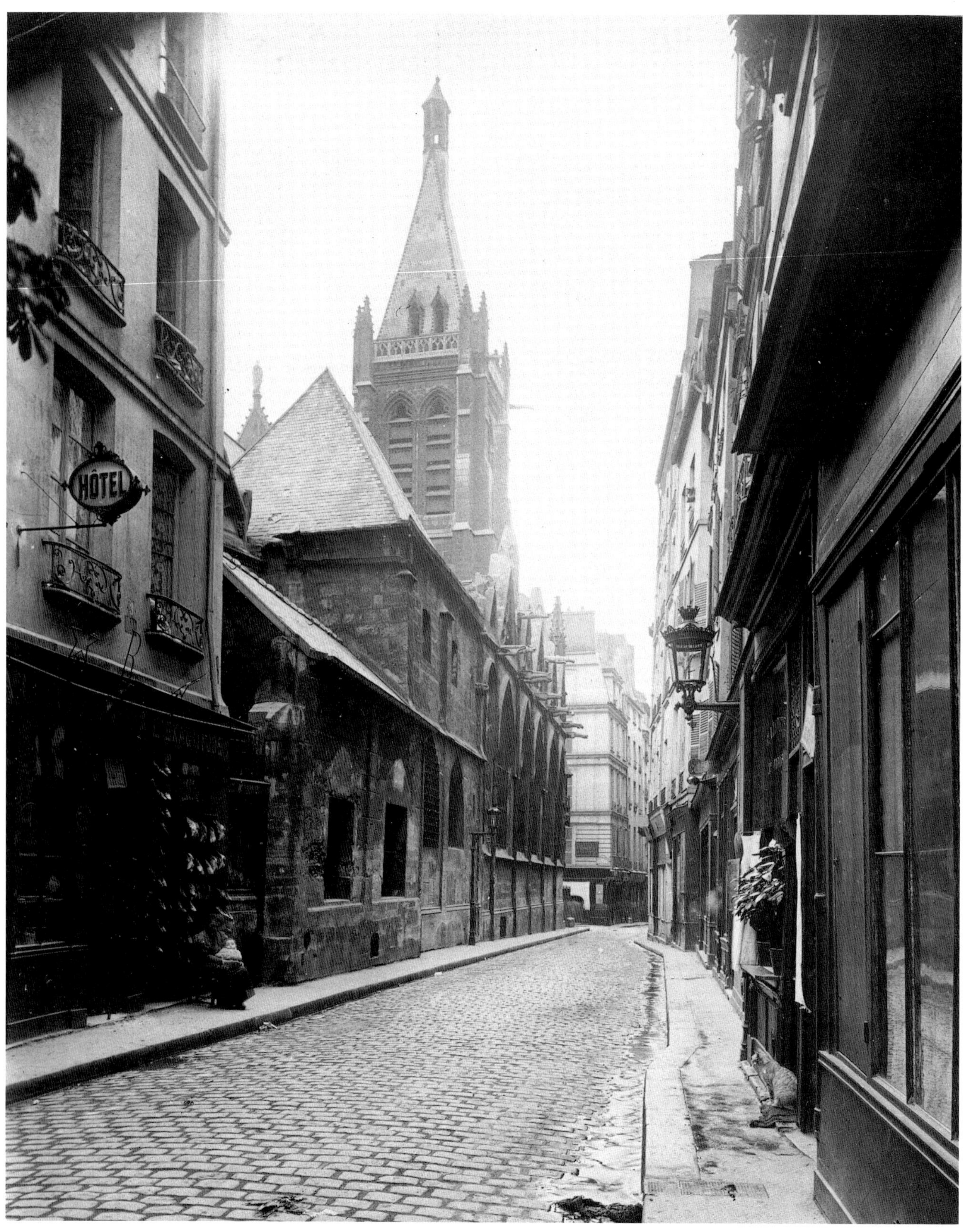

7.2 Rue Saint-Séverin, from the rue Saint-Jacques toward the church, 1898

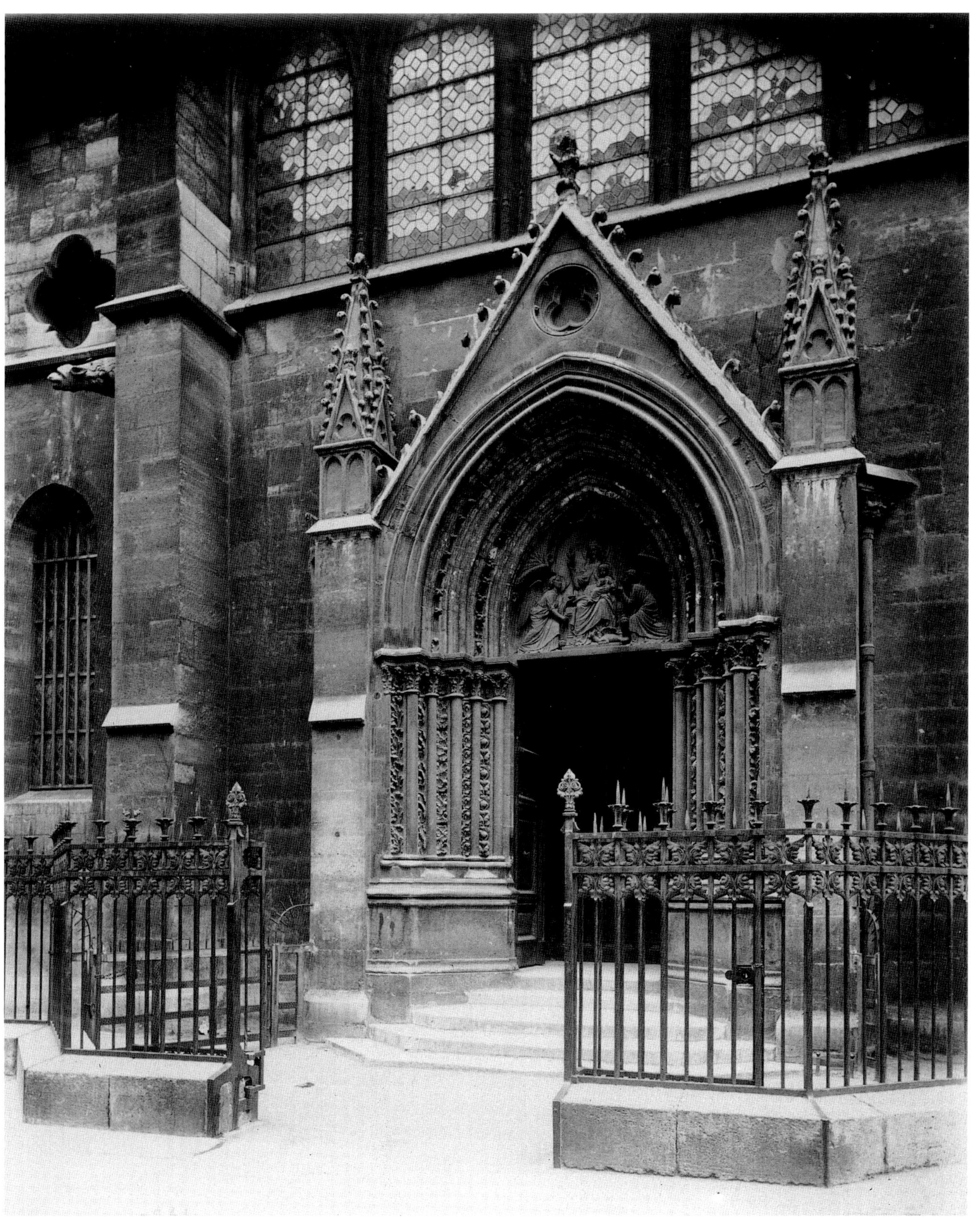

7.5 Main portal of the Church of Saint-Séverin along the rue des Prêtres-Saint-Séverin, 1898

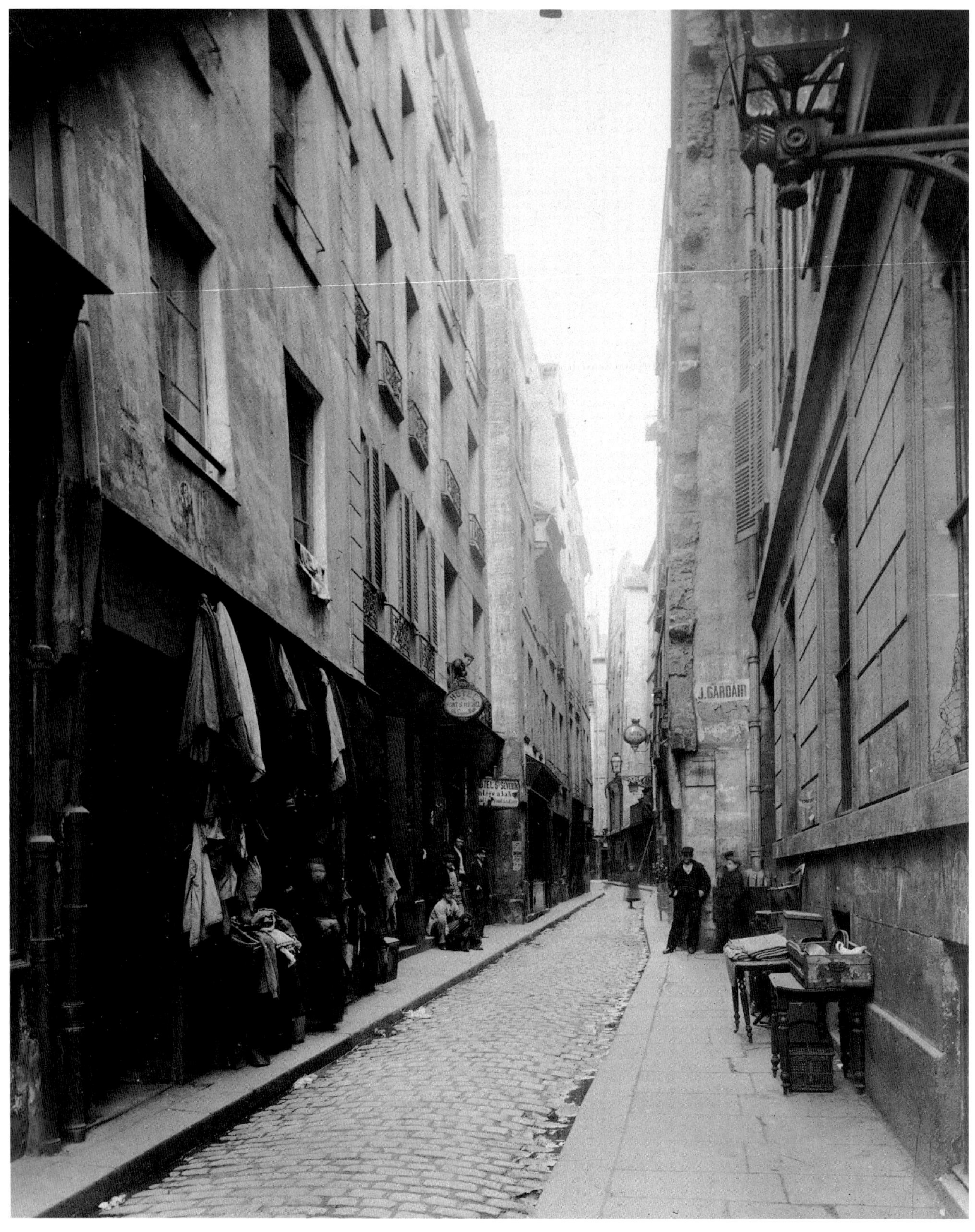

7.6 Rue de la Parcheminerie, toward the rue Saint-Jacques, May 1899

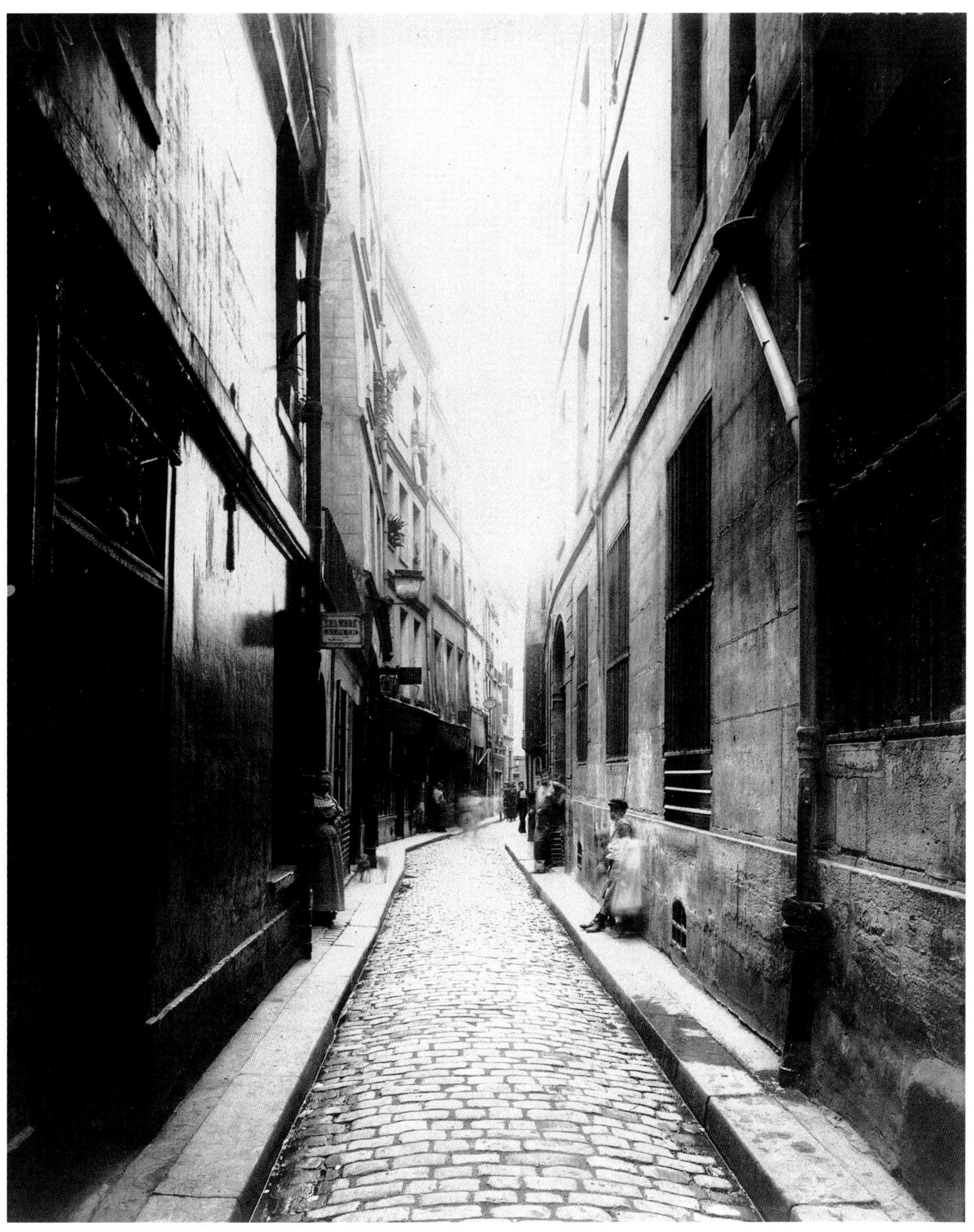

7.18 Rue de la Parcheminerie, from the rue Saint-Jacques, 1903

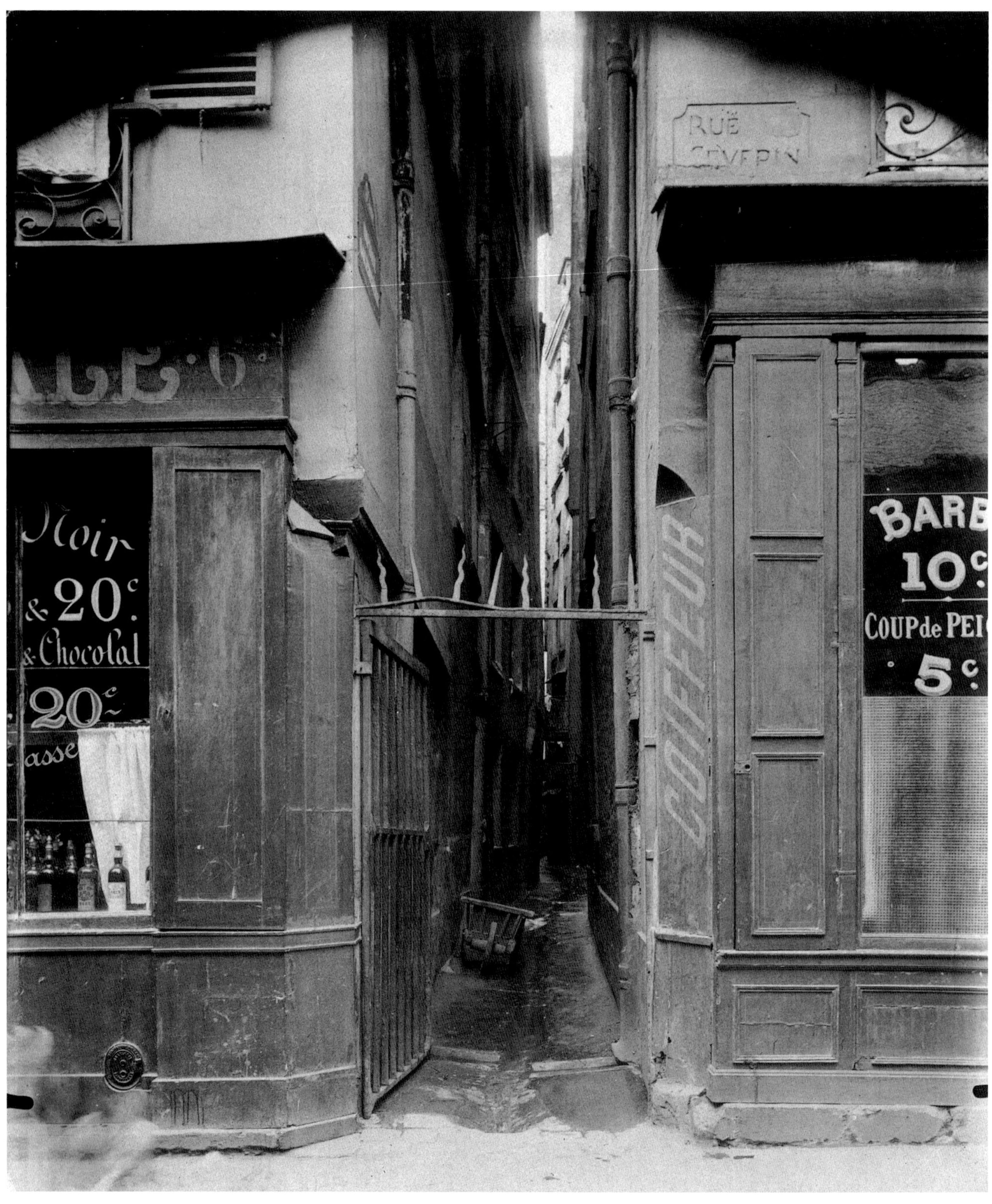

7.7 Impasse Salembrière, from the rue Saint-Séverin, May 1899

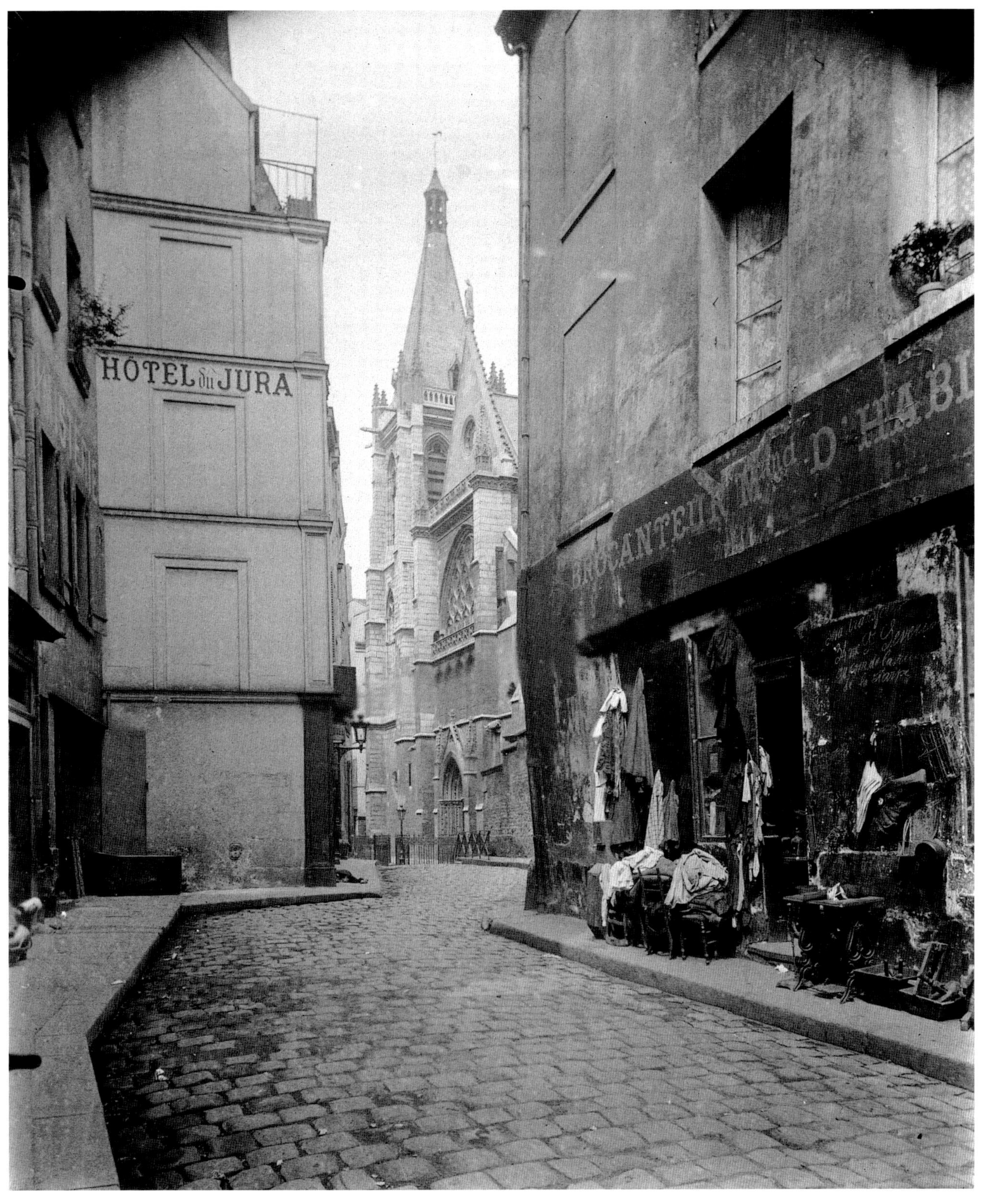

7.11 Rue des Prêtres-Saint-Séverin, toward the church, 1899

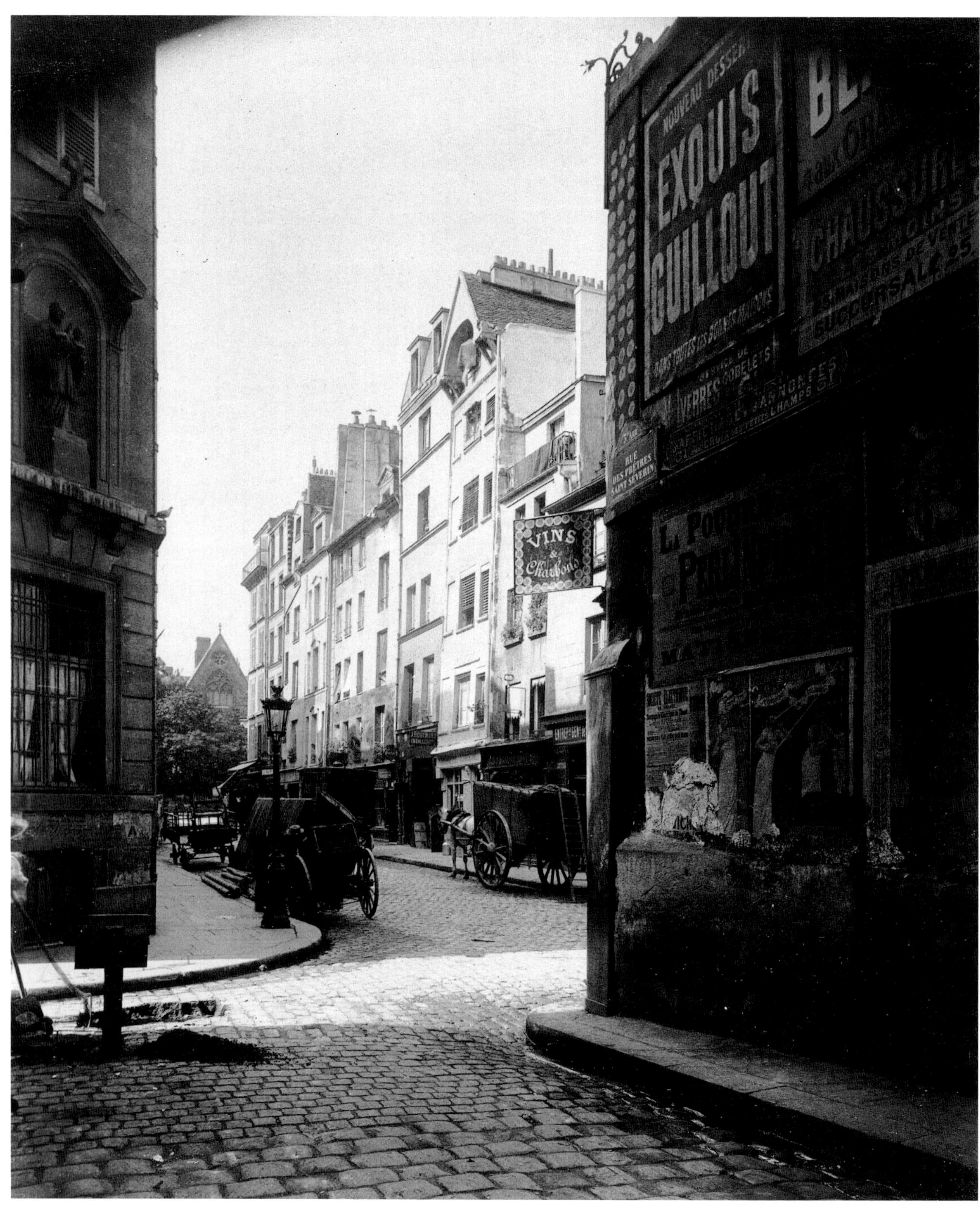

7.13 Rue des Prêtres-Saint-Séverin, toward the rue Boutebrie and the Musée de Cluny, 1899

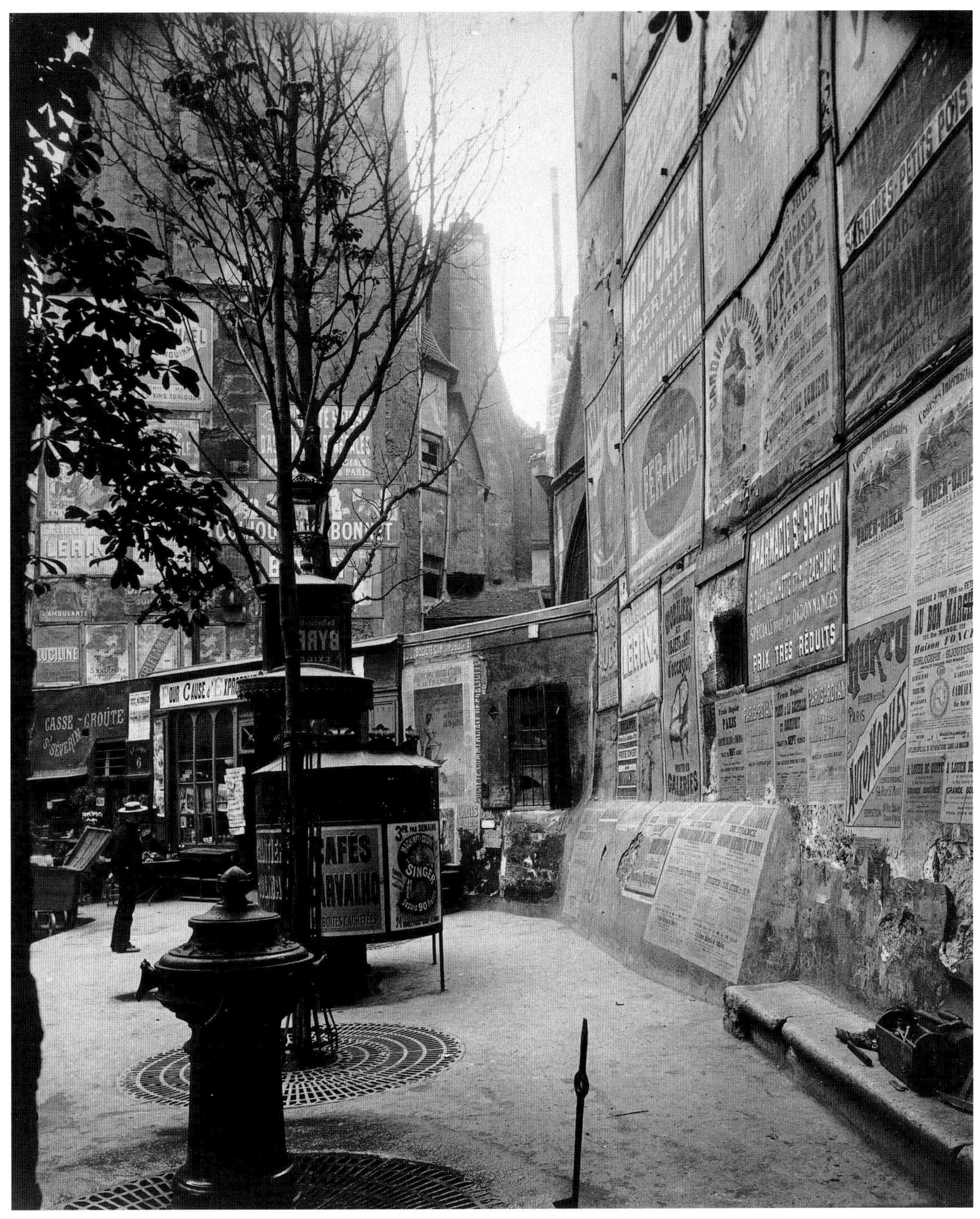

7.14 Rue Saint-Jacques, walls of the hotel abutting the apse of the Church of Saint-Séverin, August 1899

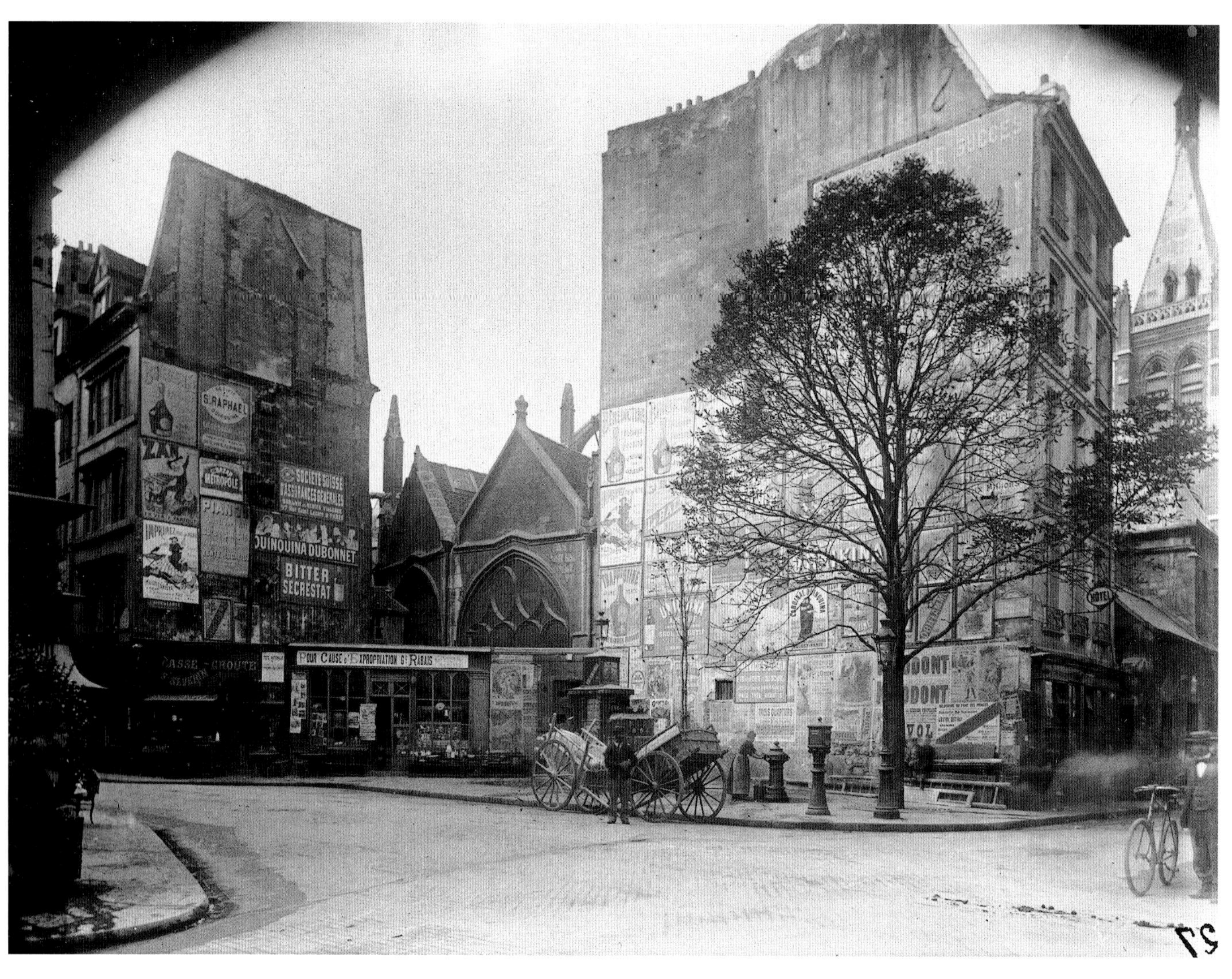

7.15 Rue Saint-Jacques from the rue Galande toward the Church of Saint-Séverin, 1899–1900

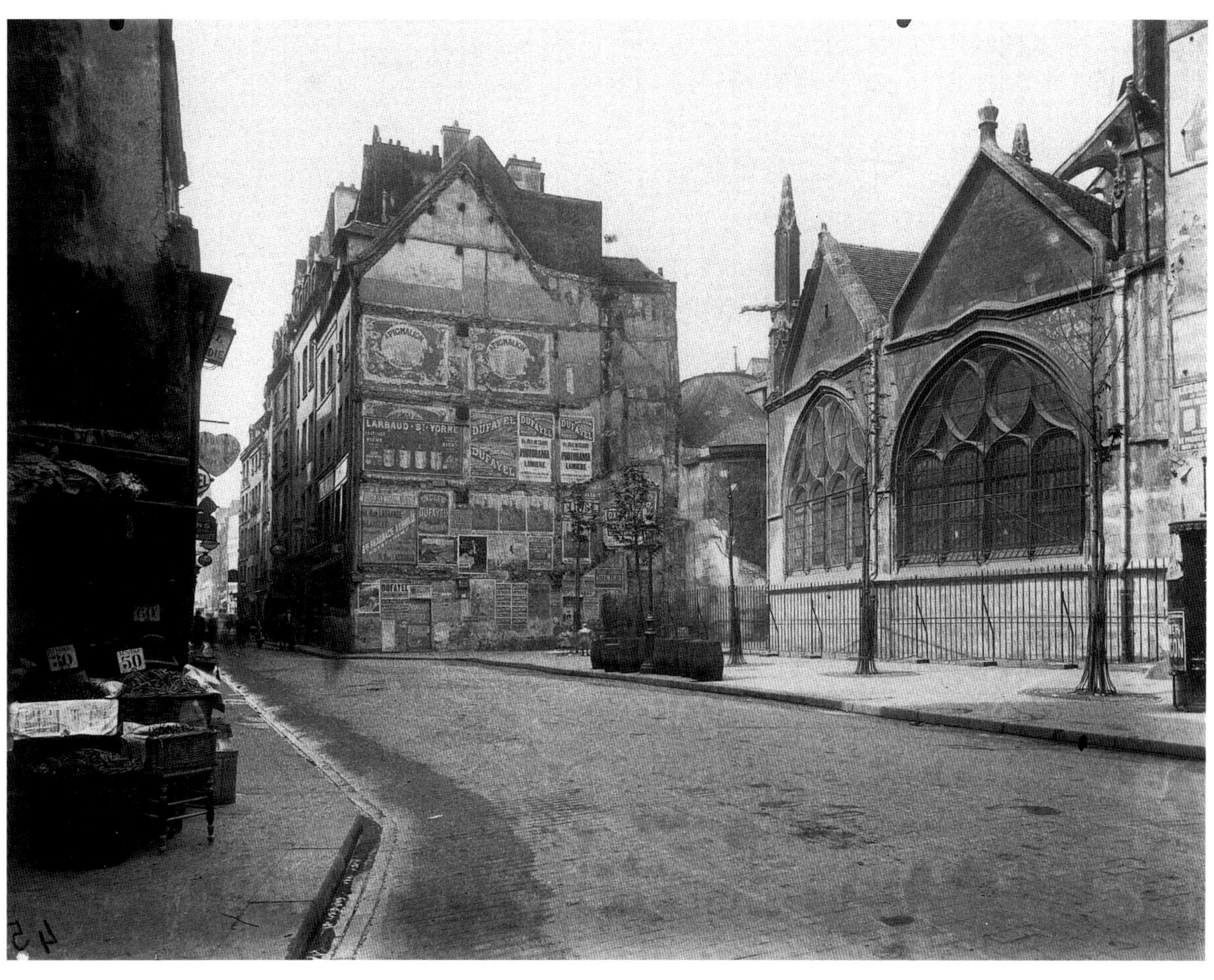

7.16 Rue Saint-Jacques, after the demolition of the stores abutting the apse of the Church of Saint-Séverin, 1902

ii. Documentation of the interior, roof, cloister, and former charnel house of the Church of Saint-Séverin, 1903

In 1903, Atget concentrated on the church itself. To photograph the interior, he selected an overcast day and, avoiding standard axial views, he made overlapping views from opposite ends of the central nave (cat. 7.21 and 7.28). He also constructed a sequence of six linked views that began near the Saint-Martin door, situated at the northwest corner of the church. Atget systematically progressed down the northernmost nave, worked around the ambulatory, and ended with a view looking back along the length of the church (cat. 7.22–7.27). During this year, he also rephotographed the space of the presbytery garden (cat. 7.34–7.37), and recorded the interior of the subsequently demolished former charnel house (cat. 7.38 and 7.39). In addition, Atget ascended the narrow stairs of the clock tower and took five views from the roof. He made a pair of photographs of the *enfilade* of flying buttresses along the northern flank of the church, seen from below and from slightly above (cat. 7.29 and 7.30). On this same visit, he moved his cumbersome equipment to the area above the ambulatory at the eastern end of the church roof and, from three closely related camera positions, photographed a further group of flying buttresses against the roof line of the surrounding buildings (cat. 7.31–7.33). The roof images are unique in Atget's work. He never sought out such inaccessible vantage points, preferring instead to describe structures from the pedestrian's viewpoint at street level.

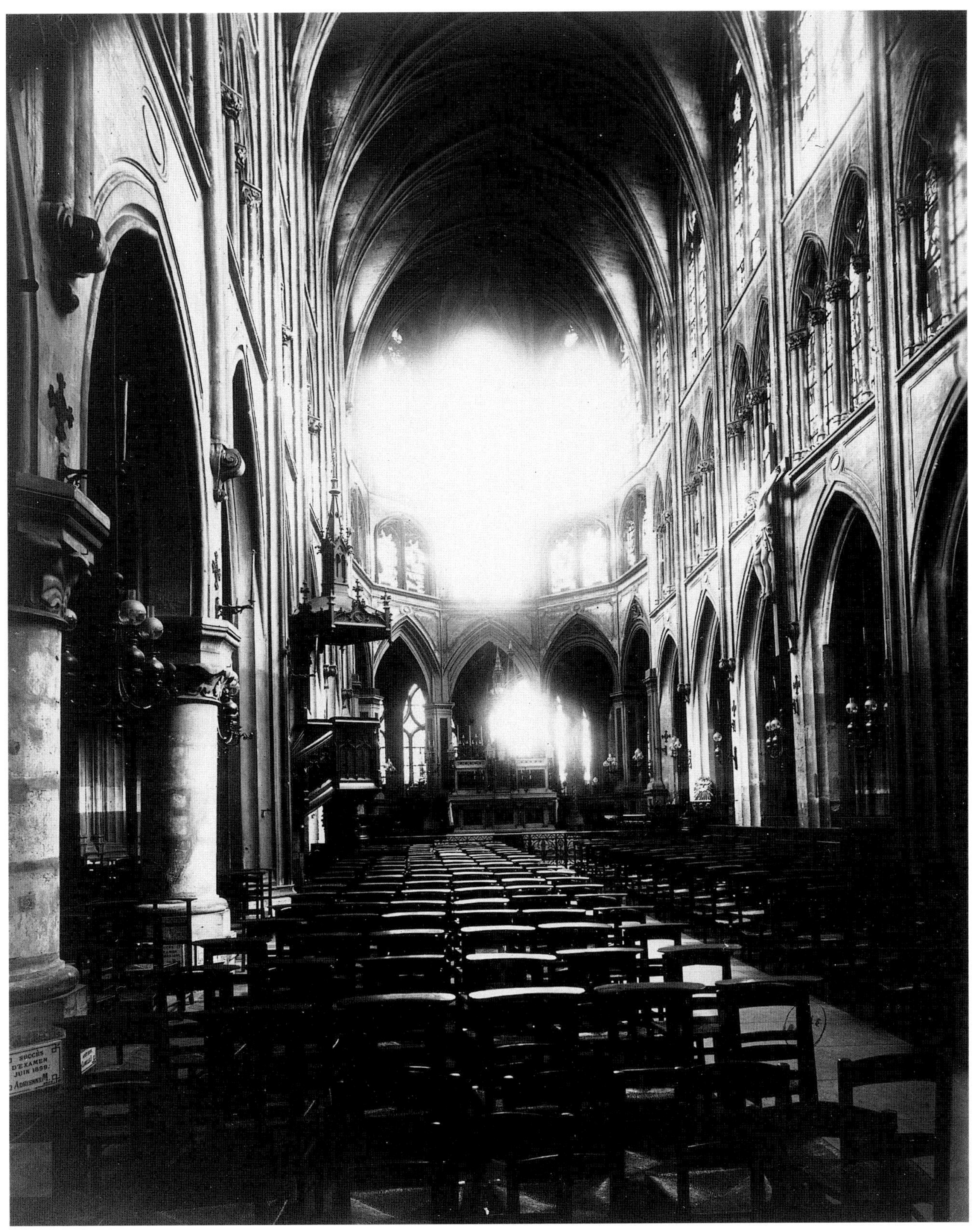

7.21 Central nave of the Church of Saint-Séverin, toward the choir, 1903

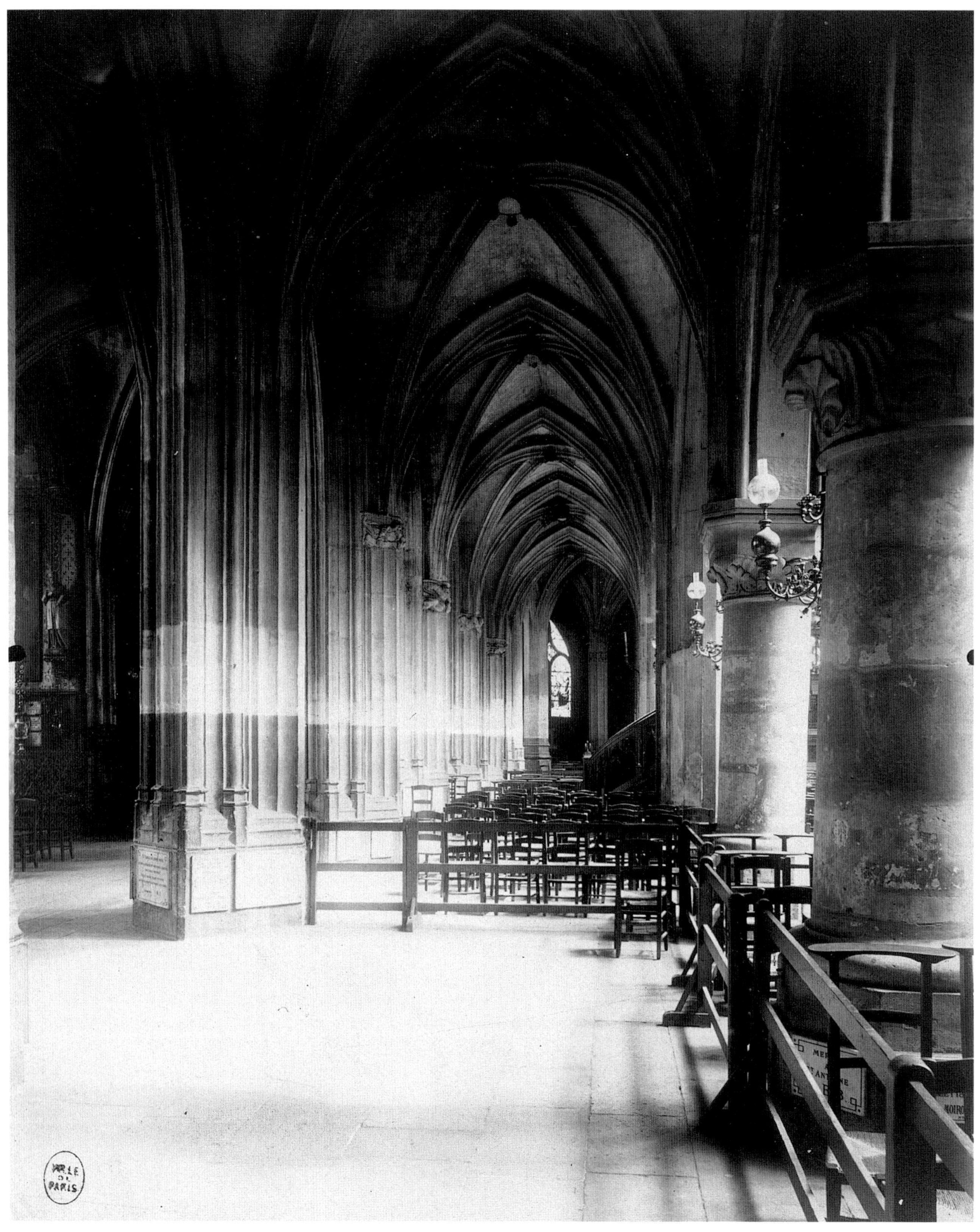

7.22 Second north nave of the Church of Saint-Séverin, toward the ambulatory, 1903

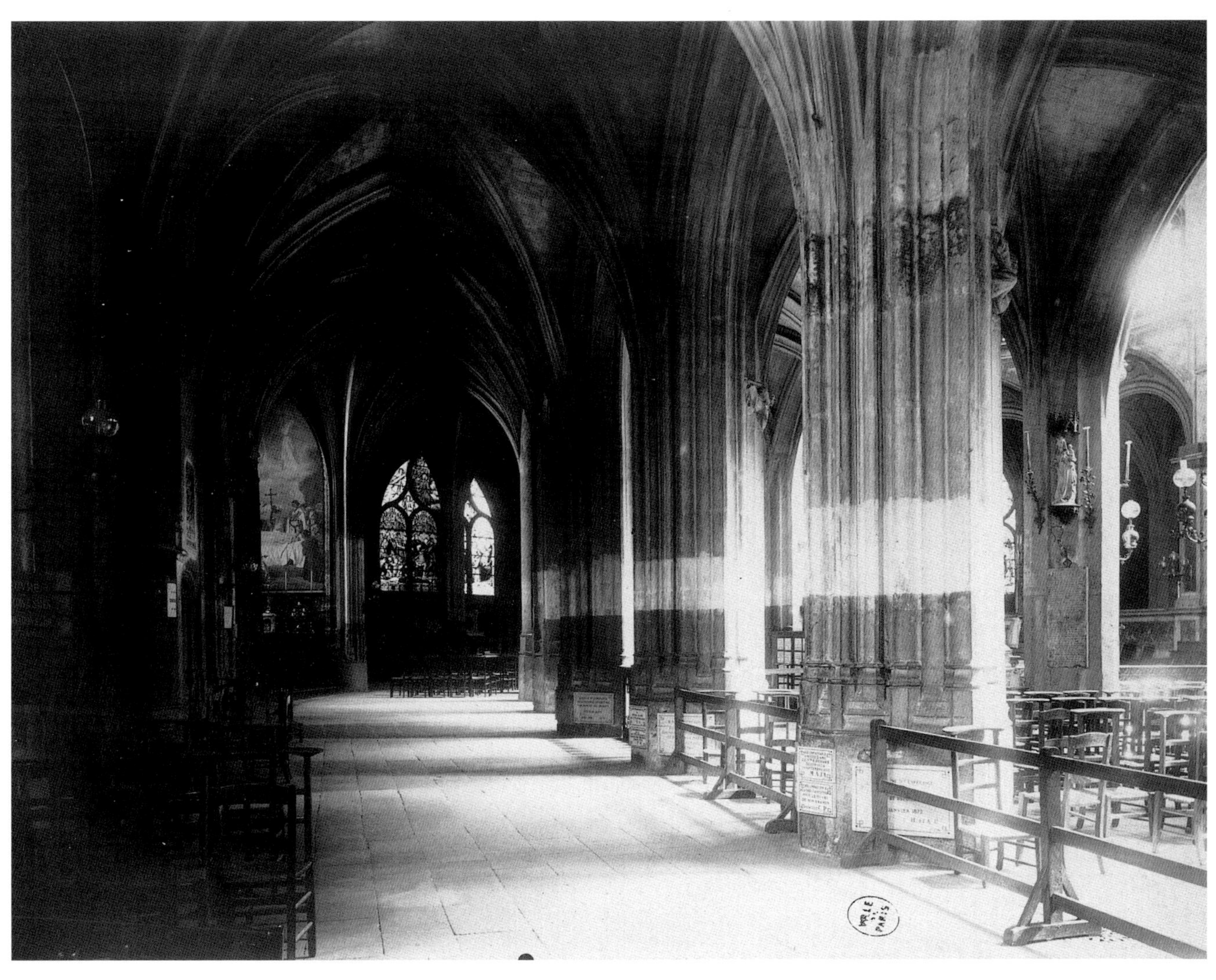

7.23 Northernmost nave of the Church of Saint-Séverin, toward the ambulatory, 1903

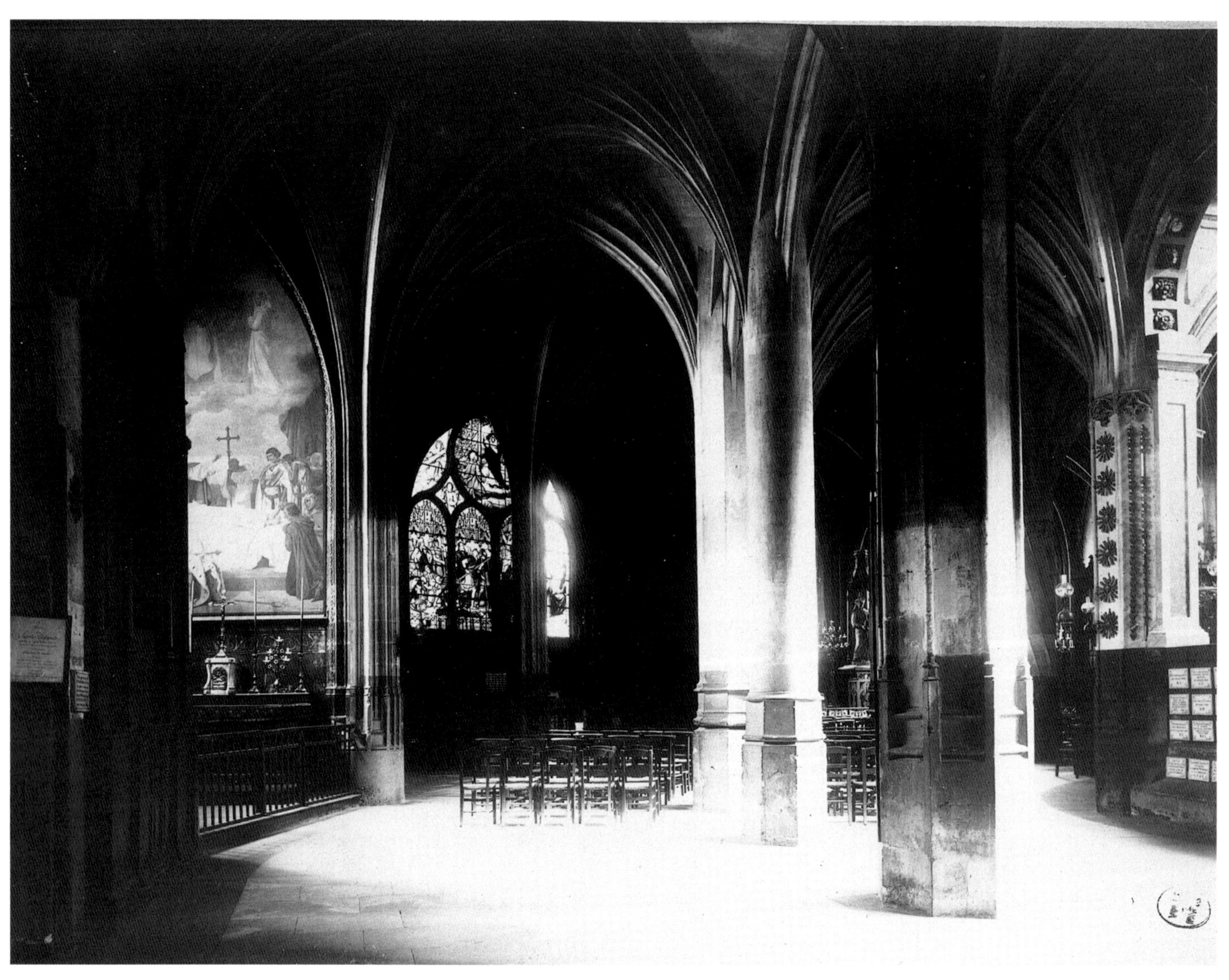

7.24 Northernmost nave of the Church of Saint-Séverin, toward the ambulatory, 1903

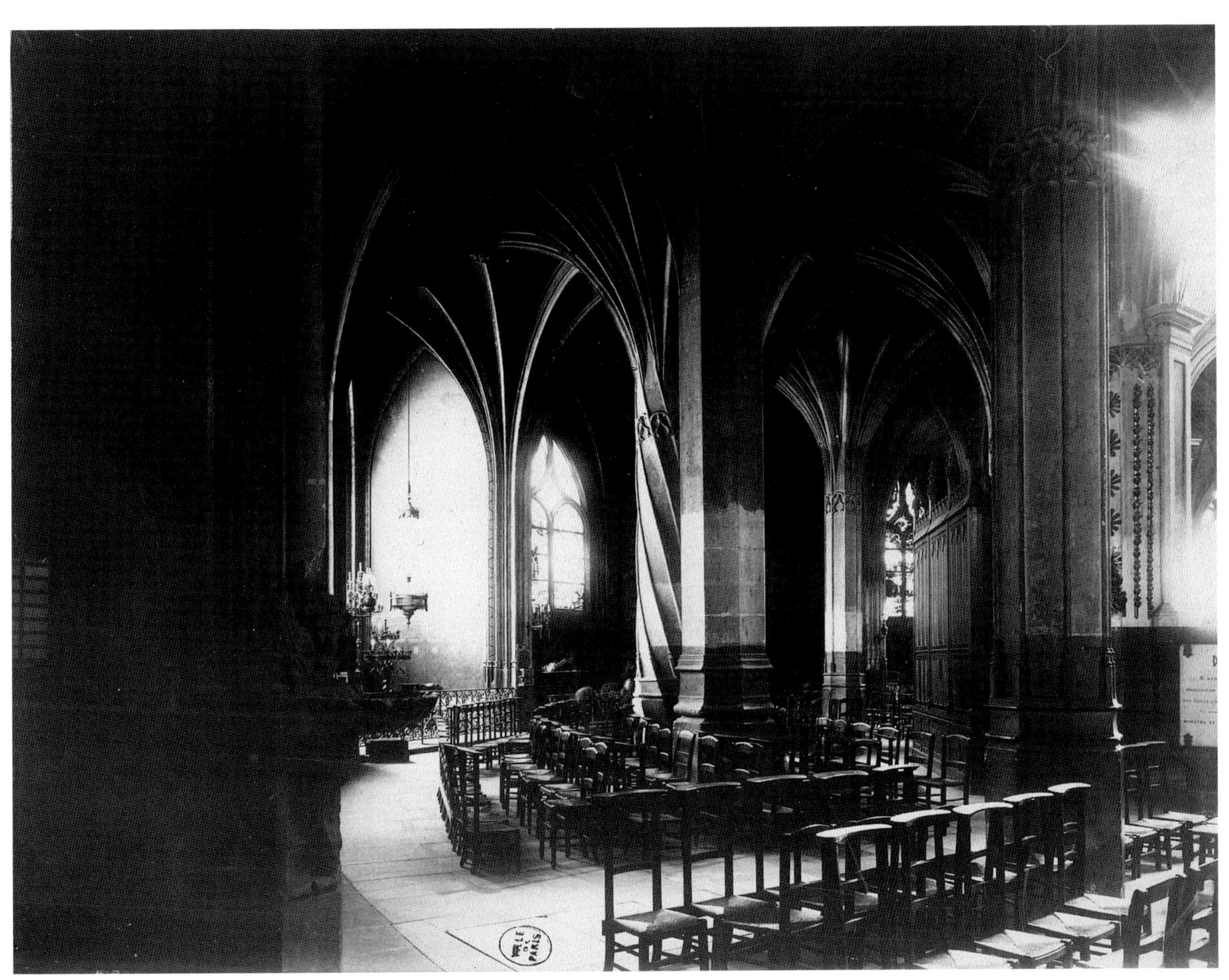

7.25 Ambulatory of the Church of Saint-Séverin, 1903

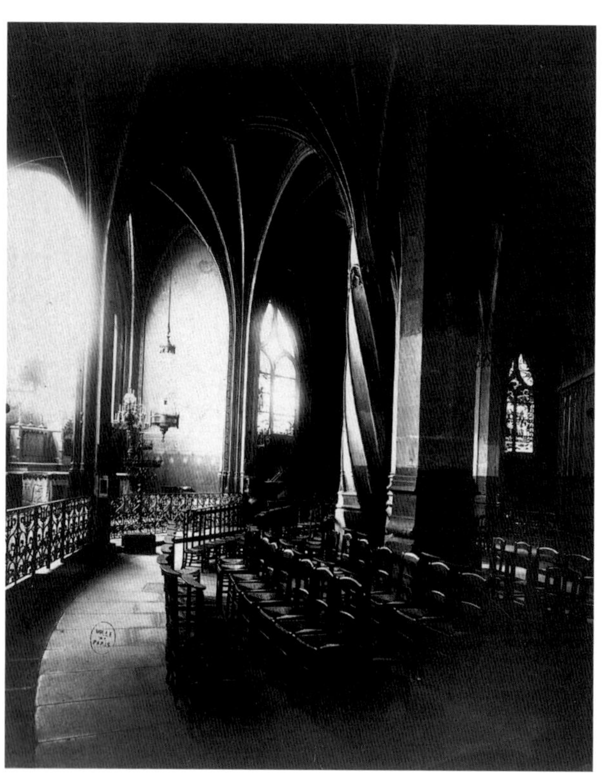

7.26 Ambulatory of the Church of Saint-Séverin, 1903

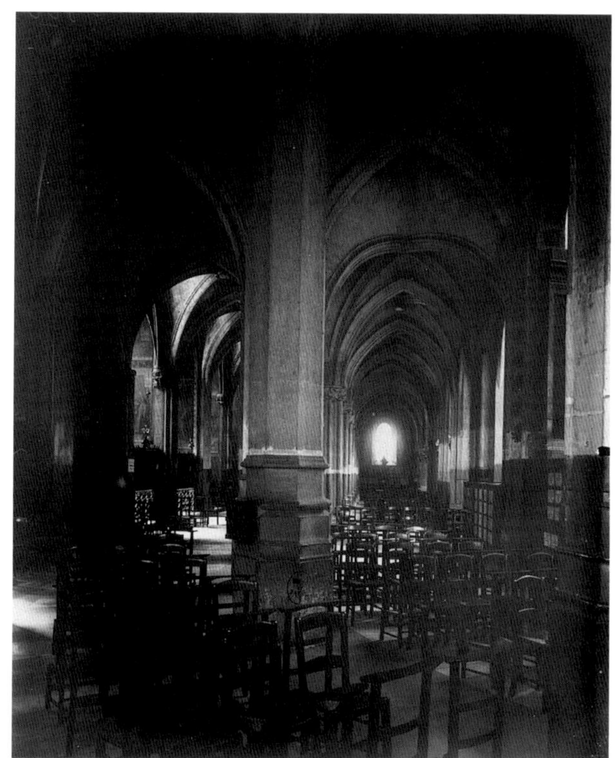

7.27 Ambulatory and south naves of the Church of Saint-Séverin, 1903

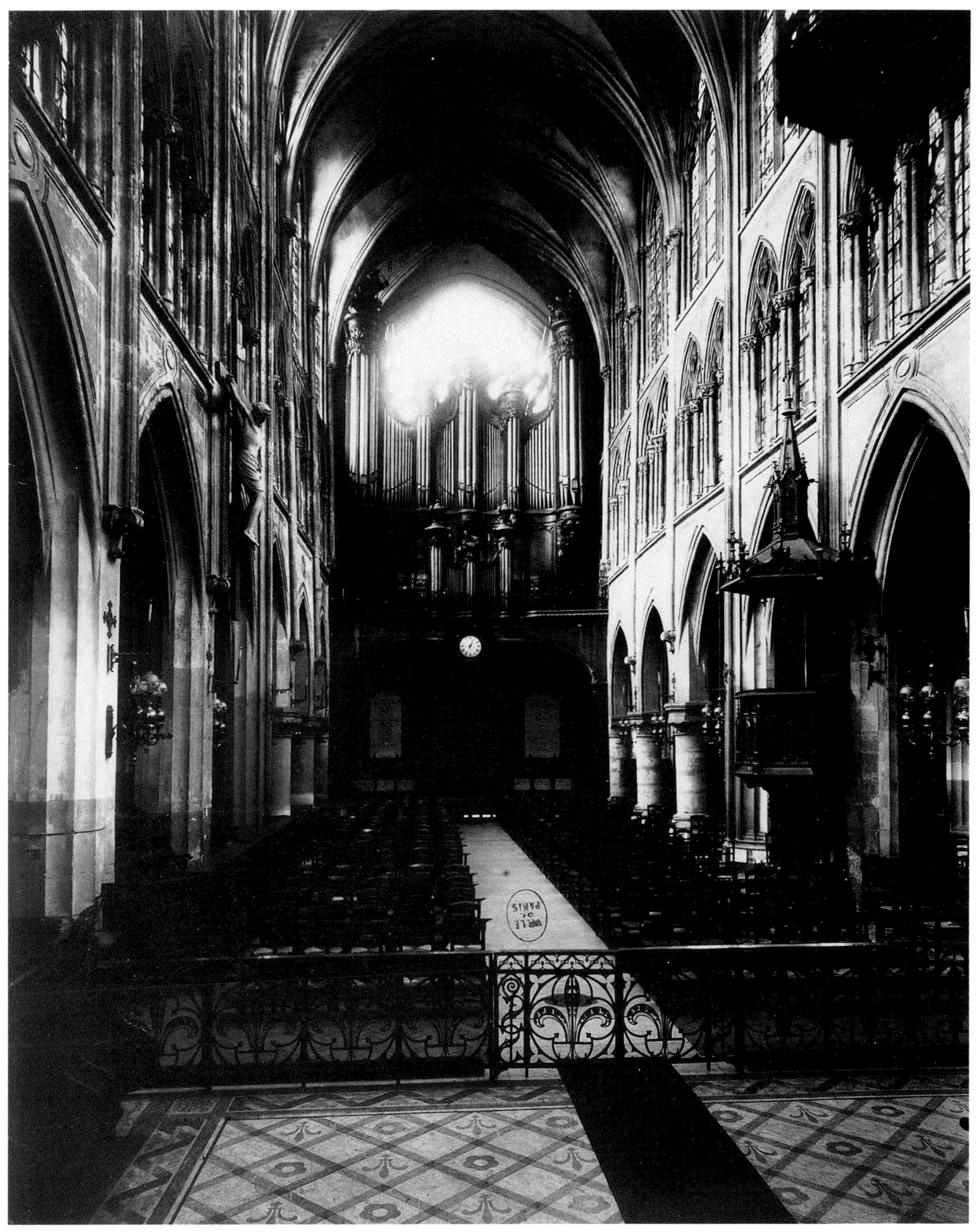

7.28 Central nave of the Church of Saint-Séverin, from the choir toward the great organ, 1903

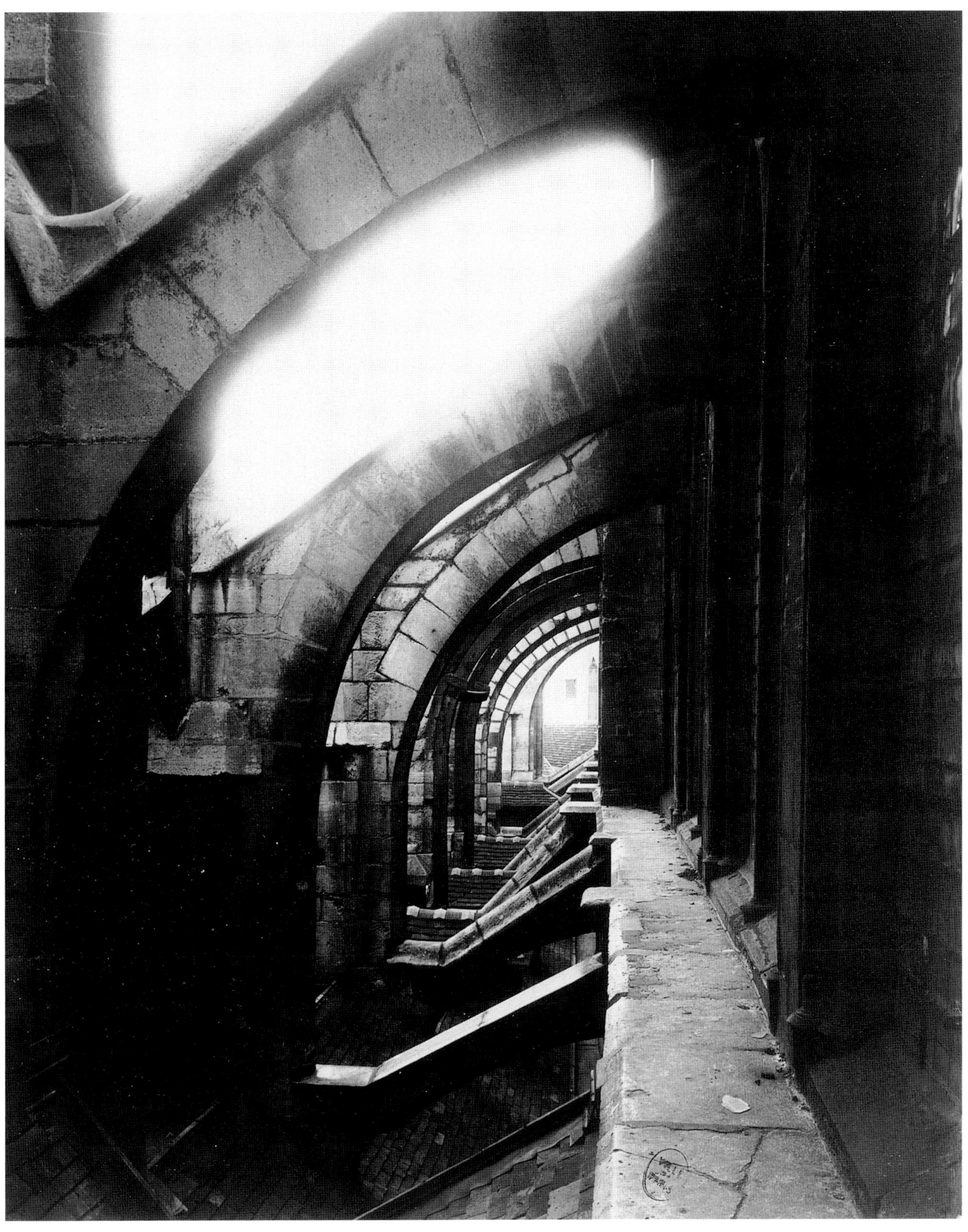

7.29 Flying buttresses, north side of the Church of Saint-Séverin, 1903

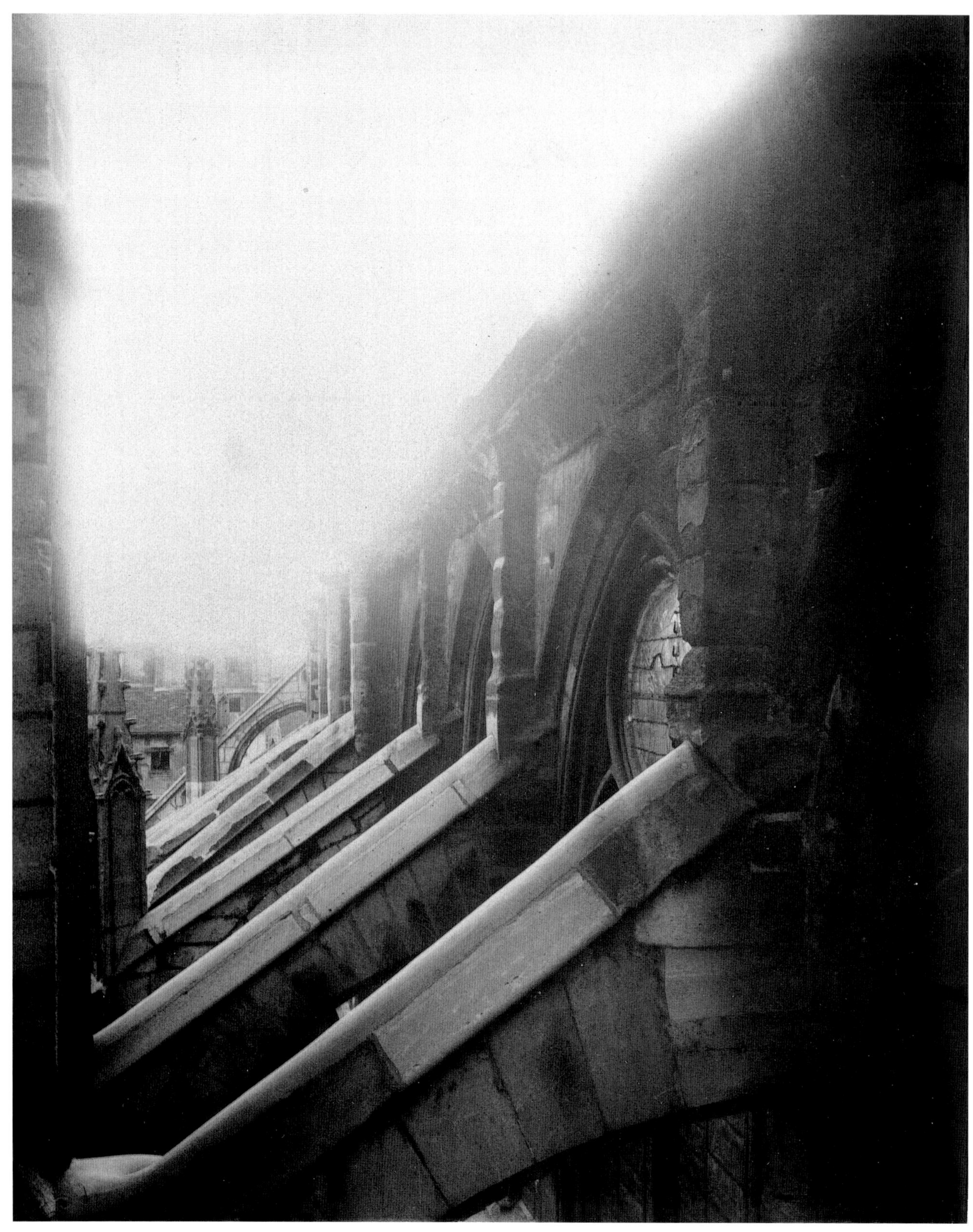

7.30 Flying buttresses (upper level), north side of the Church of Saint-Séverin, 1903

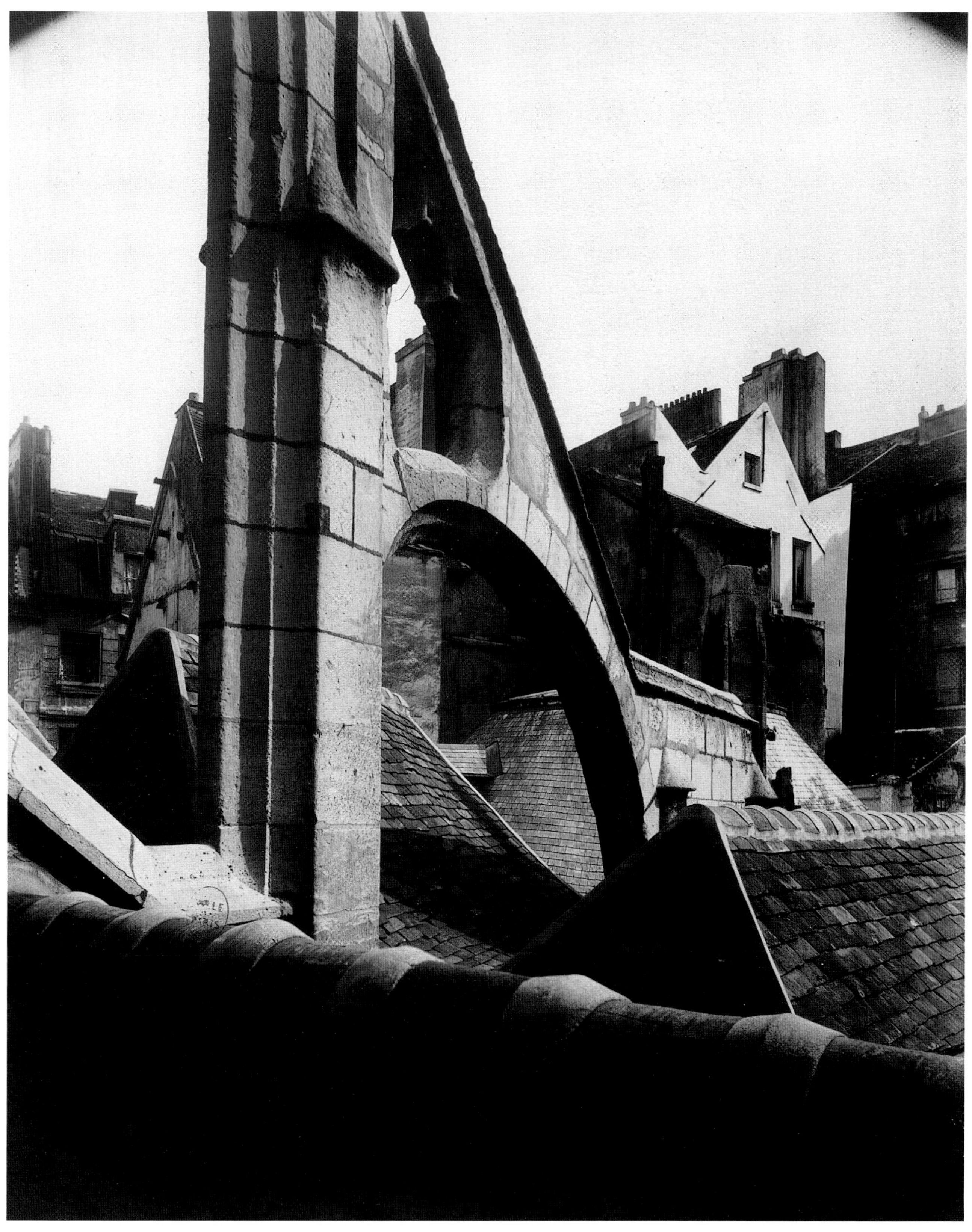

7.31 Flying buttresses above the ambulatory of the Church of Saint-Séverin, 1903

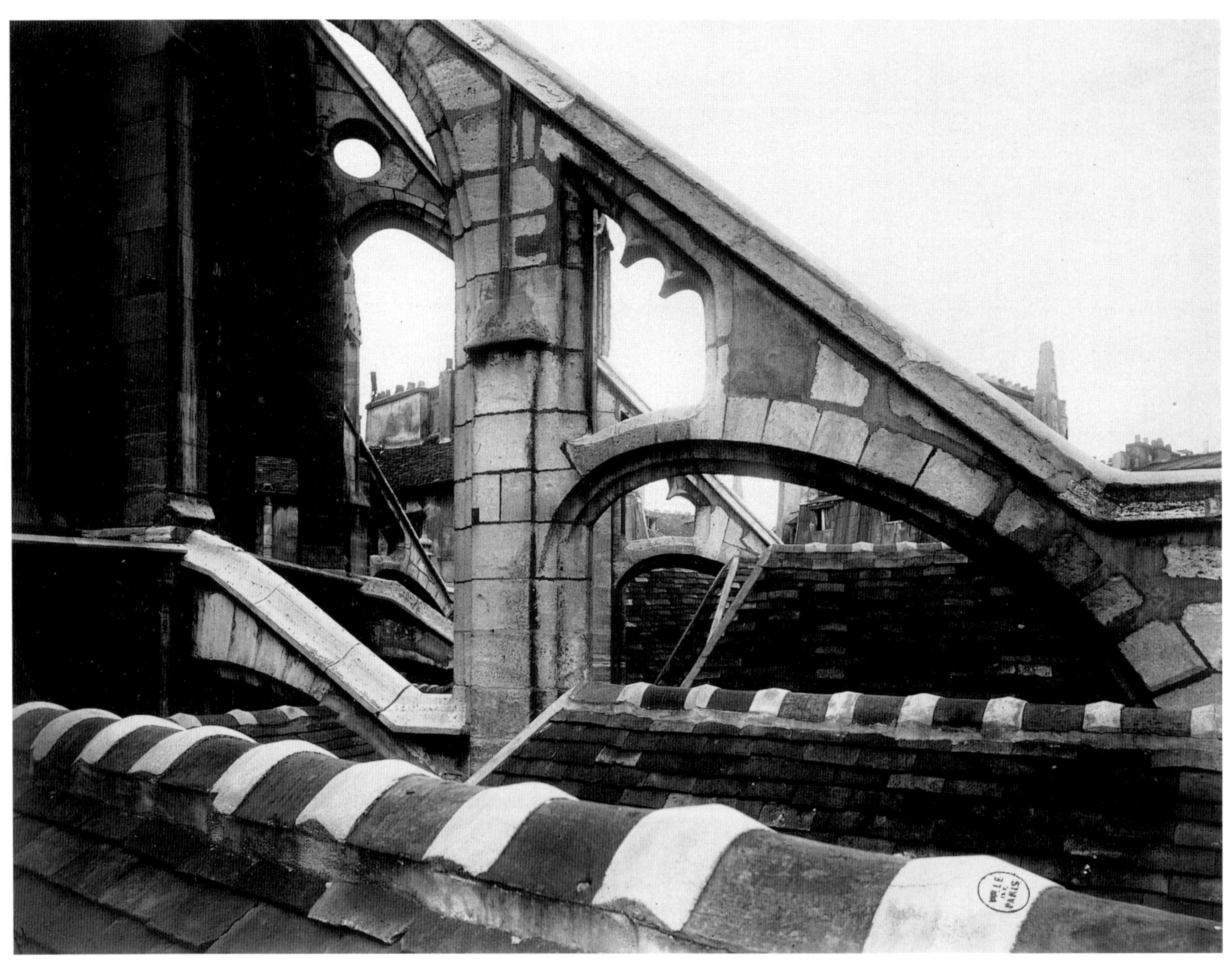

7.32 Flying buttresses above the ambulatory of the Church of Saint-Séverin, 1903

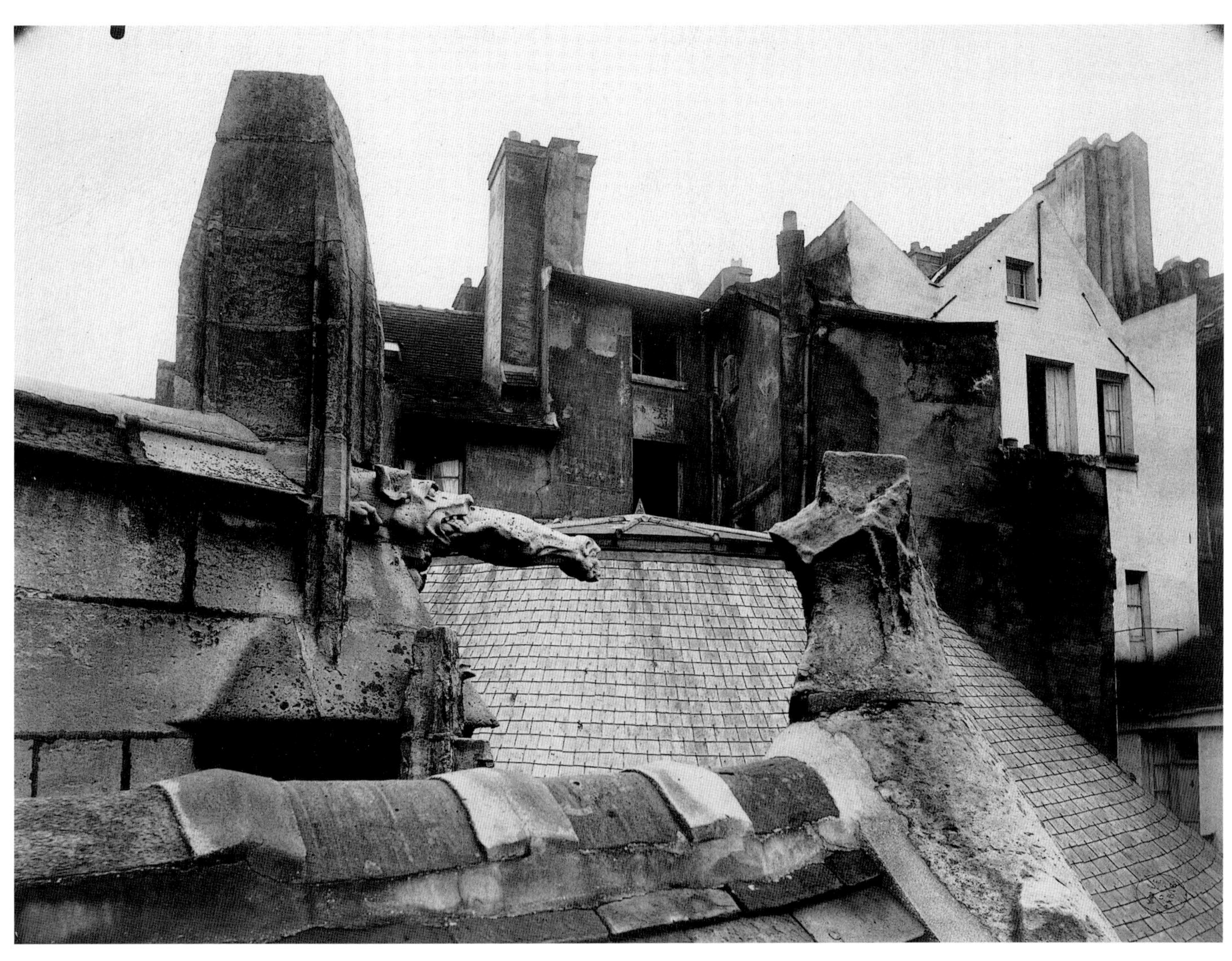

7.33 Rooftops of the radiating chapels of the Church of Saint-Séverin and buildings along the rue Saint-Jacques, 1903

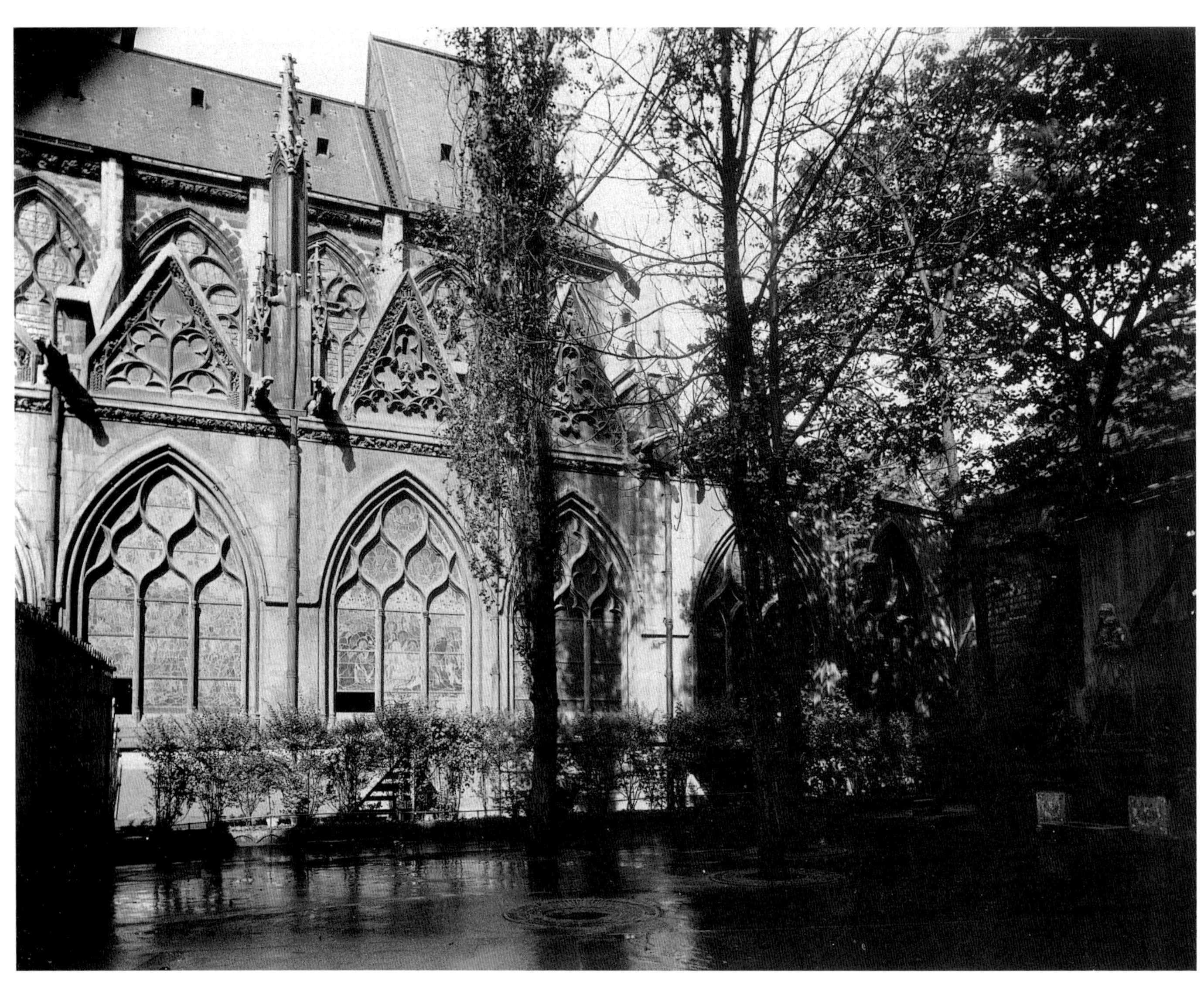

7.35 Presbytery garden and south side of the Church of Saint-Séverin, 1903

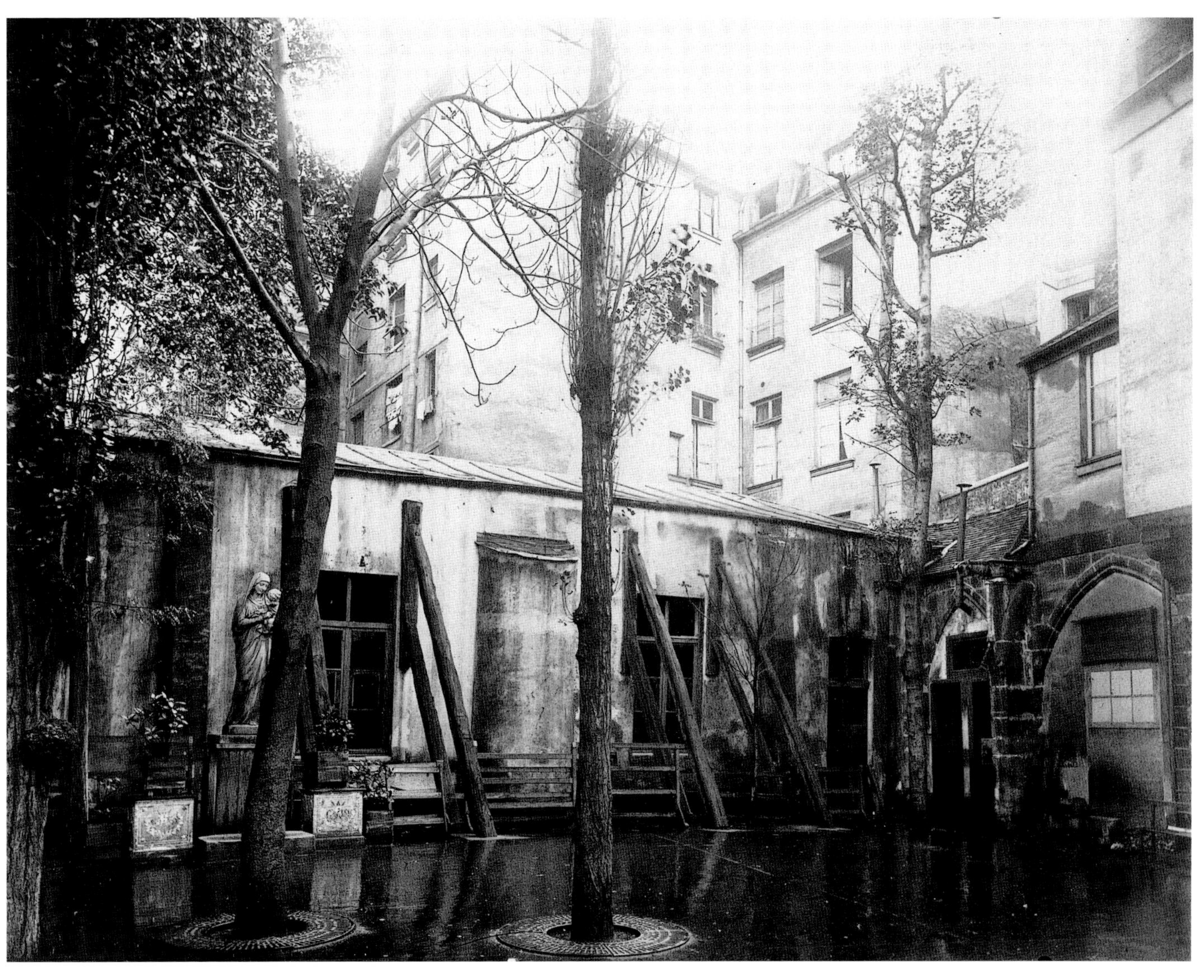

7.36 Presbytery garden and former cloister of the Church of Saint-Séverin, 1903

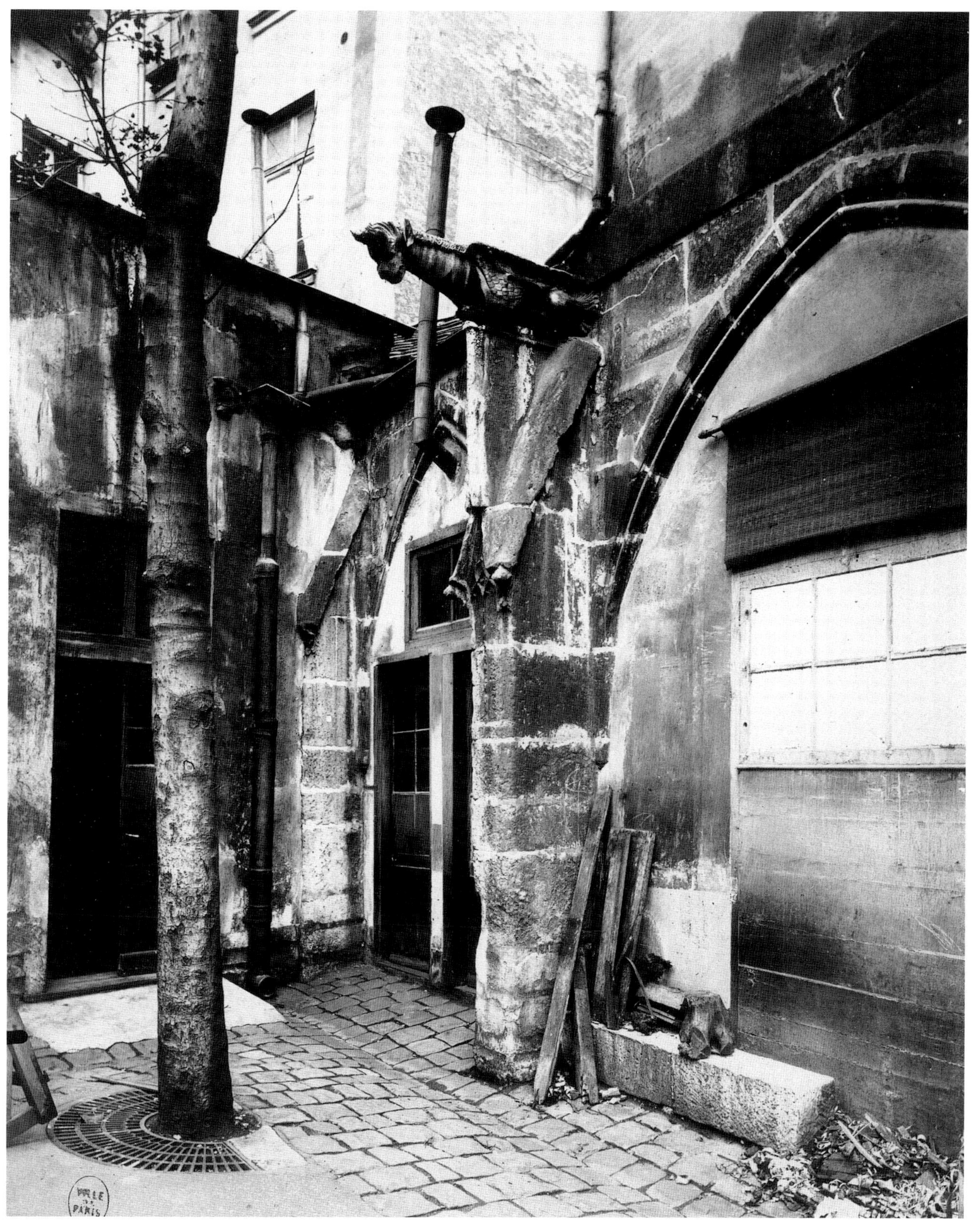

7.37 Presbytery garden, former cloister, and entrance to the former charnel house of the Church of Saint-Séverin, 1903

iii. Documentation of the Church of Saint-Séverin and the surrounding streets, 1905–1906

When Atget returned to Saint-Séverin in 1905–1906, he added previously undocumented views to his coverage, notably those of the exterior of the Saint-Martin door (cat. 7.43–7.45), the iron balustrade adjacent to the organ (cat. 7.48), and the presbytery courtyard (cat. 7.46 and 7.47). In a departure from his normal practice and possibly because he was dissatisfied with the poor quality of his 1903 negative, Atget rephotographed the view along the rue de Saint-Séverin (7.43; compare with cat. 7.41). In this later view, the softly radiant afternoon light allowed Atget to describe the north side of the church with its succession of overhanging gargoyles. However, he retained both negatives and included them in the 1920 government purchase.

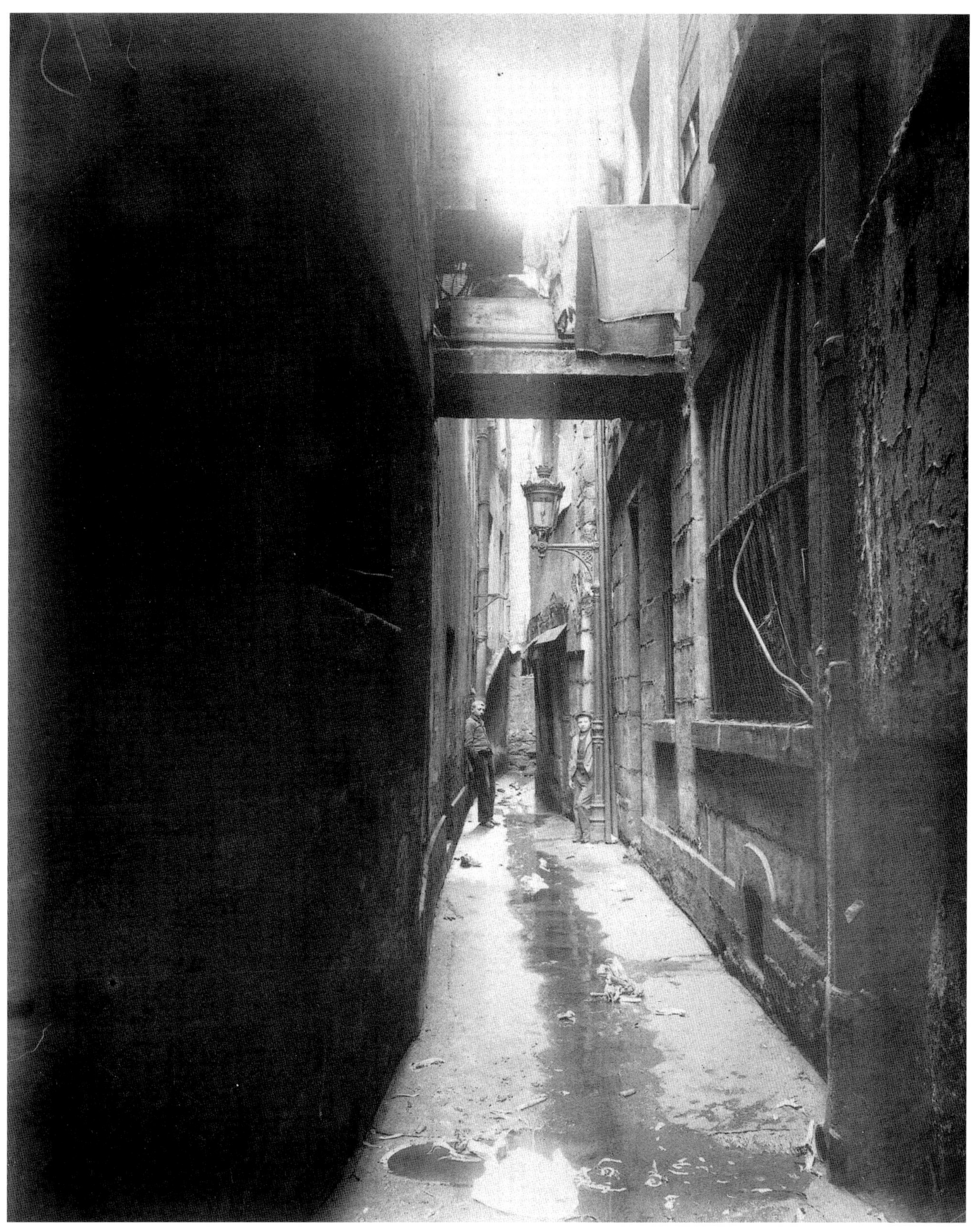

7.42 Impasse Salembrière, 1905–1906

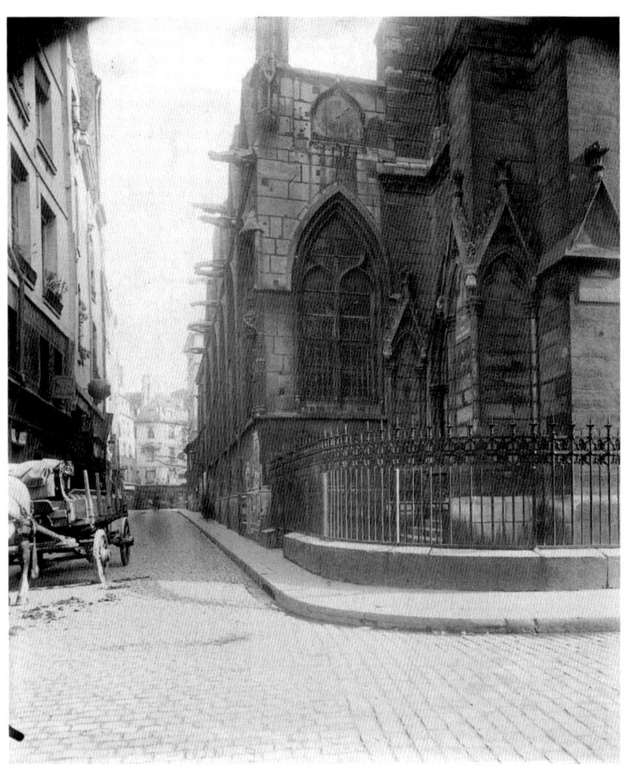

7.43 Rue Saint-Séverin at the intersection with the rue des Prêtres-Saint-Séverin, toward the rue Saint-Jacques, 1905–1906

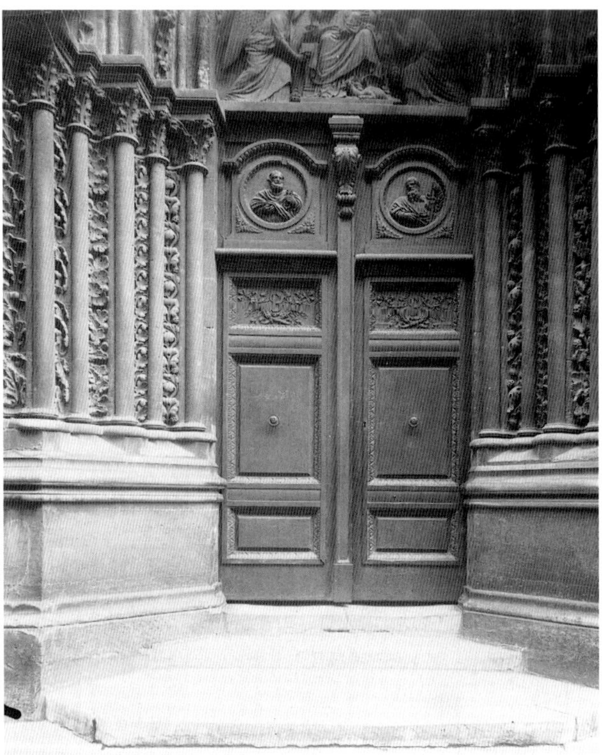

7.44 Portal of Saint-Martin of the Church of Saint-Séverin, at the corner of the rue des Prêtres-Saint-Séverin and the rue Saint-Séverin, 1905–1906

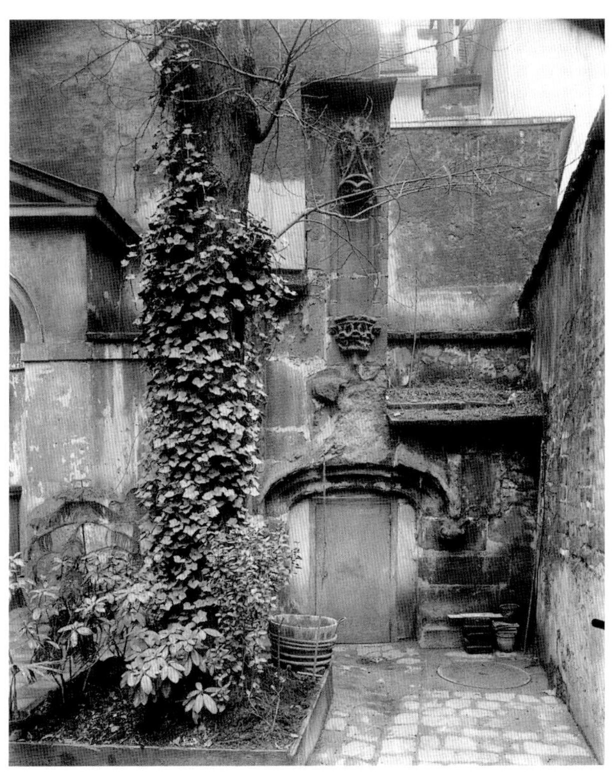

7.46 Presbytery courtyard of the Church of Saint-Séverin, 1905–1906

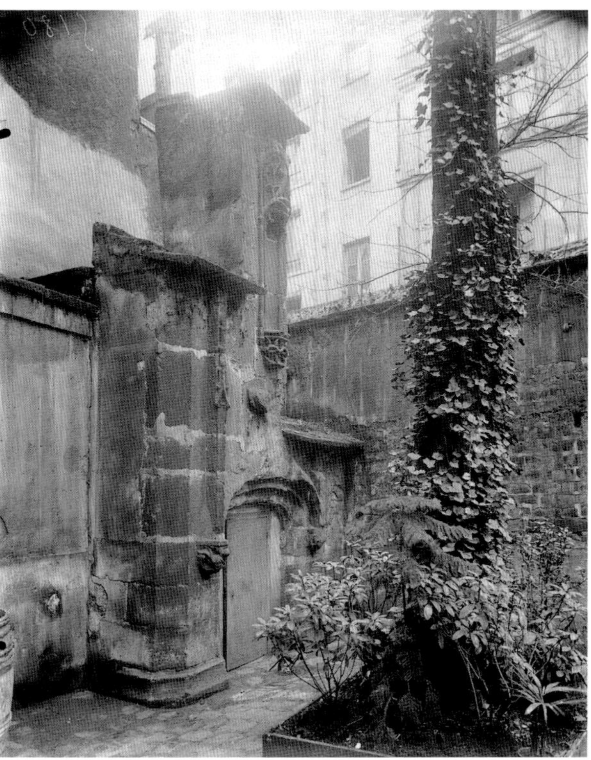

7.47 Presbytery courtyard of the Church of Saint-Séverin, 1905–1906

iv. Widening of the rue Saint-Jacques, February 1908

On an overcast day in February 1908, Atget returned to the church to record the demolition of buildings and the widening of the rue de Petit-Pont and the rue Saint-Jacques, a process that, including the widening of the rue de la Parcheminerie and the rue des Prêtres-Saint-Séverin in 1913, he would continue to document over the next six years until 1914 (see sections v and vi). From the southeast corner of the rue Galande, Atget made two views, one looking south along the rue Saint-Jacques (cat. 7.52), and the second looking northward along the rue du Petit-Pont (cat. 7.53). With this first photograph, he replicated his 1902 view (cat. 7.16). On the same day, he also made two closely related views from the rue de la Parcheminerie, one looking north toward the church (cat. 7.50) and the second along the same stretch of the rue Saint-Jacques (cat. 7.51) that he also recorded in his view from the rue Galande (cat. 7.52).

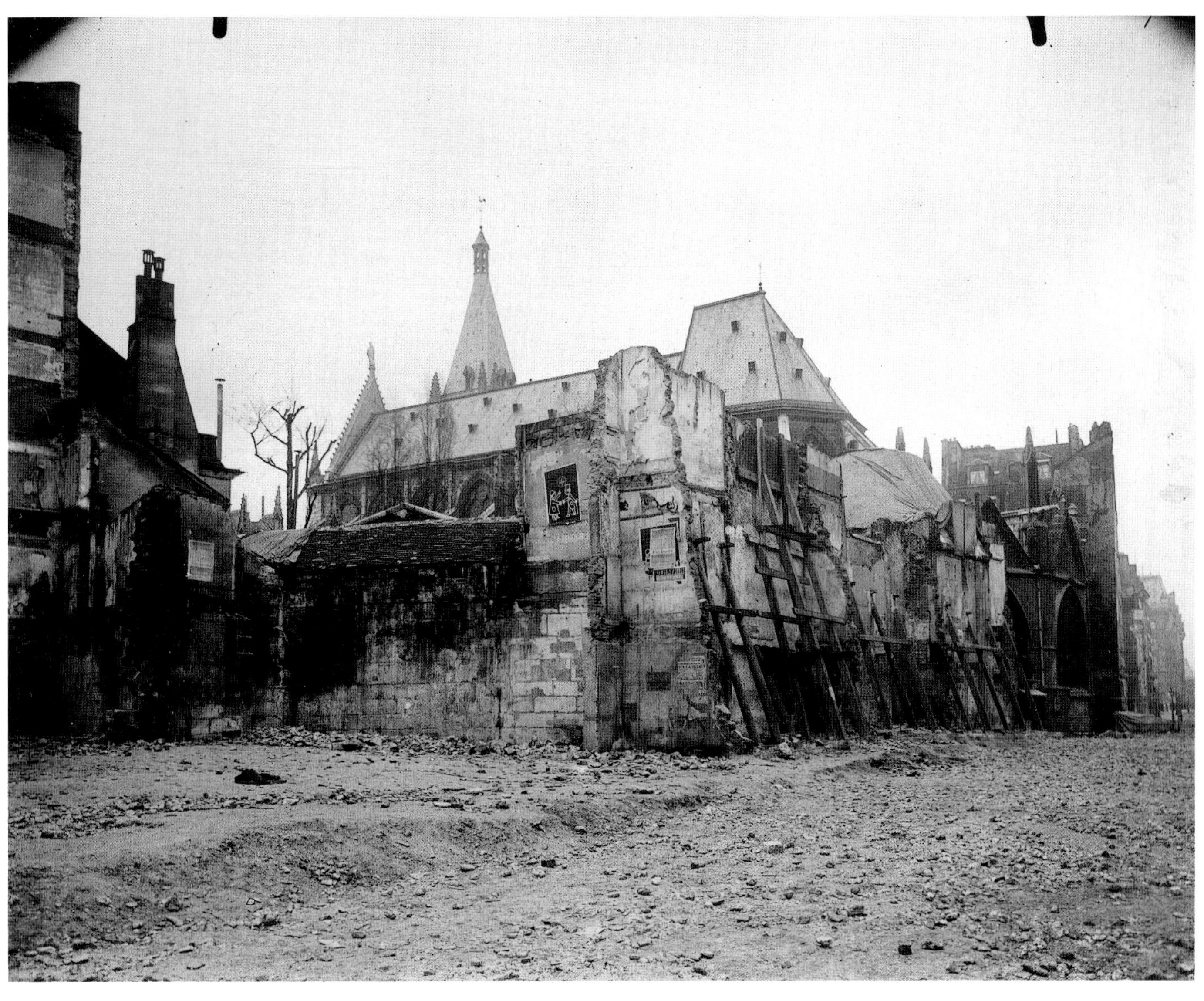

7.51 Rue Saint-Jacques after the demolition of the buildings bordering the cloister of the church, from the corner of the rue de la Parcheminerie, February 1908

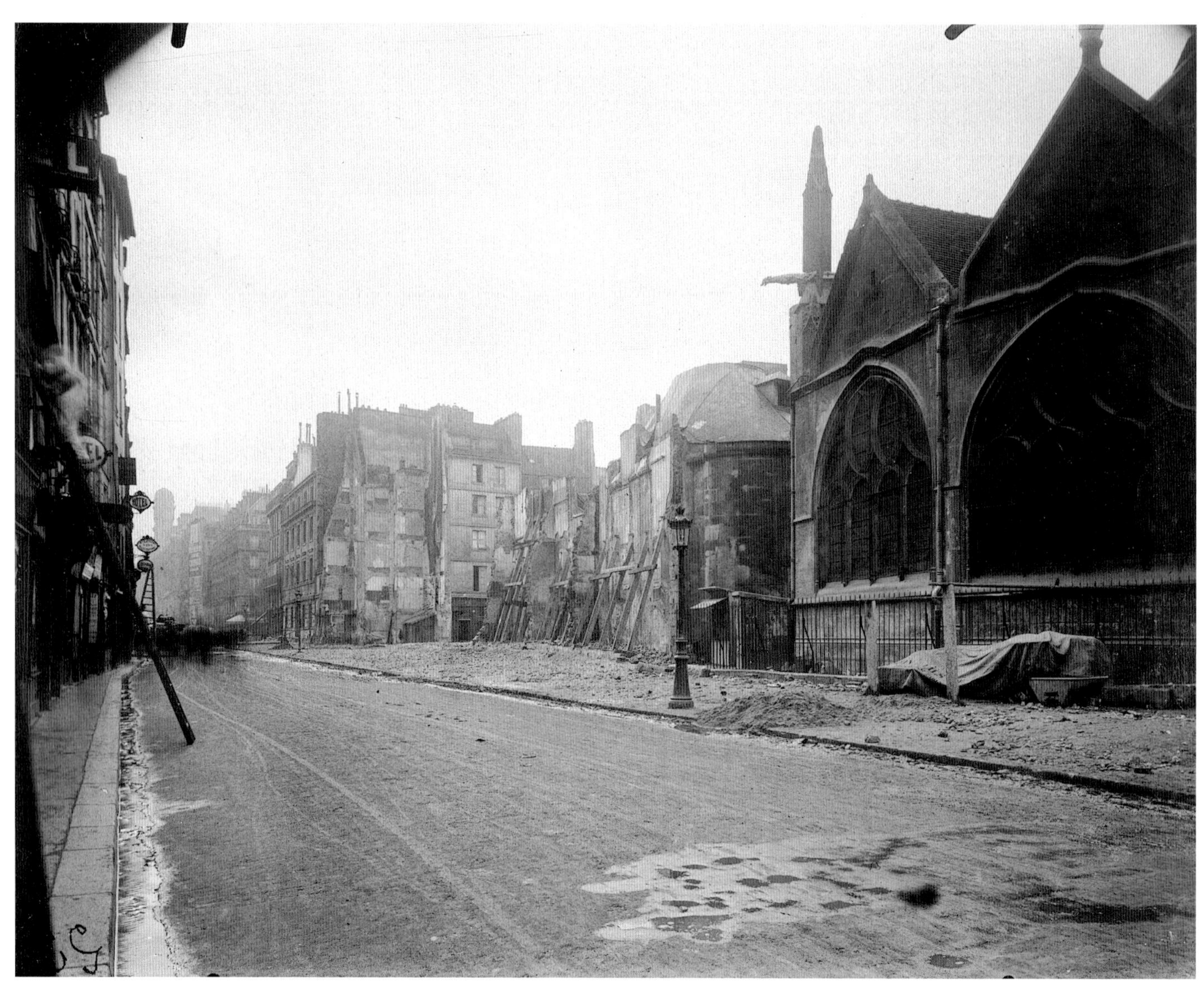

7.52 Rue Saint-Jacques after the demolition of the buildings bordering the cloister of the church, from the rue Galande, February 1908

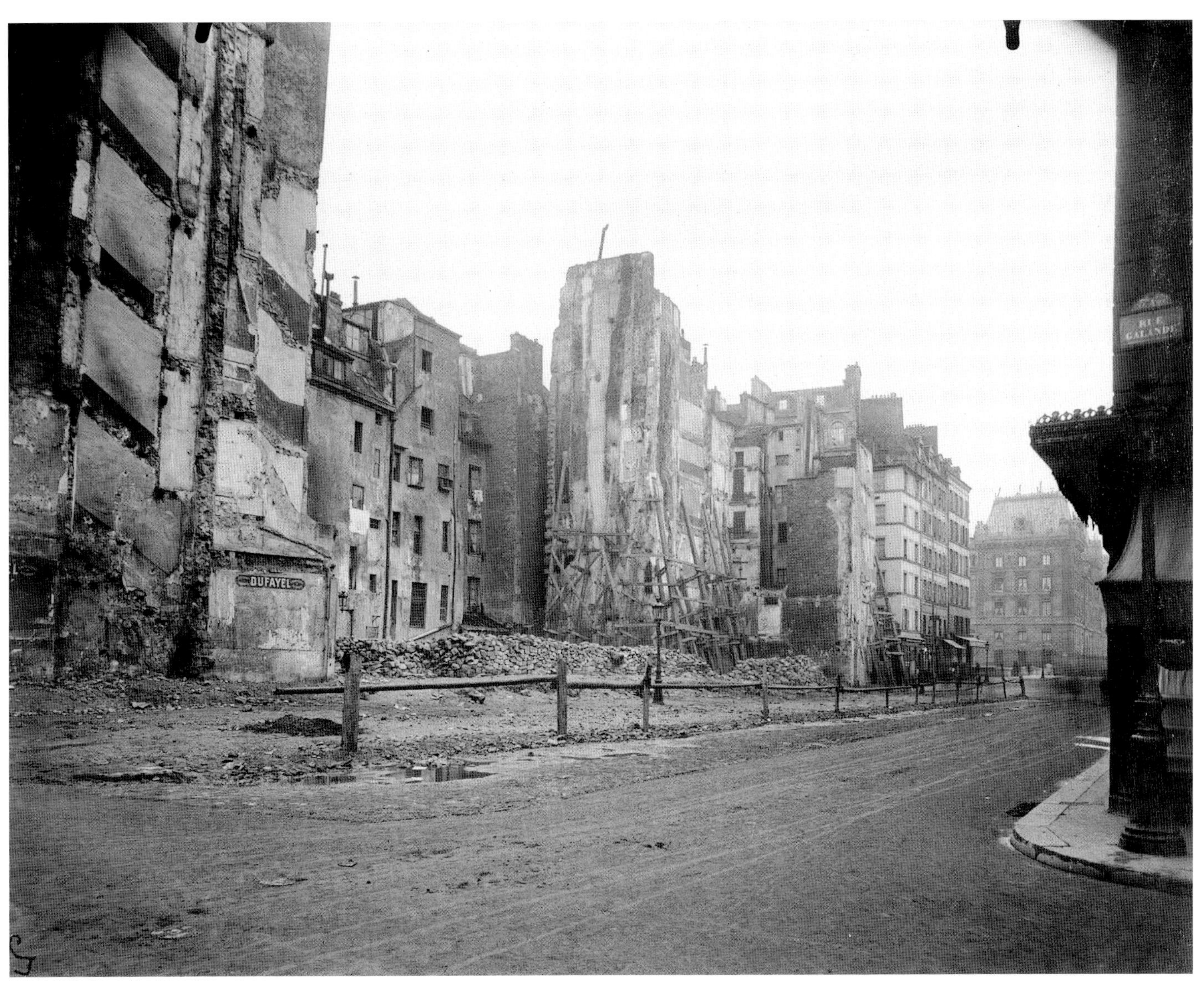

7.53 Rue du Petit-Pont after the partial demolition of buildings, from the rue Galande, February 1908

v. Documentation of rue des Prêtres-Saint-Séverin, 1912

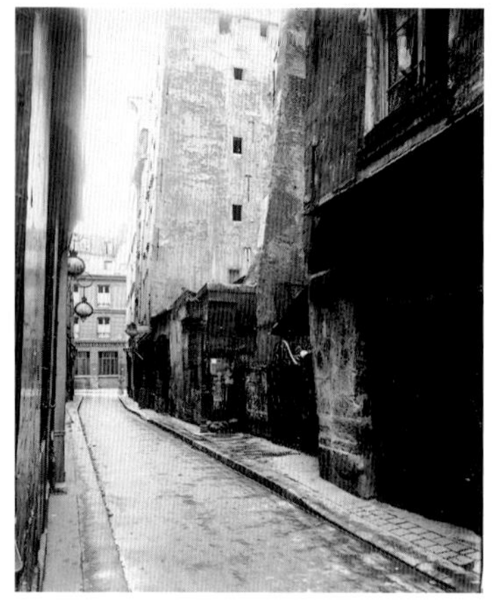

7.54 Rue de la Parcheminerie, toward the rue de la Harpe, 1912

With the knowledge that the buildings along the rue des Prêtres-Saint-Séverin, between the rue de la Parcheminerie and the church, were to be demolished in order to widen and straighten the street, Atget devoted eleven photographs from his series *Topographie du vieux Paris* to recording its appearance in 1912. Since this urban change would destroy the intimate, picturesque character of this section of the street, Atget thoroughly, almost obsessively, documented it. He made four views at the intersection formed by the rue Boutebrie, the rue de la Parcheminerie, and the rue des Prêtres-Saint-Séverin, recording the perspective along each of these streets (cat. 7.54, 7.56, 7.57, and 7.64). In an effort to preserve the pedestrian's experience of traversing the rue des Prêtres-Saint-Séverin, Atget constructed two sequences of linked views. One consists of five views which, beginning on the rue Boutebrie, pass through the intersection and continue along the rue des Prêtres-Saint-Séverin toward the church (cat. 7.56, 7.58–7.61), while the second, a sequence of only three views, covers a portion of the same section of the street but in the opposite direction, looking toward the rue Boutebrie (cat. 7.62–7.64). In each of these sequences, Atget included pairs of overlapping photographs: each pair surveyed the same stretch of the rue des Prêtres-Saint-Séverin, but from opposite sides of the road (cat. 7.60 and 7.61; 7.62 and 7.63).

Atget also made a single view from the corner of the rue de la Parcheminerie looking north along the rue Saint-Jacques from a position very close to the one that he had selected in 1908 (cat. 7.65; compare with 7.51). This last photograph documents the temporary shops that had sprung up in the intervening four years and would be swept away in 1913.

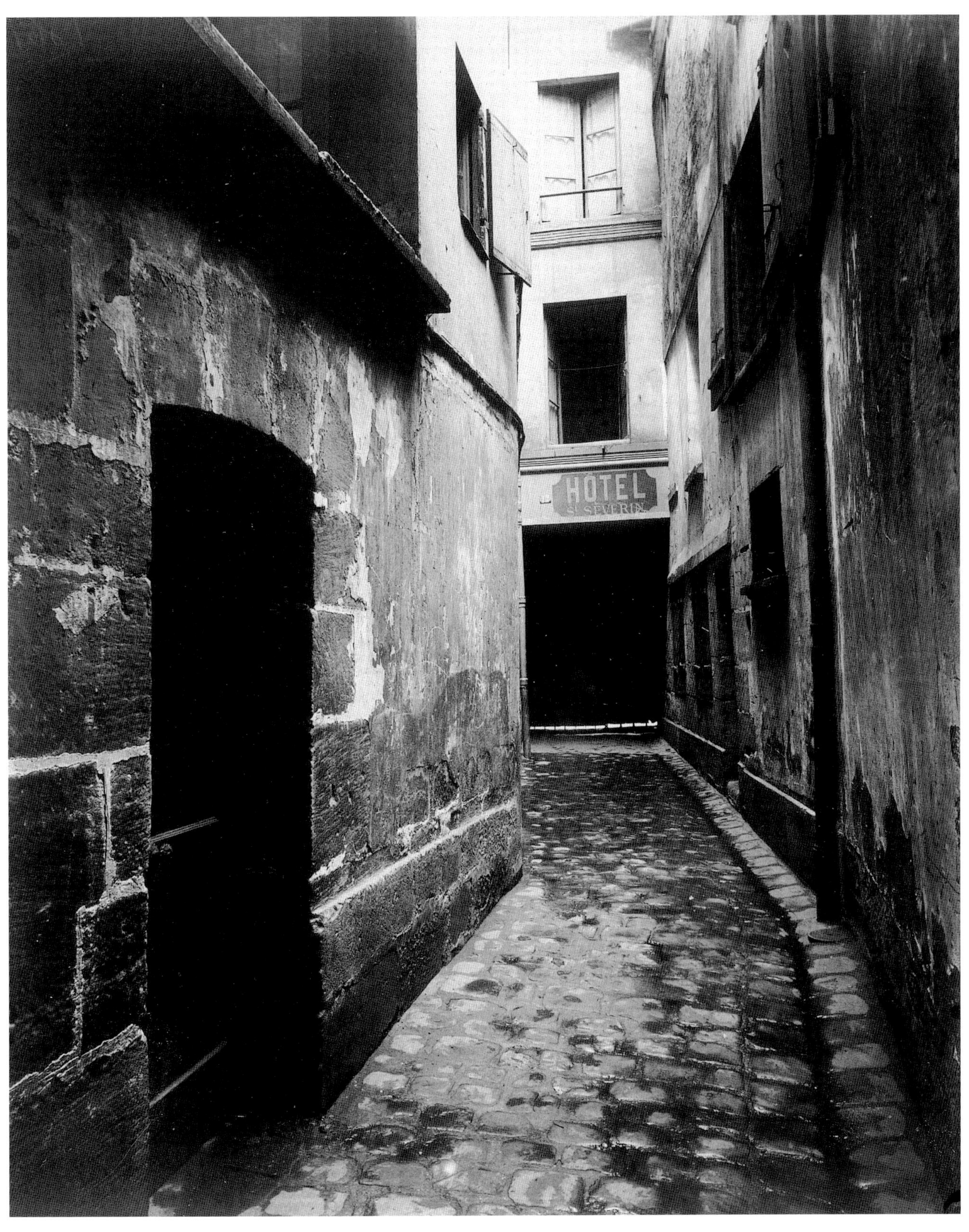

7.55 Former entrance to the presbytery of the Church of Saint-Séverin, 12 rue de la Parcheminerie, 1912

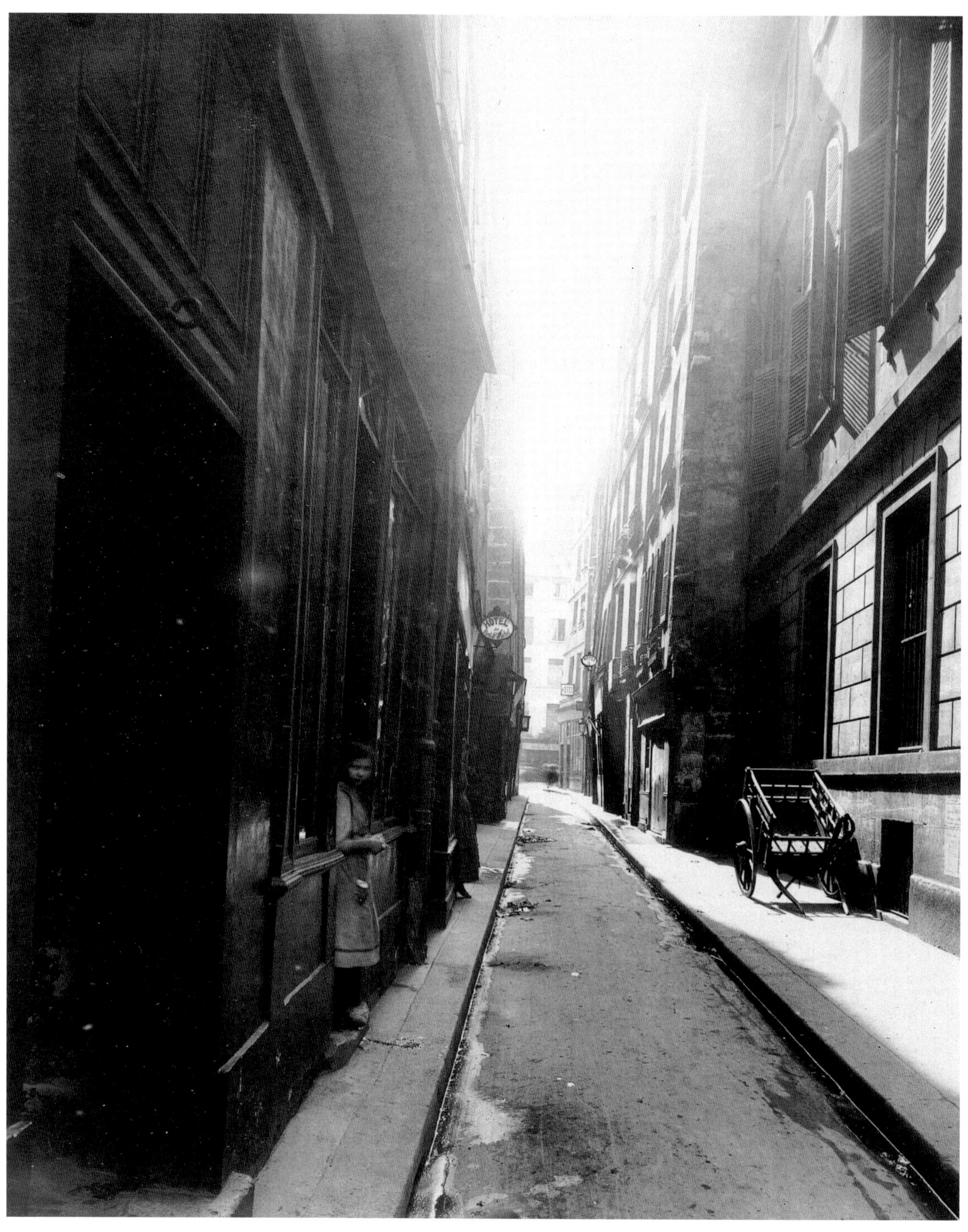

7.57 Rue de la Parcheminerie, toward the rue Saint-Jacques, 1912

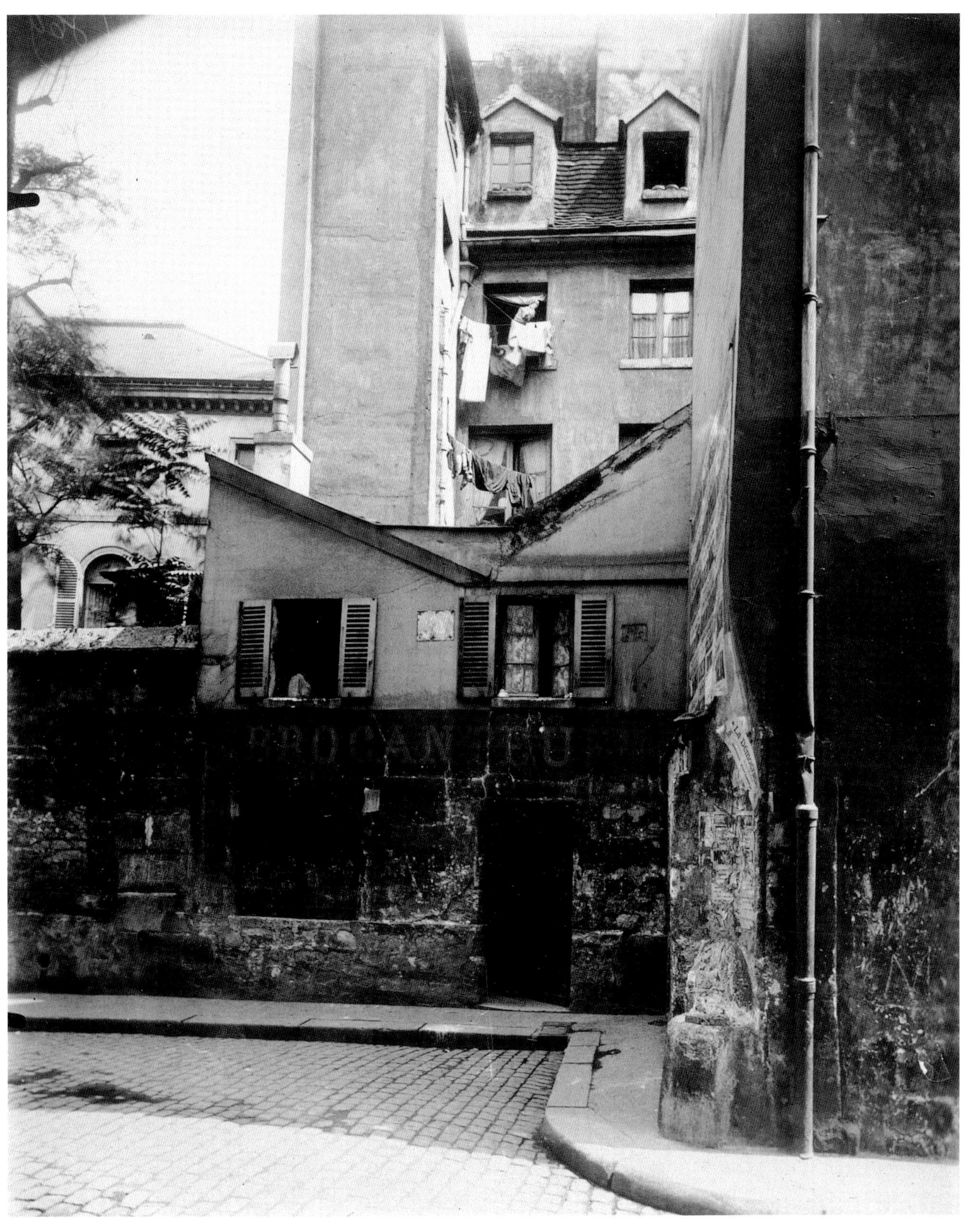

7.59 Rue des Prêtres-Saint-Séverin, old house at No. 3 and presbytery of the Church of Saint-Séverin, 1912

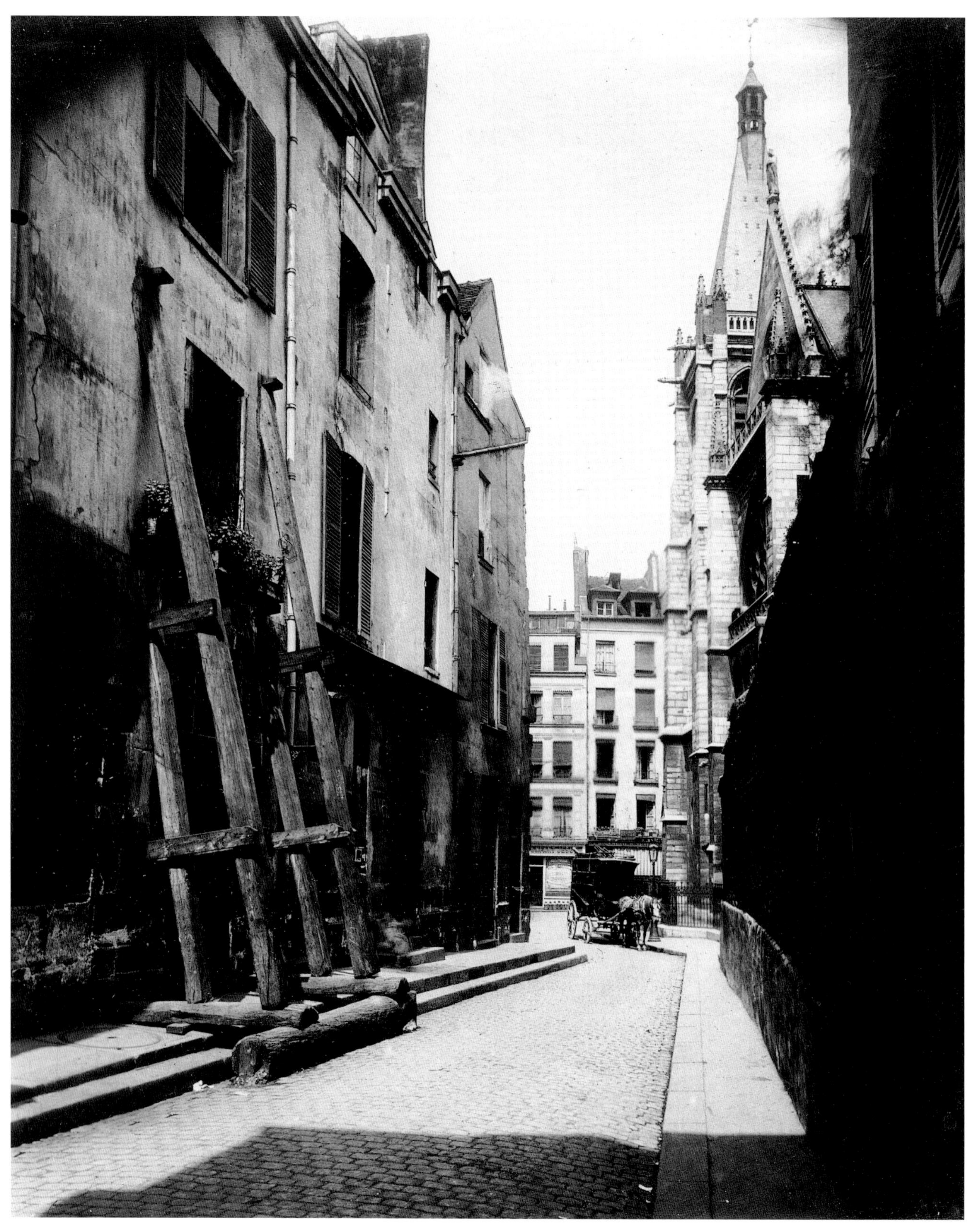

7.60 Rue des Prêtres-Saint-Séverin, toward the church, 1912

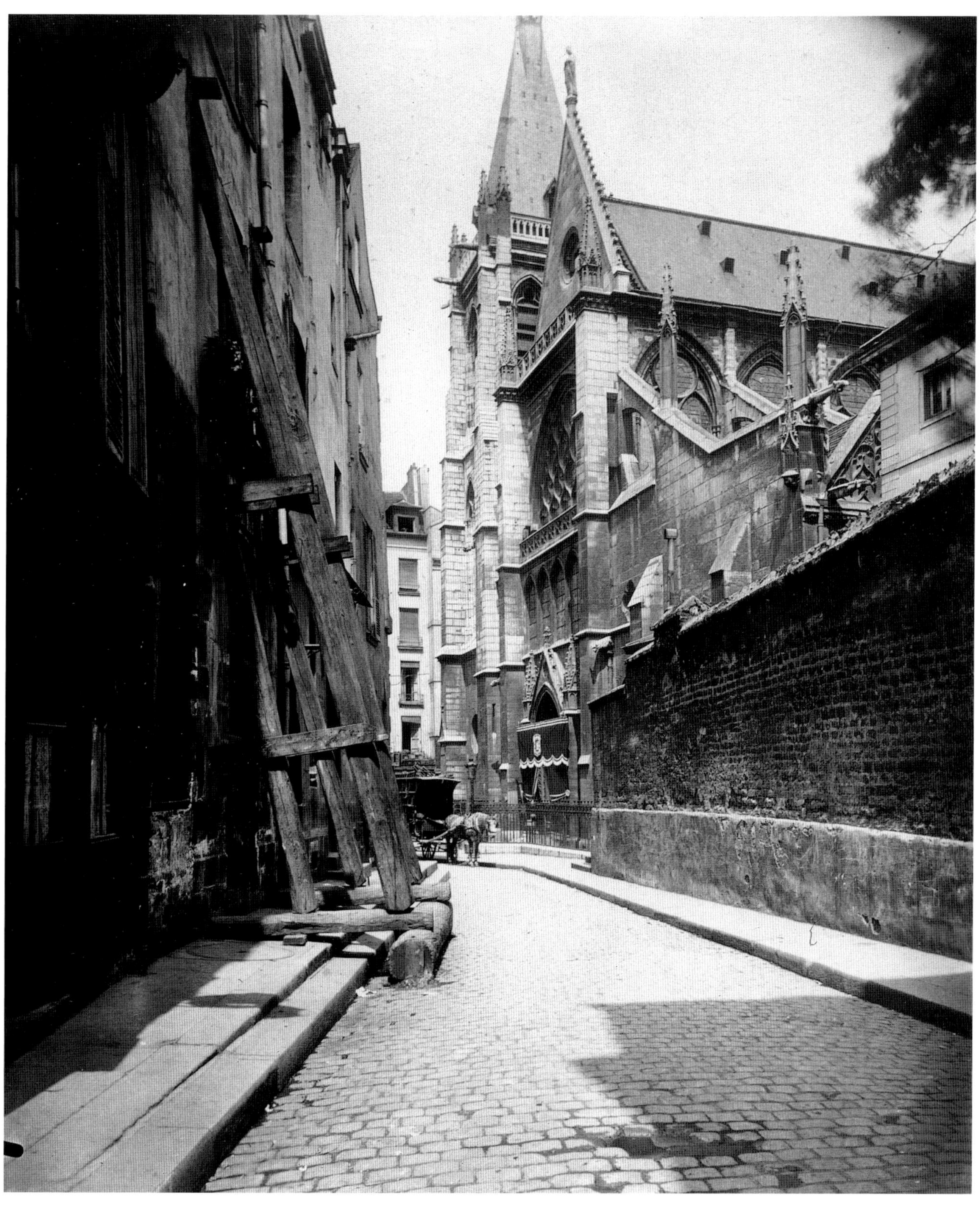

7.61 Rue des Prêtres-Saint-Séverin, toward the church, 1912

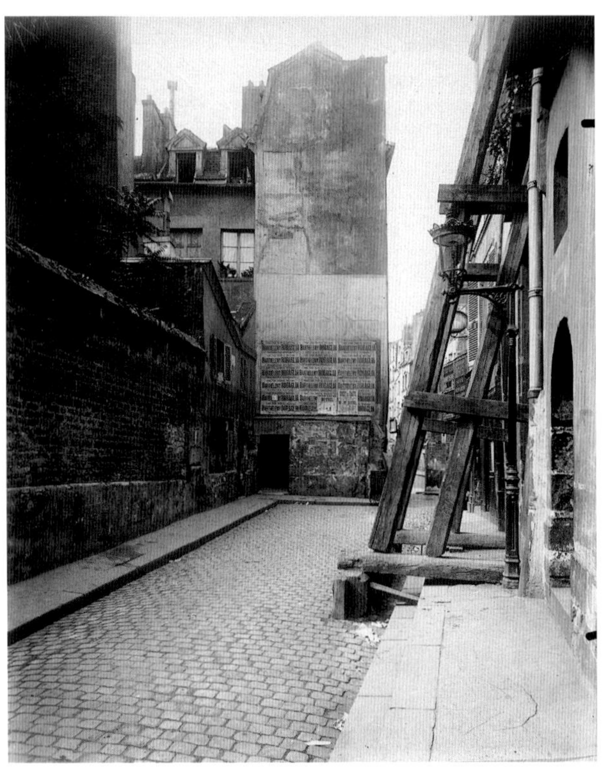

7.62 Rue des Prêtres-Saint-Séverin, toward the rue Boutebrie and the wall of the presbytery, 1912

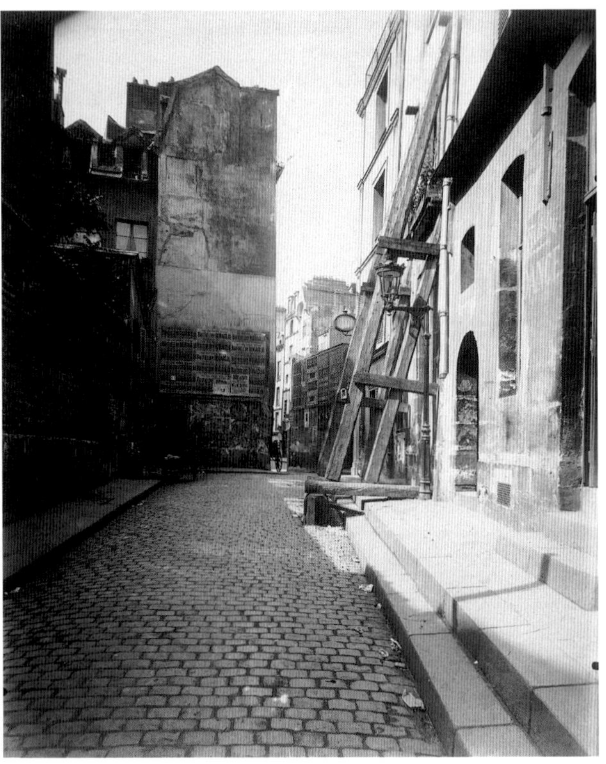

7.63 Rue des Prêtres-Saint-Séverin, toward the rue Boutebrie, 1912

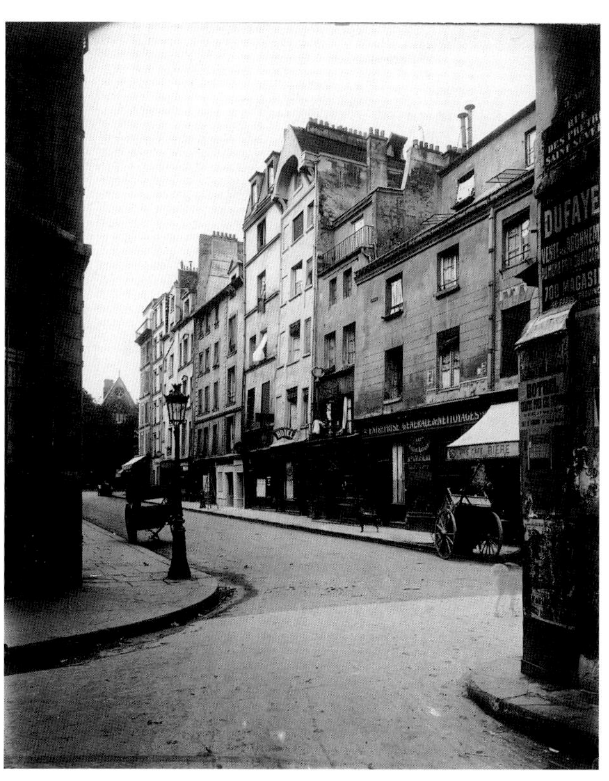

7.64 Rue Boutebrie, from the intersection of the rue de la Parcheminerie and the rue des Prêtres-Saint-Séverin, toward the Musée de Cluny, 1912

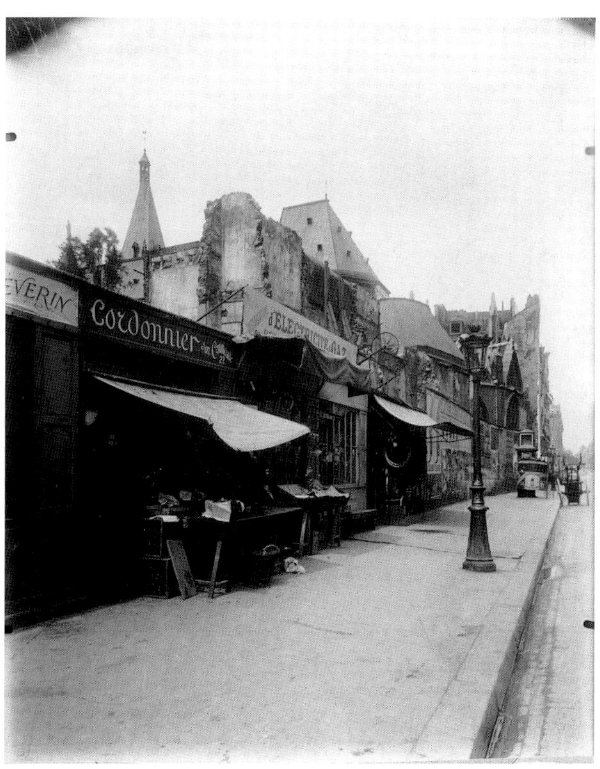

7.65 Temporary shops along the rue Saint-Jacques, 1912

vi. Documentation of the enlargement of the rue des Prêtres-Saint-Séverin and the rue de la Parcheminerie, March 1913–August 1914

Once the demolition of the buildings along the north side of rue de la Parcheminerie had begun in 1913, Atget interrupted his work on the series *Topographie du vieux Paris* to return to this street on three occasions to follow the progress, on March 15, April 8, and August 15. On his first visit he made an image of a view that he had first taken in 1899 and again in 1912—one looking north from the corner of the rue de la Parcheminerie along the rue des Prêtres-Saint-Séverin toward the church (cat. 7.67; compare with 7.11 and 7.58). On each of his subsequent visits, he repeated this view (cat. 7.75 and 7.77). In adhering to this strategy, he was providing the viewer with a point of orientation and a means of comparison. On his initial visit, he also thoroughly documented the demolition site itself, photographing it in three overlapping views: two views were made from the rue Saint-Jacques end and the third from the rue des Prêtres-Saint-Séverin (cat. 7.69–7.71). In addition, he made three views centered upon the partially demolished buildings surrounding the former lane that had led to the entrance to the presbytery (cat. 7.72–7.74; compare with 7.55).

By August 1914, almost all the buildings along the north side of the rue de la Parcheminerie had been razed and the site cleared. Over the course of probably two days, Atget made ten photographs that progressed around the church and described the state of the demolition. He repeated the comparative view from the corner of the rue de la Parcheminerie (cat. 7.83), but this time paired it with a second view (cat. 7.84), which looks along the rue de la Parcheminerie toward the rue Saint-Jacques and together forms a ninety-degree sweep. He also surveyed the site from different vantage points, a number of which closely corresponded to views made in 1913 (compare 7.81 and 7.71). Finally and presumably also for comparative purposes, he remade his 1899 view of the church from the corner of the rue Galande (cat. 7.87; compare with cat. 7.15).

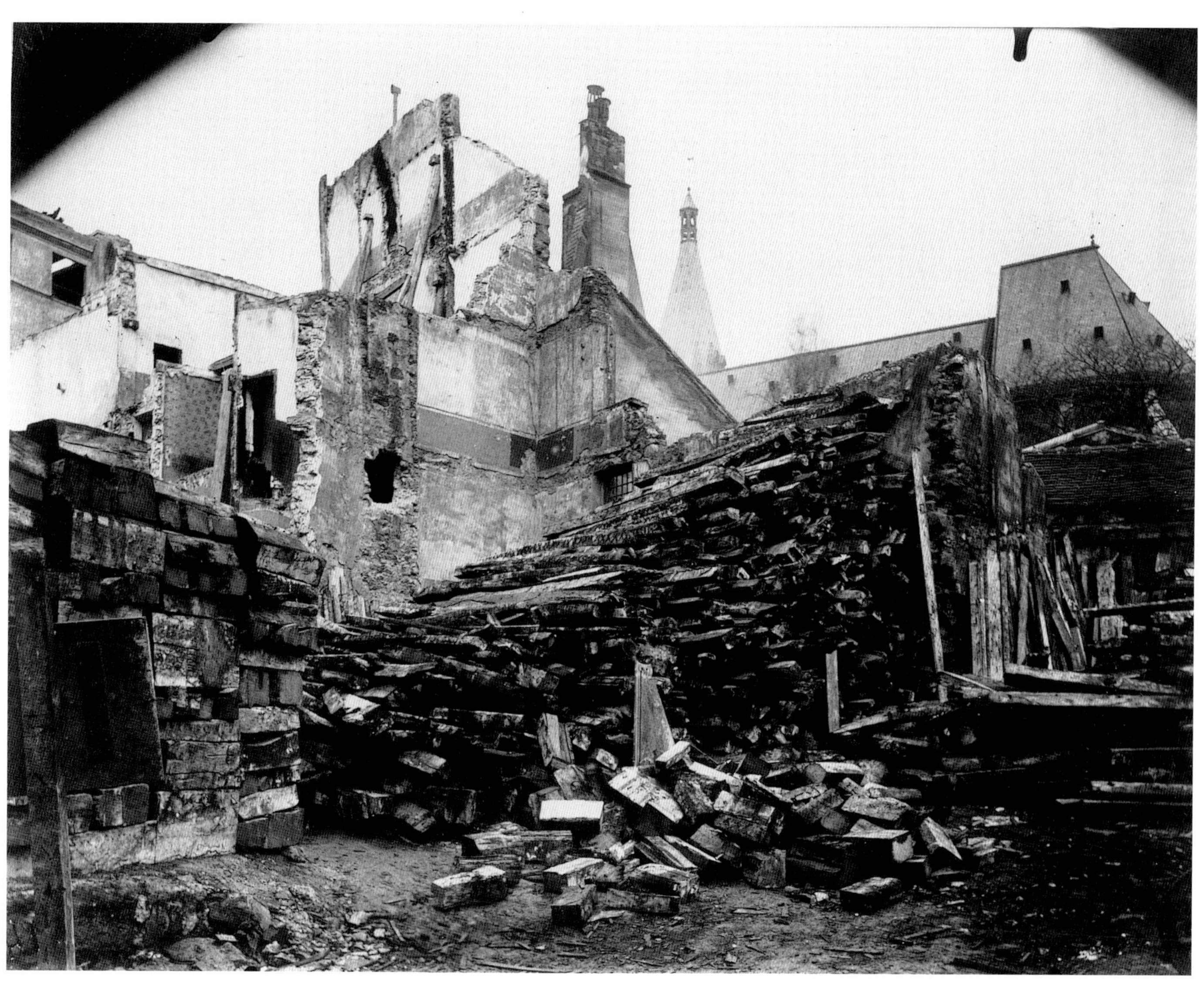

7.72 Demolitions, rue de la Parcheminerie, March 15, 1913

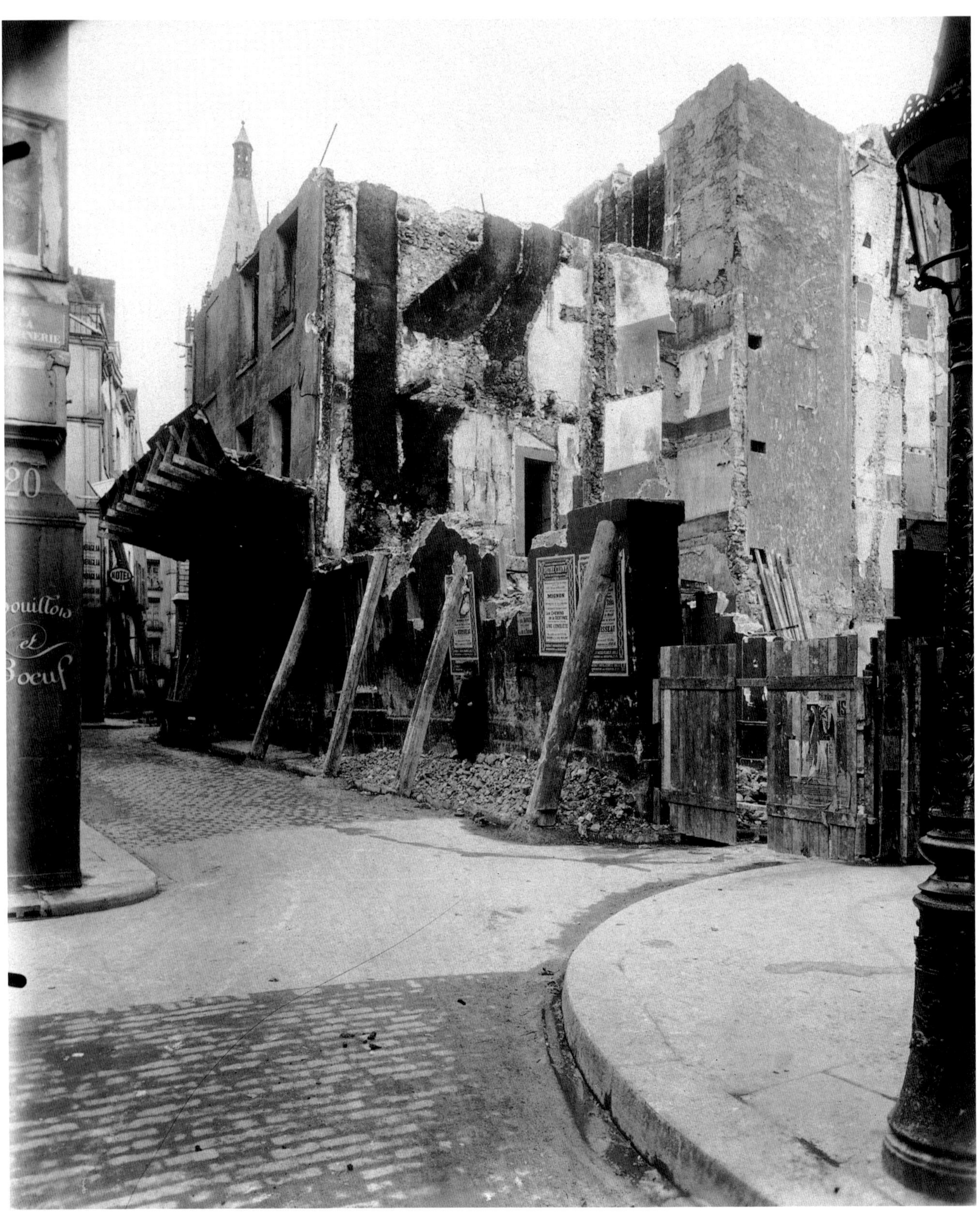

7.67 Intersection of the rue Boutebrie, the rue de la Parcheminerie, and the rue des Prêtres-Saint-Séverin, toward the church, March 15, 1913

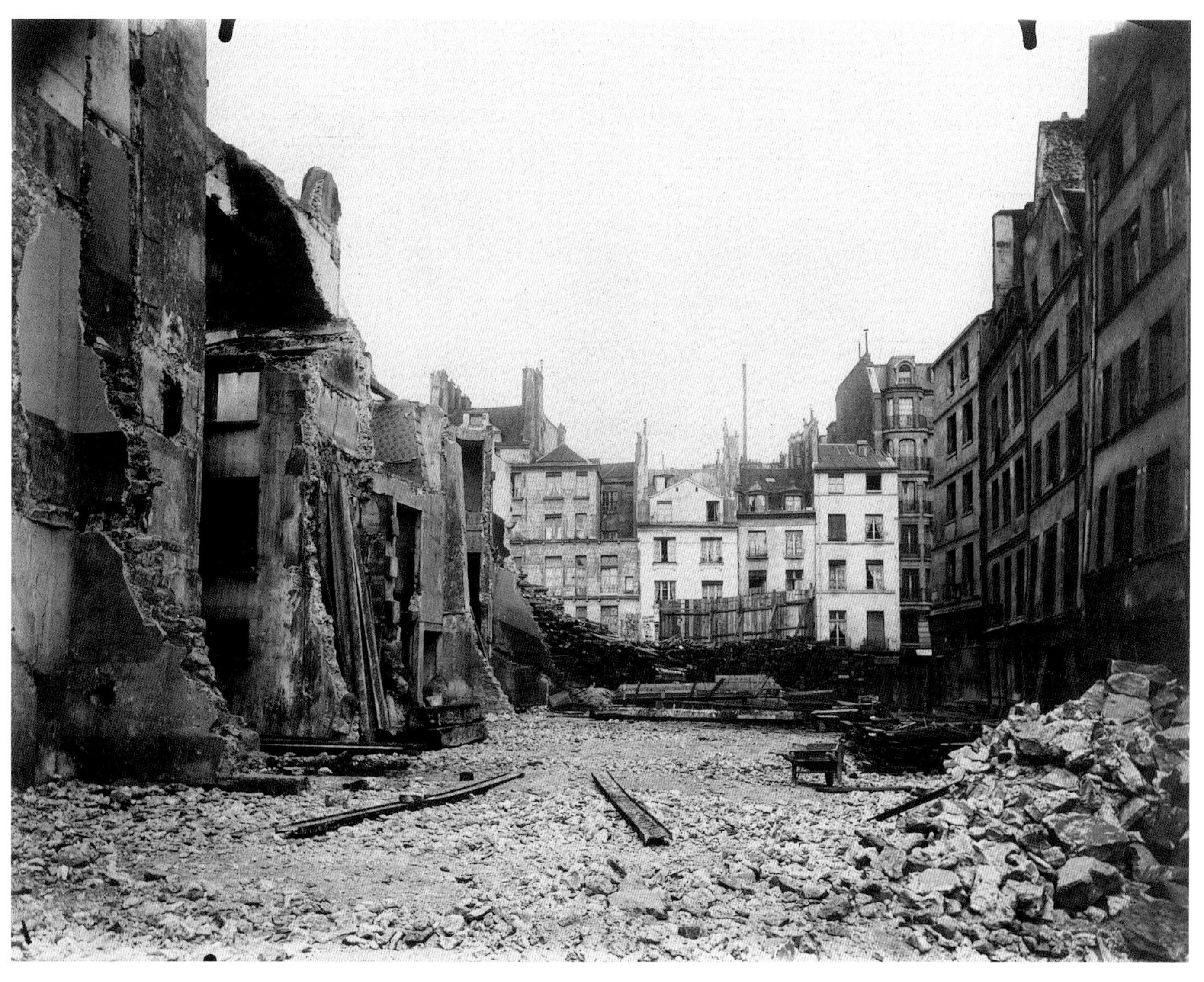

7.69 Demolition site, rue de la Parcheminerie, toward the rue Saint-Jacques, March 15, 1913

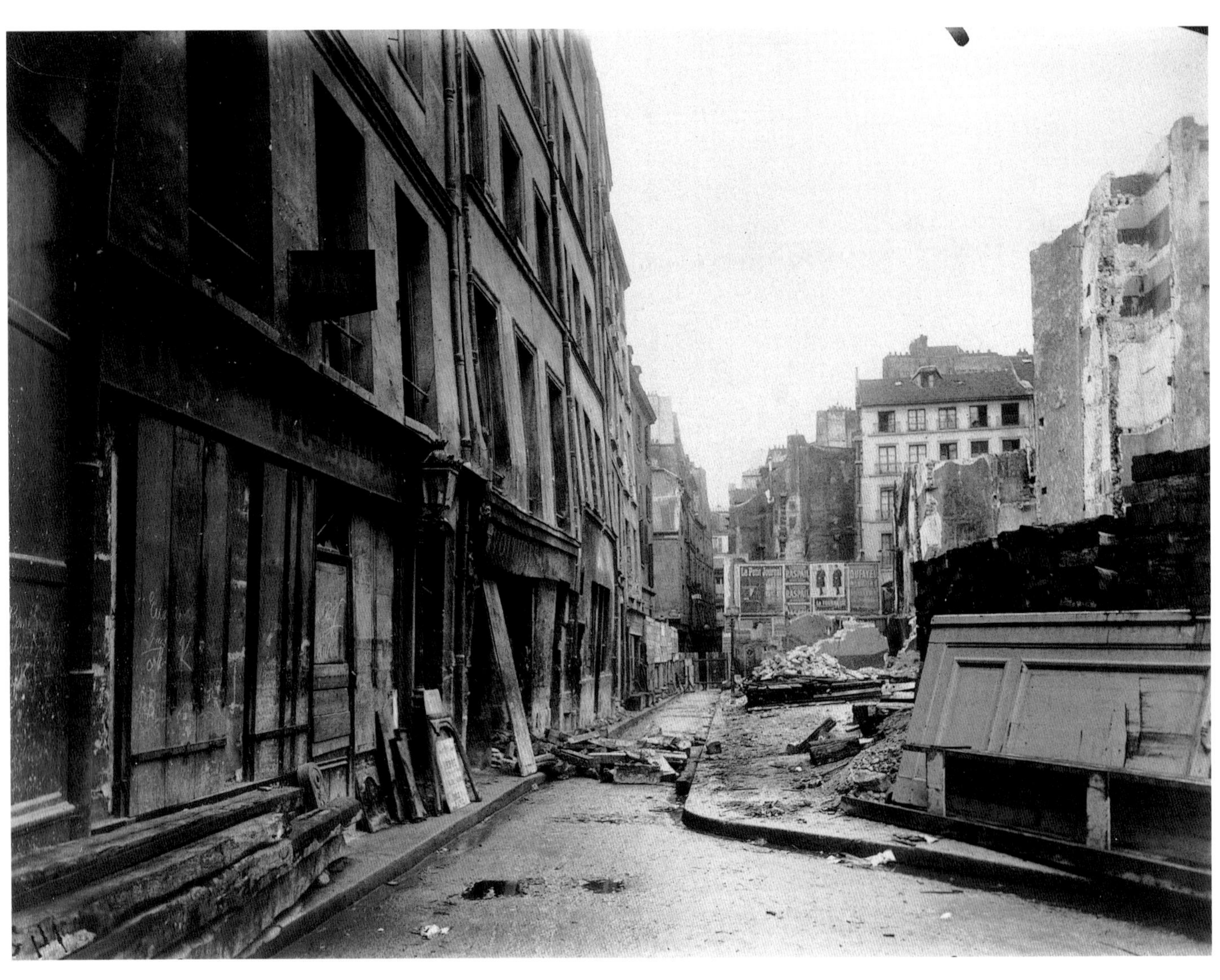

7.70 Demolitions along the rue de la Parcheminerie, from the rue Saint-Jacques toward the rue des Prêtres-Saint-Séverin, March 15, 1913

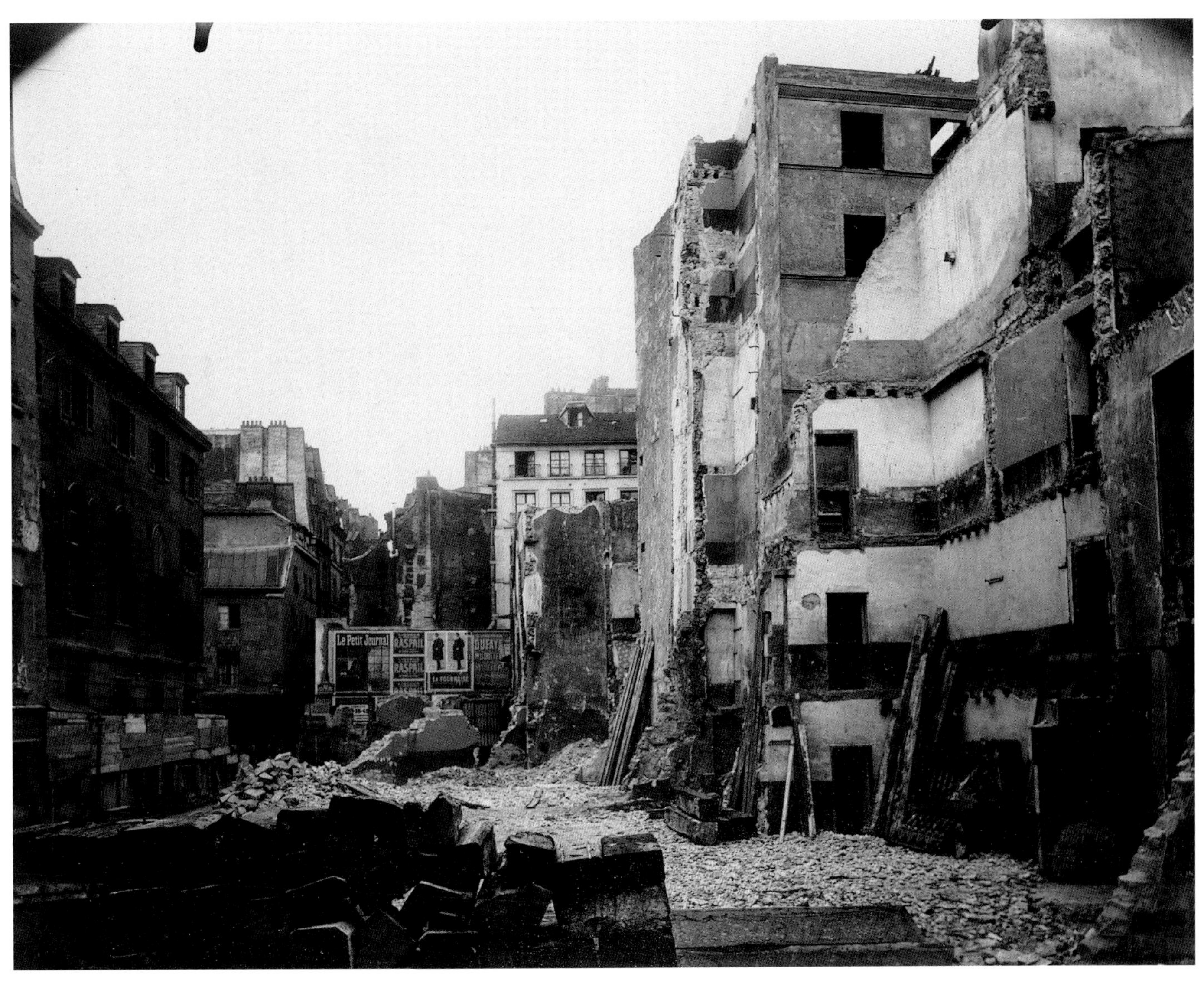

7.71 Demolitions along the rue de la Parcheminerie, from the rue Saint-Jacques toward the rue des Prêtres-Saint-Séverin, March 15, 1913

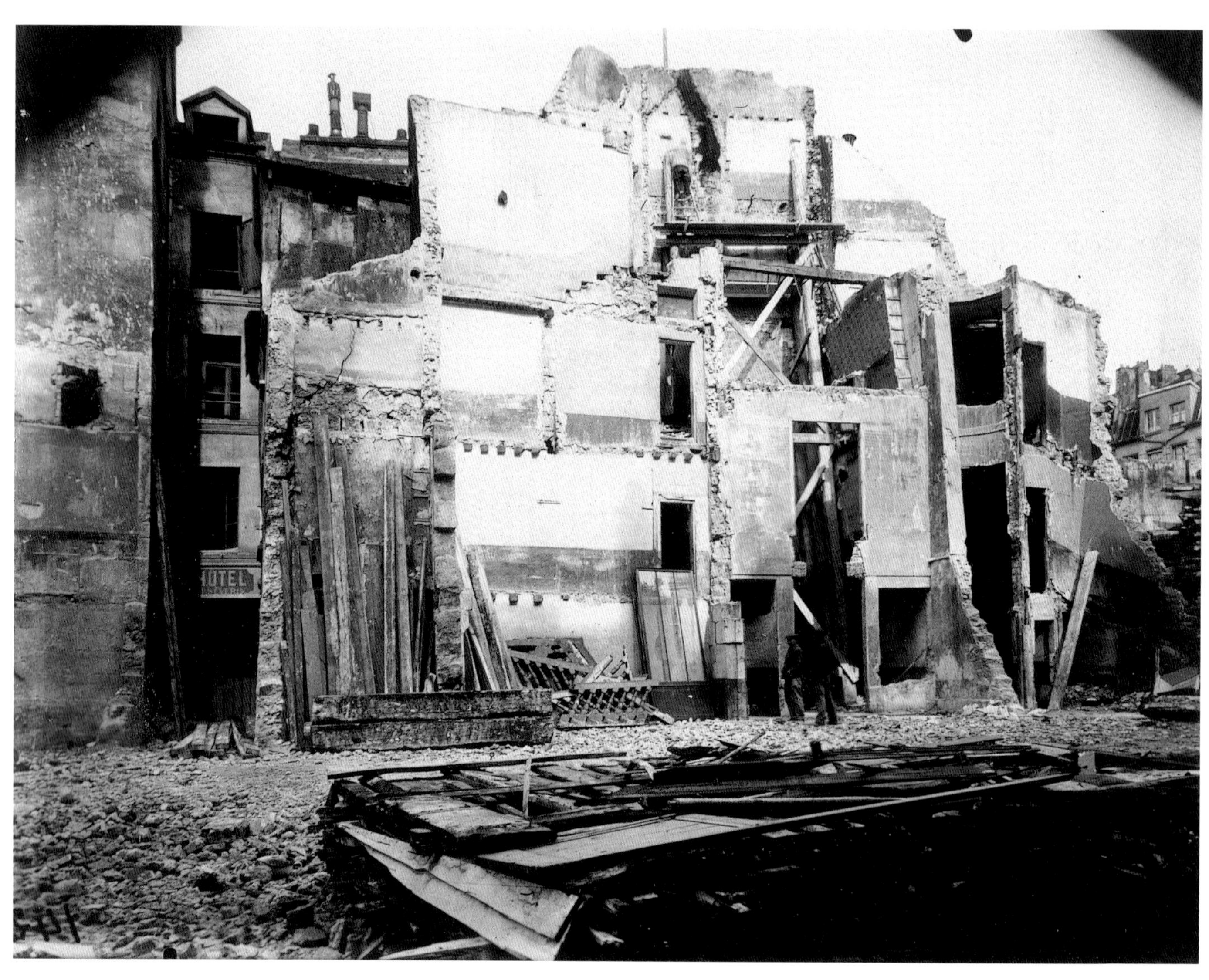

7.73 Demolitions, rue de la Parcheminerie, near the former entrance to the presbytery of the Church of Saint-Séverin, March 15, 1913

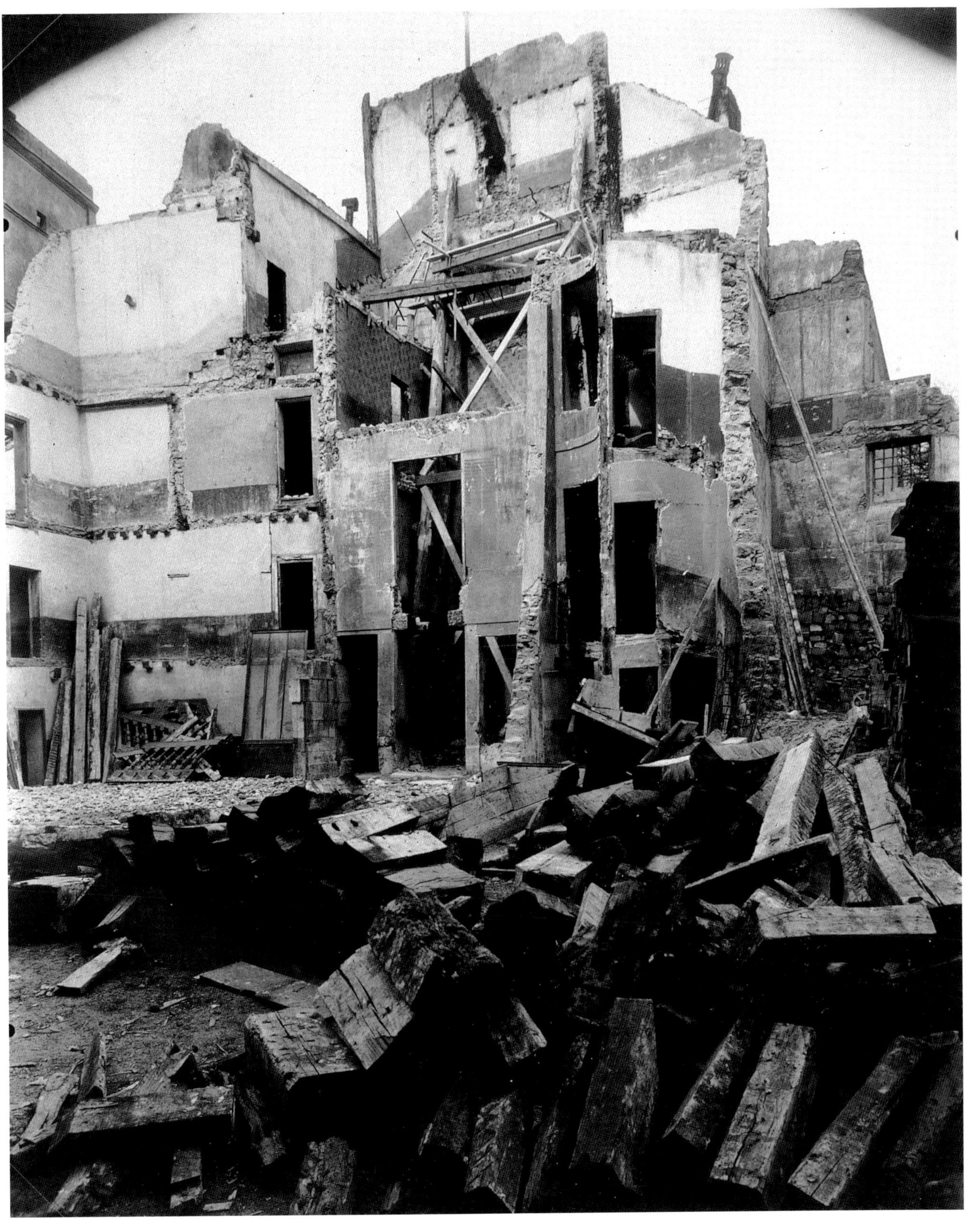

7.74 Demolitions, rue de la Parcheminerie, March 15, 1913

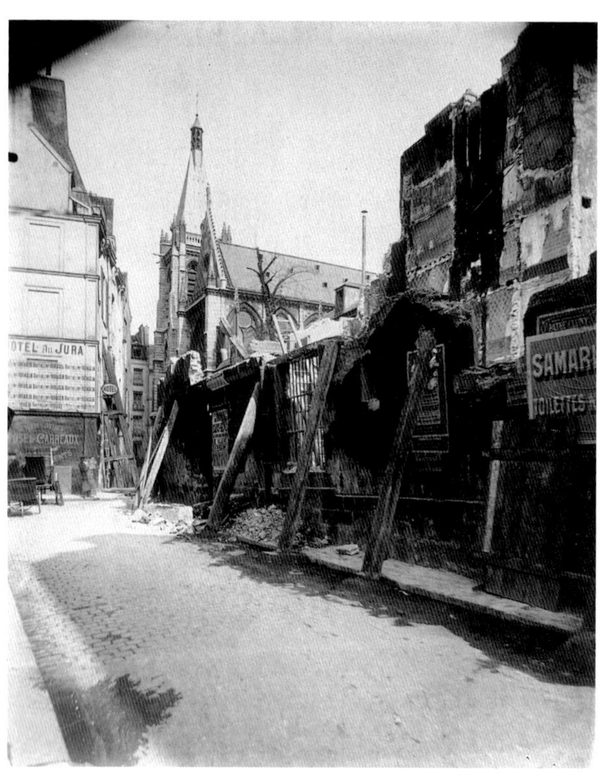

7.75 Demolitions, rue des Prêtres-Saint-Séverin, toward the church, April 8, 1913

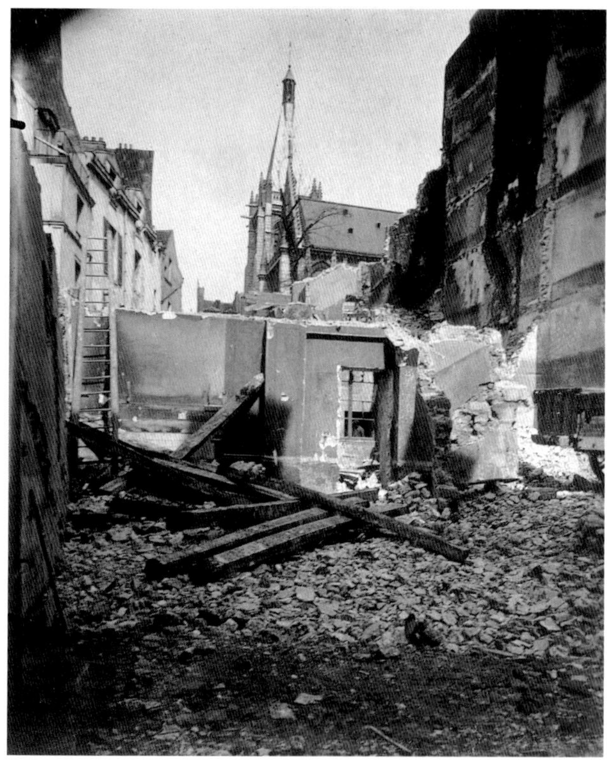

7.76 Demolition site, rue de la Parcheminerie, toward the Church of Saint-Séverin, April 8, 1913

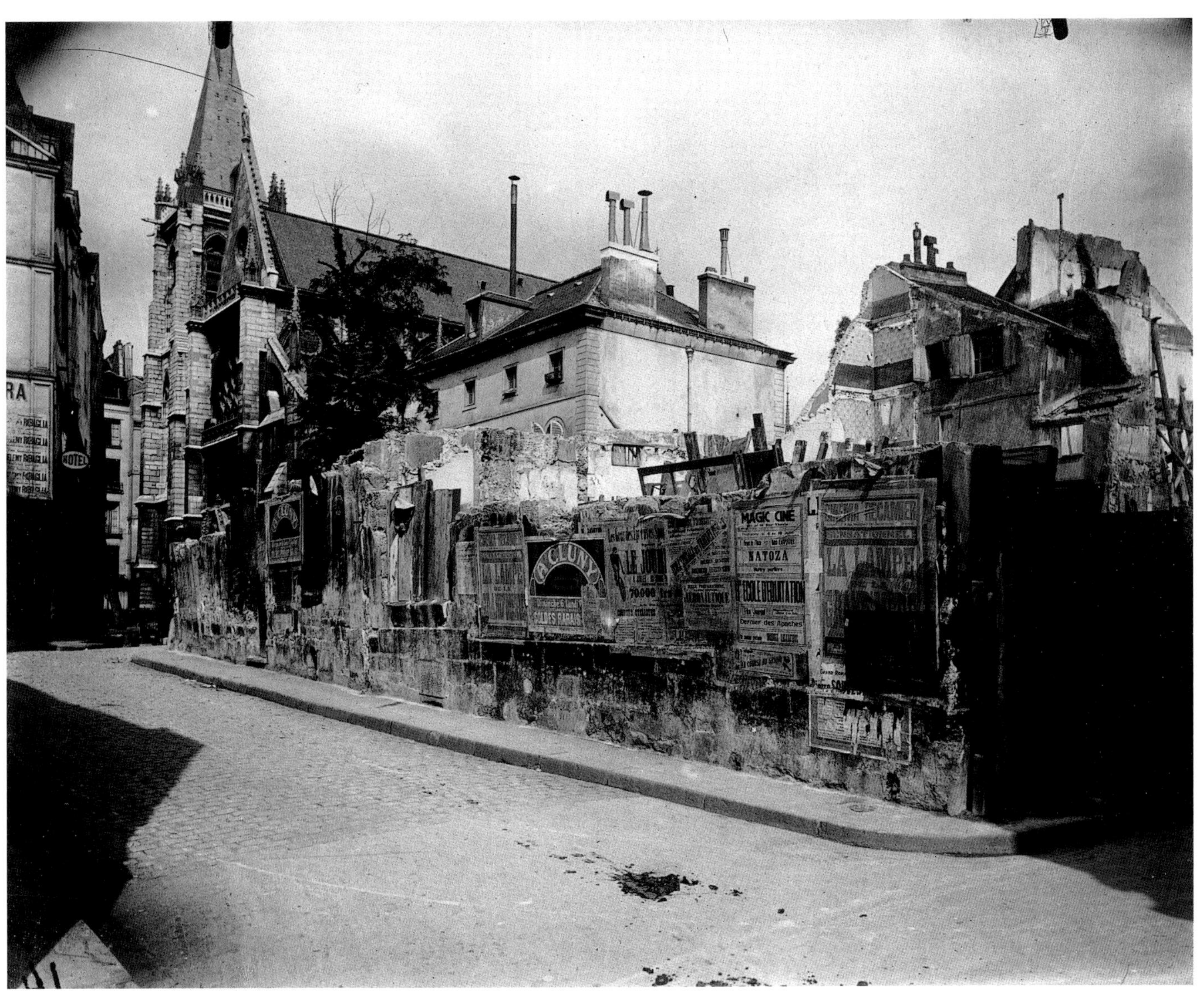

7.77 Intersection of the rue Boutebrie, the rue de la Parcheminerie, and the rue des Prêtres-Saint-Séverin, toward the presbytery and the church, August 15, 1913

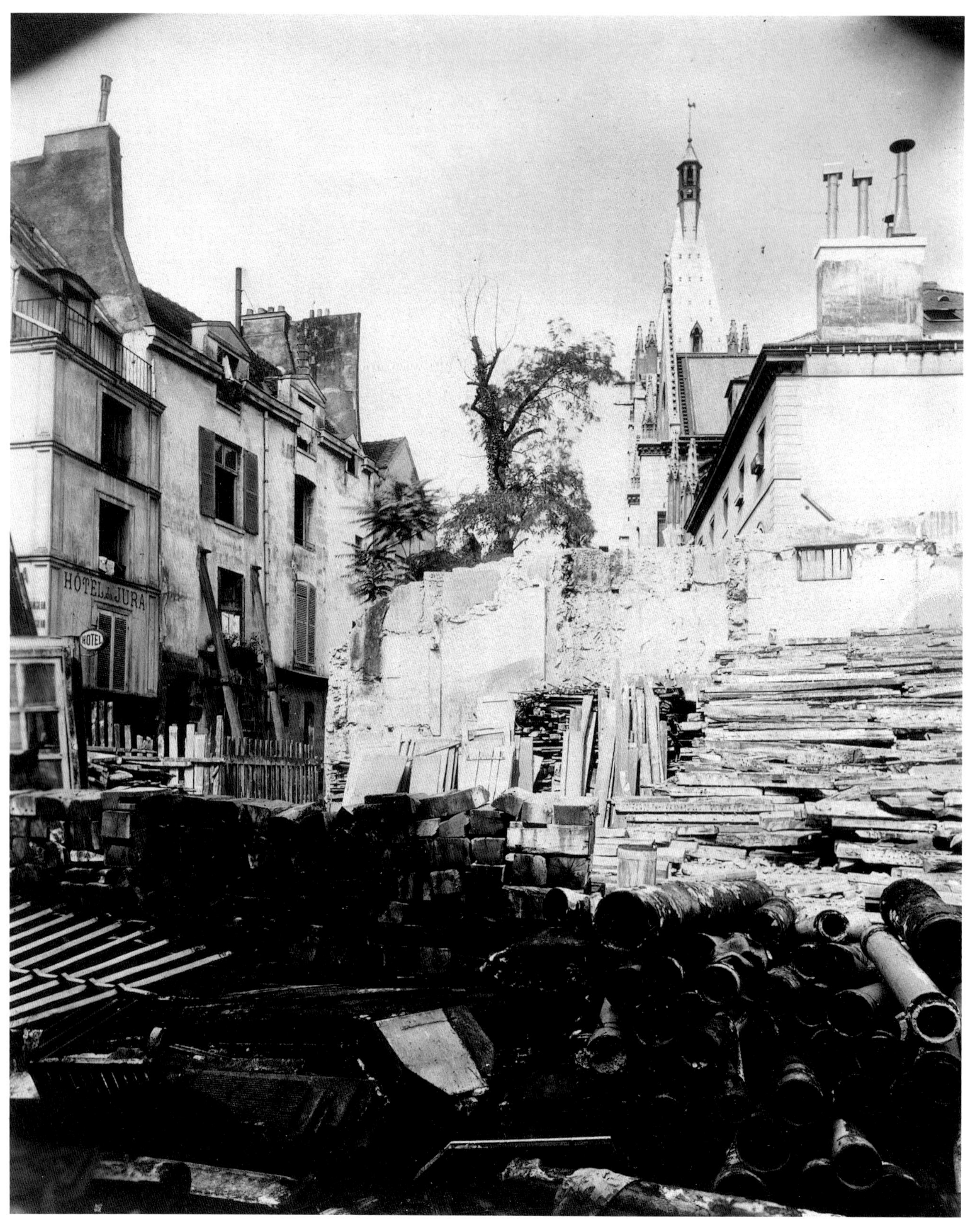

7.78 Demolition site, rue de la Parcheminerie, toward the presbytery and the church, August 15, 1913

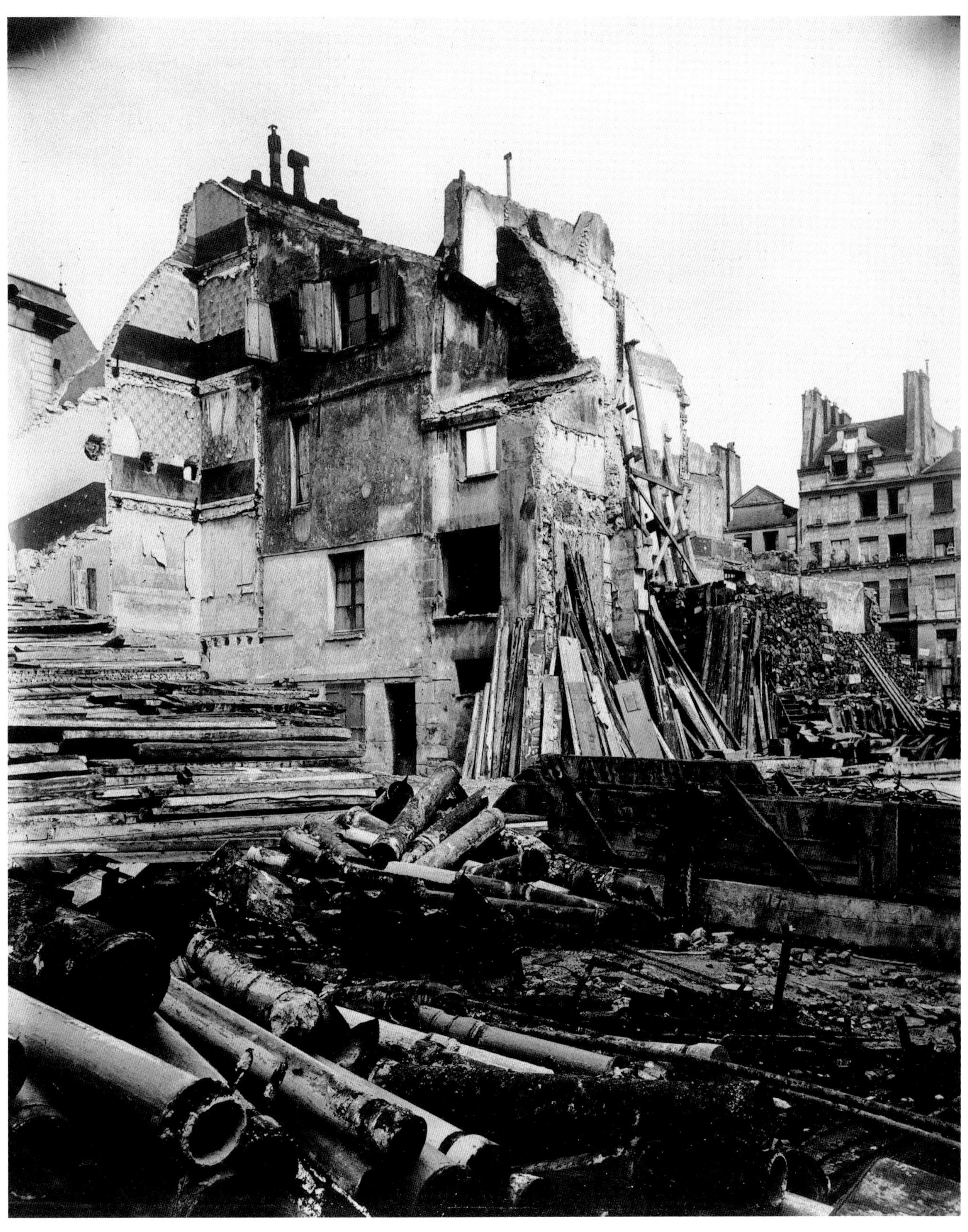

7.79 Demolition site, rue de la Parcheminerie, toward the rue Saint-Jacques, August 15, 1913

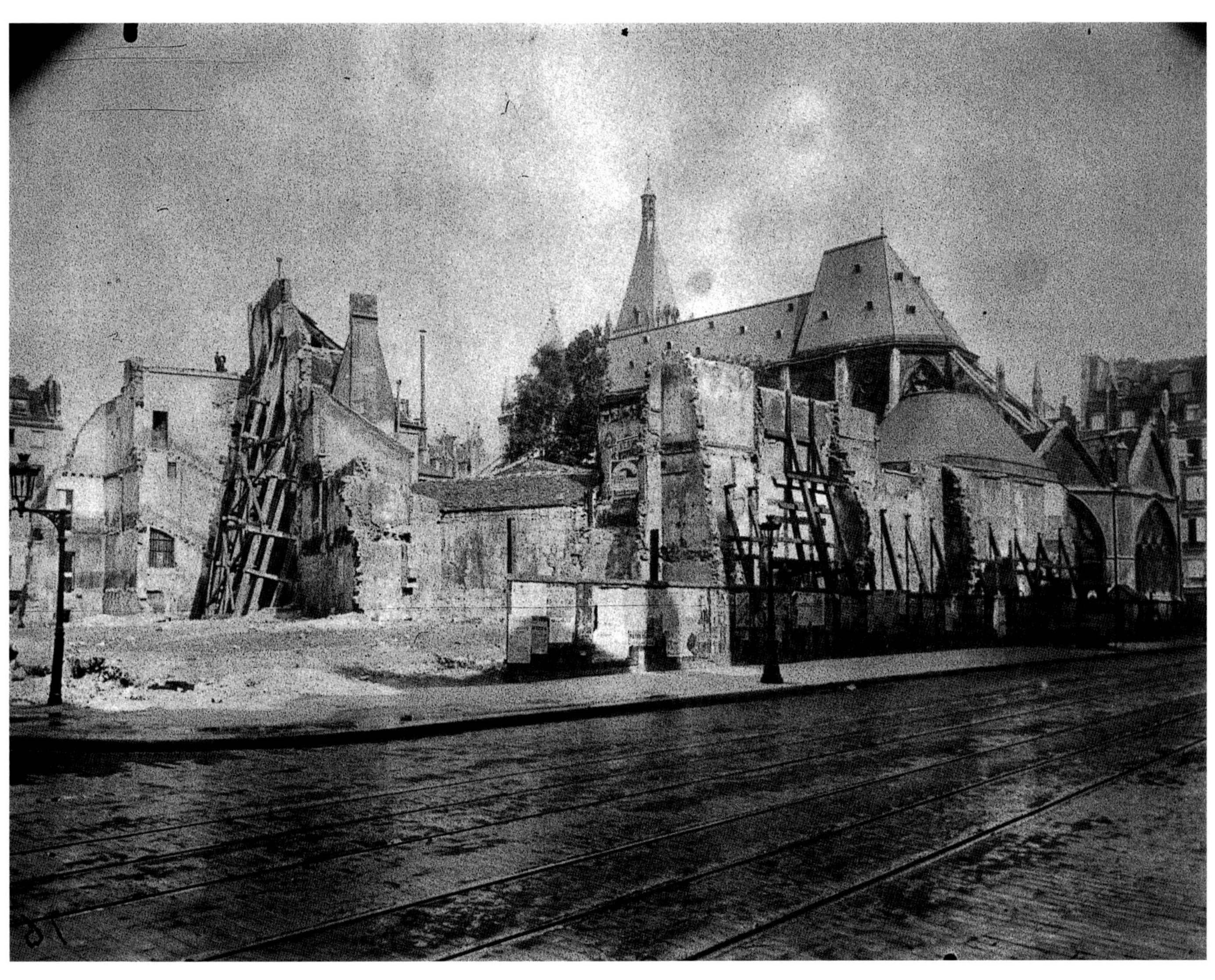

7.80 Demolitions, from the corner of the rue de la Parcheminerie and the rue Saint-Jacques, toward the Church of Saint-Séverin, August 1914

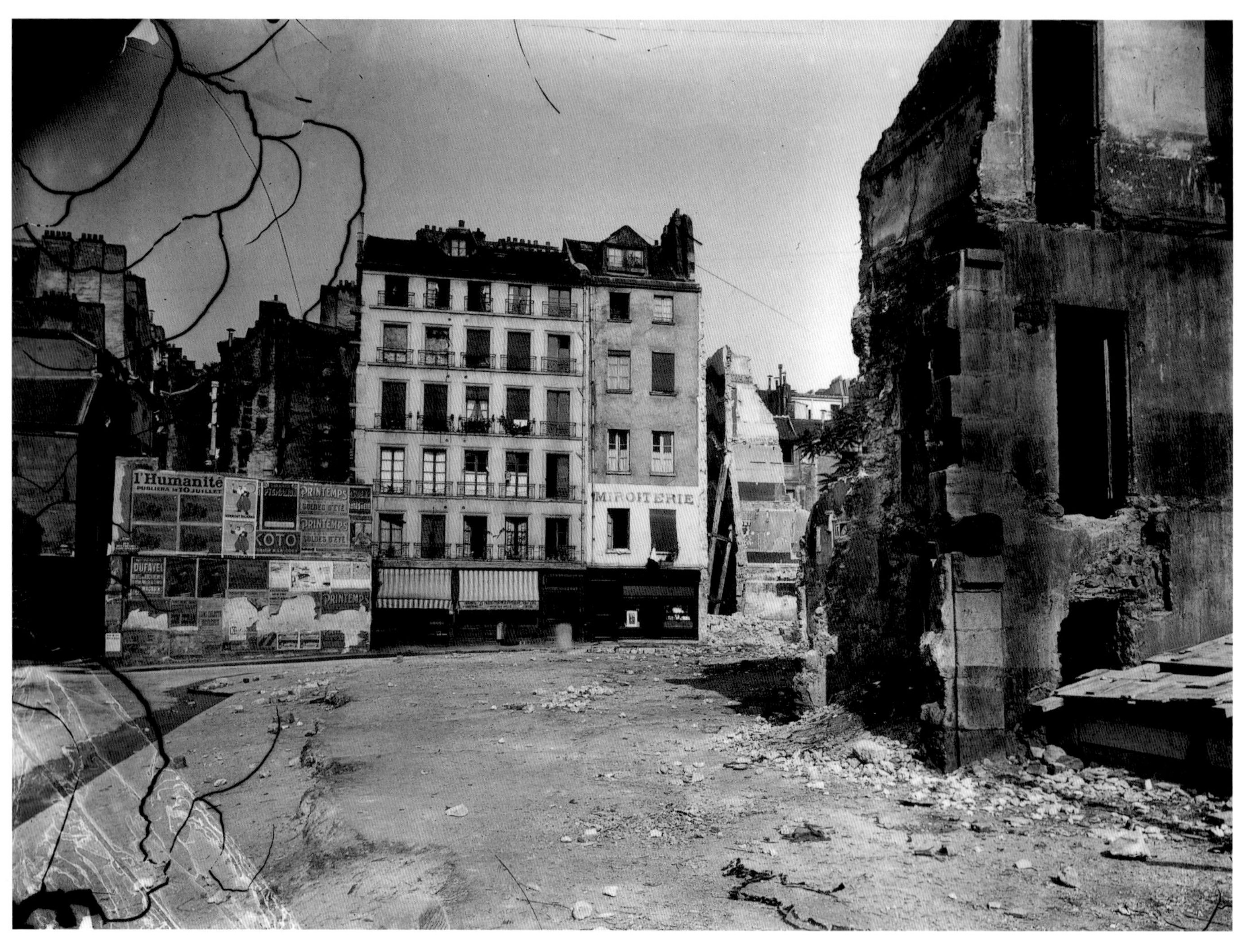

7.81 After the demolition of the buildings along the rue de la Parcheminerie, from the rue Saint-Jacques toward the rue des Prêtres-Saint-Séverin, August 1914

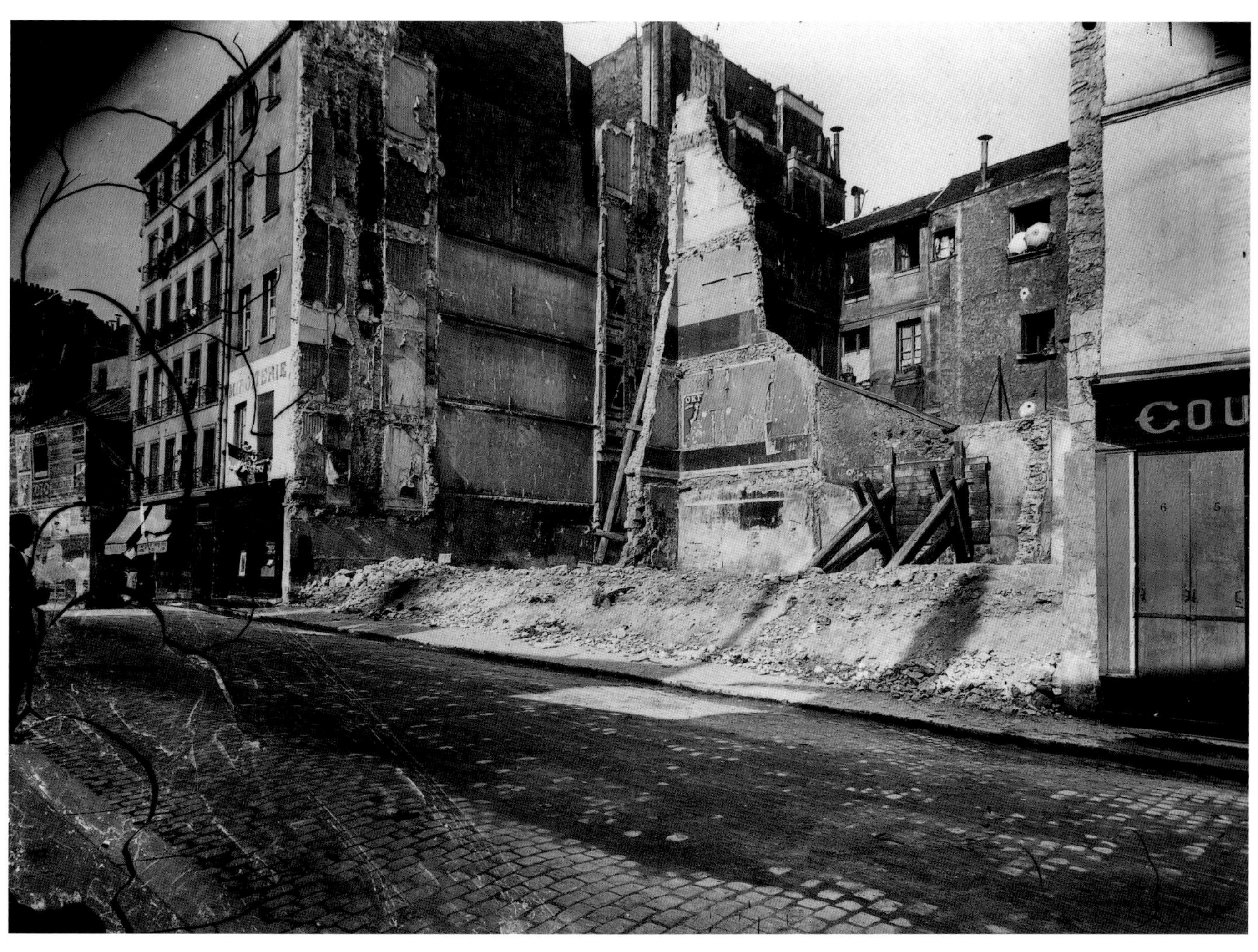

7.82 Demolition of buildings along the rue des Prêtres-Saint-Séverin, opposite the presbytery of the church, August 1914

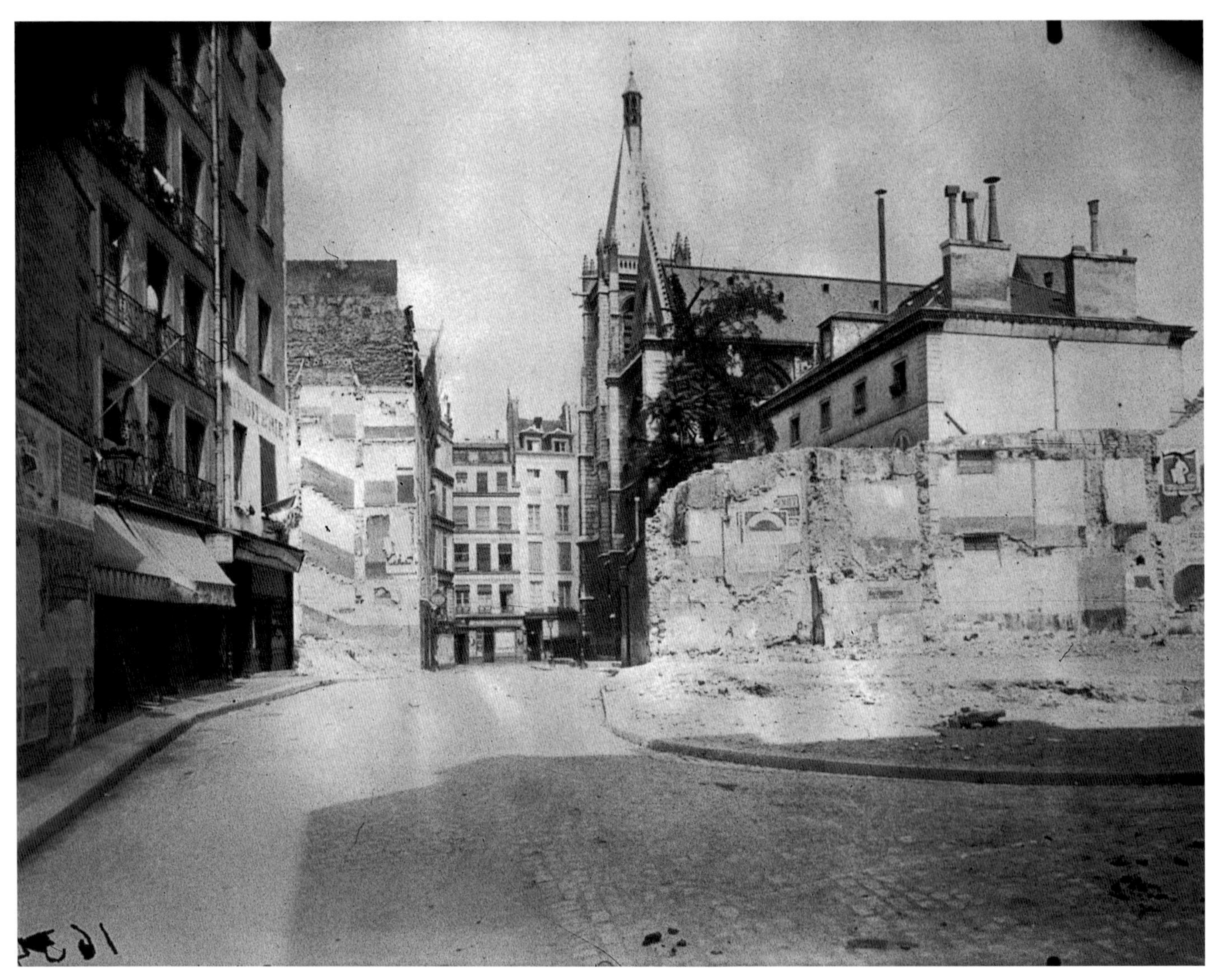

7.83 After the demolitions at the intersection of the rue Boutebrie, the rue de la Parcheminerie, and the rue des Prêtres-Saint-Séverin, toward the presbytery and the church, August 1914

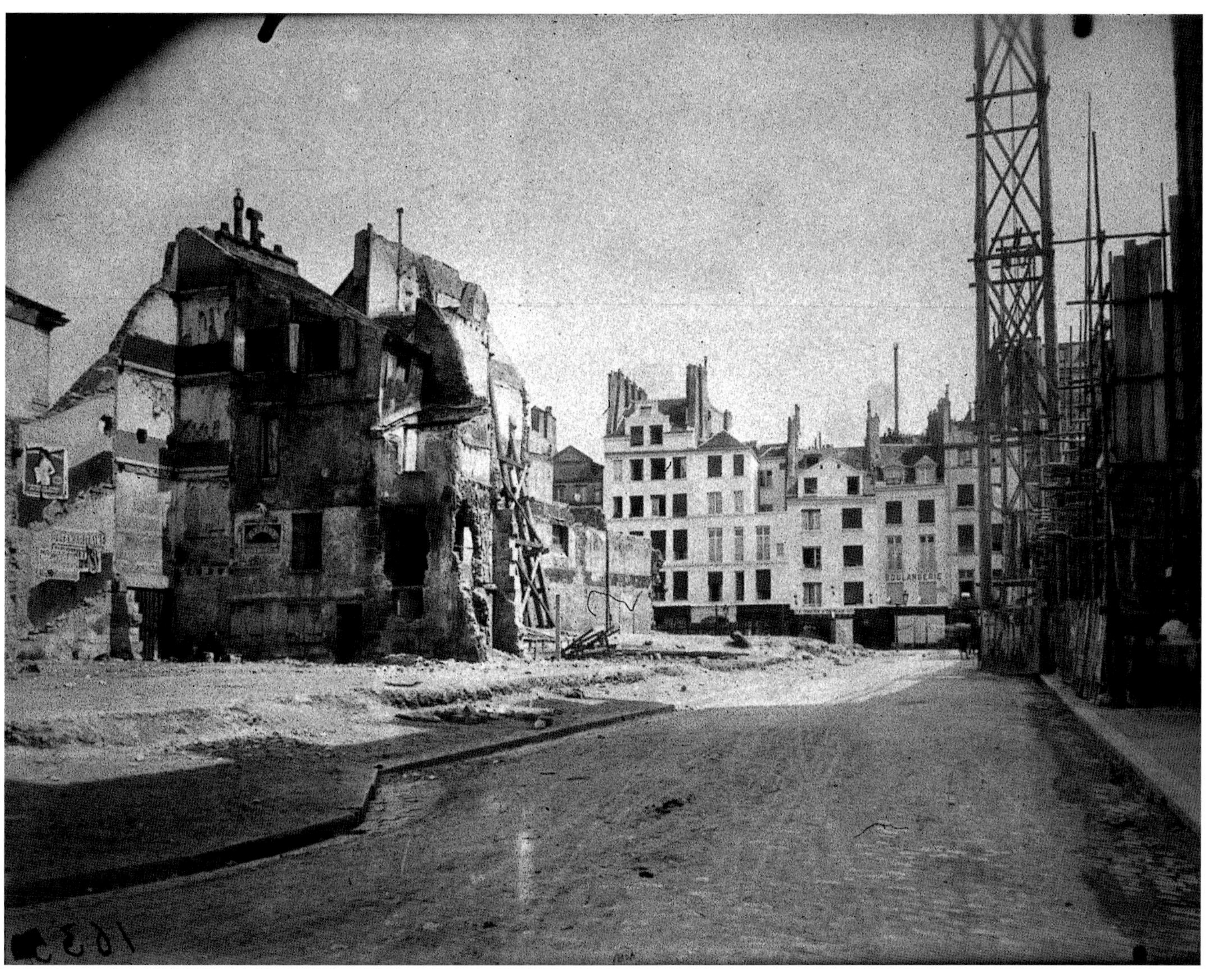

7.84 Demolitions at the intersection of the rue Boutebrie, the rue de la Parcheminerie and the rue des Prêtres-Saint-Séverin, toward the rue Saint-Jacques, August 1914

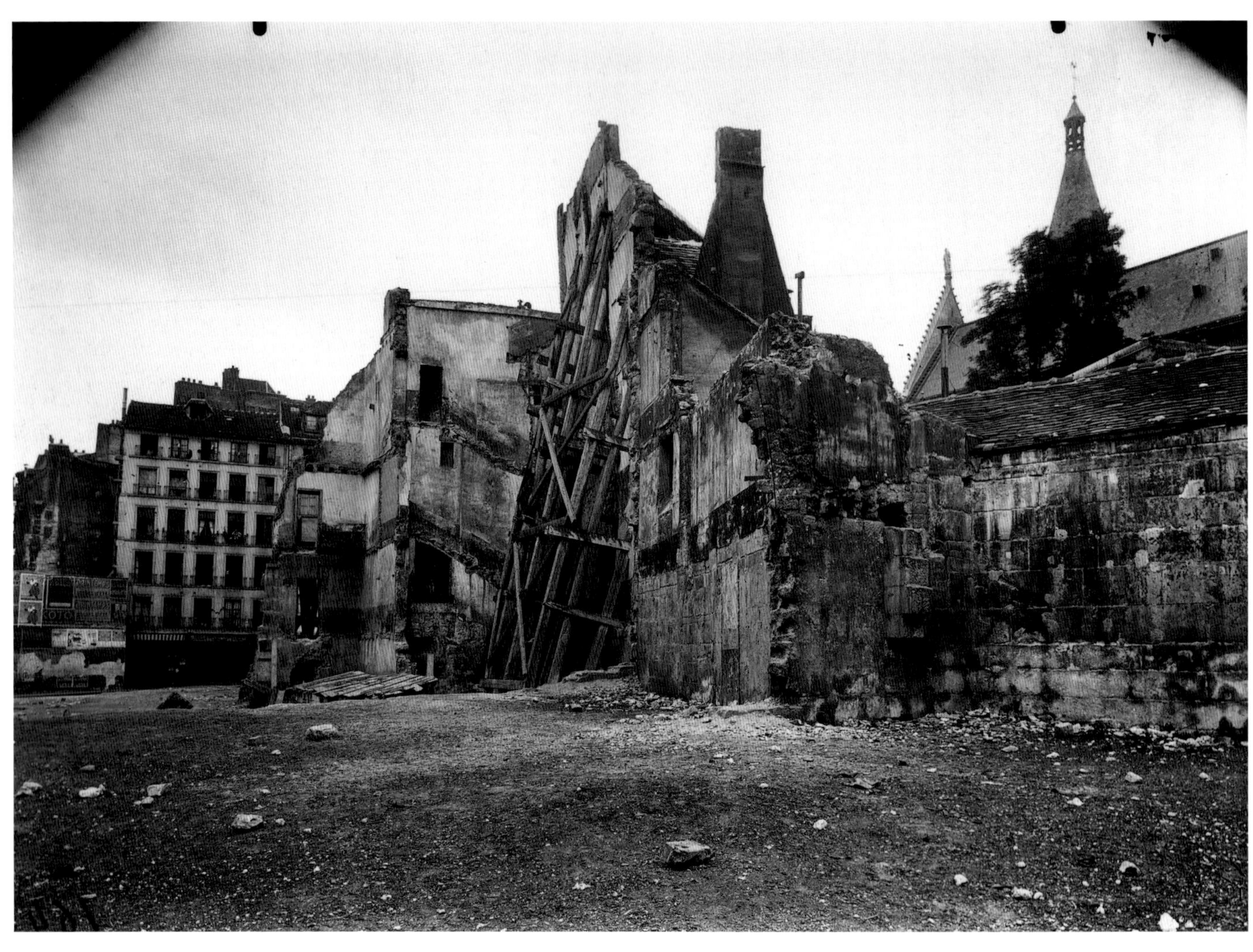

7.88 After the demolition of the buildings along the rue de la Parcheminerie, from the rue Saint-Jacques toward the rue des Prêtres-Saint-Séverin and the church, August 1914

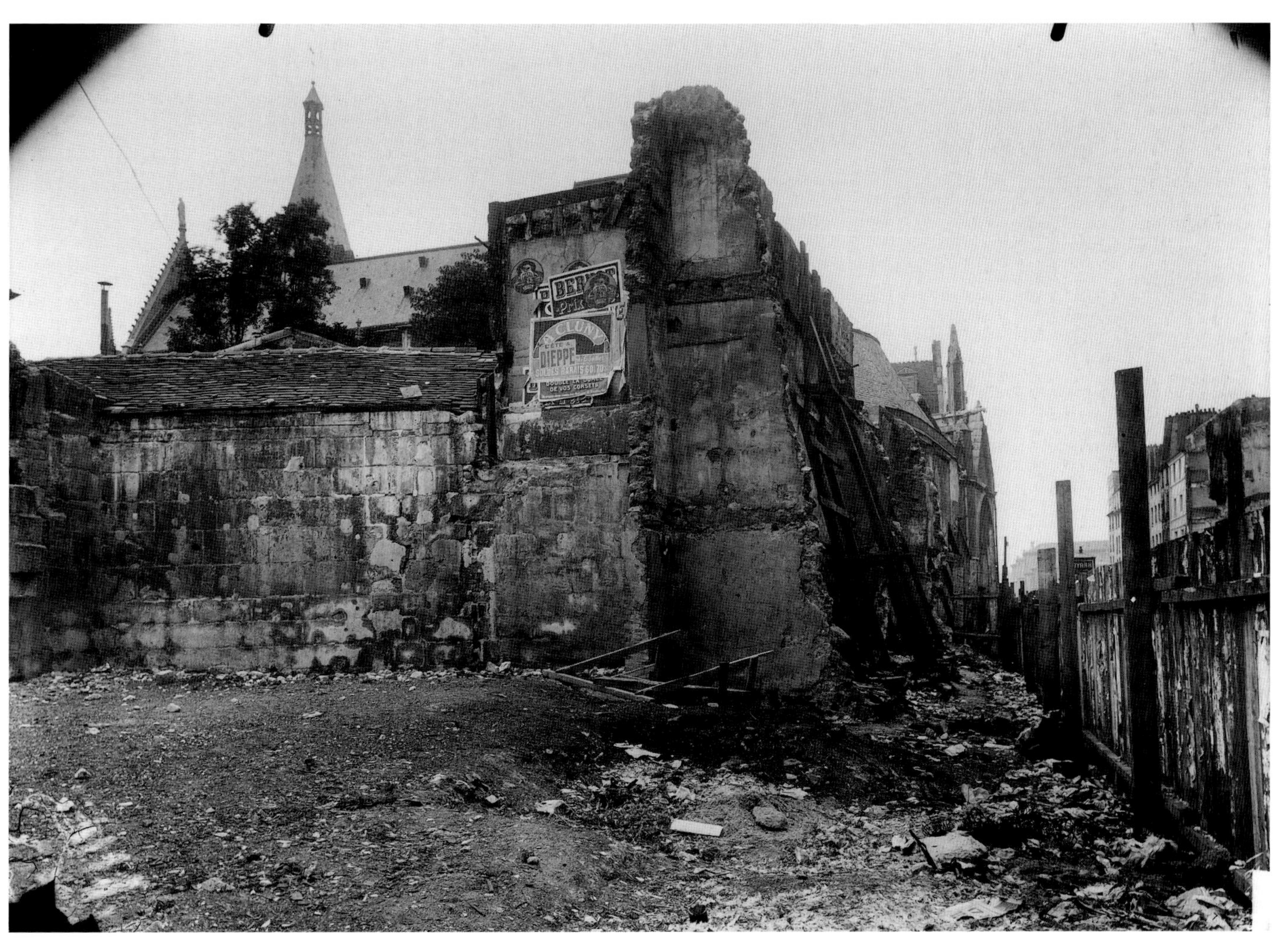

7.89 Demolition site, view along the rue Saint-Jacques, August 1914

vii. Final views, 1920–1923

When Atget returned to Saint-Séverin after World War I, it was partly to update his stock of views, since he had sold seventy-six from a total of eighty-nine negatives of the church and its neighborhood to the French government in 1920. Each time, he revisited an earlier view, some of which he had first taken in 1898 or 1899, and, in several cases, had remade over the intervening years (compare, for example, cat. 7.92 with 7.13 and 7.64). In returning to these same camera positions, Atget completed his coverage of the Church of Saint-Séverin.

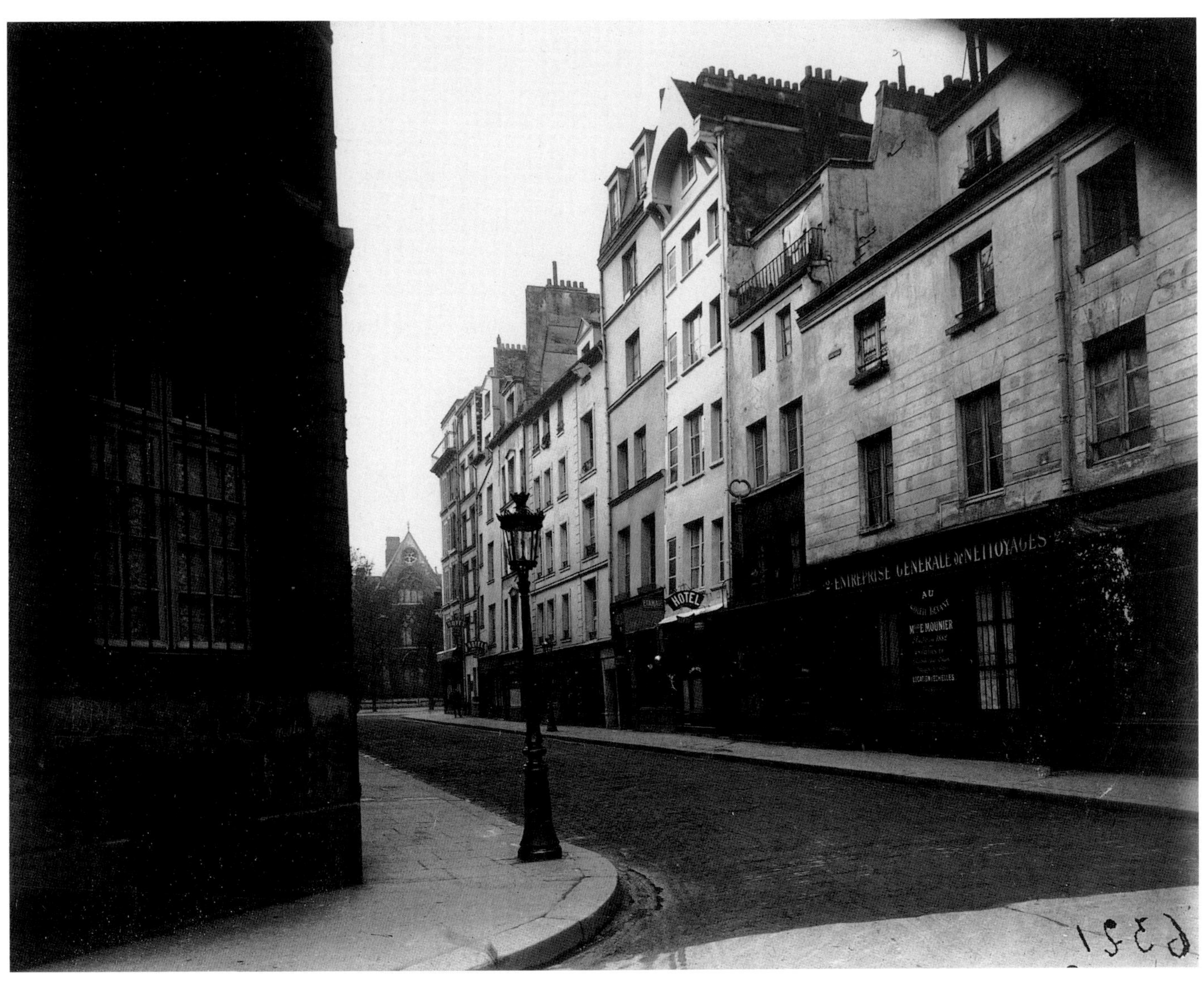

7.92 Rue Boutebrie, from the intersection of the rue de la Parcheminerie and the rue des Prêtres-Saint-Séverin toward the Musée de Cluny, March 1922

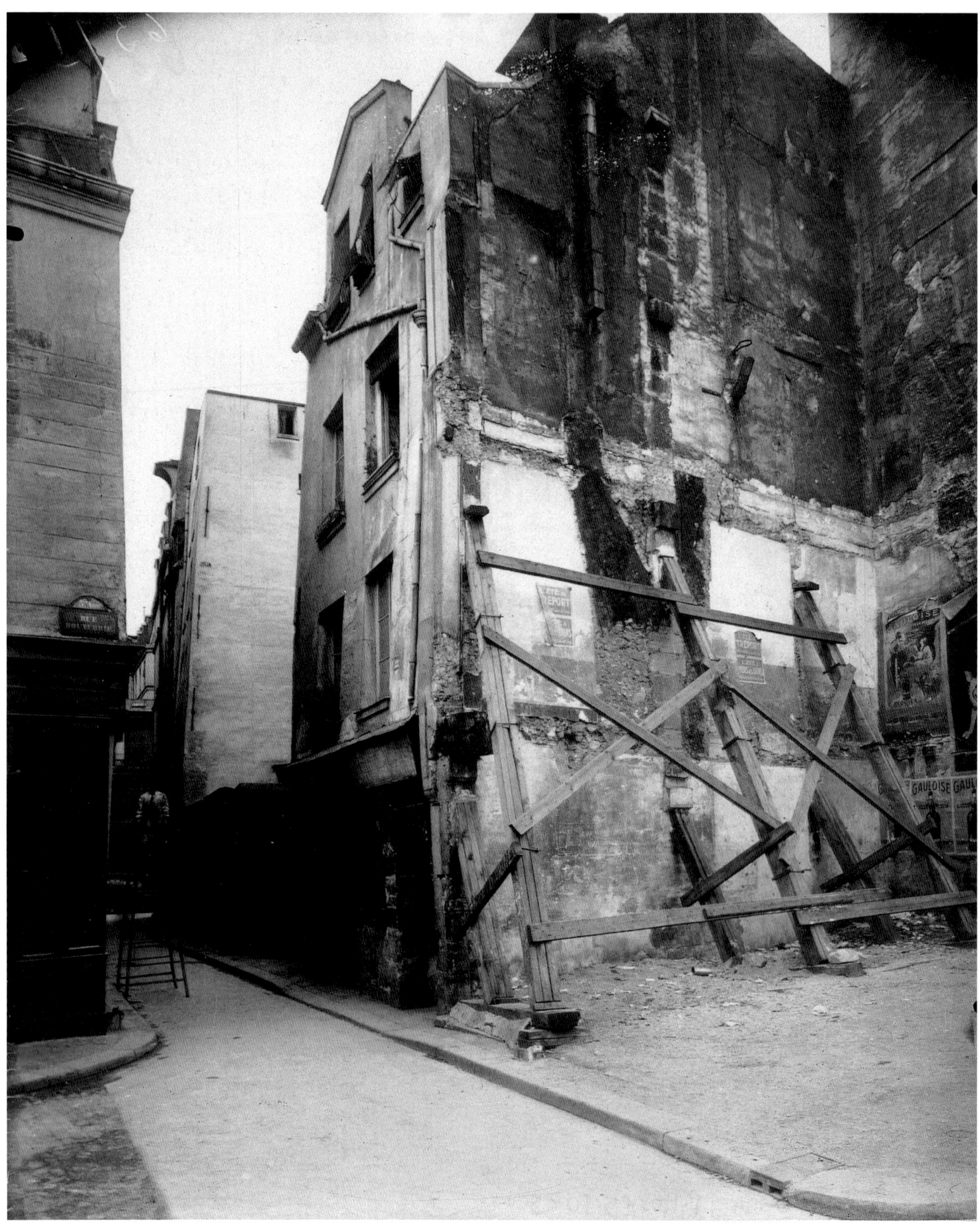

7.93 Demolition of the building at the corner of the rue de la Parcheminerie and the rue des Prêtres-Saint-Séverin, 1922

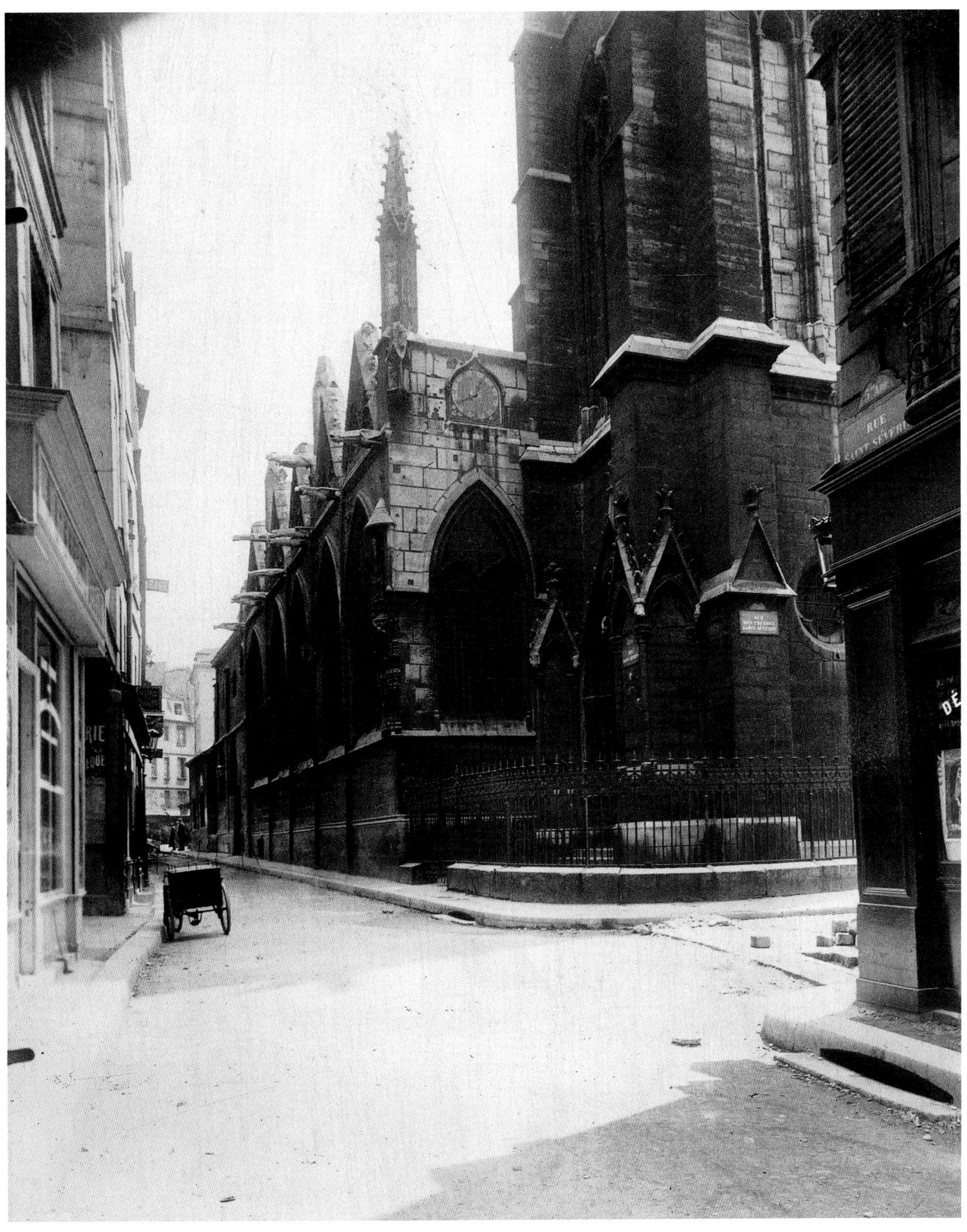

7.94 Rue Saint-Séverin at the intersection with the rue des Prêtres-Saint-Séverin, toward the rue Saint-Jacques, June 1923

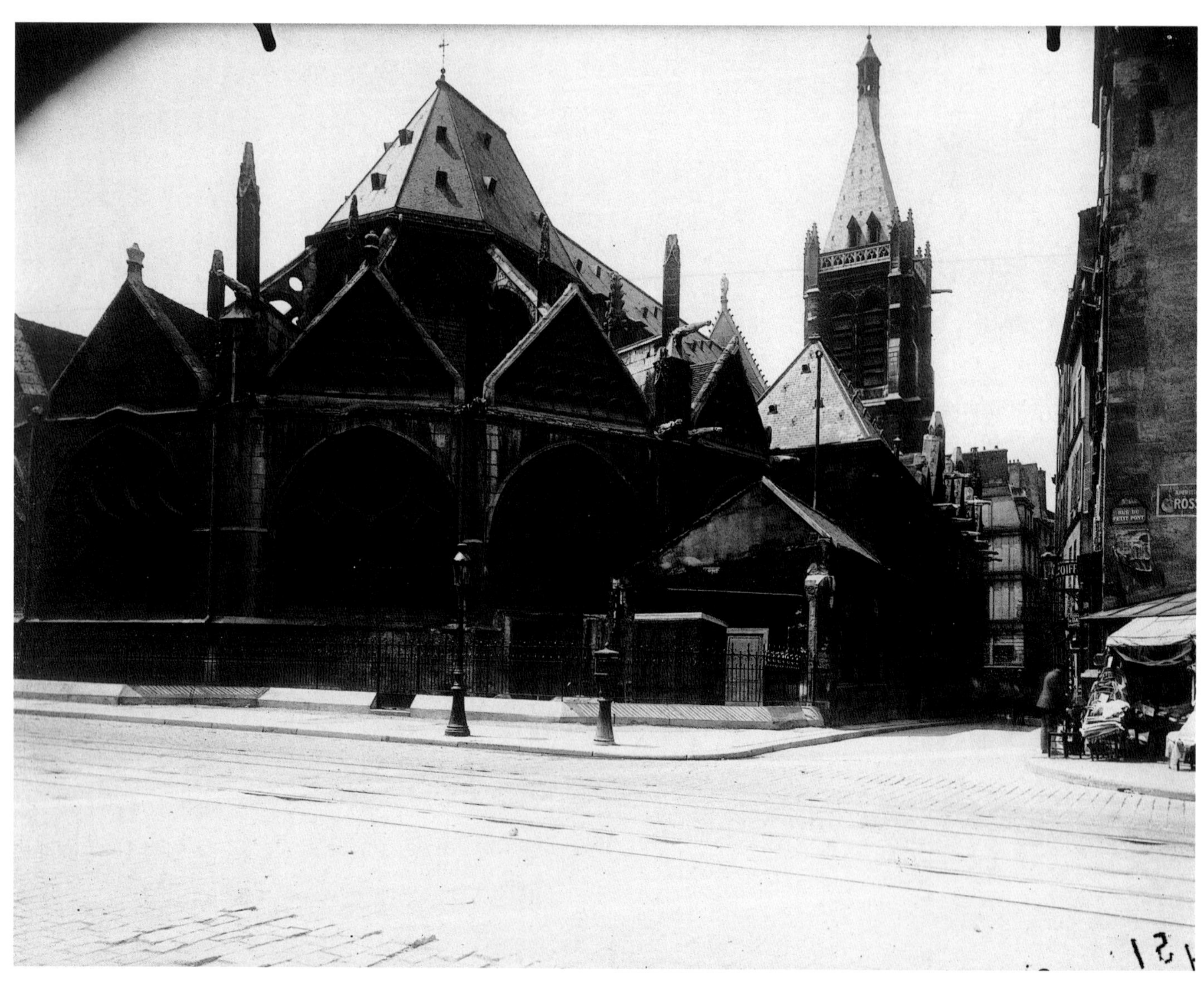

7.95 Corner of the rue Galande and the rue Saint-Jacques, toward the church and the rue Saint-Séverin, June 1923

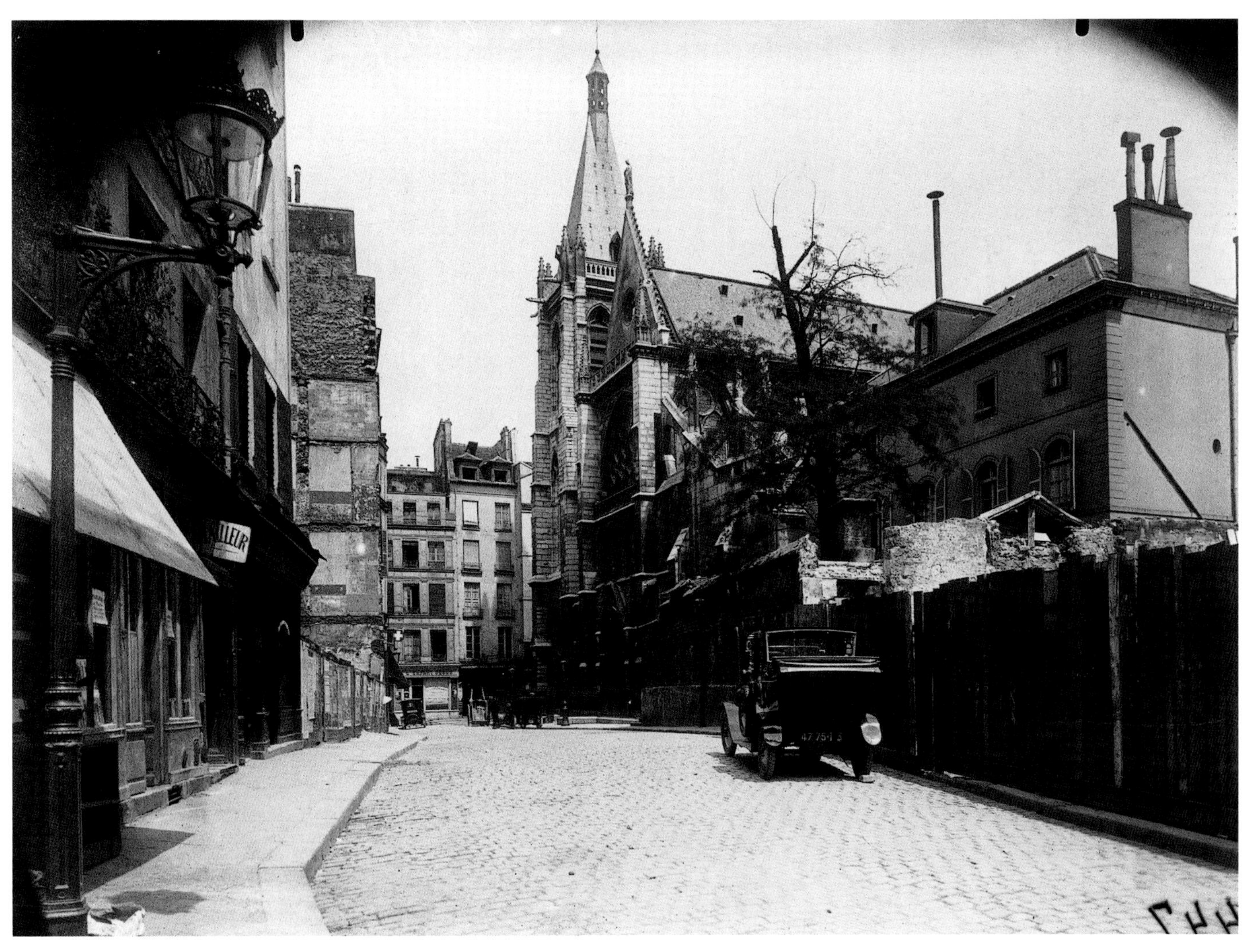

7.96 Rue des Prêtres-Saint-Séverin, toward the presbytery and the church, June 1923

Chapter 5

Conclusion

This study differs from previous publications on the work of Eugène Atget by presenting it as sequences of topographically related photographs, rather than as single magisterial images.[1] Each of the selected sites discussed in chapter 4 is portrayed by all of the known photographs Atget made of them, and not by a selection of a few representative images.

In order to understand Atget as a commercial photographer, it has been necessary to reconstruct his working method in detail, and to describe how this method was shaped by technical concerns, affected by topographical considerations, and influenced by commercial demands. Once his photographs have been reconstituted as sequential groups, one can perceive the direct and integral relationship between his working method and the subject matter of his photography, and realize the extent to which Atget's work is concerned with elucidating the character of distinctive architectural and urban spaces in Paris. In photographing a space, Atget typically moved through it, thereby automatically generating a succession of images, which allowed his viewers to imaginatively occupy and grasp, for example, the overall configuration of a church's interior space, or the more open conditions encountered at an urban intersection. Each photograph becomes firmly imbedded within an overall sequence; each image not only derives its architectural meaning from that context, but in turn contributes to the cumulative description of a site. Once a photograph is removed from the sequence to which it belongs, a part of its intrinsic meaning and original purpose is lost.

Except for the first two years of his photography in Paris, Atget produced sequences of linked images and groups of interrelated photographs throughout his entire career. As an approach, this had three obvious advantages. First, it created a simple framework within which to work, one which could be easily and readily expanded, contracted, and adapted. Second, this method of working provided him with considerable flexibility in being able to respond to the varied needs of his clients by selectively incorporating such decorative details as an iron balustrade into his overall coverage of a site. Third, it allowed Atget to carry out his trade efficiently and expediently, ensuring that he would not need to return to the site because he had omitted some aspect of it.

While all his work reveals consistencies in approach and process, Atget did modify and adapt his method when confronted with the diversity of urban subjects. The examples in this publication have been selected to indicate the variety of typical subjects he repeatedly photographed throughout his career. These ranged widely. Stairwells, entrance vestibules, and courtyards required relatively few images to describe their usually compact and confined spaces. Streets necessitated additional images to record their linear form and describe their relationship to the courtyards, *passages*, intersecting streets, and public squares found along their length. Finally, an entire neighborhood required an even greater number of photographs not only to cover the individual structures, streets, and squares but also to establish the topographical relationship between each of these distinctive elements. In one of his most complex and sustained series of photographs, Atget produced a historical record of the neighborhood of Saint-Séverin as it was transformed over a period of twenty-five years. In photographing this area over time, Atget drew upon various strategies: In addition to linked sequences of views, he recorded the same space from multiple angles and overlapping viewpoints, and made a series of views over time from a consistent camera position.

As one would surely expect from a commercial photographer who earned his livelihood from producing work in a highly competitive and specialized market, Atget's work varies considerably, revealing different levels of inspiration. His photographs are not merely those produced by an accomplished professional photographer but, as he expressed in his letters to Paul Léon in 1920, also ones that participated in a larger documentary entity. Moreover, unlike the work of most commercial architectural photographers, whose output strictly adhered to a limited set of pictorial conventions, Atget's work exhibits an astonishing degree of internal development and growth, particularly in the later work of the 1920s when he often revisited and reinterpreted earlier sites. Inevitably, a photographer as talented, independent-minded—he bluntly told Abbott that he did not work on assignment because "people did not know what to photograph"[2]—and personally motivated as Atget could never blindly adhere to a formulaic system of image-making merely for its own sake. In the process of photographing on a nearly daily basis over a period of thirty years, Atget certainly followed identifiable patterns of working. However, when he encountered unexpected atmospheric conditions or, increasingly toward the end of his life, deliberately sought out ephemeral lighting effects that altered and transformed the appearance of a site, Atget modified his process and produced images which neither could have been anticipated nor planned.

Seen in its entirety, the considerable cultural significance of Atget's body of work rests not merely upon the scope and thoroughness of its documentation, but upon the photographer's singular ability to envision and construct a complex vision of the city, at once deeply personal and elegiac in its form.

Catalogue of Photographs

This is a complete illustrated catalogue of all the photographs discussed in this publication. In the catalogue entries:

- *Reference numbers* have been assigned to the figure illustrations in chapters 1 through 3 and to each of the photographs included in chapter 4. If the image is also reproduced in the body of the publication, this is indicated by a page number.

- *Titles* are descriptive and have been created by the author. They are indicated in bold and include the numerical abbreviation for the arrondissement in which the site in located in Paris.

- *Date* corresponds to the date Atget exposed his negative.

- *Technique.* All photographs were printed from gelatin silver bromide glass-plate negatives by Atget, and are unmounted albumen silver prints unless otherwise specified.

- *Dimensions* are of the image, the photographic paper, and, where applicable, the original mount. These are given in centimeters with height preceding width.

- *Inscriptions* record all notations in Atget's hand, as well as five stamps. Inscriptions on the verso of unmounted and mounted prints are in pencil; while those on the recto of mounted prints are in black ink, unless otherwise indicated. The five stamps are:

    1) MC stamp: oval blue- or red-ink stamp, *MUSEE/CARNAVALET*
    2) BHVP stamp: circular blue-ink stamp, *BIBLIOTH·DE·LA*

VILLE·DE·PARIS, used by the Bibliothèque historique de la Ville de Paris

3) VP stamp: oval blue- or red-ink stamp, *VILLE/DE/PARIS*, used by the Musée Carnavalet and the Bibliothèque historique de la Ville de Paris

4) BN stamp: oval red stamp, *BN/EST*, used by the Bibliothèque nationale de France

5) Atget stamp: black-ink stamp, *E. ATGET/Rue Campagne-Première 17 bis*

The following abbreviations are used:
u.l. (upper left), u.c. (upper center), u.r. (upper right), c.l. (center left), c. (center), c.r. (center right), l.l. (lower left), l.c. (lower center), l.r. (lower right).

• *Series* refers to Atget's classification system of his negatives into the following series:

AP: *L'Art dans le vieux Paris* (Art in Old Paris);
PP: *Paris pittoresque* (Picturesque Paris);
T: *Topographie du vieux Paris* (Topography of Old Paris).

Atget's negative number follows the series abbreviation.

• *Negative* provides the reference number for Atget's negatives acquired by the French government. In 1920, the state purchased 2,621 negatives (numbers MH37421N–MH40020N), and in 1928 after Atget's death, a further 2,000 negatives were acquired (numbers MH87000N–MH89000N). These negatives are now held by the archives photographiques de la Médiathèque de l'architecture et du patrimoine, and are stored at the Fort de Saint-Cyr. Their public access and use is through the Caisse nationale des monuments historiques et des sites (CNMHS).

• *Collections* provides the institutional abbreviation and the accession number for photographs in the following four collections:

MC: Musée Carnavalet
BHVP: Bibliothèque historique de la Ville de Paris
BN: Bibliothèque nationale de France
APMAP: Archives photographiques de la Médiathèque de l'architecture et du patrimoine

Note: In six instances, because of the poor condition of the original photographs, the catalogue reproductions have been made from Atget's negatives (cat. 7.81, 7.82, 7.85, 7.86, 7.88, and 7.89); however, the catalogue entries describe the prints. In two instances, no surviving prints have been located; in these cases, the reproductions have been made from the negatives and the catalogue entries describe the negatives (cat. 7.90 and 7.91).

Figure Illustrations on pages ii–35

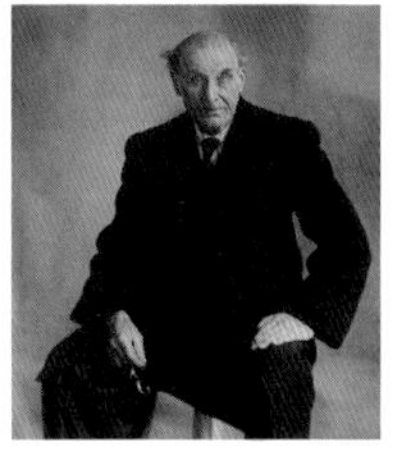

Ill. 1 page ii
Berenice Abbott
Eugène Atget, 1927
Unmounted gelatin silver print
23 x 20 cm (image and sheet)
Inscriptions. Verso: black ink stamp c., *Photograph by Eugène Atget / Copyright: Berenice Abbott / Reproduction rights reserved;* black ink stamp (twice), *PHOTOGRAPH / BY / BERENICE ABBOTT / 50 COMMERCE ST. / NEW YORK 14, N. Y.*
Private collection

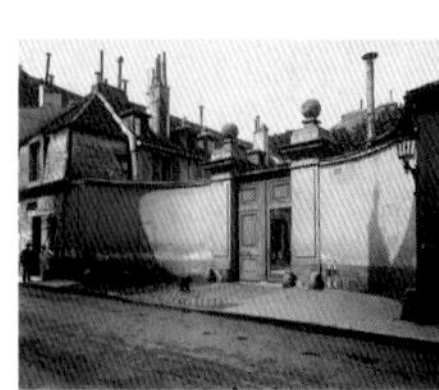

Ill. 2 page 2
Stables, Hôtel de Croy, 6 rue du Regard, 6th, 1902
17.6 x 22 cm (image);
17.7 x 22 cm (sheet)
Inscriptions. Verso: c.l., *Hôtel Rue du Regard 6 / (6e arr);* u.l., *4547*
Series AP 4547 MH38184N
MC Ph 7687

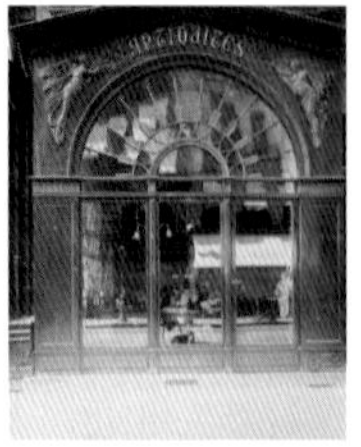

Ill. 3 page 3
Empire-style store, 21 rue Faubourg-Saint-Honoré, 8th, 1902
Albumen silver print mounted on blue-gray board
22.6 x 17.6 cm (image and sheet);
31 x 24 cm (board)
Inscriptions. Recto: l.c., *Boutique Empire 21 F^{b} St Honoré. (1902);* l.r., *Atget.* Verso: u.r., *4556*
Series AP 4556 MH38171N
MC Ph 19546

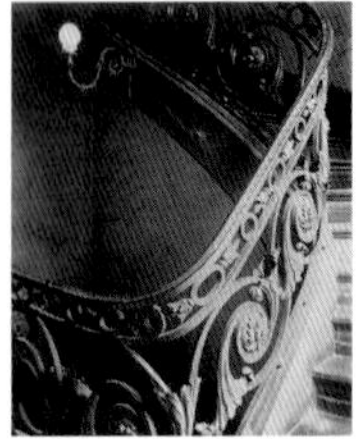

Ill. 4 page 4
Staircase, Hôtel Sully-Charost, 11 rue du Cherche-Midi, 6th, 1904–1905
22.3 x 17.5 cm (image and sheet)
Inscriptions. Verso: u.c., *Hôtel Sully charost Rue / du cherche Midi 11 / 6^{e};* u.r., *4958*
Series AP 4958 MH38914N
MC Ph 7666

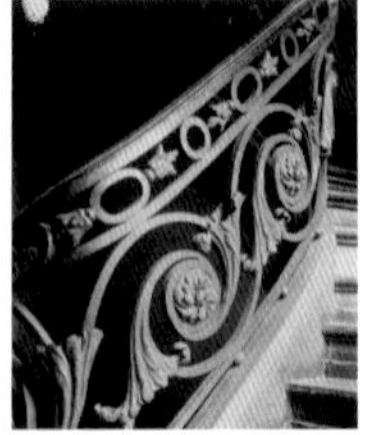

Ill. 5 page 5
Detail of banister, Hôtel Sully-Charost, 11 rue du Cherche-Midi, 6th, 1904–1905
21.8 x 17.4 cm (image and sheet)
Inscriptions. Verso: u.c, *Ancien Hôtel Sully charost / Rue du cherche Midi 11 / 6e;* u.r., *4960*
Series AP 4960 MH38921N
MC Ph 7667

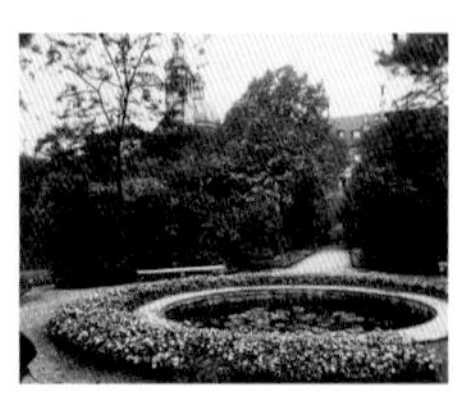

Ill. 6 page 6
Garden of the former convent of the Carmes Déchaux (now the Institut catholique de Paris), 70 rue de Vaugirard, 6th, 1914
17.7 x 22.4 cm (image);
18 x 22.4 cm (sheet)
Inscriptions. Recto: MC stamp l.l on image. Verso: l.l., *(Carmes);* u.r., *1586*
Series T 1586
MC Ph 3755 (page 42 in the album *Vieux Paris, Pittoresque ou Disparu, Parc Delessert)*

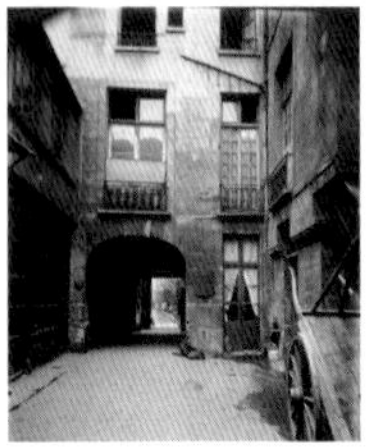

Ill. 13 page 20
Passage des Singes, toward the rue Vieille-du-Temple, 4th, 1911
21.9 x 17.8 cm (image and sheet)
Inscriptions. Verso: u.c., *Entrée du Passage coté / Rue Vieille du Temple / conduisant à la rue des / Guillemites 6 / (4e arr);* u.r., *1092*
Series T 1092 MH38034N
MC Ph 5914

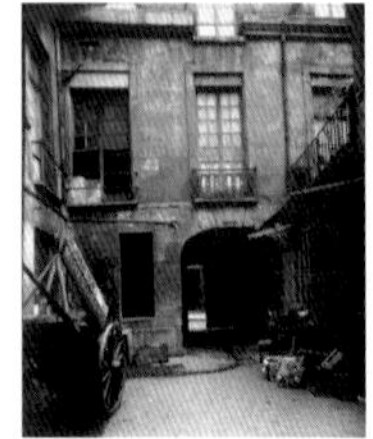

Ill. 14 page 21
Passage des Singes, toward the rue des Guillemites, 4th, 1911
22 x 17.9 cm (image);
22 x 18.1 cm (sheet)
Inscriptions. Verso: u.c., *ancien passage menant / Rue Vieille du Temple / Cote Rue des Guillemites / (4^{e} arr);* u.r., *1089*
Series T 1089
MC Ph 5915

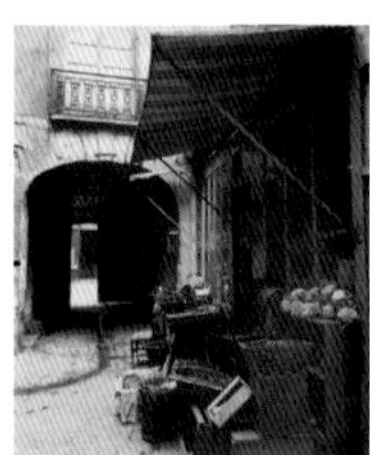

Ill. 15 page 24
Vegetable stand, passage des Singes, 4th, 1911
21.5 x 17.6 cm (image);
21.5 x 17.8 cm (sheet)
Inscriptions. Verso: u.c., *Passage conduisant à la / rue Vieille du temple / 6 Rue des Guillemites / (4e arr);* u.r., *5769*
Series AP 5769
MC Ph 5916

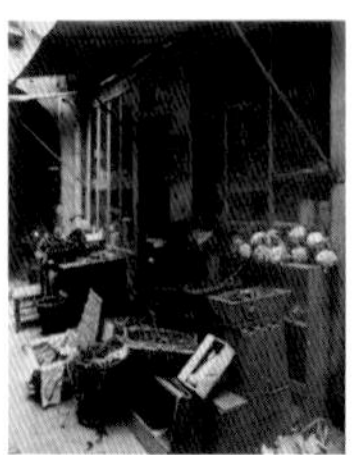

Ill. 16 page 24
Detail of vegetable stand, passage des Singes, 4th, 1911
albumen silver print mounted on blue-gray board
22.6 x 17.5 cm (image and sheet);
23.8 x 29.7 cm (mount)
Inscriptions. Recto: c., *Boutique Pittoresque dans un passage 6 Rue / des Guillemites—1911 (4^{e} arr);* l.l., *Atget;* VP stamp l.l. on print. Verso: u.r., 237
Series PP 237
BHVP XIV, 315

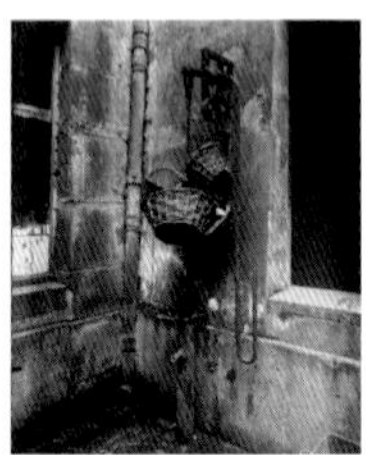

Ill. 17 page 25
Well, passage des Singes, 4th, 1911
22.6 x 17.8 cm (image);
22.6 x 18 cm (sheet)
Inscriptions. Verso: u.c., *Ancienne fontaine du Passage / 6 rue des Guillemites / 1911;* u.r., *1091*
Series T 1091 MH38033N
MC Ph 4038 (page 43 in the album *Vieux Paris Pittoresque et Disparu)*

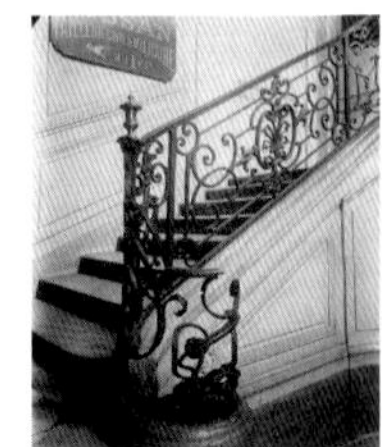

Ill. 18 page 27
Staircase, ground floor, Hôtel Dodun, 21 rue de Richelieu, 1st, 1904–1905
21.9 x 17.5 cm (image);
21.9 x 17.8 cm (sheet)
Inscriptions. Verso: u.c., *Hotel Dodun Rue / Richelieu 21 / (1^{e});* u.r., *4940*
Series AP 4940 MH38934N
MC Ph 5073

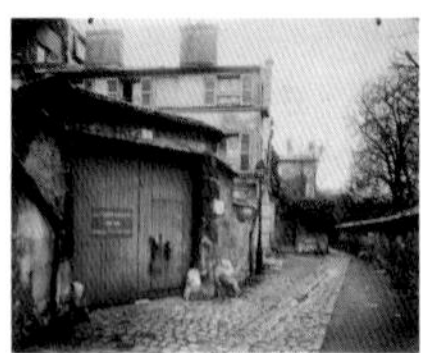

Ill. 25 page 30
Balzac's house, 24 rue Berton, 16th, 1913
17.6 x 21.2 cm (image);
18.1 x 21.2 cm (sheet)
Inscriptions. Verso: l.l., *Maison de Balzac / 24 Rue Berton / 1840–48 (16^{e} arr);* u.l., *1406*
Series T 1406 MH38321N
MC Ph 8440

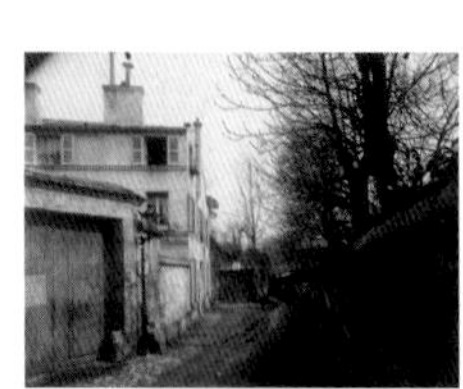

Ill. 26 page 31
Balzac's house, 24 rue Berton, 16th, March 1922
17.6 x 22.3 cm (image);
18 x 22.4 cm (sheet)
Inscriptions. Verso: u.l., *6318*
Series AP 6318
MC Ph 4601 (Page 32 in the album *Vieux Paris, Coins Pittoresque, Vieux Montmartre)*

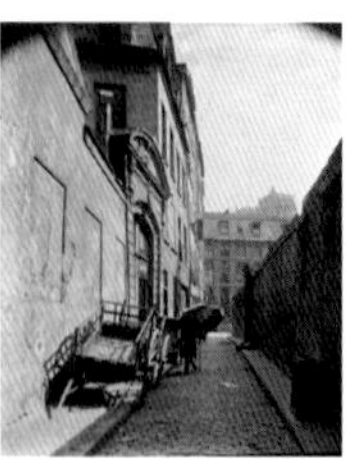

Ill. 27 page 32
Rue Saint-Julien-le-Pauvre, toward the rue de la Bûcherie and the former annex of the Hôtel-Dieu, 5th, August 1899
21.7 x 17.6 cm (image);
21.8 x 17.7 cm (sheet)
Inscriptions. Verso: u.c., *R St Julien le Pauvre;* u.r., *3685 / 3685*
Series AP3685 MH38220N
MC Ph 6897

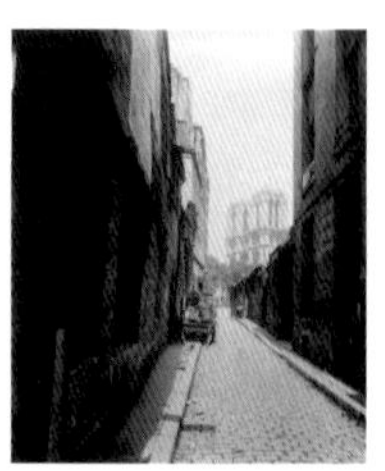

Ill. 28 page 33
Rue Saint-Julien-le-Pauvre, toward the quai de Montebello and Notre-Dame, 5th, 1912
21.9 x 17.7 cm (image);
21.9 x 18 cm (sheet)
Inscriptions. Verso: u.c., *Rue St Julien le Pauvre / de la rue Galande / 5^{e} arr);* u.r., *1362*
Series T 1362 MH38037
MC Ph 6905

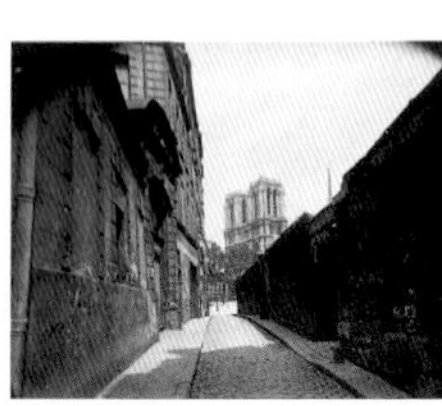

Ill. 29 page 16
Rue Saint-Julien-le-Pauvre, toward the quai de Montebello and Notre-Dame, 5th, June 1923
17.2 x 22.4 cm (image);
17.7 x 22.5 cm (sheet)
Inscriptions. Verso: c.l., *Rue S^{t} tJulien le Pauvre;* u.l., *6448;* Atget stamp c.r.; beside stamp r., *17 bis.*
Series AP 6448 MH87007N
MC Ph 3836 (page 11 in the album *Vieux Paris, Coins Pittoresque)*

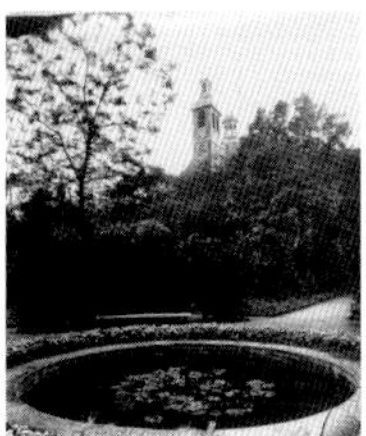

Ill. 7 page 7
Garden of the former convent of the Carmes Déchaux (now the Institut catholique de Paris), 70 rue de Vaugirard, 6th, 1914
21.5 x 17.7 cm (image);
21.5 x 18.1 cm (sheet)
Inscriptions. Recto: MC stamp l.r. on image. Verso: u.c., *(Carmes)*; u.r., *1587*
Series T 1587
MC Ph 3756 (page 43 in the album *Vieux Paris, Pittoresque ou Disparu, Parc Delessert*)

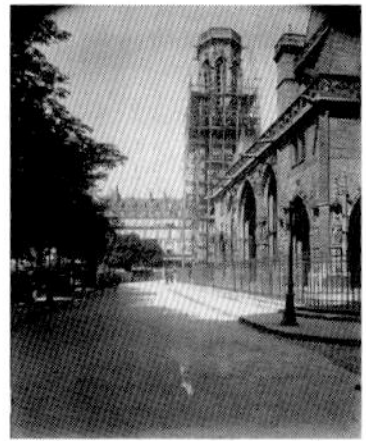

Ill. 8 page 18
Place du Louvre and the Church of Saint-Germain-l'Auxerrois, 1st, 1902
22.1 x 17.8 cm (image and sheet)
Inscriptions. Verso: u.c., *La Place du Louvre et St Germain L'auxerrois / 1^e arr.*; u.r., *4506*
Series AP 4506
MC Ph 5213

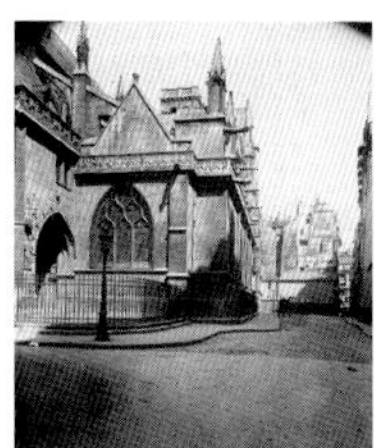

Ill. 9 page 18
Rue des Prêtres-Saint-Germain-l'Auxerrois, from place du Louvre, 1st, 1902
21.9 x 17.5 cm (image);
21.9 x 17.7 cm (sheet)
Inscriptions. Verso: u.c., *Rue des Pretres St Germain / L'auxerrois / 1^e arr.*; u.r., *4507*
Series AP 4507
MC Ph 5214

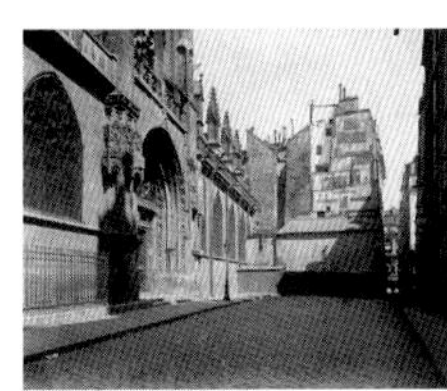

Ill. 10 page 18
Rue des Prêtres-Saint-Germain-l'Auxerrois, 1st, 1902
17.5 x 21.3 cm (image);
17.6 x 21.3 cm (sheet)
Inscriptions. Verso: c.l., *Rue des Pretres St Germain / L'auxerrois (1^e arr)*; u.l., *4505*
Series AP 4505 MH38197N
MC Ph 5215

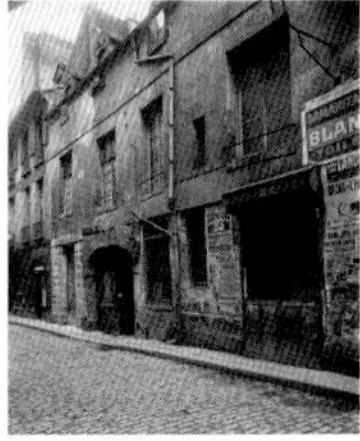

Ill. 11 page 19
6 rue des Guillemites, 4th, 1911
21.8 x 17.7 cm (image);
21.8 x 17.8 cm (sheet)
Inscriptions. Verso: u.c., *Maison et Entrée du / Curieux passage Rue des / Guillemites 6 / (4e arr)*; u.r., *1090*
Series T 1090 MH38032N
MC Ph 5912

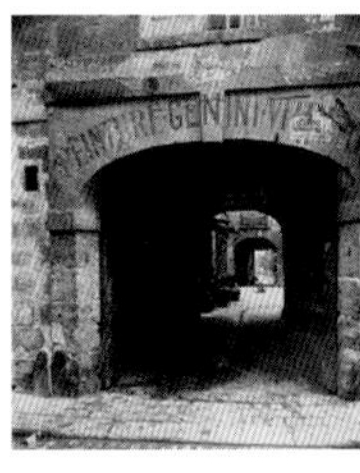

Ill. 12 page 19
Entrance, passage des Singes, 6 rue des Guillemites, 4th, 1911
22 x 17.7 cm (image);
22 x 17.8 cm (sheet)
Inscriptions. Verso: u.c., *Entrée du passage 6 Rue / des Guillemites / (4e arr)*; u.r., *1093*
Series T 1093
MC Ph 5913

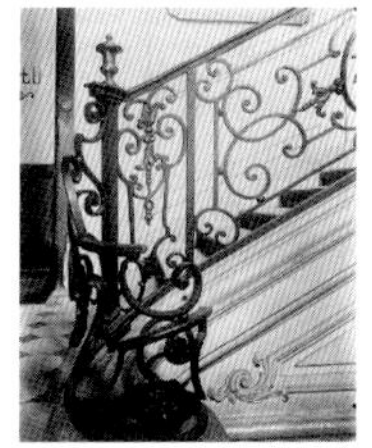

Ill. 19 page 27
Detail of staircase, ground floor, Hôtel Dodun, 21 rue de Richelieu, 1st, 1904–1905
22.2 x 17.5 cm (image);
22.2. x 17.7 cm (sheet)
Inscriptions. Verso: u.c., *Hotel Dodun—Rue/Richelieu 21 / (1^e)*; u.r., *4941*
Series AP 4941
MC Ph 5074

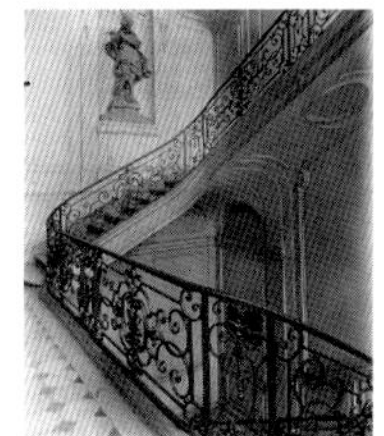

Ill. 20 page 27
Staircase, first-floor landing, Hôtel Dodun, 21 rue de Richelieu, 1st, 1904–1905
22 x 17.5 cm (image);
22 x 17.6 cm. (sheet)
Inscriptions. Verso: u.c., *Hotel Dodun Contrôleur / des Finances / R. Richelieu 21 / (1^e)*; u.r., *4946*
Series AP 4946 MH38920N
MC Ph 5079

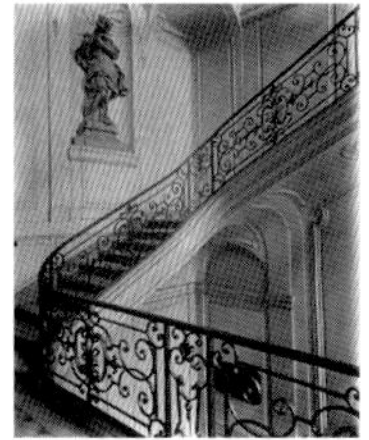

Ill. 21 page 27
Staircase, first-floor landing, Hôtel Dodun, 21 rue de Richelieu, 1st, 1904–1905
21.9 x 17.7 cm (image);
21.9x 17.9 cm (sheet)
Inscriptions. Verso: u.c., *Hotel Dodun—Rue / Richelieu 21—/ (1^e)*; u.r., *4943*
Series AP 4943 MH38936N
MC Ph 5076

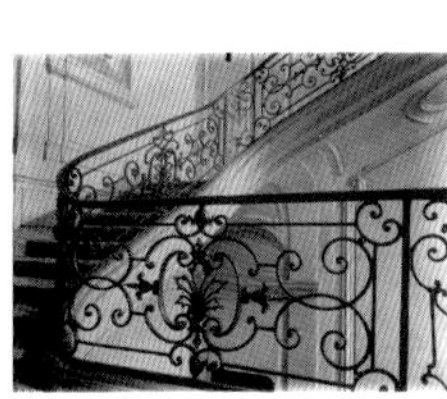

Ill. 22 page 28
Detail of banister, first-floor landing, Hôtel Dodun, 21 rue de Richelieu, 1st, 1904–1905
17.6 x 22.3 cm (image);
17.7 x 22.4 cm (sheet)
Inscriptions. Verso: c.l., *Hotel Dodun—Rue / Richelieu 21 / (1^e)*; u.l., *4942*
Series AP 4942 MH38935N
MC Ph 5075

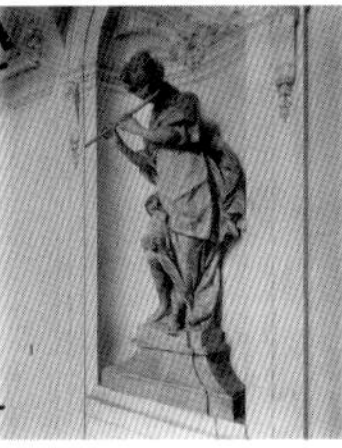

Ill. 23 page 29
Statue in niche between first and second floors, Hôtel Dodun, 21 rue de Richelieu, 1st, 1904–1905
21.9 x 17.6 cm (image);
21.9 x 17.7 cm (sheet)
Inscriptions. Verso: u.c., *Hotel Dodun—R Richelieu / 21—(Statue par Coustou)/ (1^e)*; u.r., *4944*
Series AP 4944 MH87386N
MC Ph 5077

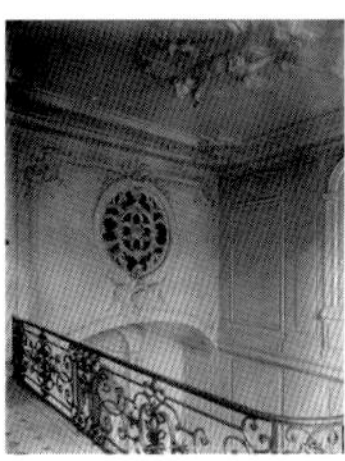

Ill. 24 page 29
Staircase, second-floor landing, Hôtel Dodun, 21 rue de Richelieu, 1st, 1904–1905
22.1 x 17.5 cm (image);
21.1 x 17.6 cm (sheet)
Inscriptions. Verso: u.c., *Hotel Dodun—R /Richelieu 21 / (1e)*; u.r., *4945*
Series AP 4945 MH38937N
MC Ph 5078

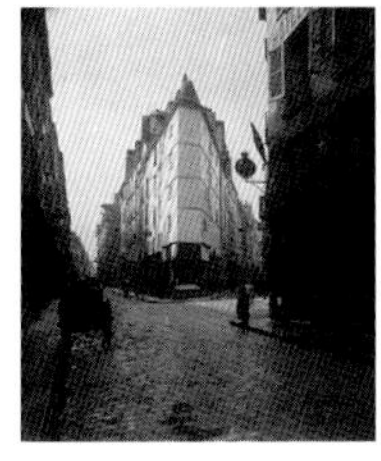

Ill. 30 page 16
Corner of the rue de Seine and the rue de l'Échaudé, 6th, 1905
21.7 x 17.8 (image and sheet)
Inscriptions. Verso: u.c., *coin Rue de Seine et / Echaudé St Germain*; u.r., *5063*
Series AP 5063 MH38851N
MC Ph 3876 (page 1 in the album *Coins du Vieux Paris*)

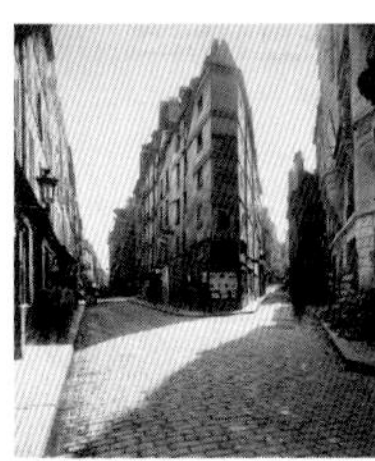

Ill. 31 page 34
Corner of the rue de Seine and the rue de l'Échaudé, 6th, 1910–1911
21.7 x 17.8 cm (image);
21.7 x 18.2 cm (sheet)
Inscriptions. Verso: u.c., *coin Rue de Seine et / Echaudé St Germain; u.r., 5746*
Series AP 5746 MH39641N
MC Ph 3924 (page 49 in the album *Coins du Vieux Paris*)

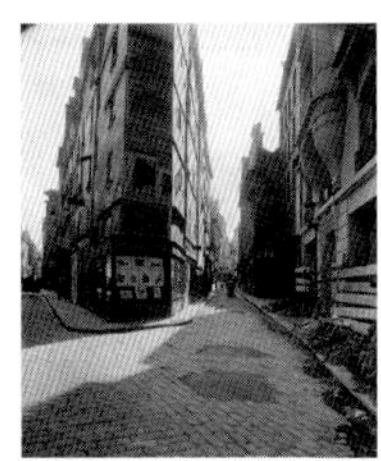

Ill. 32 page 46
Corner of the rue de Seine and the rue de l'Échaudé, 6th, 1910–1911
21.9 x 17.7 cm (image);
21.9 x 17.8 cm (sheet)
Inscriptions. Verso: u.c., *coin Rue de Seine et / Echaudé St Germain*; u.r., *1017*
Series T 1017
MC Ph 7391

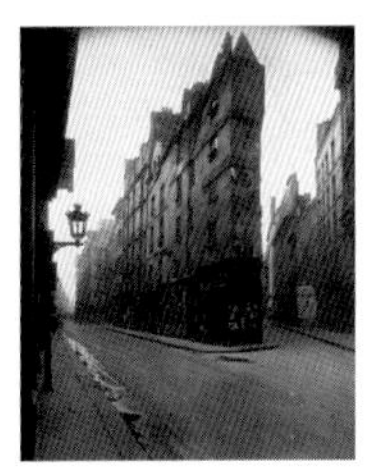

Ill. 33 page 35
Corner of the rue de Seine and the rue de l'Échaudé, 6th, May 1924
Unmounted mat albumen silver print
22.3 x 17.4 cm (image);
22.5 x 17.4 cm (sheet)
Inscriptions. Verso: u.c., *Coin Rue de Seine*; u.r., *6486*; Atget stamp c.; below stamp c., *17 bis*
Series AP 6486
MC Ph 3868 (page 43 in the album *Vieux Paris-Coins Pittoresques*)

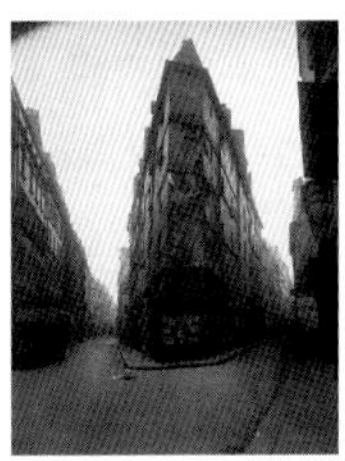

Ill. 34 page 35
Corner of the rue de Seine and the rue de l'Échaudé, 6th, May 1924
Unmounted mat albumen silver print
22.3 x 17.8 cm (image);
22.7 x 17.8 cm (sheet)
Inscriptions. Verso: u.c., *Coin Rue de Seine*; u.r., *6487*; Atget stamp c.; below stamp c., *17 bis*
Series AP 6487
MC Ph 3869 (page 44 in the album *Vieux Paris–Coins Pittoresques*)

1. Hôtel de Beauvais, 68 rue François-Miron, 4th arrondissement, 1900 and 1902

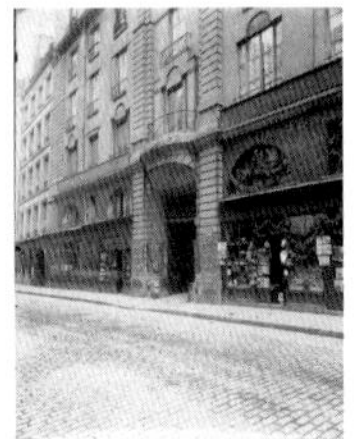

1.1
Entrance facade, August 1900
21.8 x 17.6 cm (image);
21.8 x 17.8 cm (sheet)
Inscriptions. Verso: u.r., *4068*
Series AP 4068 MH37856N
MC Ph 5977

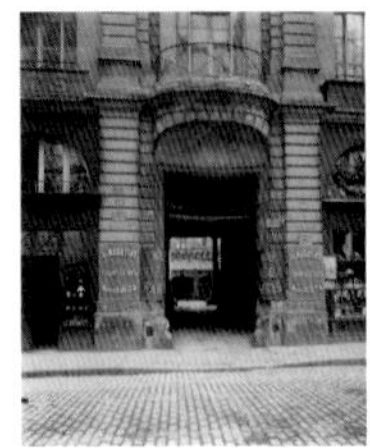

1.2 page 39
Entrance portal, August 1900
21.4 x 17.5 cm (image);
21.4 x 17.8 cm (sheet)
Inscriptions. Verso: u.c., *Hotel de Beauvais—/ Rue François Miron (IVe)*; u.r., *4069*
Series AP 4069 MH37857N
MC Ph 5978

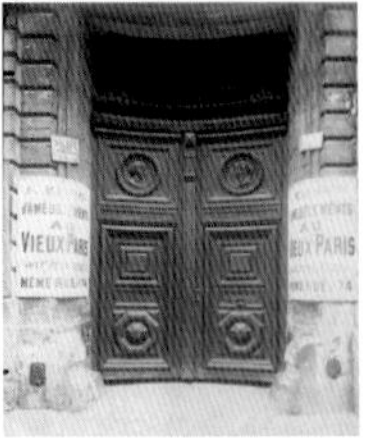

1.3 page 40
Entrance door, 1902
22.1 x 17.6 cm (image);
22.1 x 17.9 cm (sheet)
Inscriptions. Verso: u.c., *Ancien Hotel de Beauvais / 68 Rue François Miron / (4 ^{e} arr)*; u.r., *4521*
Series AP 4521 MH38166N
MC Ph 5979

1.4
Detail of entrance door, 1902
22 x 17.6 cm (image);
22 x 17.8 cm (sheet)
Inscriptions. Verso: u.c., *Ancien Hotel de Beauvais—/ 68 Rue François Miron / (4^{e} arr)*; u.r., *4522*
Series AP 4522 MH38142N
MC Ph 5980

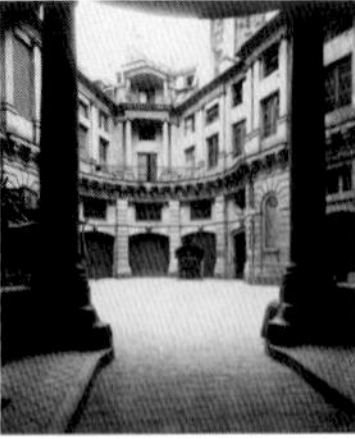

1.5 page 41
View from the entrance portal into courtyard, 1902
21.7 x 17.7 cm (image and sheet)
Inscriptions. Verso: u.c., *Hotel de Beauvais 68 / R François Miron / (4^{e} arr)*; u.r., *4508*
Series AP 4508 MH38200N
MC Ph 5984

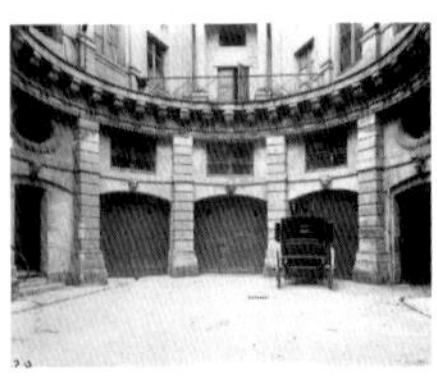

1.6
Coach house at rear of courtyard, 1902
17.6 x 21.9 cm (image);
18.3 x 21.9 cm (sheet)
Inscriptions. Verso: c.l., *Hotel de Beauvais—68 / R. François Miron / (4^{e} arr)*; u.l., *4509*
Series AP 4509 MH88506N
MC Ph 5985

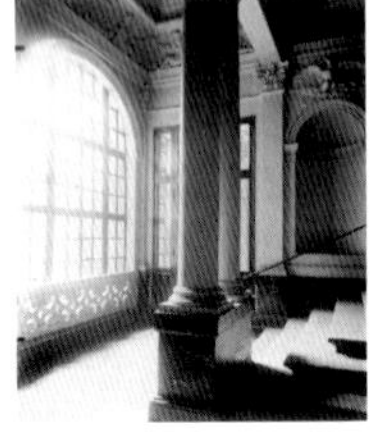

1.13 page 44
Vestibule and grand staircase, 1902
21.9 x 17.7 cm (image);
21.9 x 18.2 cm (sheet)
Inscriptions. Verso: u.c., *Ancien Hotel de Beauvais / 68 Rue François Miron / (4^{e} arr)*; u.r., *4520*
Series AP 4520 MH38141N
MC Ph 5988

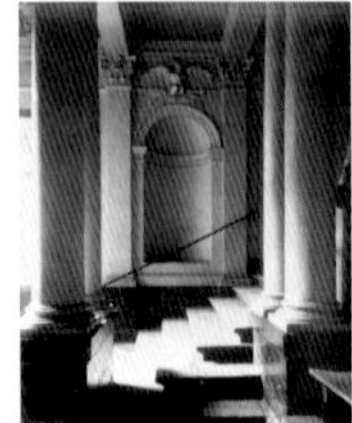

1.14 page 44
Vestibule, grand staircase with niche, 1902
21.8 x 17.7 cm (image and sheet)
Inscriptions. Verso: u.c., *Ancien Hotel de Beauvais / 68 Rue François Miron / (4^{e} arr)*; u.r., *4519*
Series AP 4519 MH38211N
MC Ph 5990

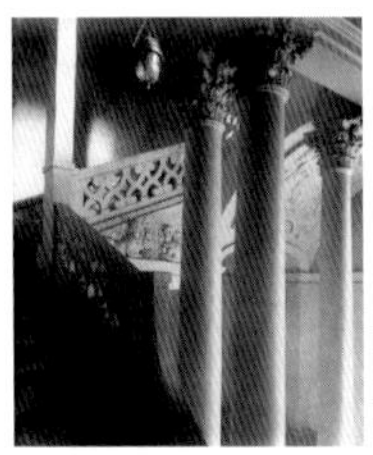

1.15 page 45
Grand staircase, first flight, 1902
21.3 x 17.8 cm (image);
21.3 x 18.1 cm (sheet)
Inscriptions. Verso: u.c., *Ancien Hotel de Beauvais—/ 68 Rue François Miron / (4^{e} arr)*; u.r., *4516*
Series AP 4516 MH38208N
MC Ph 5993

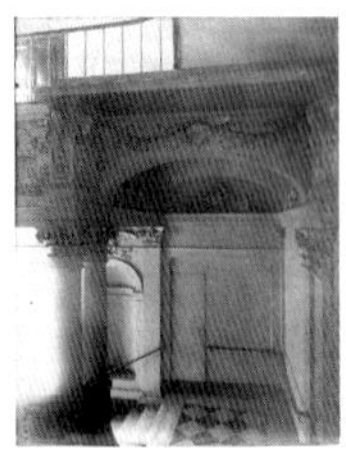

1.16
Sculptural relief at top of grand staircase, 1902
22 x 17.5 cm (image);
22 x 17.8 cm (sheet)
Inscriptions. Verso: u.c., *Ancien Hotel de Beauvais / 68 Rue François Miron / (4^{e} arr)*; u.r., *4517*
Series AP 4517 MH38209N
MC Ph 5991

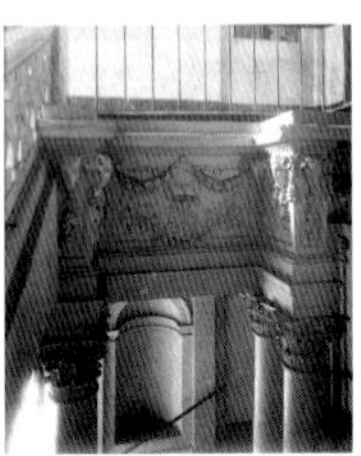

1.17
Sculptural relief at top of grand staircase, 1902
21.6 x 17.7 cm (image);
21.6 x 18.0 cm (sheet)
Inscriptions. Verso: u.c., *Hotel de Beauvais— 68 / Rue François Miron / 4^{e} arr*; u.r., *4518*
Series AP 4518 MH38210N
MC Ph 5992

2. Hôtel de Ranes and the rue Visconti, 6th arrondissement, 1910

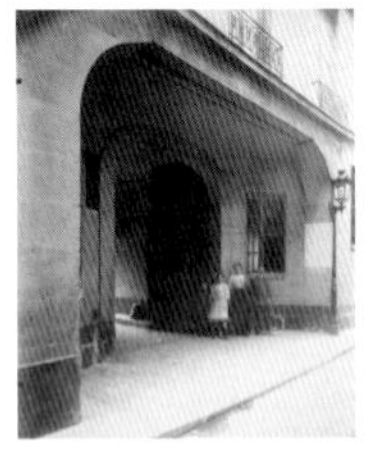

2.1 page 47
Entrance portal, Hôtel de Ranes, 21 rue Visconti
albumen silver print mounted on blue-gray board
22. x 17.5 cm (image and sheet); 29.8 x 23.8 cm (mount)
Inscriptions. Recto: l.c., *Hotel de Ranes 21 Rue Visconti—1910—6^{e} arr*; l.r., *Atget*; VP stamp l.r. on print.
Verso: u.r., [102]5
Series T 1025
BHVP XXIV, 184

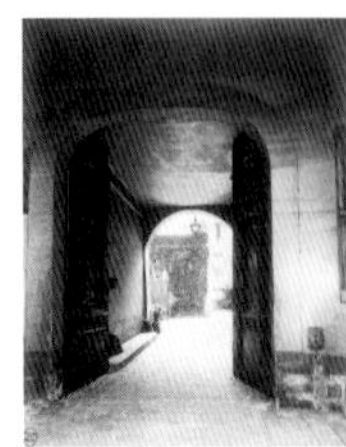

2.2
View from entrance portal into courtyard, Hôtel de Ranes, 21 rue Visconti
albumen silver print mounted on blue-gray board
21.7 x 17.6 cm (image and sheet);
29.9 x 23.8 cm (mount)
Inscriptions. Recto: l.c., *Hotel de Ranes 21 Rue Visconti—1910—6^{e} arr*; l.r., *Atget*; VP stamp l.l. on print.
Verso: u.r., *1028*
Series T 1028 MH39862N
BHVP XXIV, 185

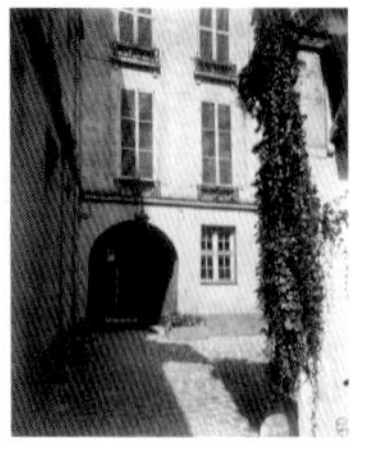

2.3
Courtyard, toward entrance portal and street, Hôtel de Ranes, 21 rue Visconti
albumen silver print mounted on blue-gray board
21.8 x 17.6 cm (image and sheet);
29.9 x 23.8 cm (mount)
Inscriptions. Recto: l.c., *Hotel de Ranes 21 Rue Visconti—1910—6^{e} arr*; l.r., *Atget*; VP stamp l.r. on print.
Verso: u.r., *1027*
Series T 1027 MH39864N
BHVP XXIV, 187

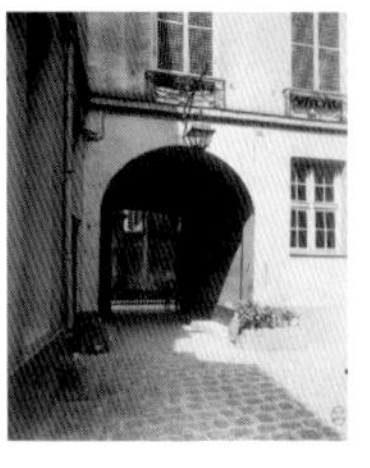

2.4 page 48
Courtyard, toward entrance portal and street, Hôtel de Ranes, 21 rue Visconti
albumen silver print mounted on blue-gray board
21.9 x 17.9 cm (image and sheet);
29.9 x 23.8 cm (mount)
Inscriptions. Recto: l.c., *Hotel de Ranes 21 Rue Visconti—1910—6^{e} arr*; l.r., *Atget*; VP stamp l.r. on print.
Verso: u.r., *1026*
Series T 1026 MH39861N
BHVP XXIV, 186

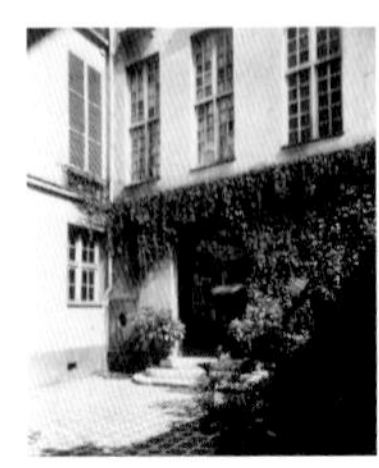

2.5 page 49
Courtyard entrance, Hôtel de Ranes, 21 rue Visconti
albumen silver print mounted on blue-gray board
22 x 16.6 cm (image and sheet);
29.9 x 23.9 cm (mount)
Inscriptions. Recto: l.c., *Hotel de Ranes 21 Rue Visconti—1910—6^{e} arr*; l.r., *Atget*; VP stamp l.l. on print.
Verso: u.r., *5748*
Series AP 5748 MH39643N
BHVP XXIV, 188

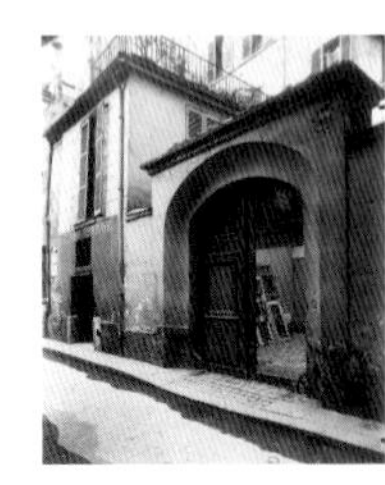

2.6
Hôtel facing the Hôtel de Ranes, 24 rue Visconti
albumen silver print mounted on blue-gray board
22.2 x 17.5 cm (image and sheet);
29.9 x 23.7 cm (mount)
Inscriptions. Recto: l.c., *Hotel de Ranes 21 Rue Visconti—1910—6^{e} arr*; l.r., *Atget*; VP stamp l.r. on print.
Verso: u.r., *1029*
Series T 1029
BHVP XXIV, 163

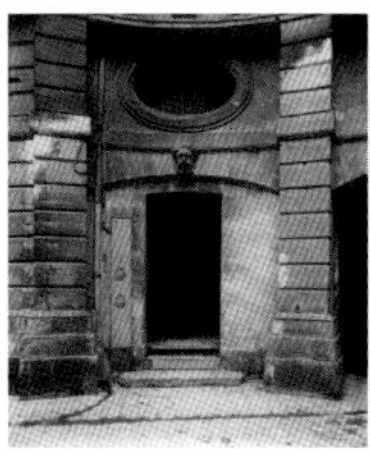

1.7 page 42
Courtyard, entrance to back staircase, 1902
20.9 x 17.6 cm (image);
20.9 x 17.9 cm (sheet)
Inscriptions. Verso: u.c., *Hotel de Beauvais—68 Rue / François Miron / (4^e arr)*; u.r., *4511*
Series AP 4511 MH38203N
MC Ph 5986

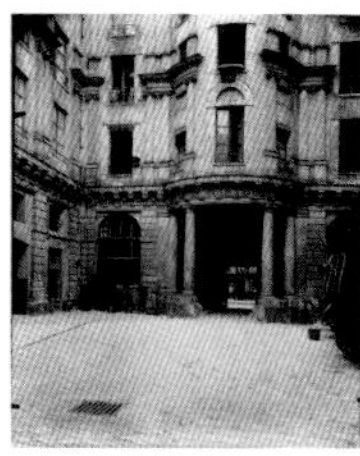

1.8
Courtyard, toward the entrance portal and street, 1902
21.7 x 17.4 cm (image);
21.7 x 17.7 cm (sheet)
Inscriptions. Verso: u.c., *Hotel de Beauvais—68 / Rue François Miron/ (4^e arr)*; u.r., *4510*
Series AP 4510
MC Ph 5981

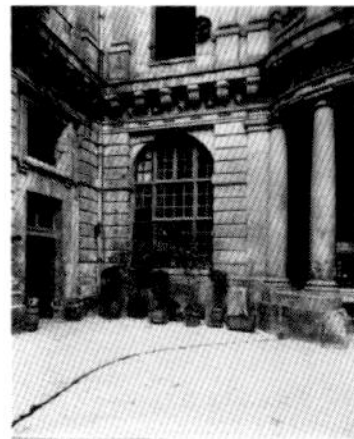

1.9 page 53
Corner of courtyard to the left of entrance portal, 1902
21.3 x 17.5 cm (image);
21.3 x 17.9 cm (sheet)
Inscriptions. Verso: u.c., *Hotel de Beauvais—68 / Rue François Miron (4^e arr)*; u.r., *4512*
Series AP 4512 MH38204N
MC Ph 5983

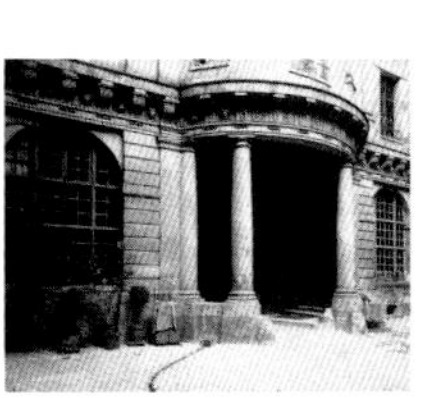

1.10
Entrance portal, courtyard side, 1902
albumen silver print mounted on blue-gray board
17.4 x 21.1 cm (image and sheet);
23.8 x 29.9 cm (mount)
Inscriptions. Recto: below print l.c., *Hotel de Beauvais—68 R. François Miron—4^e arr / 1902*; l.r., *Atget.*; BHVP stamp l.r. on print and mount. Verso: l.r., *4513*
Series AP 4513 MH88507N
BHVP XIV, 52

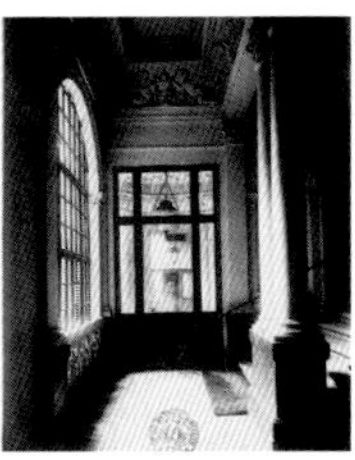

1.11 page 44
Vestibule of the grand staircase, 1902
albumen silver print mounted on blue-gray board
22.4 x 17.1 cm (image and sheet);
29.8 x 23.8 cm (mount)
Inscriptions. Recto: below print l.c., *Hotel de Beauvais—68 Rue François Miron*; l.l., *Atget.*; l.r., *4^e arr*; BHVP stamp l.c. of print. Verso: u.r., *4515*
Series AP 4515 MH38207N
BHVP XIV, 57

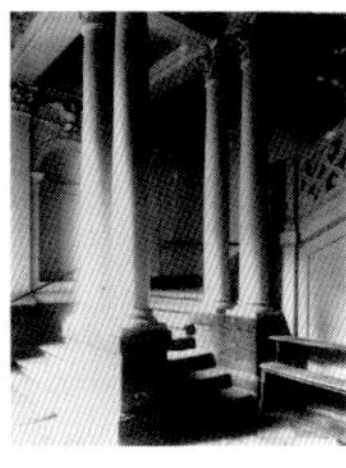

1.12 page 44
Vestibule and grand staircase, 1902
22 x 17.7 cm (image);
22 x 17.9 cm (sheet)
Inscriptions. Verso: u.c., *Ancien Hotel de Beauvais / 68 Rue François Miron / (4^e arr)*; u.r., *4514*
Series AP 4514 MH38206N
MC Ph 5989

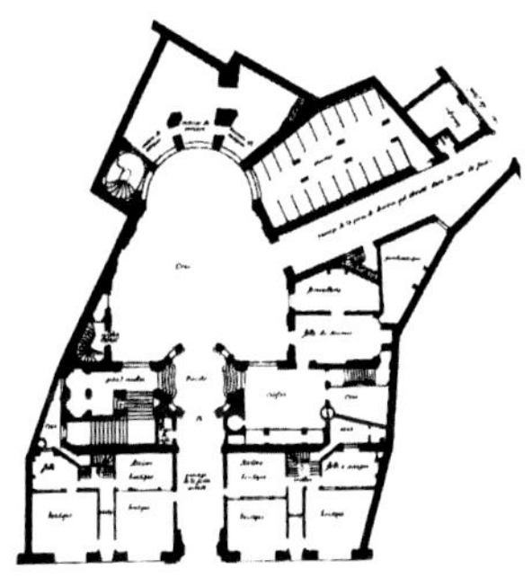

Hôtel de Beauvais, plan of the ground floor

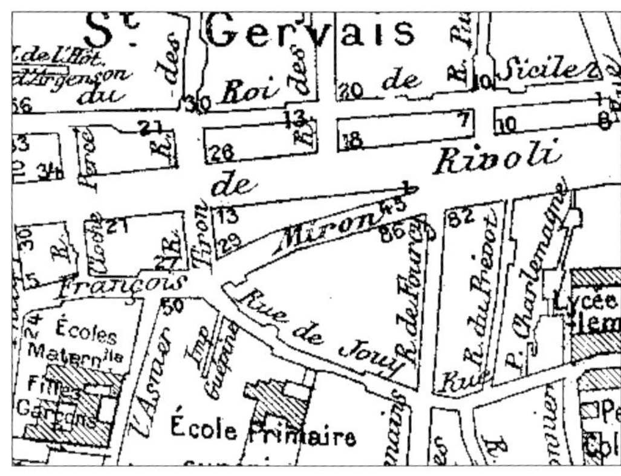

Detail of 1900 map, showing the Hôtel de Beauvais

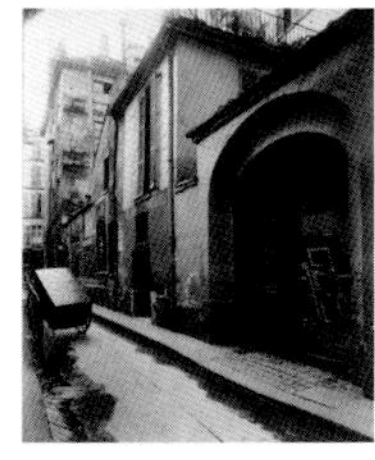

2. page 50
24 rue Visconti and view toward the rue Bonaparte
albumen silver print mounted on blue-gray board
22.6 x 17.5 cm (image and sheet);
29.9 x 23.8 cm (mount)
Inscriptions. Recto: l.c., *Un coin de la rue Visconti au N° 24—6^e arr*; l.r., *Atget*; VP stamp l.r. on print. Verso: u.r., *1030*
Series T 1030
BHVP XXIV, 192

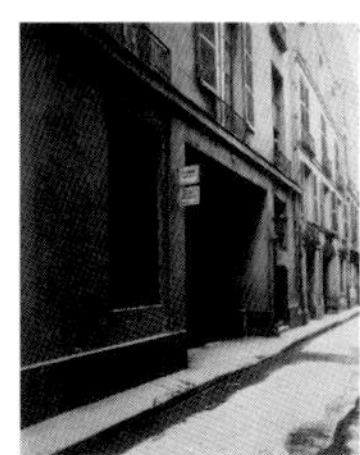

2.8 page 51
22 rue Visconti and view toward the rue de Seine
albumen silver print mounted on blue-gray board
22 x 17.4 cm (image and sheet);
29.9 x 23.7 cm (mount)
Inscriptions. Recto: l.l., *Hotel 22 Rue Visconti—1910—6^e arr*; l.r., *Atget*; VP stamp l.r. on print.
Verso: u.r., *1031*
Series T 1031
BHVP XXIV, 190

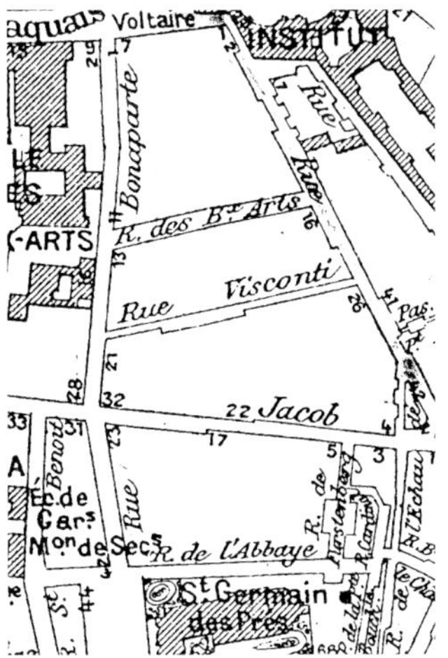

Detail of 1900 map, showing the rue Visconti

3. The rue du Parc-Royal, the rue de Sévigné, and the rue de Jarente, 3rd and 4th arrondissements, 1911

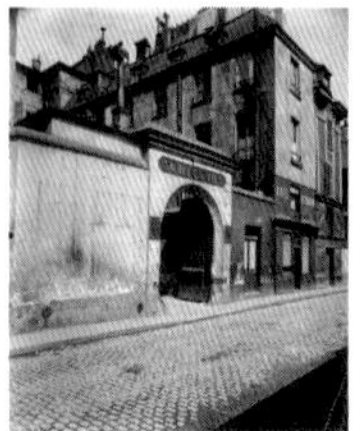

3.1 page 53
Hôtel de Vigny, 10 rue du Parc-Royal, 3rd
21.7 x 17.6 cm (image and sheet)
Inscriptions. Verso: u.c., *Hotel de Vigny 10 Rue / du Parc Royal (3^e arr)*; u.r., *1138*
Series T 1138
MC Ph 5634

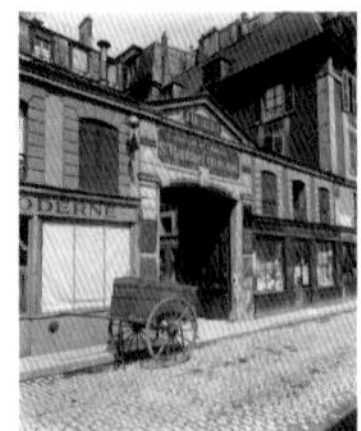

3.2 page 53
Hôtel Graux Marly, 8 rue du Parc-Royal, 3rd
21.7 x 17.7 cm (image and sheet)
Inscriptions. Verso: u.c., *Hotel construit par Graux Marly / 8 Rue du Parc Royal (3^e arr)*; u.r., *1139*
Series T 1139
MC Ph 5633

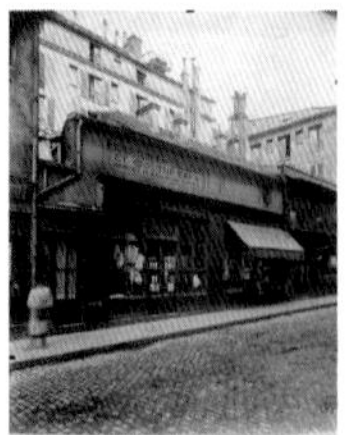

3.3 page 53
Old house and shops, 2 rue du Parc-Royal, 3rd
21.8 x 17.8 cm (image and sheet)
Inscriptions. Verso: u.c., *Vieille maison 2 Rue du / Parc Royal (3e arr)*; u.r., *1143*
Series T 1143
MC Ph 5628

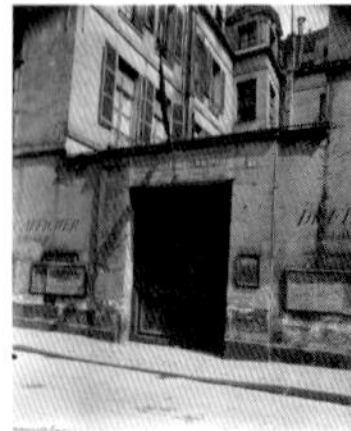

3.4 page 54
Hôtel de Joncquières, 48 rue de Sévigné, 3rd
21.9 x 17.9 cm (image and sheet)
Inscriptions. Verso: u.c., *Hôtel 48 Rue de Sevigné / (3e arr*; u.r., *1140*
Series T 1140
MC Ph 6133

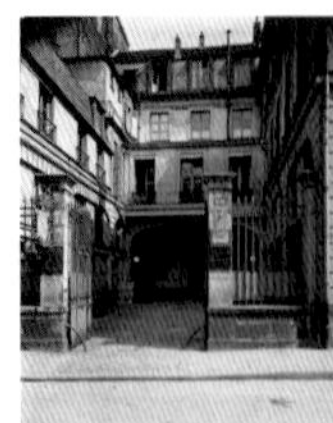

3.5 page 54
Hôtel de Joncquières, 46 rue de Sévigné, 3rd
21.5 x 17.7 cm (image and sheet)
Inscriptions. Verso: u.c., *Hotel 46 Rue de Sevigné / (3e arr)*; u.r., *1141*
Series T 1141
MC Ph 6132

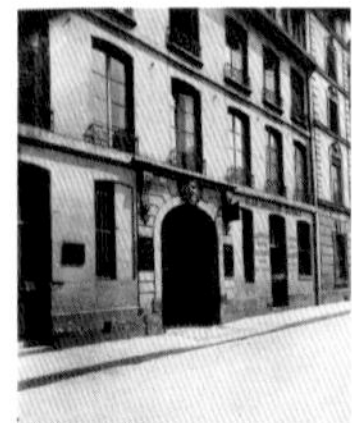

3.6 page 54
Hôtel, 40 rue de Sévigné, 3rd
albumen silver print mounted on blue-gray board
21.5 x 17.7 cm (image and sheet);
29.7 x 23.7 cm (board)
Inscriptions. Recto: below image l.c., *Hôtel ~~49~~ 40 Rue de Sevigné—1911 / (3e arr)*; l.r., *Atget*; VP stamp l.r. on print. Verso; u.r., *1142*
Series T 1142
BHVP XI, 226

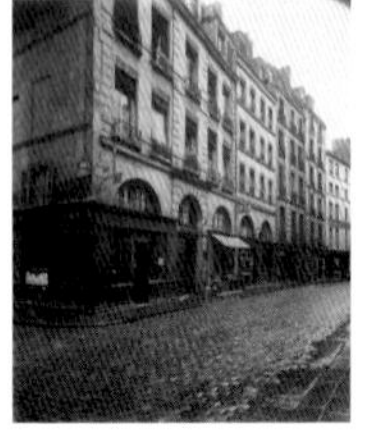

3.13 page 56
Rue de Sévigné, even-numbered side of the street, from the corner of the rue de Jarente toward the rue Saint-Antoine, 4th
21.6 x 17.8 cm (image and sheet)
Inscriptions. Verso: u.c., *Un coin au 12 de la rue / de Sevigné / (4e arr)*; u.r., *1150*
Series T 1150
MC Ph 6137

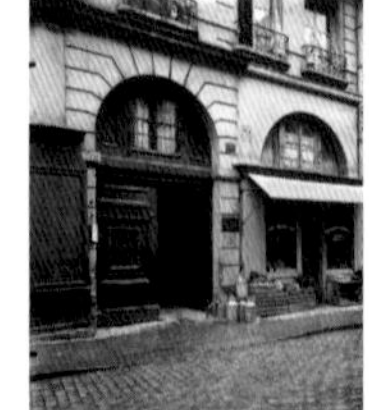

3.14 page 56
Hôtel, 12 rue de Sévigné, 4th
21.7 x 17.6 cm (image);
21.7 x 17.7 cm (sheet)
Inscriptions. Verso: u.c., *Ancien Hotel 12 Rue / de Sévigné / (4e arr)*; u.r., *1151*
Series T 1151
MC Ph 6136

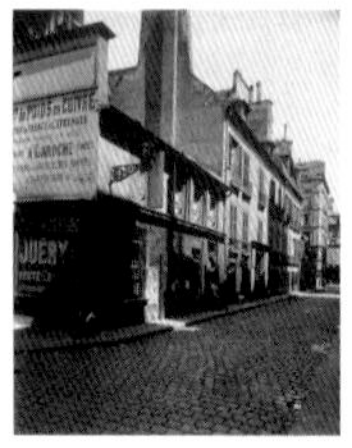

3.15 page 57
Buildings along the north side of the rue de Jarente, toward the rue de Turenne, 4th
21.6 x 17.8 cm (image);
21.6 x 18 cm (sheet)
Inscriptions. Verso: u.c., *Un coin de la rue Jarente / au N° 8 (4^e arr)*; u.r., *1154*
Series T 1154
MC Ph 6146

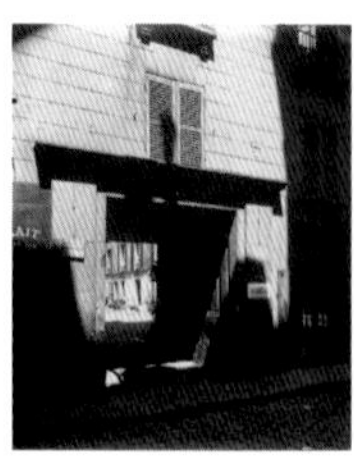

3.16 page 57
Old house, 6 rue de Jarente, 4th
21.8 x 17.6 cm (image and sheet)
Inscriptions. Verso: u.c., *Vieille maison 6 Rue / Jarente (4^e arr)*; u.r., *1155*
Series T 1155
MC Ph 6145

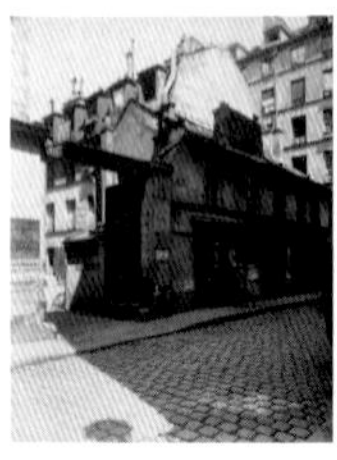

3.17 page 57
4 rue de Jarente, from the rue Caron, 4th
albumen silver print mounted on blue-gray board
22.2 x 17.8 cm (image and sheet);
29.7 x 23.8 cm (board)
Inscriptions. Recto: below print l.c., *Vieille maison 4 Rue Jarente—1911 (4^e arr)*; l.r., *Atget*; VP stamp l.l. on print. Verso: u.r., *1156*
Series T 1156
BHVP XIV, 335

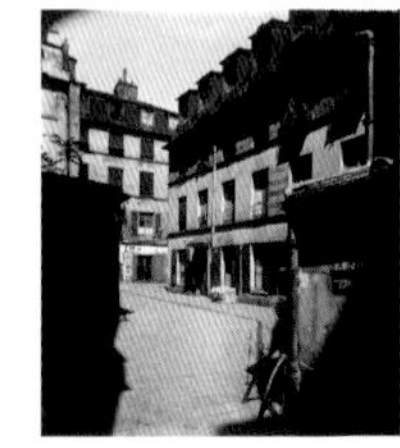

3.18 page 57
Courtyard, 4 rue de Jarente, 4th
21.8 x 17.9 cm (image and sheet)
Inscriptions. Verso: u.c., *La cour du 4 de la rue / Jarente / (4 arr)*; u.r., *1157*
Series T 1157
MC Ph 6144

4. Intersection of the rue de l'Abbaye, the rue Cardinale, the rue de l'Échaudé, the passage de la Petite-Boucherie, and the rue Bourbon-le-Château, 6th arrondissement, 1910

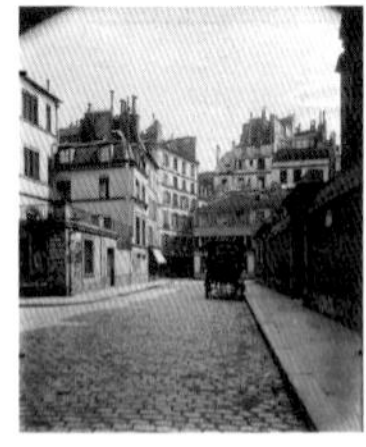

4.1 page 58
Rue de l'Abbaye, toward the passage de la Petite-Boucherie with the intersection of the rue de Furstenberg on the left
21.8 x 17.7 cm (image);
21.8 x 17.9 cm (sheet)
Inscriptions. Verso: u.c., *Coin Rue de L'abbaye et / Passage de la petite Boucherie / 6e*; u.r., *987*
Series T 987
MC Ph 7126

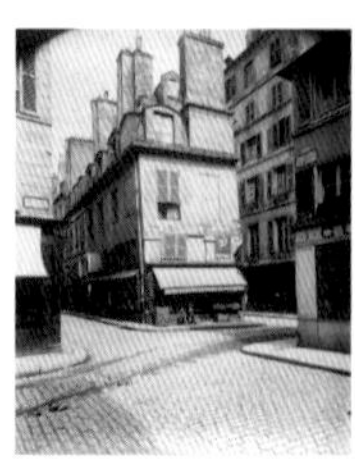

4.2 page 59
Épicerie de l'Abbaye, at the intersection of the rue de l'Abbaye, the rue Cardinale, the rue de l'Échaudé, and the passage de la Petite-Boucherie
21.5 x 17.6 cm (image);
21.5 x 17.8 cm (sheet)
Inscriptions. Verso: u.c., *Vieille maison Coin Rue / Cardinale et abbaye / 6e*; u.r., *992*
Series T 992
MC Ph 7122

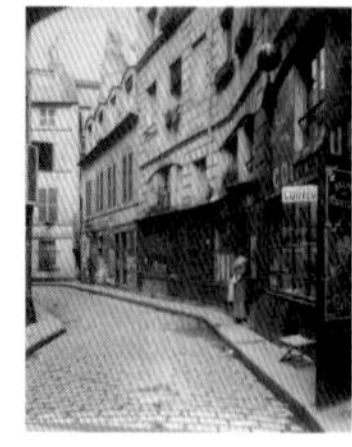

4.3 page 60
Rue Cardinale
22 x 18 cm (image and sheet)
Inscriptions. Verso: u.c., *Vieille maison 5 Rue Cardinale / 6^e*; u.r., *991*
Series T 991
MC Ph 7124

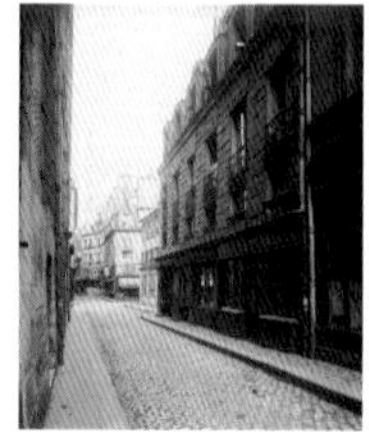

4.4
Passage de la Petite-Boucherie, toward the rue Cardinale
21.8 x 17.7 cm (image);
21.8 x 17.8 cm (sheet)
Inscriptions. Verso: u.c., *Vieille maisons—Boutiques / 1 Passage de la petite Boucherie / 6^e*; u.r., *994*
Series T 994
MC Ph 7127

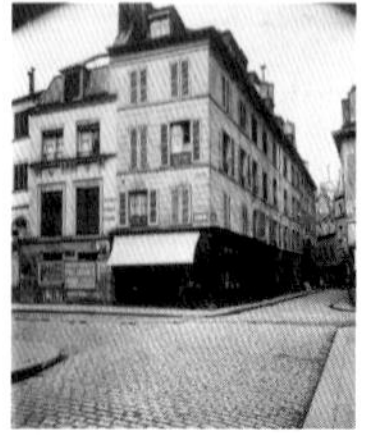

4.5
Passage de la Petite-Boucherie, toward the intersection of the rue de l'Abbaye and rue Cardinale
21.7 x 17.6 cm (image);
21.7 x 17.9 cm (sheet)
Inscriptions. Verso: u.c., *Vieille maison Rue de / L'Abbaye 2 Bis—coin / Rue Cardinale / 6e*; u.r., *993*
Series T 993
MC Ph 7121

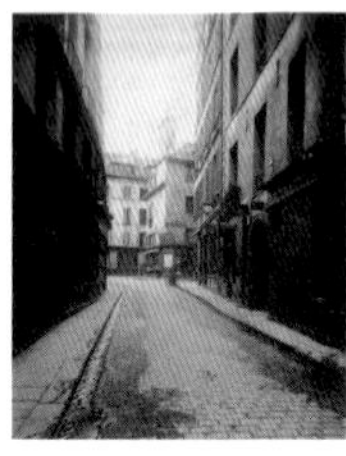

4.6 page 61
Rue Bourbon-le-Château, from the rue de Buci toward the rue de l'Échaudé and the rue Cardinale
21.8 x 17.6 cm (image and sheet)
Inscriptions. Verso: u.c., *Vue prise de la rue de Buci / 6e*; u.r., *1000*
Series T 1000
MC Ph 7120

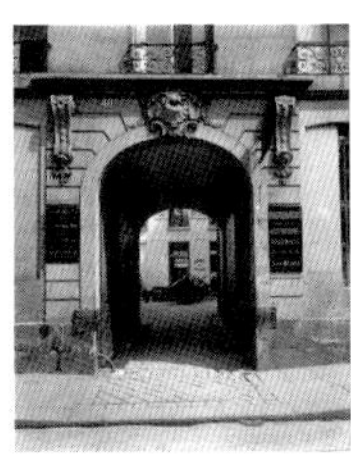

3.7 page 54
Entrance portal, 40 rue de Sévigné, 3rd
21.8 x 17.7 cm (image and sheet)
Inscriptions. Verso: u.c., *40 Rue de Sévigné (Porte) / (3ᵉ arr)*; u.r., *1144*
Series T 1144 MH 39074N
MC Ph 6131

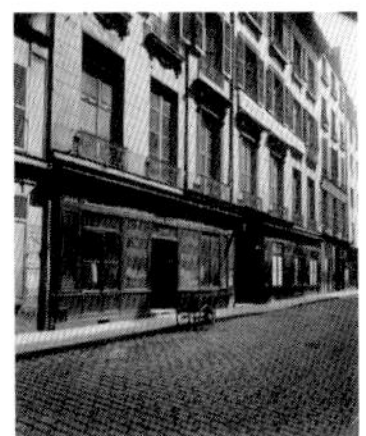

3.8 page 55
22–28 rue de Sévigné, 4th
21.1 x 17.9 cm (image and sheet)
Inscriptions. Verso: u.c., *Ancien Hotel 26 Rue de / Sévigné (4ᵉ arr)*; u.r., *1145*
Series T 1145
MC Ph 6139

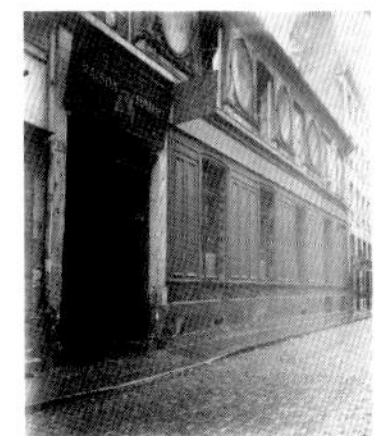

3.9
Hôtel, 13 rue de Sévigné, 4th
albumen silver print mounted on blue-gray board
22.8 x 17.6 cm (image and sheet);
29.7 x 23.8 cm (board)
Inscriptions. Recto: below print l.c., ~~*Hôtel de Chavigny*~~ *13 Rue de Sevigné / 1911 (4ᵉ arr)*; l.r., *Atget*; VP stamp l.r. on print. Verso: u.r., *1148*
Series T 1148
BHVP XIV, 332

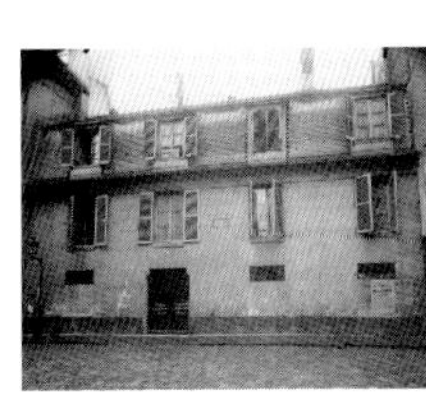

3.10
Hôtel of Nicolas Pinon de Quincy, 9 rue de Sévigné, 4th
17.8 x 22.3 cm (image);
17.9 x 22.3 cm (sheet)
Inscriptions. Verso: c.l., *Hotel de Nicolas Pinon / 9 Rue de Sévigné / (4ᵉ arr)*; u.l., *1149*
Series T 1149
MC Ph 6140

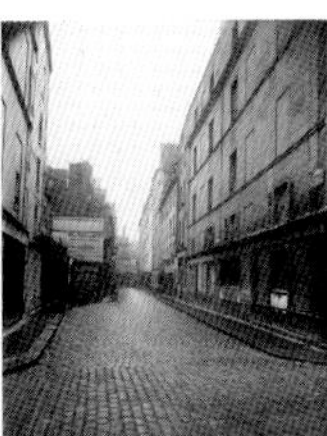

3.11 page 56
Rue de Jarente, from the corner of the rue de Sévigné toward the rue de Turenne, 4th
21.1 x 17.7 cm (image and sheet)
Inscriptions. Verso: u.c., *La rue Jarente de la / rue de Sévigné / (4ᵉ arr)*; u.r., *1153*
Series T 1153
MC Ph 6142

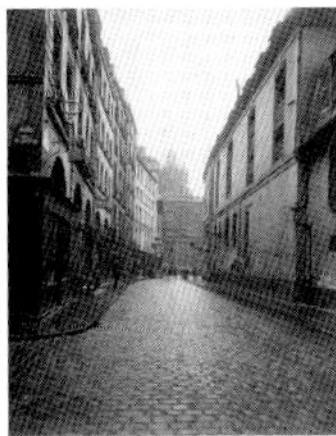

3.12 page 56
Rue de Sévigné, from the corner of the rue de Jarente toward the Church of Saint-Paul-Saint-Louis, 4th
21.1 x 17.7 cm (image and sheet)
Inscriptions. Verso: u.c., *Coin de la rue de Sévigné / du coin de la rue / Jarente / (4ᵉ arr)*; u.r., *1152*
Series T 1152
MC Ph 6141

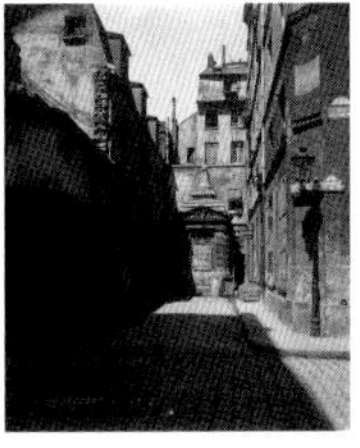

3.19
Impasse de la Poissonnerie, from the rue de Jarente, 4th
21.4 x 18.1 cm (image and sheet)
Inscriptions. Verso: u.c., *Impasse de la Poissonnerie / (4ᵉ arr)*; u.r., *1158*
Series T 1158
MC Ph 6147

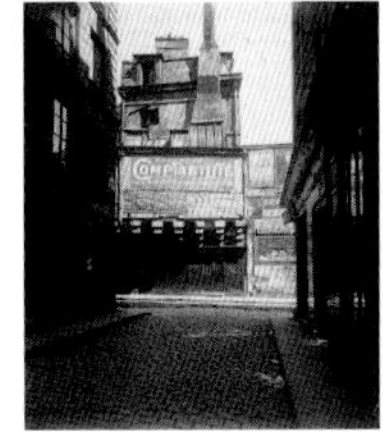

3.20
Corner of the rue de Turenne and the rue de Jarente, 4th
21.6 x 17.9 cm (image and sheet)
Inscriptions. Verso: u.c., *Un coin de la rue de / Turenne de la rue Necker / (4ᵉ arr)*; u.r., *1159*
Series T 1159
MC Ph 6266

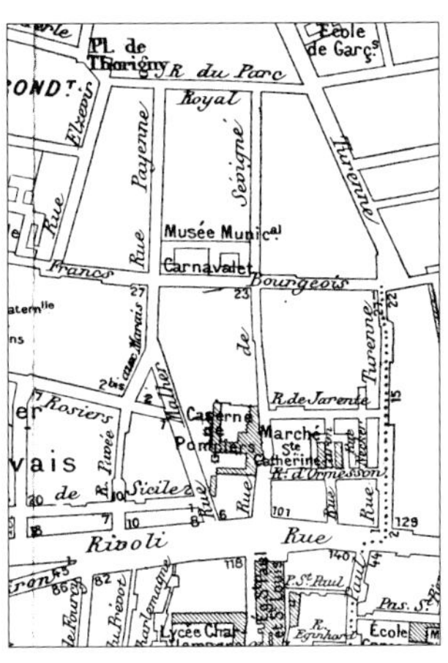

Detail of 1900 map, showing the rue du Parc-Royal, the rue de Sévigné, and the rue de Jarante

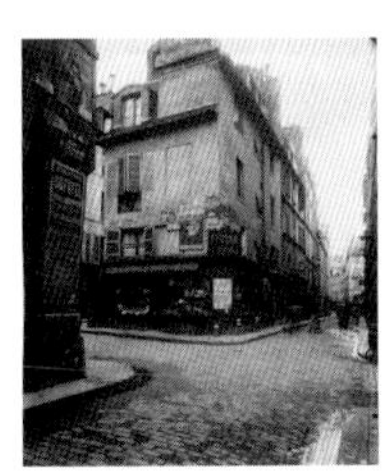

4.7 page 62
Épicerie de l'Abbaye, corner of the rue de l'Abbaye and the rue de l'Échaudé
21.7 x 17.5 cm (image);
21.7 x 17.8 cm (sheet)
Inscriptions. Verso: u.c., *Coin de la rue de L'Echaudé / Sᵗ Germain et abbaye—Vue / prise du 23 de la rue / de L'Echaudé Sᵗ Germain / 6ᵉ*; u.r., *999*
Series T 999
MC Ph 7051

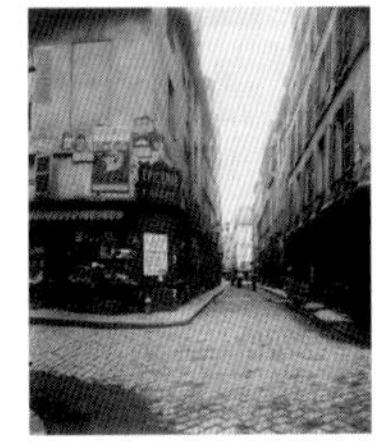

4.8 page 63
Rue de l'Échaudé, from the intersection of the rue de l'Abbaye and the rue Bourbon-le-Château
21.7 x 17.8 cm (image);
21.7 x 18 cm (sheet)
Inscriptions. Verso: u.c., *Rue de L'Echaude Sᵗ Germain / de la rue de L'abbaye 6ᵉ*; u.r., *998*
Series T 998
MC Ph 7052

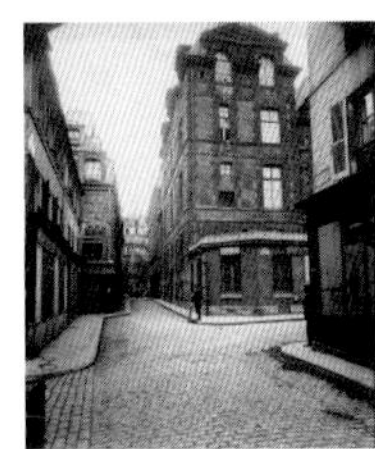

4.9 page 64
Passage de la Petite-Boucherie, from the corner of the rue de l'Abbaye and the rue Cardinale
22.1 x 17.8 cm (image and sheet)
Inscriptions. Verso: u.c., *Coin de la rue de L'abbaye / et de la petite Boucherie / 6ᵉ*; u.r., *1001*
Series T 1001
MC Ph 7125

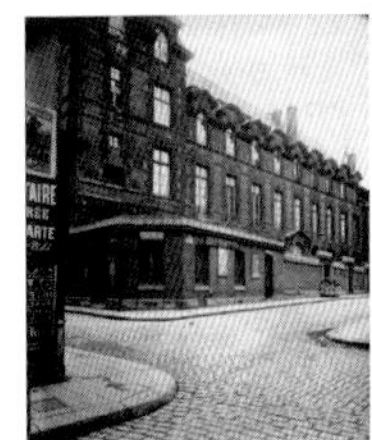

4.10 page 65
Former Abbey Palace of Saint-Germain-des-Prés, 3 rue de l'Abbaye, from the Épicerie de l'Abbaye
21.8 x 17.8 cm (image and sheet)
Inscriptions. Verso: u.c., *Ancien Palais abbatial 3 / Rue de L'abbaye / Vue prise de la rue Bourbon / le château 6ᵉ*; u.r., *1002*
Series T 1002
MC Ph 7119

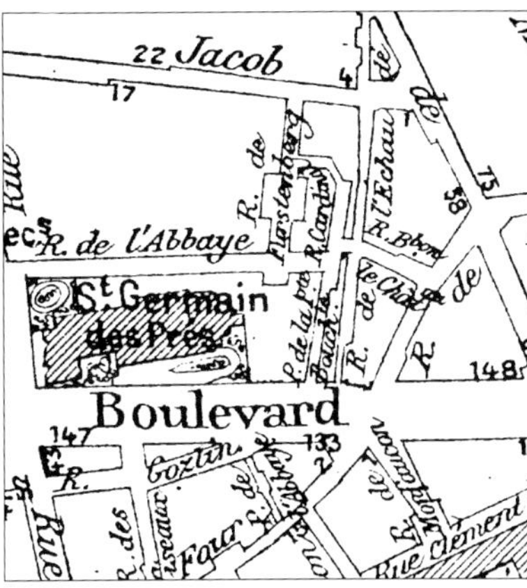

Detail of 1900 map, showing the rue de l'Abbaye, the rue Cardinale, the rue de l'Échaudé, the passage de la Petite-Boucherie, and the rue Bourbon-le-Château

5. The quays surrounding the Pont-Neuf, 1st and 6th arrondissements, 1911

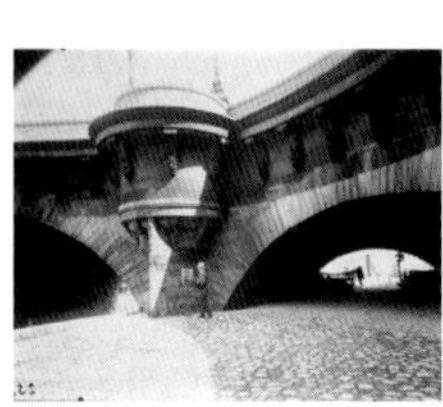

5.1 page 67
Pont-Neuf, from the écluse de la Monnaie, 6th, 1911
17.6 x 22 cm (image); 17.9 x 22 cm (sheet)
Inscriptions. Verso: c.r., *L'Ecluse de la Monnaie / Pont Neuf / (6e arr)*; l.r., *225*
Series PP 255 MH37641N
MC Ph 6967

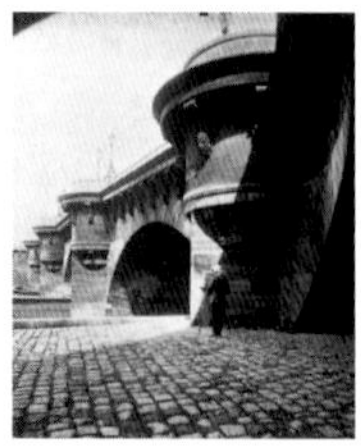

5.2 page 68
Pont-Neuf, from the écluse de la Monnaie, 6th, 1911
21.6 x 17.7 cm (image);
21.6 x 18.1 cm (sheet)
Inscriptions. Verso: u.c., *L'Ecluse de la Monnaie— / Pont Neuf (6e arr)*; u.r., *256*
Series PP 256 MH37642N
MC Ph 6968

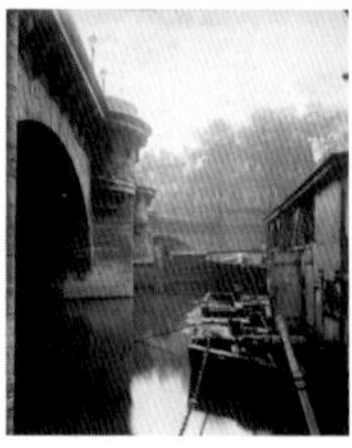

5.3 page 69
Pont-Neuf, from the banks of the Vert-Galant, south side, toward the quai de Conti, 1st, 1911
22.2 x 17.5 cm (image and sheet)
Inscriptions. Verso: u.c., *Pont Neuf / (1^e arr)*; u.r., *266*
Series PP 266 MH87093N
MC Ph 5353

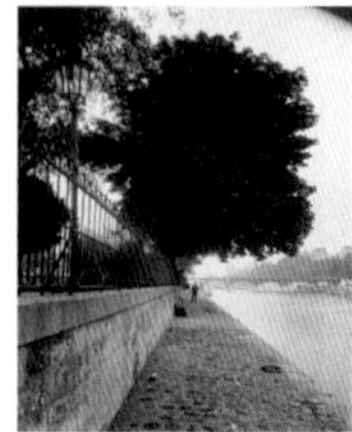

5.4 page 70
Banks of the Vert-Galant, north side, toward the pont des Arts, 1st, 1911
21.9 x 17.8 cm (image and sheet)
Inscriptions. Verso: u.c., *Terre plein du Pont / Neuf / (1^e arr)*; u.r., *273*
Series PP 273
MC Ph 5363

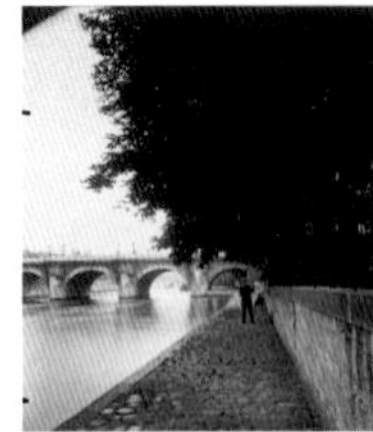

5.5 page 71
Banks of the Vert-Galant, north side, toward the Pont-Neuf, 1st, 1911
21.7 x 17.7 cm (image);
21.7 x 18 cm (sheet)
Inscriptions. Verso: u.c., *Terre plein du Pont / Neuf / (1^e arr)*; u.r., *274*
Series PP 274
MC Ph 5362

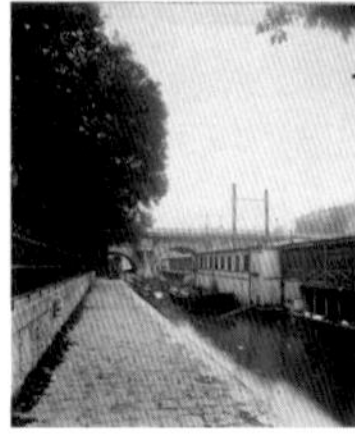

5.6 page 72
Banks of the Vert-Galant, south side, toward the Pont-Neuf, 1st, 1911
21.8 x 17.8 cm (image and sheet)
Inscriptions. Verso: u.c., *Terre plein du Pont Neuf / (1e arr)*; u.r., *275*
Series PP 275 MH37639N
MC Ph 5359

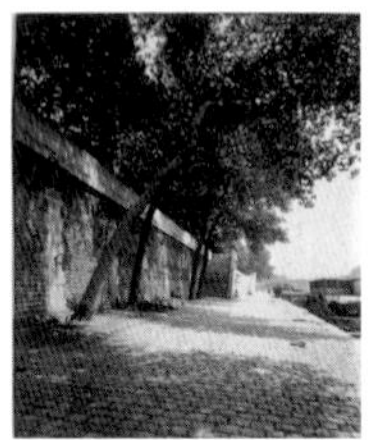

5.13 page 79
Port de la Mégisserie, toward the pont au Change, 1st, 1911
22.1 x 17.7 cm (image);
22.1 x 17.8 cm (sheet)
Inscriptions. Verso: u.c., *Port de la Megisserie / (1e arr)*; u.r., *304*
Series PP 304
MC Ph 5377

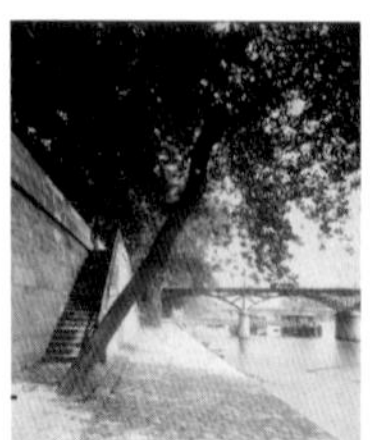

5.14 page 80
Port du Louvre, toward the pont des Arts, 1st, 1911
21.9 x 17.7 cm (image);
21.9 x 17.9 cm (sheet)
Inscriptions: Verso: u.c., *Port du Louvre / (1^e arr)*; u.r., *312*
Series PP 312
MC Ph 5344

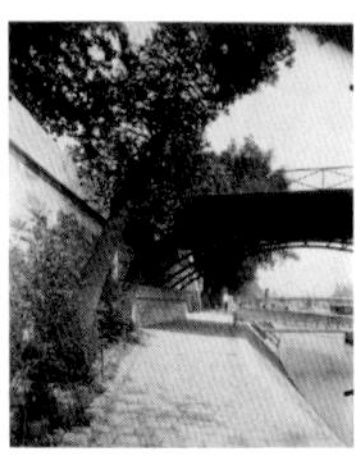

5.15 page 81
Port du Louvre, toward the pont des Arts and the Pont-Neuf, 1st, 1911
21.8 x 17.6 cm (image);
21.8 x 17.8 cm (sheet)
Inscriptions. Verso: u.c., *Port du Louvre / (1^e arr)*; u.r., *309*
Series PP 309 MH37811N
MC Ph 5345

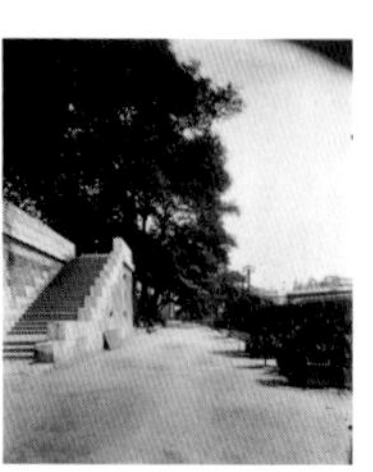

5.16 page 82
Port du Louvre, toward the Pont-Neuf, 1st, 1911
21.7 x 17.4 cm (image);
21.7 x 17.7 cm (sheet)
Inscriptions. Verso: u.c., *Port du Louvre / (1^e arr)*; u.r., *311*
Series PP 311
MC Ph 5346

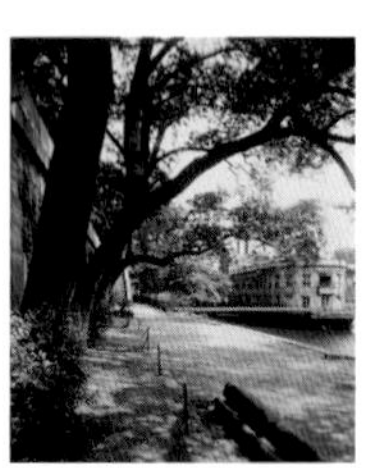

5.17 page 83
Port du Louvre, toward the Pont-Neuf, 1st, 1911
22 x 17.7 cm (image);
22 x 18 cm (sheet)
Inscriptions. Verso: u.c., *Port du Louvre / (1^e arr)*; u.r., *310*
Series PP 310
MC Ph 5348

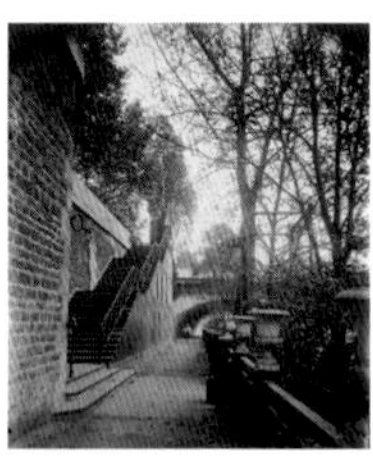

5.18 page 84
Port du Louvre, toward the Pont-Neuf, 1st, 1911
22 x 17.7 cm (image);
22 x 18 cm (sheet)
Inscriptions. Verso: u.c., *Port du Louvre / (1^e arr)*; u.r., *326*
Series PP 326
MC Ph 5349

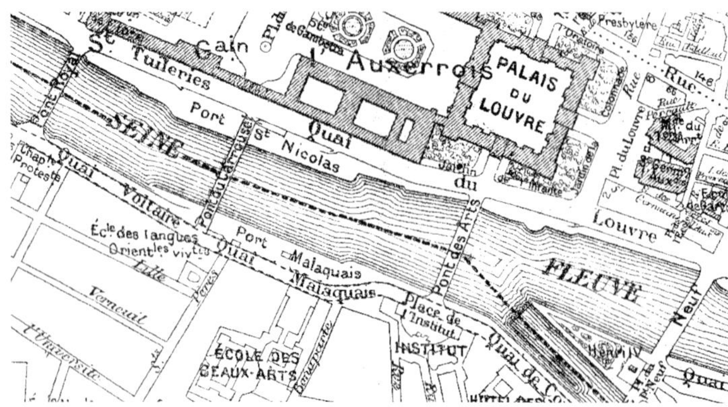

Detail of 1900 map, showing the Pont-Neuf

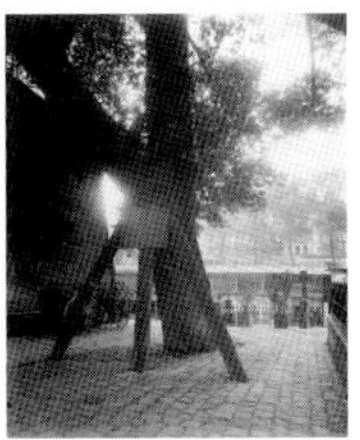

5.7 page 73
Near the entrance of the garden of the Vert-Galant, toward the quai de Conti, 1st, 1911
21.9 x 17.7 cm (image);
21.9 x 18.1 cm (sheet)
Inscriptions. Verso: u.c., *Terre plein du Pont / Neuf / (1e arr)*; u.r., *1146*
Series T 1146
MC Ph 5361

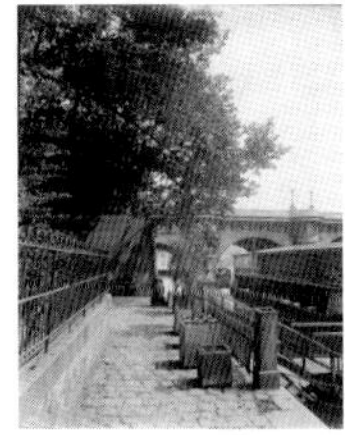

5.8 page 74
Banks of the Vert-Galant, south side, toward the Pont-Neuf, 1st, 1911
22.2 x 17.8 cm (image and sheet)
Inscriptions. Verso: u.c., *Le Pont Neuf—les quais / (1e arr)*; u.r., *280*
Series PP 280 MH37700N
MC Ph 5355

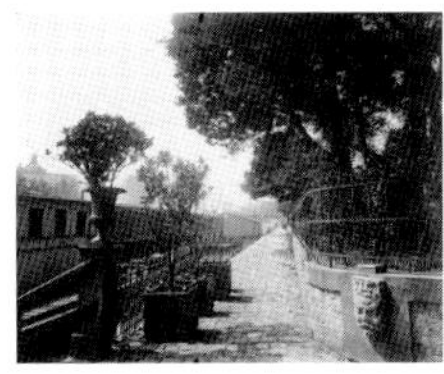

5.9 page 75
Banks of the Vert-Galant, south side, toward the pont des Arts, 1st, 1911
17.8 x 22 cm (image);
17.8 x 22.1 cm (sheet)
Inscriptions. Verso: c.l., *Les quais au Pont / Neuf (1e arr)*; u.l., *281*
Series PP 281 MH37817N
MC Ph 5354

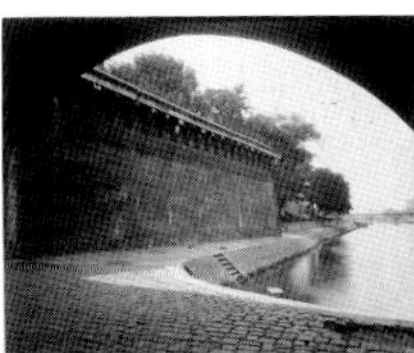

5.10 page 76
Beneath the Pont-Neuf, north side, toward the Vert-Galant and the pont des Arts, 1st, 1911
18.1 x 21.7 cm (image and sheet)
Inscriptions. Verso: c.l., *Vue prise sous le / Pont Neuf / (1e arr)*; u.l., *282*
Series PP 282 MH87086N
MC Ph 5357

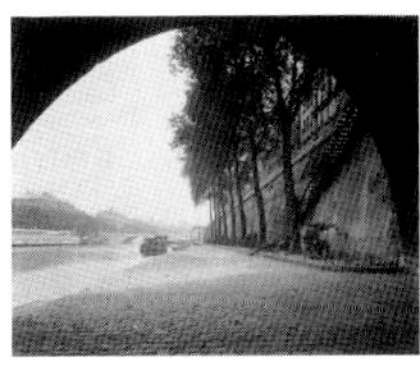

5.11 page 77
Beneath the Pont-Neuf, north side, toward the quai de l'Horloge and the pont au Change, 1st, 1911
17.9 x 22.4 cm (image and sheet)
Inscriptions. Verso: c.l., *Vue prise sous le / Pont Neuf / (1e arr)*; u.l., *283*
Series PP 283 MH37818N
MC Ph 5358

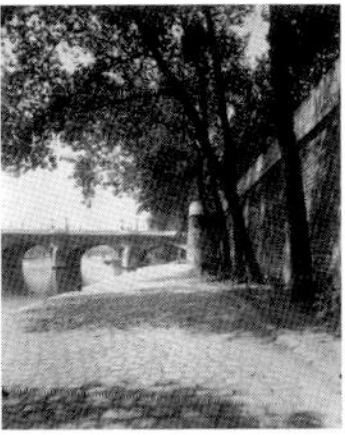

5.12 page 78
Port de la Mégisserie, toward the Pont-Neuf, 1st, 1911
22.4 x 17.7 cm (image);
22.4 x 18 cm (sheet)
Inscriptions. Verso: u.c., *Port de la Megisserie / (1e arr)*; u.r., *303*
Series PP 303 MH87091N
MC Ph 5374

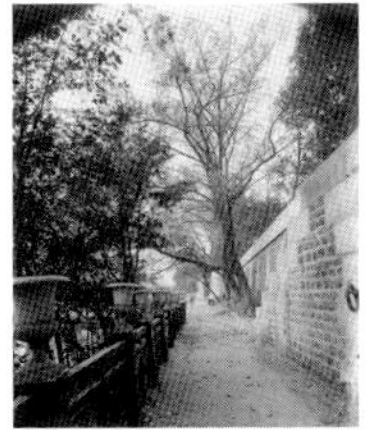

5.19 page 84
Port du Louvre, toward the pont des Arts, 1st, 1911
22 x 17.7 cm (image and sheet)
Inscriptions. Verso: u.c., *Port du Louvre au / Pont Neuf / (1e arr)*; u.r., *327*
Series PP 327
MC Ph 5350

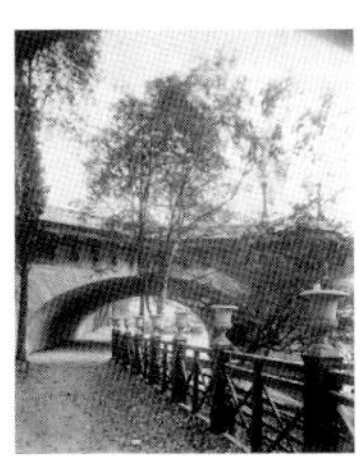

5.20 page 84
Port du Louvre, near the Pont-Neuf, toward the quai de la Mégisserie, 1st, 1911
22.9 x 17.7 cm (image);
22.9 x 17.9 cm (sheet)
Inscriptions. Verso: u.c., *Port du Louvre / Pont Neuf / (1e arr)*; u.r., *325*
Series PP 325 MH87090N
MC Ph 5351

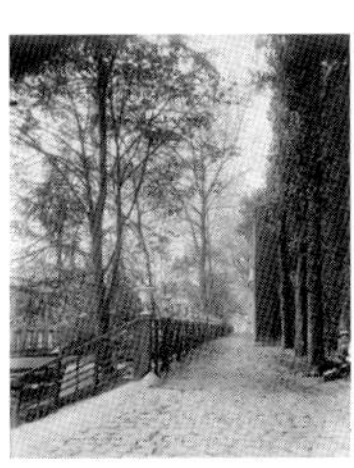

5.21 page 84
Port du Louvre, near the Pont-Neuf, toward the pont des Arts, 1st, 1911
22.3 x 17.7 cm (image);
22.3 x 18.2 cm (sheet)
Inscription. Verso: u.c., *Port du Louvre / (1e arr)*; u.r., *328*
Series PP 328
MC Ph 5347

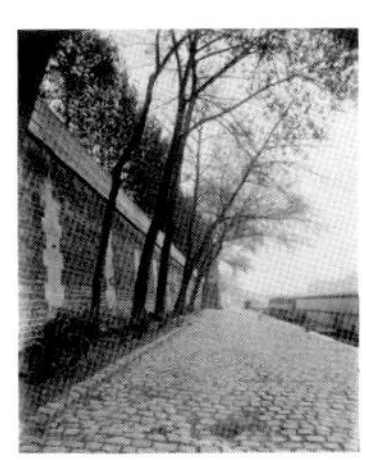

5.22 page 85
Port de la Mégisserie, toward the pont au Change, 1st, 1911
22.5 x 17.6 cm (image);
22.5 x 18 cm (sheet)
Inscriptions. Verso: u.c., *Port de la Megisserie / (1e arr)*; u.r., *329*
Series PP 329 MH37703N
MC Ph 5376

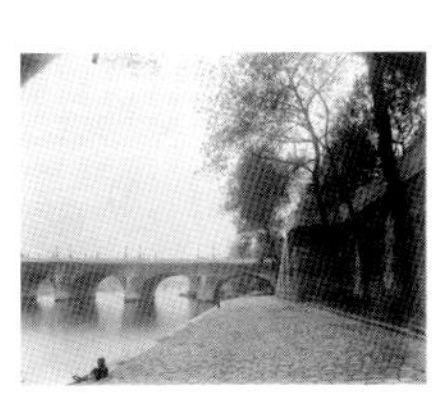

5.23 page 86
Port de la Mégisserie, toward the Pont-Neuf, 1st, 1911
17.7 x 21.8 cm (image);
18 x 21.8 cm (sheet)
Inscriptions. Verso: c.l., *Port de la Megisserie / (1e arr)*; u.l., *331*
Series PP 331 MH87087N
MC Ph 5378

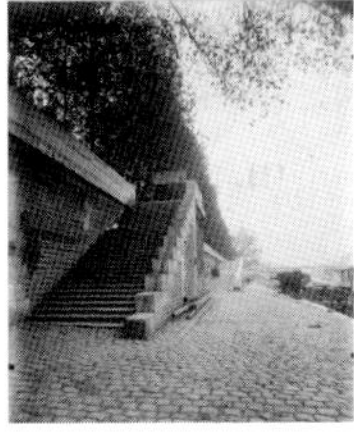

5.24 page 87
Port de la Mégisserie, toward the pont au Change, 1st, 1911
22.1 x 17.7 cm (image);
22.1 x 18 cm (sheet)
Inscriptions. Verso: u.c., *Port de la Megisserie / (1e arr)*; u.r., *330*
Series PP 330
MC Ph 5375

6. Place Bernard Halpern, 5th arrondissement, 1898, 1923, and 1924

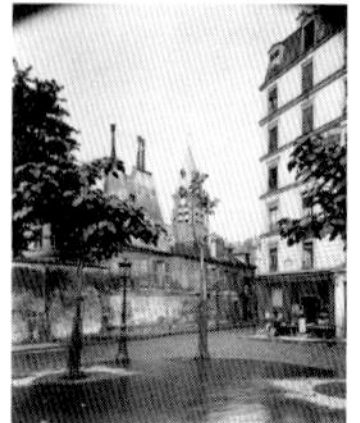

6.1 page 89
Place Bernard Halpern, toward the rue Daubenton and the Church of Saint-Médard, May 1898
21.1 x 17.3 cm (image);
21.4 x 17.3 cm (sheet)
Inscriptions. Verso: u.l., *St Medard*; u.r., *3043*
Series PP 3043 MH38477N
MC Ph 6703

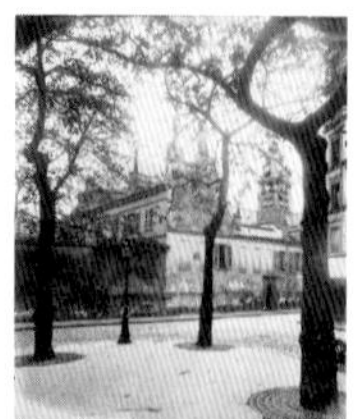

6.2 page 90
Place Bernard Halpern, toward the rue Daubenton and the Church of Saint-Médard, 1923
Unmounted gelatin silver chloride print
22.5 x 17.7 cm (image);
22.9 x 17.9 cm (sheet)
Inscriptions. Verso: u.c., *Coin de la rue / Daubanton*; u.r., *6437*; Atget stamp l.c.
Series AP 6437
MC Ph 3826 (page 1 in the album *Vieux Paris, Coins Pittoresques*)

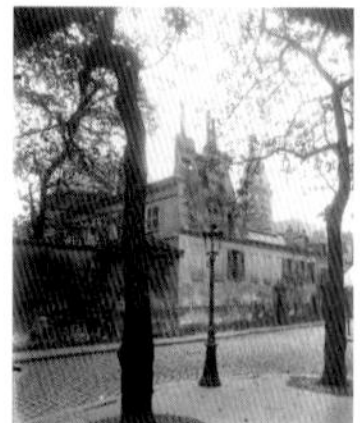

6.3 page 90
Place Bernard Halpern, toward the rue Daubenton and the Church of Saint-Médard, 1923
Unmounted mat albumen silver print
21.8 x 17.6 cm (image);
22.1 x 18.1 cm (sheet)
Inscriptions. Verso: u.c., *Coin Rue Daubanton*; u.r., *6438*
Series AP 6438 MH87316N
MC Ph 3827 (page 2 in the album *Vieux Paris, Coins Pittoresques*)

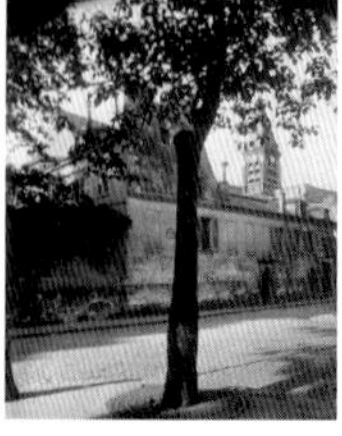

6.4 page 91
Place Bernard Halpern, toward the rue Daubenton and the Church of Saint-Médard, 1924
Unmounted mat albumen silver print
21.9 x 17.5 cm (image);
22.4 x 17.7 cm (sheet)
Inscriptions. Recto: BN stamp l.c. on print; inscribed in ink on print l.r., *A8996*. Verso: u.l., *St Medard*; u.r., *6501*
Series AP 6501 MH87031N
BN T040391

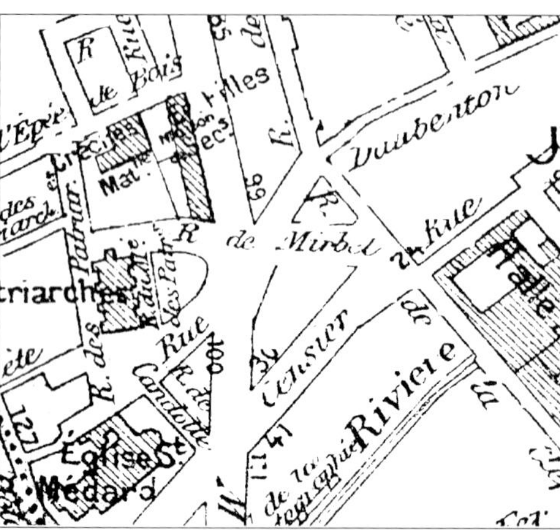

Detail of 1900 map, showing Place Bernard Halpern

7. The Church of Saint-Séverin, 5th arrondissement, 1898–1923

i. Earliest views of the Church of Saint-Séverin and environs, 1898–1903 (7.1–7.20)

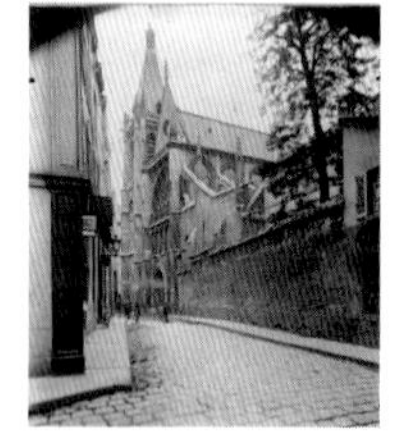

7.1 page 95
Rue des Prêtres-Saint-Séverin, toward the church, 1898
21.8 x 17.5 cm (image);
21.8 x 17.8 cm (sheet)
Inscriptions. Verso: u.l., *St Severin*; in blue pencil u.r., *3037*
Series PP 3037 MH38449N
MC Ph 6828

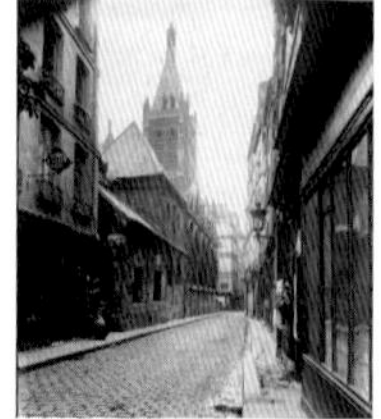

7.2 page 96
Rue Saint-Séverin, from the rue Saint-Jacques toward the church, 1898
21 x 17.5 cm (image);
22.2 x 17.6 cm (sheet)
Inscriptions. Verso: u.l., *Ve*; u.c., *Rue St Séverin*; u.r., *3038*
Series PP 3038 MH38367N
MC Ph 6818

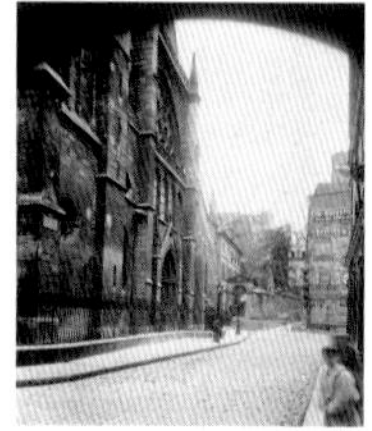

7.3
West front of the church along the rue des Prêtres-Saint-Séverin, 1898
21.7 x 17.5 cm (image);
22.6 x 17.8 cm (sheet)
Inscriptions. Verso: u.l., *St Severin*; u.r., *3040*
Series PP 3040 MH38368N
MC Ph 6829

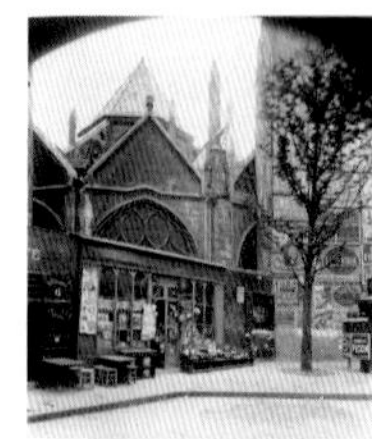

7.4
Shop abutting the apse of the church, rue Saint-Jacques, 1898
21.4 x 17.6 cm (image);
22.2 x 17.8 cm (sheet)
Inscriptions. Verso: u.c., *St Severin*; u.r., *3041*
Series PP 3041
MC Ph 6859

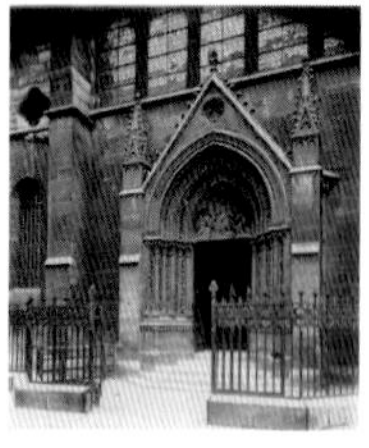

7.5 page 97
Main portal of the church, rue des Prêtres-Saint-Séverin, 1898
21.3 x 17.4 cm (image);
21.7 x 17.4 cm (sheet)
Inscriptions. Verso: u.l., *St Severin*; u.r., *3569*
Series AP 3569
MC Ph 6830

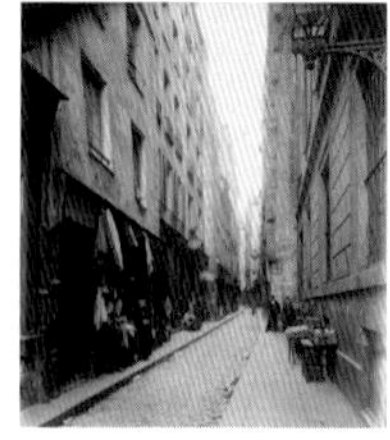

7.6 page 98
Rue de la Parcheminerie, toward the rue Saint-Jacques, May 1899
21.8 x 17.7 cm (image);
21.8 x 17.8 cm (sheet)
Inscriptions. Verso: u.l., *Ve*; u.c., *R de la Parcheminerie*; u.r., *3602*
Series AP 3602
MC Ph 6809

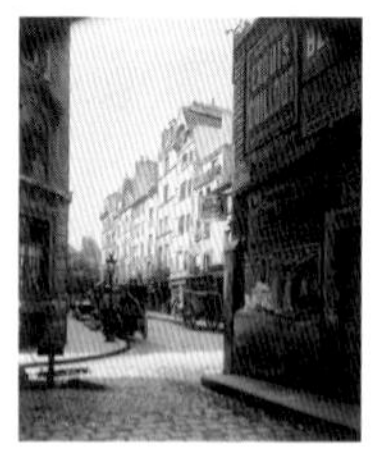

7.13 page 102
Rue des Prêtres-Saint-Séverin, toward the rue Boutebrie and the Musée de Cluny, 1899
21.5 x 17.5 cm (image and sheet)
Inscriptions. Verso: u.c., *R Boutebrie*; u.r., *3684*
Series AP 3684 MH38219N
MC Ph 6814

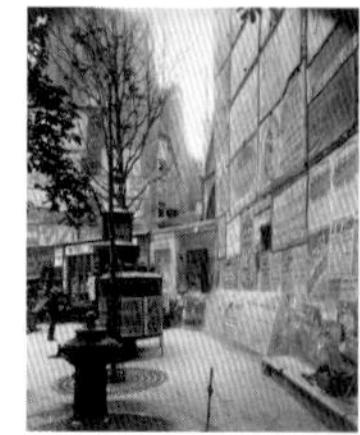

7.14 page 103
Rue Saint-Jacques, walls of the hotel abutting the apse of the church, August 1899
22.5 x 17.8 cm (image);
22.6 x 18.4 cm (sheet)
Inscriptions. Verso: u.c., *St Severin*; u.r., *3689*
Series AP 3689 MH38236N
MC Ph 6858

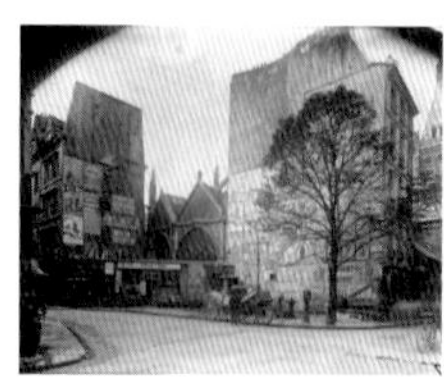

7.15 page 104
Rue Saint-Jacques from the rue Galande toward the church, 1899 or 1900
17.6 x 21.4 cm (image);
17.8 x 22.2 cm (sheet)
Inscriptions. Verso: c.r., *St Severin*; l.r., *3727*
Series AP 3727 MH38225N
MC Ph 6857

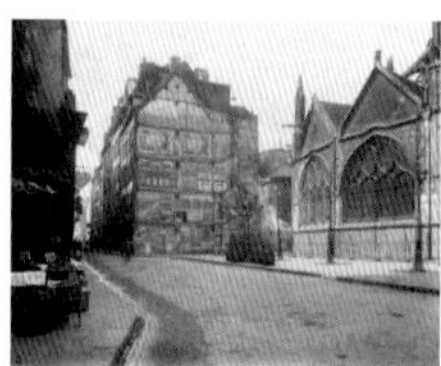

7.16 page 105
Rue Saint-Jacques, after the demolition of the stores abutting the apse of the church, 1902
17.7 x 22 cm (image);
17.8 x 22 cm (sheet)
Inscriptions. Verso: c.l., *St Severin en 1902. Rue / St Jacques—après le / Dégagement de L'Eglise / 5e arr) / (Voir la 1e série)*; u.l., *4529*
Series AP 4529 MH38112N
MC Ph 6862

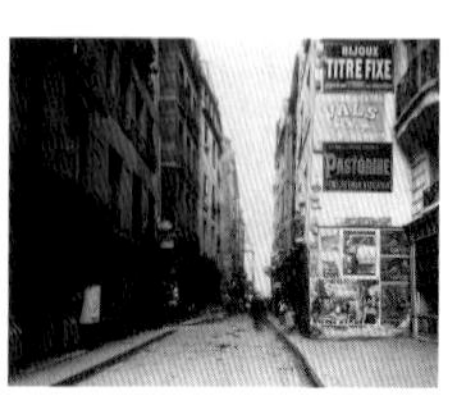

7.17
Rue Saint-Jacques, toward the quays with the intersection of the rue de la Parcheminerie at the left, 1903
17.8 x 21.9 cm (image);
17.9 x 21.9 cm (sheet)
Inscriptions. Verso: c.l., *La Rue St Jacques entre / le Bd St Germain et la / Rue du petit pont / (va disparaitre) / (5e)*; u.l., *4789*
Series AP 4789
MC Ph 6365

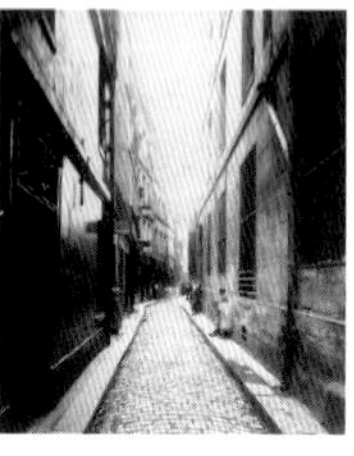

7.18 page 99
Rue de la Parcheminerie, from the rue Saint-Jacques, 1903
22 x 17.4 cm (image and sheet)
Inscriptions. Verso: u.c., *Rue de la Parcheminerie / Vue prise de la St Jacques / (5e)*; u.r., *4790*
Series AP 4790
MC Ph 6812

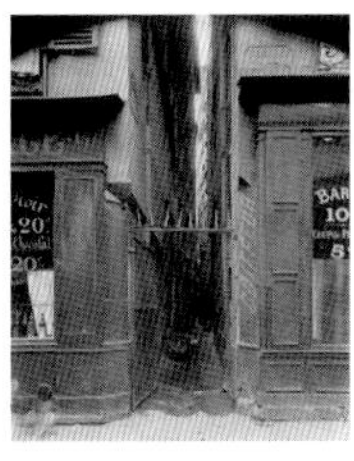

7.7 page 100
Impasse Salembrière, from the rue Saint-Séverin, May 1899
21.6 x 17.7 cm (image);
21.9 x 17.9 cm (sheet)
Inscriptions. Verso: u.l., *V*ᵉ; u.c., *Cul de sac de la Salambière*; u.r., *3603*
Series AP 3603 MH38429N
MC Ph 6863

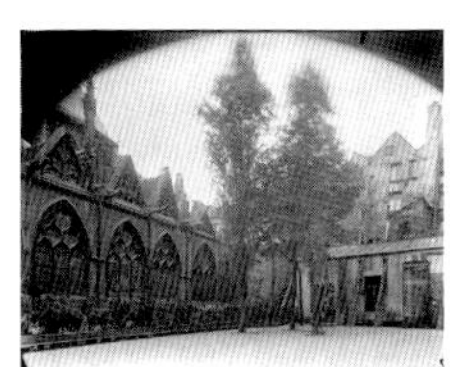

7.8
Presbytery garden, toward the south side of the church, May 1899
17.7 x 22.2 cm (image);
17.8 x 22.2 cm (sheet)
Inscriptions. Verso: l.l., *V*ᵉ; c.l., *S*ᵗ *Séverin*; u.l., *3617*
Series AP 3617 MH38488N
MC Ph 6851

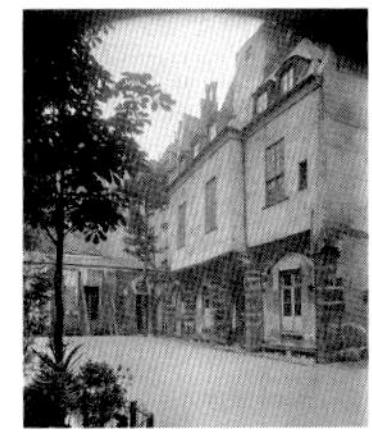

7.9
Presbytery garden, toward the former cloister and charnel house, May 1899
21.1 x 17.6 cm (image);
22.1 x 17.7 cm (sheet)
Inscriptions. Verso: u.r., *3616*
Series AP 3616 MH38488N
MC Ph 6852

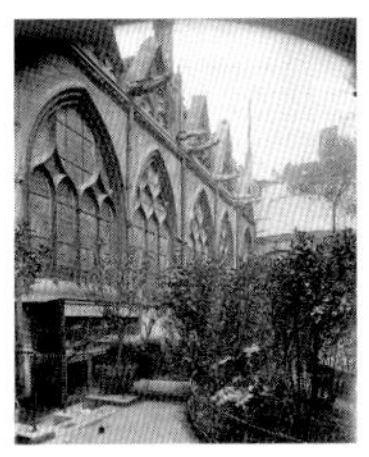

7.10
Presbytery garden and south side of the church, May 1899
21.8 x 17.7 cm (image);
22.1 x 17.9 cm (sheet)
Inscriptions. Verso: u.r., *3618*
Series AP 3618
MC Ph 6849

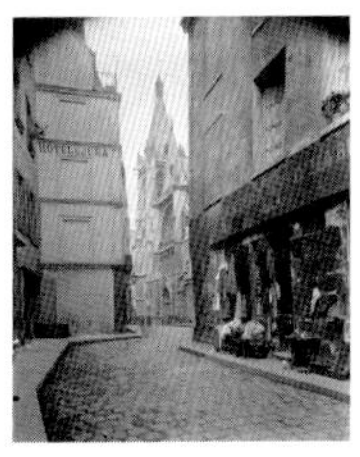

7.11 page 101
Rue des Prêtres-Saint-Séverin, toward the church, 1899
21.3 x 17 cm (image);
21.3 x 17.4 cm (sheet)
Inscriptions. Verso: u.r., *3663*
Series AP 3663 MH38254N
MC Ph 6817

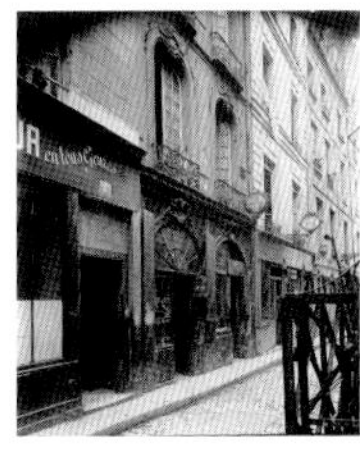

7.12
Louis XV facade [Hôtel Dubisson], 29 rue de la Parcheminerie, 1899
21.3 x 17.4 cm (image);
21.5 x 17.4 cm (sheet)
Inscriptions. Verso: u.c., *R de la Parcheminerie*; u.r., *3675*
Series AP 3675 MH38263N
MC Ph 6810

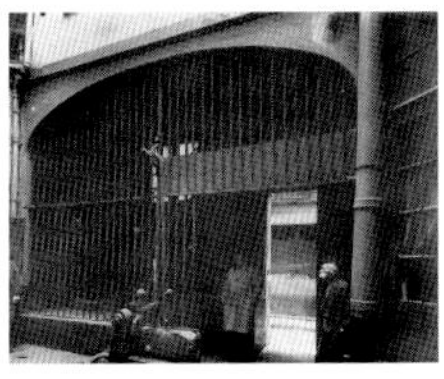

7.19
Old courtyard with grill, 2 rue de la Parcheminerie, 1903
17.5 x 22.1 cm (image and sheet)
Inscriptions. Verso: c.l., *Grille d'une vieille maison Rue / de la parcheminerie / (V*ᵉ*)*; u.l., *4791*
Series AP 4791 MH39040N
MC Ph 6792

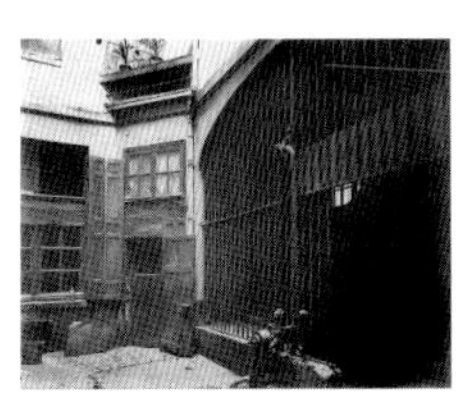

7.20
Old courtyard with grill, 2 rue de la Parcheminerie, 1903
17.6 x 21.9 cm (image);
17.9 x 21.9 cm (sheet)
Inscriptions. Verso: c.l., *Cour et Grille d'une Vieille / maison R de la parcheminerie 2 / (5*ᵉ*)*; u.l., *4792*
Series AP 4792 MH39041N
MC Ph 6813

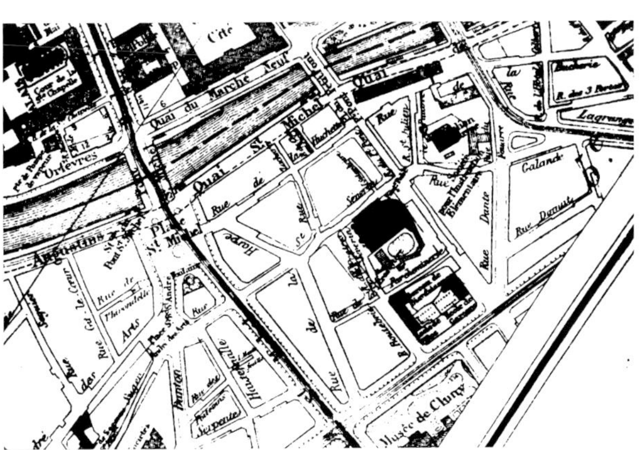

Detail of 1900 map, showing the Church of Saint-Séverin

ii. Documentation of the interior, roof, cloister, and former charnel house of the Church of Saint-Séverin, 1903 (7.21–7.41)

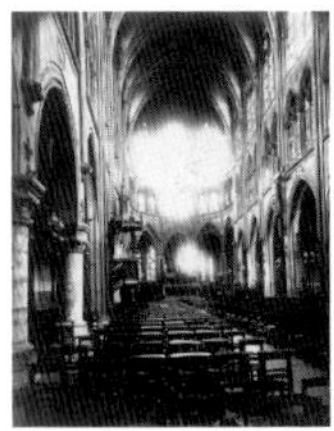

7.21 page 107
Central nave of the church, toward the choir, 1903
Albumen silver print mounted on blue-gray board
22.6 x 17.5 cm (image and sheet); 30 x 24 cm (board)
Inscriptions. Recto: below print, l.c., *Eglise St Séverin 1903–5e arr*; l.r., *Atget*; VP stamp l.r. on print. Verso: u.r., *4801*
Series AP 4801 MH39054N
MC Ph 13368

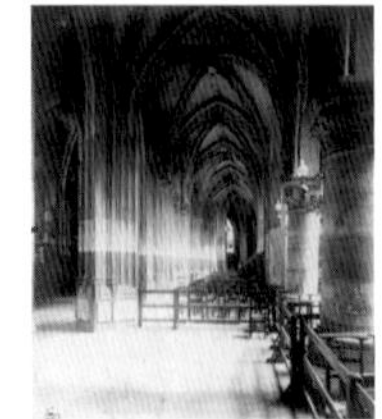

7.22 page 108
Second north nave of the church, toward the ambulatory, 1903
Albumen silver print mounted on blue-gray board
22.3 x 17.4 cm (image and sheet); 30 x 24 cm (board)
Inscriptions. Recto: below print, l.c., *Eglise St Séverin—1903—5e arr*; l.r., *Atget*; VP stamp l.l. on print. Verso: u.r., *4795*
Series AP 4795 MH39048N
MC Ph 13371

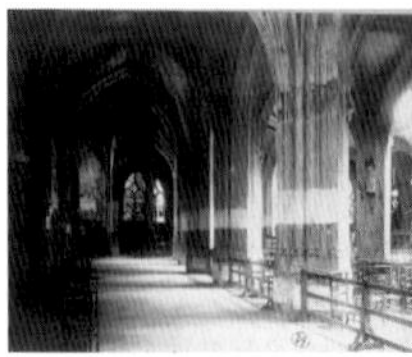

7.23 page 109
Northernmost nave of the church, toward the ambulatory, 1903
Albumen silver print mounted on blue-gray board
17.6 x 22.1 cm (image and sheet); 24 x 30 cm (board)
Inscriptions. Recto: below print, l.c., *Eglise St Séverin—1903—5e arr*; l.r., *Atget*; VP stamp l.r. on print. Verso: l.r., *4796*
Series AP 4796 MH39049N
MC Ph 13372

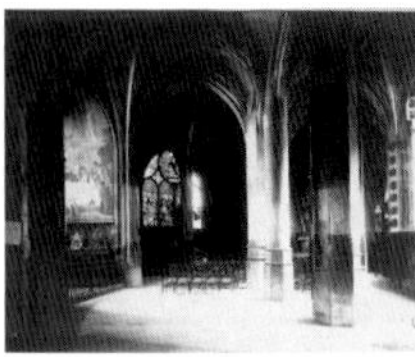

7.24 page 110
Northernmost nave of the church, toward the ambulatory, 1903
Albumen silver print mounted on blue-gray board
17.8 x 22.1 cm (image and sheet); 24 x 30 cm (board)
Inscriptions. Recto: below print, l.c., *Eglise St Séverin—1903—5e arr*; l.r., *Atget*; VP stamp l.r. on print. Verso: l.r., *4797*
Series AP 4797
MC Ph 13373

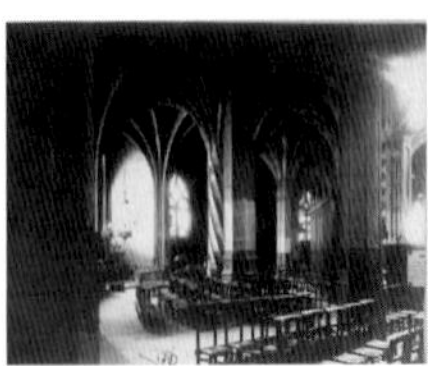

7.25 page 111
Ambulatory of the church, 1903
Albumen silver print mounted on blue-gray board
17.5 x 22.1 cm (image and sheet); 24 x 30 cm (board)
Inscriptions. Recto: below print, l.c., *Eglise St Séverin—1903—5e arr*; l.r., *Atget*; VP stamp l.c. on print. Verso: l.r., *4798*
Series AP 4798
MC Ph 13374

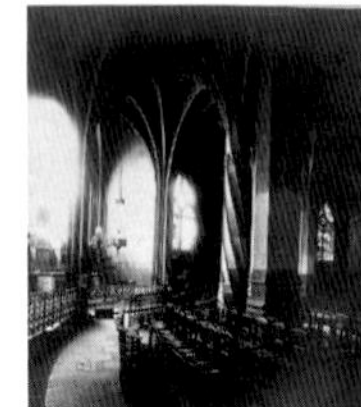

7.26 page 112
Ambulatory of the church, 1903
Albumen silver print mounted on blue-gray board
22.5 x 17.7 cm (image and sheet); 30 x 24 cm (board)
Inscriptions. Recto: below print, l.c., *Eglise St Séverin—1903—5e arr*; l.r., *Atget*; VP stamp l.l. on print. Verso: u.r., *4799*
Series AP 4799 MH39052N
MC Ph 13375

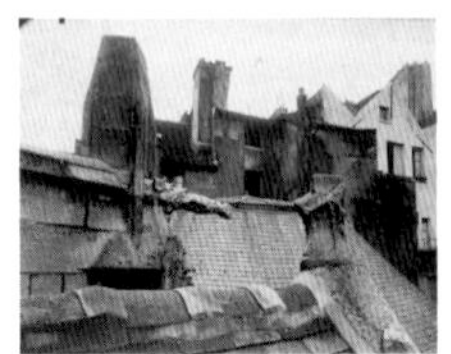

7.33 page 119
Rooftops of the radiating chapels of the church and buildings along the rue Saint-Jacques, 1903
Albumen silver print mounted on blue-gray board
17.5 x 22.3 cm (image and sheet); 24 x 30 cm (board)
Inscriptions. Recto: below print, c.l., *St Séverin—Vue prise sur les toits—1903—5e arr*; l.r., *Atget*; VP stamp l.r. on print. Verso: u.l., *4815*
Series AP 4815 MH39584N
MC Ph 4116

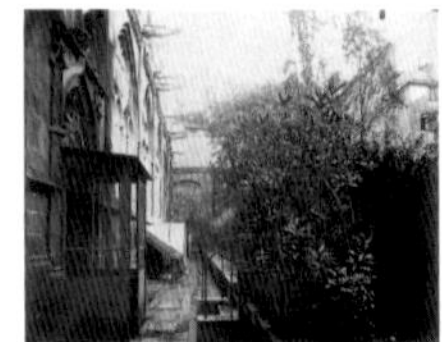

7.34
Presbytery garden and south side of the church, 1903
17.6 x 21.5 cm (image); 17.9 x 21.5 cm (sheet)
Inscriptions. Verso: c.l., *Eglise St Séverin / (Presbytere) / (5e)*; u.l., *4806*
Series AP 4806 MH39043N
MC Ph 6846

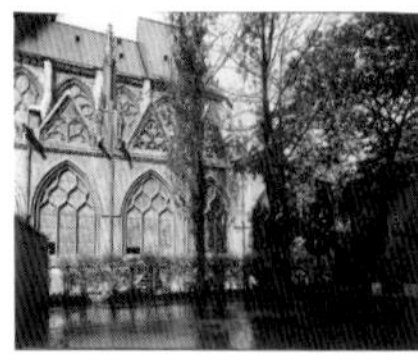

7.35 page 120
Presbytery garden and south side of the church, 1903
17.5 x 21.9 cm (image); 17.6 x 21.9 cm (sheet)
Inscriptions. Verso: c.l., *Eglise St Séverin) / (5e)*; u.l., *4805*
Series AP 4805 MH39042N
MC Ph 6850

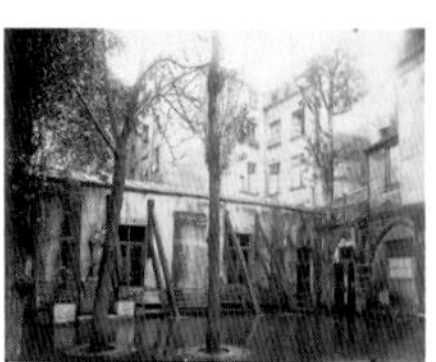

7.36 page 121
Presbytery garden and former cloister of the church, 1903
17.6 x 21.7 cm (image); 17.8 x 21.7 cm (sheet)
Inscriptions. Verso: c.l., *Petit batiment dans lequel / se trouve le cloitre ancien charnier / de St Séverin et qui Va disparaitre / (5e)*; u.l., *4804*
Series AP 4804
MC Ph 6853

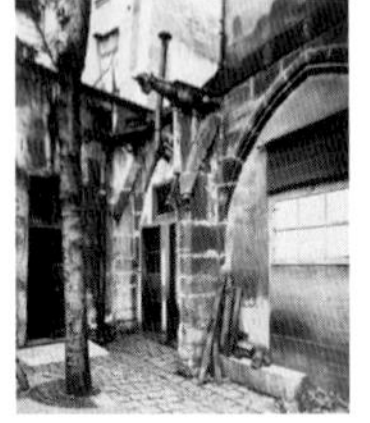

7.37 page 123
Presbytery garden, former cloister, and entrance to the former charnel house of the church, 1903
Albumen silver print mounted on blue-gray board
22.6 x 17.5 cm (image and sheet); 29.4 x 24 cm (board)
Inscriptions. Recto: below print l.c., *Entree du batiment dans lequel se trouve l'ancien charnier / de St Séverin et suite du cloitre dans le jardin du presbytere / 1903*; l.r., *Atget*; VP stamp l.l. on print. Verso: l.l., *4803*
Series AP 4803 MH39045N
MC Ph 19550

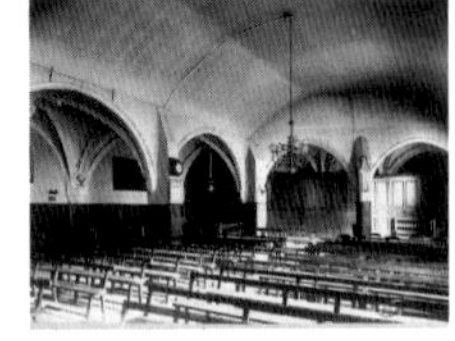

7.38
Interior of the former charnel house of the church, 1903
Albumen silver print mounted on blue-gray board
17.5 x 22.5 cm (image and sheet); 24 x 30 cm (board)
Inscriptions. Recto: below print, l.c., *Eglise St Séverin—Ancien charnier—en 1903—*; l.r., *Atget*; VP stamp l.r. on print. Verso: l.r., *4808*
Series AP 4808 MH39596N
MC Ph 13376

III. Documentation of the Church of Saint-Séverin and the surrounding streets, 1905–1906 (7.42–7.49)

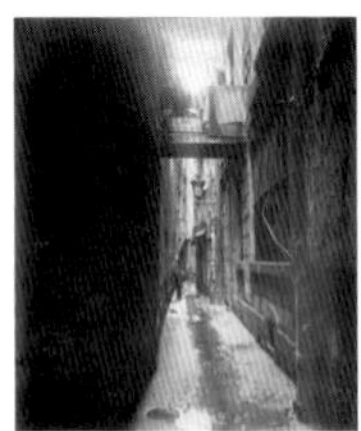

7.42 page 125
Impasse Salembrière, 1905–1906
21.8 x 17.7 cm (image); 21.8 x 17.9 cm (sheet)
Inscriptions. Verso: u.c., *Impasse Salambière Rue / St Severin / (Va Disparaitre) (5e)*; u.r., *5175*
Series AP 5175 MH39542N
MC Ph 6864

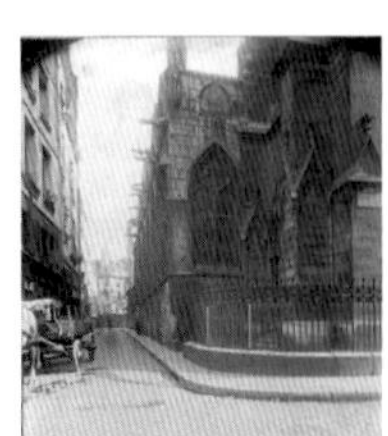

7.43 page 126
Rue Saint-Séverin at the intersection with the rue des Prêtres-Saint-Séverin, toward the rue Saint-Jacques, 1905–1906
21.6 x 17.6 cm (image); 21.6 x 17.7 cm (sheet)
Inscriptions. Verso: u.c., *Rue St Severin / (5e)*; u.r., *5178*
Series AP 5178 MH39545N
MC Ph 6827

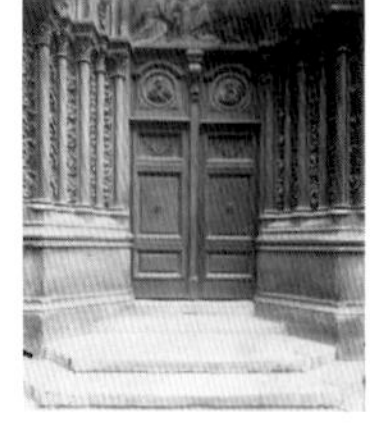

7.44 page 126
Portal of Saint-Martin, at the corner of the rue des Prêtres-Saint-Séverin and the rue Saint-Séverin, 1905–1906
21.8 x 17.6 cm (image); 21.8 x 18 cm (sheet)
Inscriptions. Verso: u.c., *Porte St Severin / (5e)*; u.r., *5176*
Series AP 5176 MH39543N
MC Ph 6831

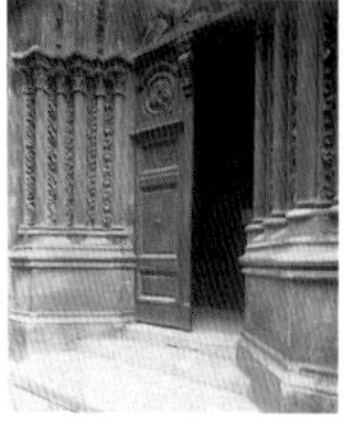

7.45
Detail of the Portal of Saint-Martin, 1905–1906
21.8 x 17.6 cm (image); 21.8 x 18 cm (sheet)
Inscriptions. Verso: u.c., *St Severin / (5^{e})*; u.r., *5177*
Series AP 5177 MH39544N
MC Ph 6832

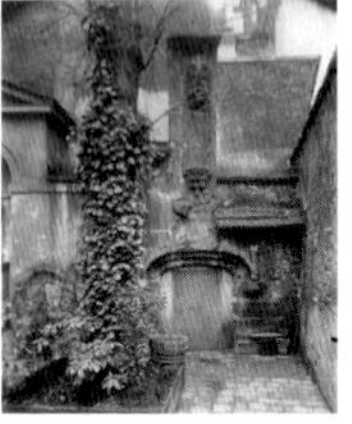

7.46 page 127
Presbytery courtyard of the church, 1905–1906
22 x 17.7 cm (image); 22 x 17.9 cm (sheet)
Inscriptions. Verso: u.c., *Presbytere St Severin / (5^{e})*; u.r., *5179*
Series AP 5179 MH39546N
MC Ph 6848

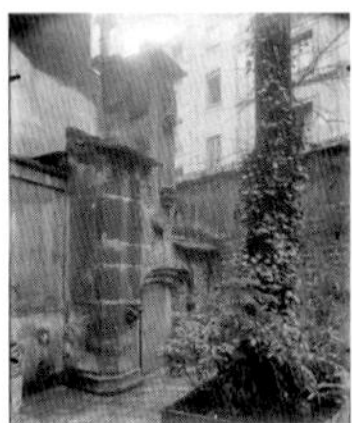

7.47 page 127
Presbytery courtyard of the church, 1905–1906
21.7 x 17.6 cm (image); 21.7 x 17.7 cm (sheet)
Inscriptions. Verso: u.c., *Presbytère St Severin / (5e)*; u.r., *5180*
Series AP 5180 MH39550N
MC Ph 6847

7.27 page 112
Ambulatory and south naves of the church, 1903
Albumen silver print mounted on blue-gray board
22.3 x 17.4 cm (image and sheet); 30 x 24 cm (board)
Inscriptions. Recto: below print, l.c., *Eglise St Séverin—1903*; l.r., *Atget*; VP stamp l.c. on print. Verso: u.r., *4800*
Series AP 4800 MH39053N
MC Ph 13370

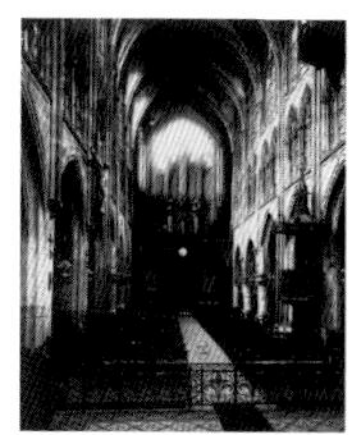

7.28 page 113
Central nave of the church, from the choir toward the great organ, 1903
Albumen silver print mounted on blue-gray board
22.6 x 17.6 cm (image and sheet); 30 x 24 cm (board)
Inscriptions. Recto: below print, l.c., *Intérieur St Séverin—1903—5e arr*; l.r., *Atget*; VP stamp l.c. on print. Verso: u.r., *4807*
Series AP 4807 MH39047N
MC Ph 13369

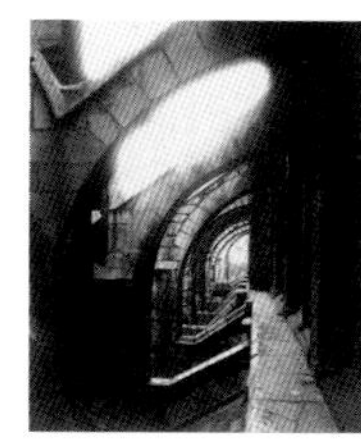

7.29 page 115
Flying buttresses, north side of the church, 1903
Albumen silver print mounted on blue-gray board
22.2 x 17.7 cm (image and sheet); 30 x 24 cm (board)
Inscriptions. Recto: below print, l.c., *Eglise St Séverin—Vue prise sur les toits—1903*; l.r., *Atget*; VP stamp l.r. on print. Verso: u.r., *4809*
Series AP 4809 MH39580N
MC Ph 13359

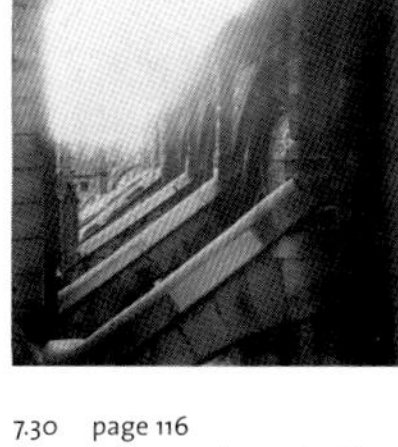

7.30 page 116
Flying buttresses (upper level), north side of the church, 1903
22 x 17.3 cm (image); 22 x 17.4 cm (sheet)
Inscriptions. Verso: u.c., *St Séverin—Vue prise sur / les toits—(5e)*; u.r., *4812*
Series AP 4812 MH39578N
MC Ph 6844

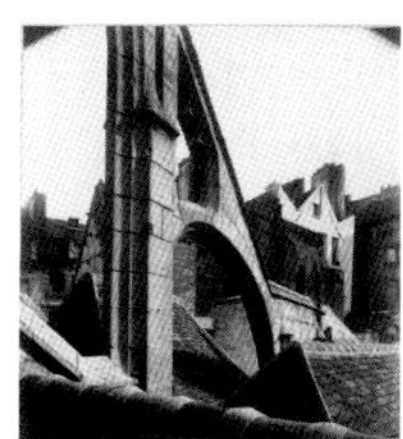

7.31 page 117
Flying buttresses above the ambulatory of the church, 1903
Albumen silver print mounted on blue-gray board
22.5 x 17.5 cm (image and sheet); 30 x 24 cm (board)
Inscriptions. Recto: below print, l.c., *Eglise St Séverin—Vue prise sur les toits—1903/ 5e arr*; l.r., *Atget*; VP stamp l.l. on print. Verso: u.r., *4810*
Series AP 4810 MH39581N
MC Ph 13360

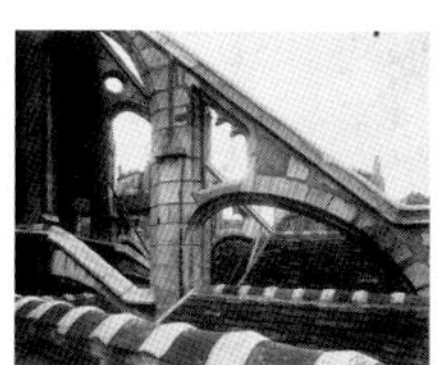

7.32 page 118
Flying buttresses above the ambulatory of the church, 1903
Albumen silver print mounted on blue-gray board
17.4 x 22.6 cm (image and sheet); 24 x 30 cm (board)
Inscriptions. Recto: below print, c.l., *Eglise St Séverin—Vue prise sur les toits—1903—5e arr*; l.r., *Atget*; VP stamp l.r. on print. Verso: u.r., *4811*
Series AP 4811 MH39579N
MC Ph 13362

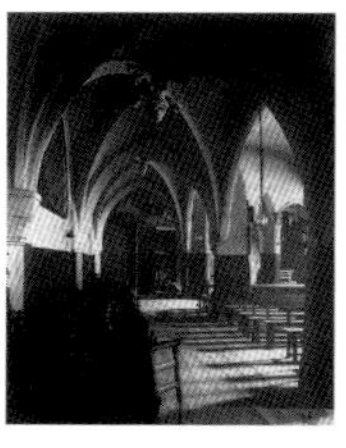

7.39
Interior of the former charnel house of the church, 1903
Albumen silver print mounted on blue-gray board
22.2 x 17.5 cm (image and sheet); 24 x 30 cm (board)
Inscriptions. Recto: below print, l.c., *St Séverin—Ancien charnier—1903—*; l.r., *Atget*; VP stamp l.r. on print. Verso: u.r., *4802*
Series AP 4802 MH39046N
MC Ph 13377

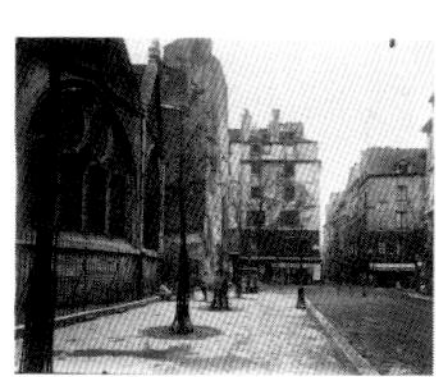

7.40
Rue Saint-Jacques, toward the quais, after the demolition of the shops abutting the apse of the church, 1903
17.4 x 21.8 cm (image); 17.5 x 21.8 cm (sheet)
Inscriptions. Verso: c.l., *St Séverin—Carrefour des / rues St Séverin St Jacques / et Galande / (5e)*; u.l., *4813*
Series AP 4813 MH39582N
MC Ph 6860

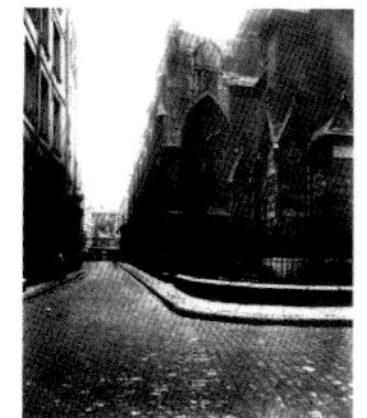

7.41
Rue Saint-Séverin at the intersection with the rue des Prêtres-Saint-Séverin, toward the rue Saint-Jacques, 1903
Albumen silver print on blue-gray board
22.1 x 17.4 cm (image and sheet); 30 x 26 cm (board)
Inscriptions. Recto: below print, l.c., *Un Coin Rue St Severin—5e arr—1903*; l.r., *Atget*; VP stamp c. on print. Verso: u.r., *4814*
Series AP 4814 MH39583N
MC Ph 13356

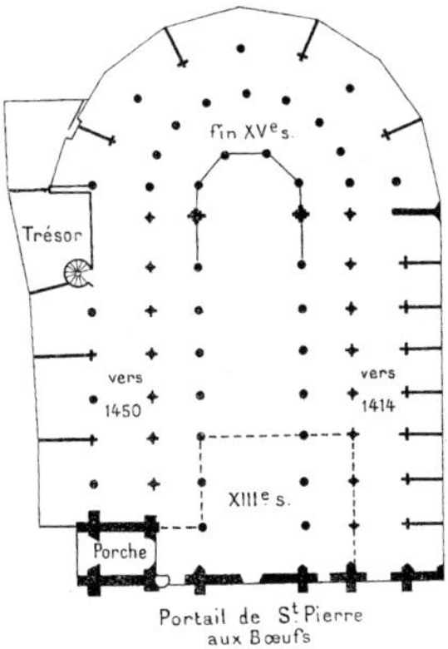

The Church of Saint-Séverin, ground plan

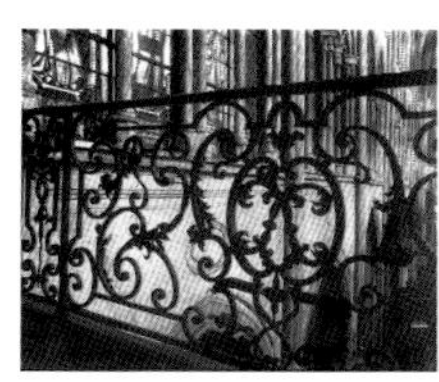

7.48
Iron balustrade of the great organ, 1905–1906
17.7 x 22 cm (image); 17.8 x 22 cm (sheet)
Inscriptions. Verso: c.1., *S Séverin Grille / (5e)*; u.l., *5181*
Series AP 5181 MH39551N
MC Ph 6833

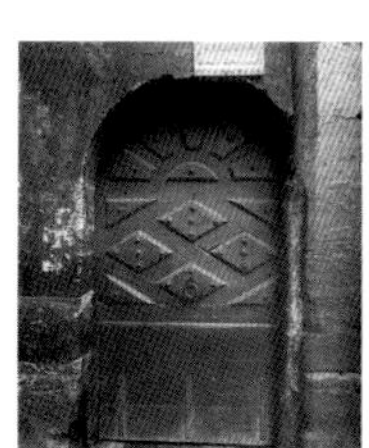

7.49
Old door, 22 rue de la Parcheminerie, 1905–1906
21.6 x 17.6 cm (image); 21.6 x 18.1 cm (sheet)
Inscriptions. Verso: u.c., *Porte 22 Rue de la / Parcheminerie / va disparaître (5^{e})*; u.r., *5190*
Series AP 5190 MH39478N
MC Ph 6811

IV. **Widening of the rue Saint-Jacques,** 1908 (7.50–7.53)

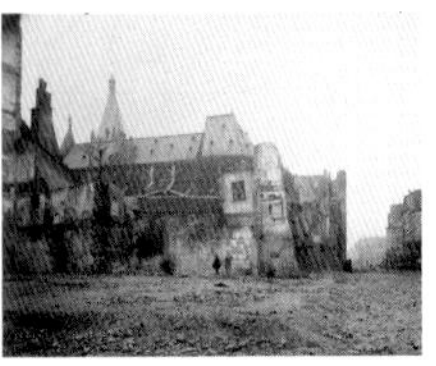

7.50
Rue Saint-Jacques after the demolition of the buildings bordering the cloister of the church, from the corner of the rue de la Parcheminerie, February 1908
17.7 x 22.2 cm (image and sheet)
Inscriptions: c.l., *Eglise St Séverin après la demolition cote / Rue de la Parcheminerie / (1908)*; u.l., *248*
Series T 248 MH37648N
MC Ph 3663 (page 10 in the album *Vieux Paris, Coins Pittoresques et Disparus—1907–1908–1909*)

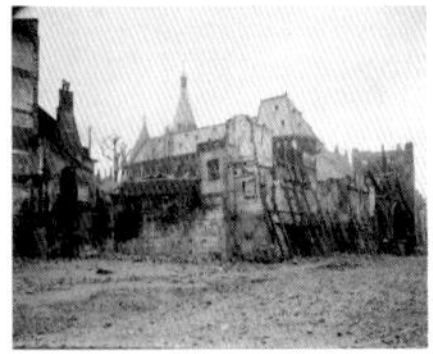

7.51 page 129
Rue Saint-Jacques after the demolition of the buildings bordering the cloister of the church, from the corner of the rue de la Parcheminerie, February 1908
17.6 x 22 cm (image);
17.7 x 22 cm (sheet)
Inscriptions. Verso: c.l., *Rue St Jacques apres La / demolition—Vue prise du coin / de la rue de la Parcheminerie / (5e)*; u.l., *249*
Series T 249 MH37649N
MC Ph 6791

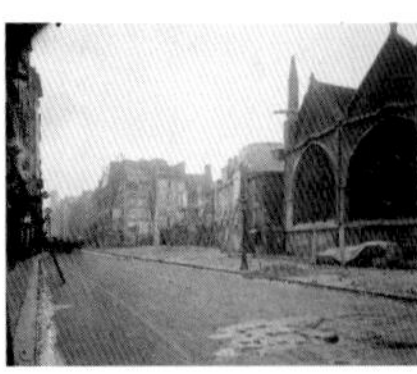

7.52 page 130
Rue Saint-Jacques after the demolition of the buildings bordering the cloister of the church, from the rue Galande, February 1908
17.7 x 20.9 cm (image);
17.8 x 22 cm (sheet)
Inscriptions. Verso: c.r., *St Séverin et Rue St Jacques /Vue prise de la Rue Galande / (5e)*; l.r., *250*
Series T 250 MH37643N
MC Ph 6861

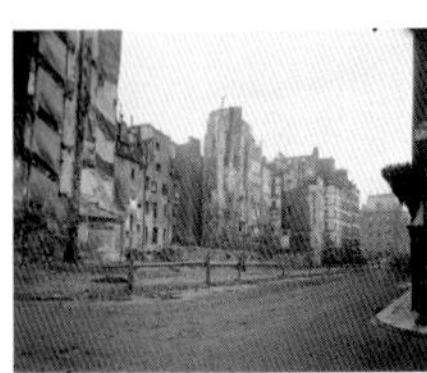

7.53 page 131
Rue du Petit-Pont after the partial demolition of buildings, from the rue Galande, February 1908
17.7 x 21.9 cm (image and sheet)
Inscriptions. Verso: c.l., *Rue du Petit Pont après la / démolition—Vue prise coin Rue / Galande / (5e)*; u.l., *251*
Series T 251 MH37644N
MC Ph 6868

V. **Documentation of the rue des Prêtres-Saint-Séverin,** 1912 (7.54–7.65)

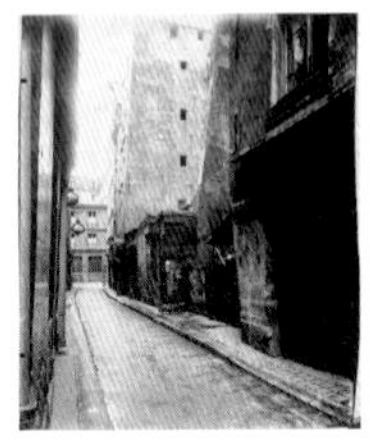

7.54 page 132
Rue de la Parcheminerie, toward the rue de la Harpe, 1912
22 x 17.6 cm (image and sheet)
Inscriptions. Verso: u.c., *Coin de la rue de la Parcheminerie / de la rue Boutebrie à partir du / No 23*; u.r., *1360.*
Series T 1360 MH38332N
MC Ph 6815

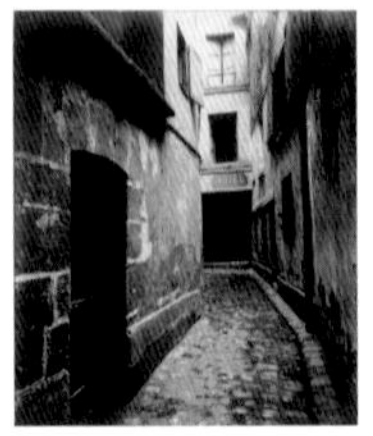

7.55 page 133
Former entrance to the presbytery of the church, 12 rue de la Parcheminerie, 1912
22.1 x 17.8 cm (image);
22.1 x 17.9 cm (sheet)
Inscriptions. Verso: u.c., *ancienne entrée du Presbytere / St Séverin, 12 Rue de la / Parcheminerie / (5e arr)*; u.r., *1361.*
Series T 1361 MH38331N
MC Ph 6795

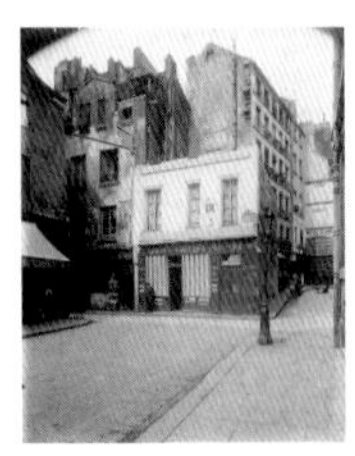

7.56
Rue Boutebrie, toward the intersection of the rue de la Parcheminerie and the rue des Prêtres-Saint-Séverin, 1912
22. x 17.7 cm (image);
22 x 17.9 cm (sheet)
Inscriptions. Verso: u.c., *Coin Rue de la / Parcheminerie / et Boutebrie / Va Disparaître*; u.r., *1380*
Series T 1380 MH38081N
MC Ph 6794

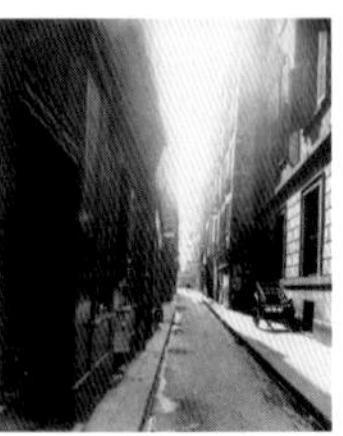

7.57 page 134
Rue de la Parcheminerie, toward the rue Saint-Jacques, 1912
21.9 x 17.7 cm (image);
21.9 x 18 cm (sheet)
Inscriptions. Verso: u.c., *Rue de la Parcheminerie / (5e arr)*; u.r., *1376*
Series T 1376 MH38329N
MC Ph 6793

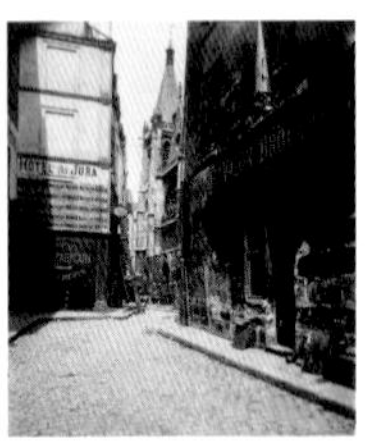

7.58
Rue des Prêtres-Saint-Séverin, toward the church, 1912
x 17.6 cm (image);
22.1 x 17.8 cm (sheet)
Inscriptions. Verso: u.c., *Rue des Prètres St / Severin / (5e arr)*; u.r., *1372*
Series T 1372 MH38279N
MC Ph 6819

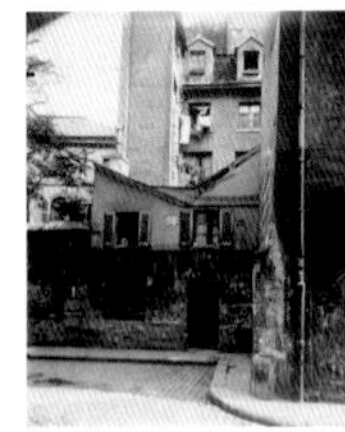

7.59 page 135
Rue des Prêtres-Saint-Séverin, old house at No. 3 and presbytery of the church, 1912
21.9 x 17.7 cm (image);
21.9 x 17.9 cm (sheet)
Inscriptions. Verso: u.c., *Vieille maison, donnant sur / le Presbytere et / 3 Rue de Prêtres / St Severin / (5e arr)*; u.r., *1369.*
Series T 1369 MH38274N
MC Ph 6822

VI. **Documentation of the destruction and enlargement of the rue des Prêtres-Saint-Séverin and the rue de la Parcheminerie,** March 1913–August 1914 (7.66–7.89)

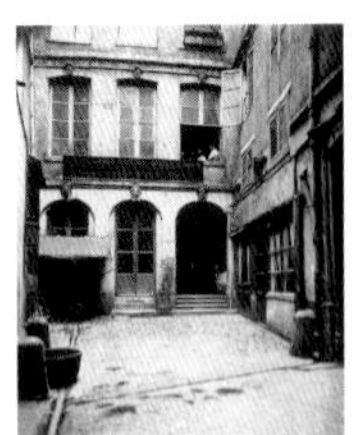

7.66
Courtyard, 34 rue Saint-Séverin, 1913
22.1 x 17.6 cm (image);
22 x 17.8 cm (sheet)
Inscriptions. Verso: u.c., *Vieille cour 34 Rue / St Severin (5e arr)*; u.r., *1418*
Series T 1418 MH87532N
MC Ph 6825

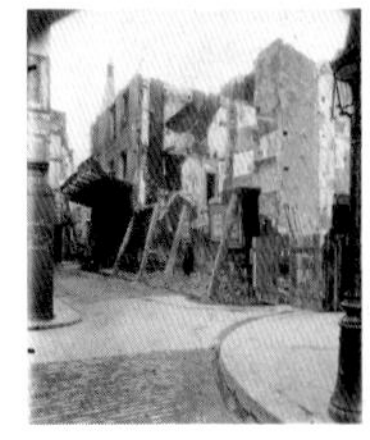

7.67 page 142
Intersection of the Rue Boutebrie, the rue de la Parcheminerie, and the rue des Prêtres-Saint-Séverin, toward the church, March 15, 1913
22.5 x 17.7 cm (image);
22.5 x 18 cm (sheet)
Inscriptions. Verso: u.c., *Un coin de la rue de la / Parcheminerie et des Prêtres / St Severin 15 Mars 1913 / (5e arr)*; u.r., *1424*
Series T 1424 MH38306N
MC Ph 6804

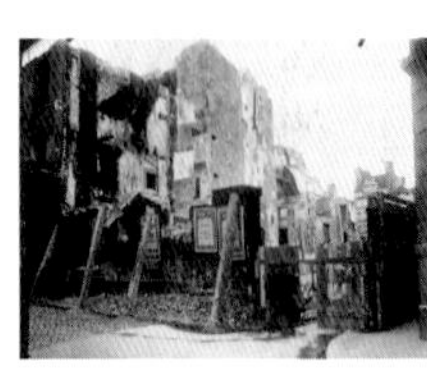

7.68
Intersection of the rue Boutebrie, the rue de la Parcheminerie, and the rue des Prêtres-Saint-Séverin, toward the rue Saint-Jacques, March 15, 1913
17.7 x 22.2 cm (image);
17.9 x 22.2 cm (sheet)
Inscriptions. Verso: c.l., *Un coin de la rue de / la Parcheminerie / Mars 1913 / (5e arr)*; u.l., *1425*
Series T 1425 MH38307N
MC Ph 6805

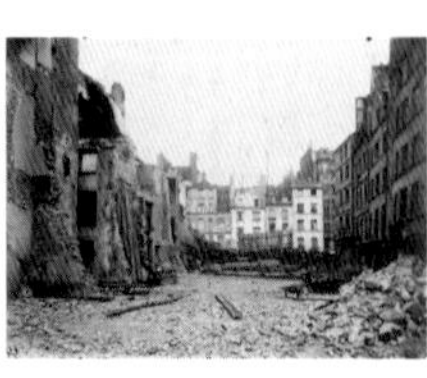

7.69 page 143
Demolition site, rue de la Parcheminerie, toward the rue Saint-Jacques, March 15, 1913
17.5 x 22.2 cm (image);
17.7 x 22.2 cm (sheet)
Inscriptions. Verso: c.l., *La rue de la Parcheminerie / apres sa demolition. Vue / prise de la rue Boutebrie / 15 Mars 1913 / (5e arr)*; u.l., *1423*
Series T 1423 MH38305N
MC Ph 6800

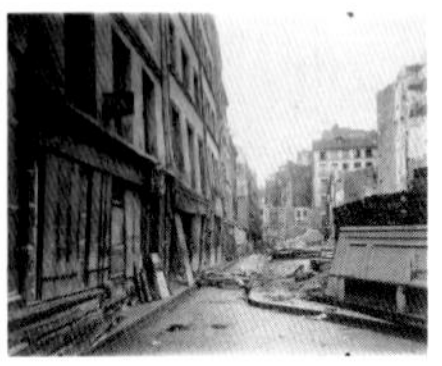

7.70 page 144
Demolitions along the rue de la Parcheminerie, from the rue Saint-Jacques toward the rue des Prêtres-Saint-Séverin, March 15, 1913
17.7 x 22.7 cm (image);
18.3 x 22.7 cm (sheet)
Inscriptions. Verso: c.l., *La rue de la Parcheminerie / après sa demolition / 15 Mars 1913 / (5e arr)*; u.l., *1422*
Series T 1422 MH38304N
MC Ph 6801

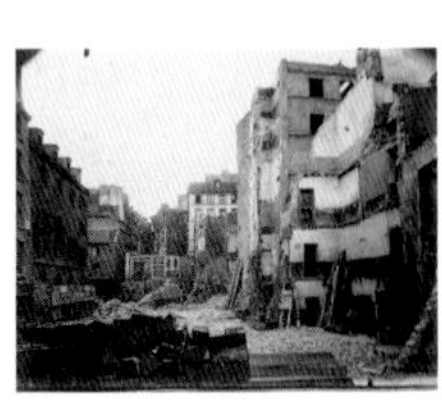

7.71 page 145
Demolitions along the rue de la Parcheminerie, from the rue Saint-Jacques toward the rue des Prêtres-Saint-Séverin, March 15, 1913
17.8 x 21.2 cm (image);
18 x 21.2 cm (sheet)
Inscriptions. Verso: c.l., *Rue de la Parcheminerie / Mars 1913 / apres la demolition 15 Mars 1913 / (5e arr)*; u.l., *1420*
Series T 1420 MH38301N
MC Ph 6802

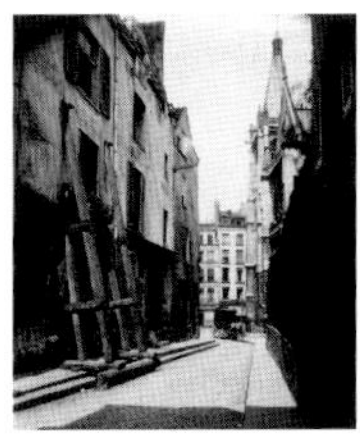

7.60 page 136
Rue des Prêtres-Saint-Séverin, toward the church, 1912
22.2 x 17.7 cm (image);
22.2 x 17.8 cm (sheet)
Inscriptions. Verso: u.c., *Un coin de la rue des / Prêtres St Severin / Vue prise du mur du / Presbytere / (5e arr)*; u.r., *1370*
Series T 1370 MH38278N
MC Ph 6820

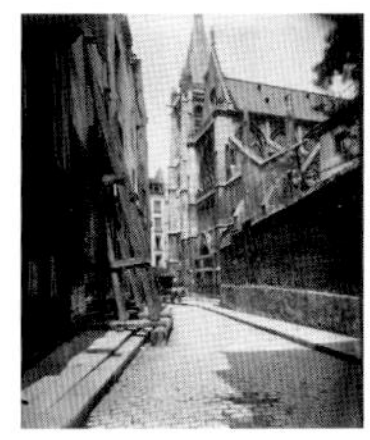

7.61 page 137
Rue des Prêtres-Saint-Séverin, toward the church, 1912
21.9 x 17.7 cm (image);
21.9 x 17.9 cm (sheet)
Inscriptions. Verso: u.c., *Rue des Prêtres S^t / Severin / (5e arr)*; u.r., *1371*
Series T 1371
MC Ph 6823

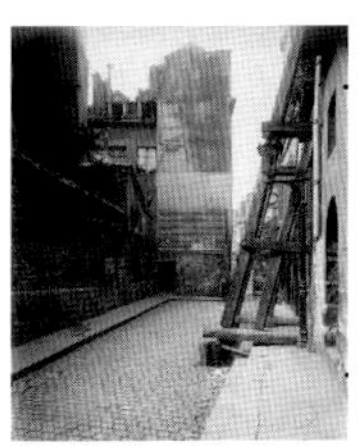

7.62 page 138
Rue des Prêtres-Saint-Séverin, toward the rue Boutebrie and the wall of the presbytery, 1912
21.9 x 17.6 cm (image);
21.9 x 17.8 cm (sheet)
Inscriptions. Verso: u.c., *La Maison, 3 Rue des Prètres / St Severin donnant sur le / Jardin du Presbytere St Severin / (5e arr)*; u.r., *1374*
Series T 1374 MH38281N
MC Ph 6826

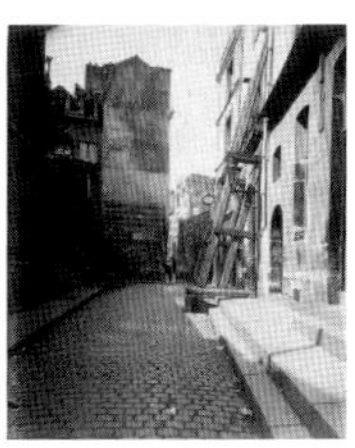

7.63 page 138
Rue des Prêtres-Saint-Séverin, toward the rue Boutebrie, 1912
22 x 17.7 cm (image);
22 x 18.2 cm (sheet)
Inscriptions. Verso: u.c., *La rue des Prêtres S^t / Severin, au fond les maisons / de la rue Boutebrie / (5e arr)*; u.r., *1373*
Series T 1373 MH38280N
MC Ph 6824

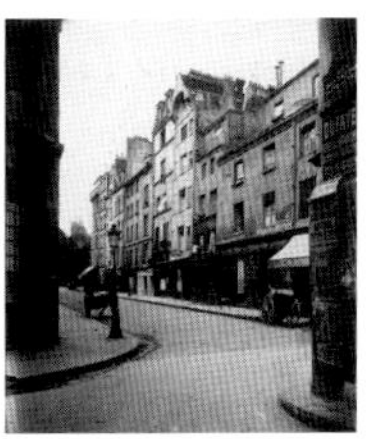

7.64 page 139
Rue Boutebrie, from the intersection of the rue la Parcheminerie and the rue des Prêtres-Saint-Séverin toward the Musée de Cluny, 1912
21.8 x 17.6 cm (image);
21.8 x 17.7 cm (sheet)
Inscriptions. Verso: u.c., *Les maisons de la Boutebrie / (N^o* pairs) Vue de la rue des / Prètres / *St Séverin / (5e arr)*; u.r., *1375*
Series T 1375 MH38080N
MC Ph 6816

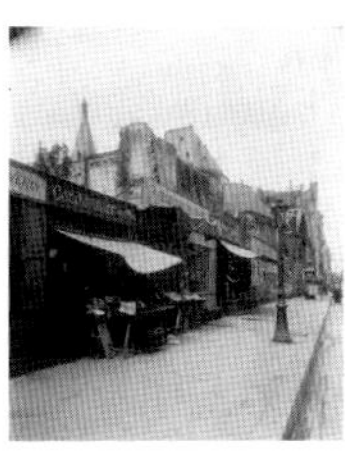

7.65 page 139
Temporary shops along the rue Saint-Jacques, 1912
22.1 x 17.7 cm (image);
22.1 x 17.9 cm (sheet)
Inscriptions. Verso: u.c., *Coin de St Severin / Rue St Jacques/ Va disparaitre (5^e)*; u.r., *1379*
Series T 1379 MH38326N
MC Ph 6821

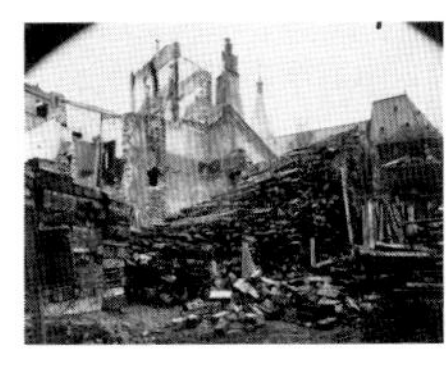

7.72 page 141
Demolitions, rue de la Parcheminerie, March 15, 1913
17.8 x 22.5 cm (image and sheet)
Inscriptions. Verso: c.l., *La Rue de la Parcheminerie / Mars 1913 / (5^e arr)*; u.l., *1421*
Series T 1421
MC Ph 6803

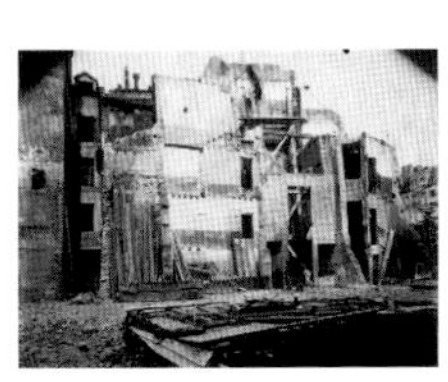

7.73 page 146
Demolitions, rue de la Parcheminerie, near the former entrance to the presbytery of the church, March 15, 1913
17.7 x 22.2 cm (image);
17.8 x 22.2 cm (sheet)
Inscriptions. Verso: c.l., *Un coin de la rue de / la Parcheminerie / Mars 1913 / (5^e arr)*; u.l., *1426*
Series T 1426 MH38308N
MC Ph 6806

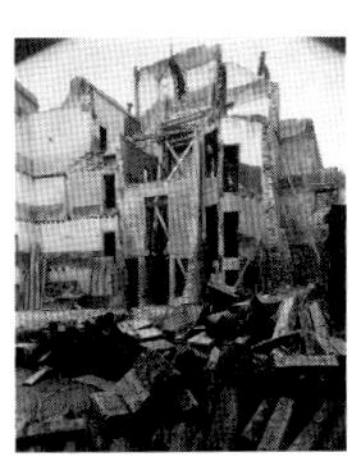

7.74 page 147
Demolitions, rue de la Parcheminerie, March 15, 1913
21.9 x 17.9 cm (image);
22 x 18.1 cm (sheet)
Inscriptions. Verso: u.l., *La rue de la Parcheminerie / 15 Mars 1913*; u.r., *1427*
Series T 1427 MH38320N
MC Ph 11087 (page 8 in the album *Coins du Vieux Paris, Pittoresques et Disparus)*

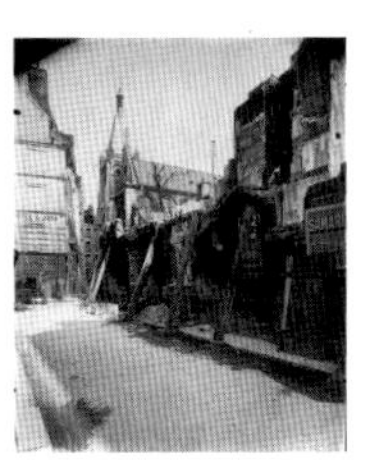

7.75 page 148
Demolitions, rue des Prêtres-Saint-Séverin, toward the church, April 8, 1913
22 x 17.6 cm (image);
22 x 18.1 cm (sheet)
Inscriptions. Verso: u.c., *Coin de la rue de la / Parcheminerie le 8 avril / 1913/ (5e arr)*; u.r., *1435*
Series T 1435 MH38155N
MC Ph 6799

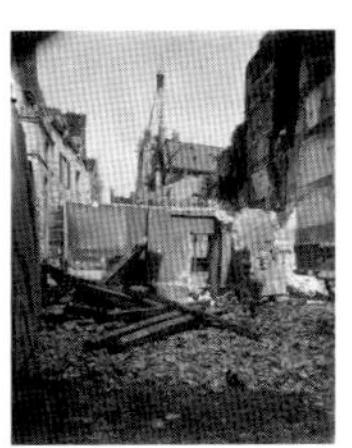

7.76 page 148
Demolition site, rue de la Parcheminerie, toward the church, April 8, 1913
22.5 x 17.5 cm (image);
22.5 x 17.6 cm (sheet)
Inscriptions. Verso: u.c., *Un coin de la rue de la / Parcheminerie le / 8 avril 1913 / (5^e arr)*; u.r., *1434*
Series T 1434
MC Ph 6798

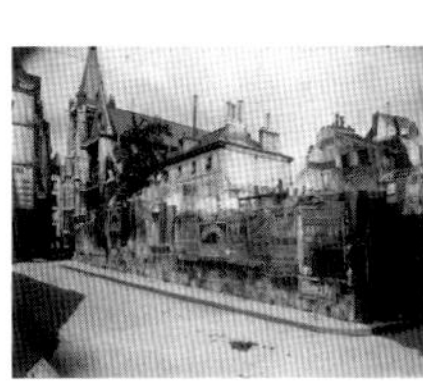

7.77 page 149
Intersection of the rue Boutebrie, the rue de la Parcheminerie, and the rue des Prêtres-Saint-Séverin, toward the presbytery and the church, August 15, 1913
17.6 x 21.7 cm (image and sheet)
Inscriptions. Verso: c.l., *Le coin de la rue de la / Parcheminerie le 15 aout / 1913 après sa demolition / (5e arr)*; u.l., *1483*
Series T 1483 MH38132N
MC Ph 6797

Continuation of the documentation of the destruction and enlargement of the rue des Prêtres-Saint-Séverin and the rue de la Parcheminerie, March 1913–August 1914 (7.66–7.89)

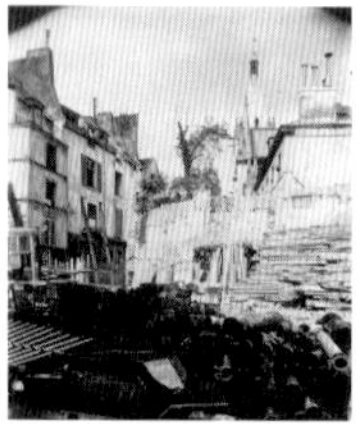

7.78 page 150
Demolition site, rue de la Parcheminerie, toward the presbytery and the church, August 15, 1913
21.5 x 17.6 cm (image);
21.5 x 18 cm (sheet)
Inscriptions. Verso: u.c., *Le coin de la rue* [des Prêtres-] *St Severin / et de la rue de la Parcheminerie, / le 15 aout 1913 / (5^e arr)*; u.r., *1481*
Series T 1481 MH38133N
MC Ph 6808

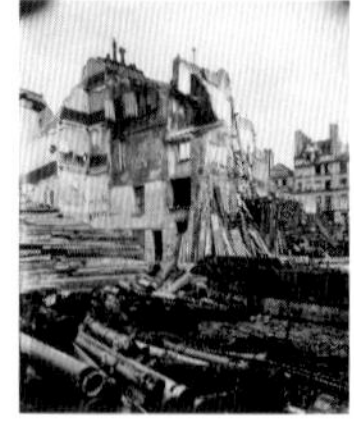

7.79 page 151
Demolition site, rue de la Parcheminerie, toward the rue Saint-Jacques, August 15, 1913
22.7 x 17.7 cm (image and sheet)
Inscriptions. Verso: u.c., *Une épave de la rue de / la Parcheminerie après / la demolition le 15 aout / 1913 / (5e arr)*; u.r., *1482*
Series T 1482 MH38346N
MC Ph 6796

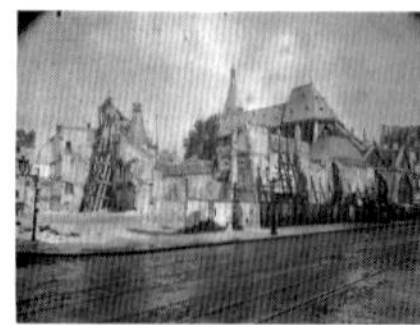

7.80 page 153
Demolitions, from the corner of the rue de la Parcheminerie and the rue Saint-Jacques, toward the church, August 1914
Unmounted gelatin silver chloride print
17.6 x 22.4 cm (image);
18 x 22.4 cm (sheet)
Inscriptions. Recto: BN stamp l.c. on print. Verso: c.l., *Eglise St Séverin / en Aout 1914*; u.l., *1640*
Series T 1640 MH38585N
BN T42416

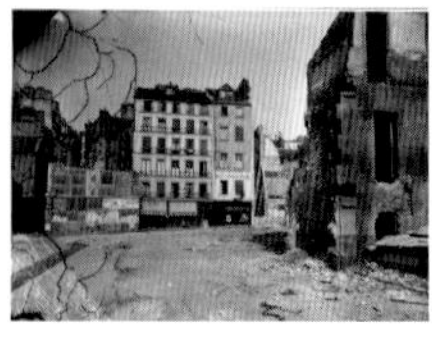

7.81 page 154
After the demolition of the buildings along the rue de la Parcheminerie, from the rue Saint-Jacques toward the rue des Prêtres-Saint-Séverin, August 1914
Unmounted gelatin silver chloride print
17.4 x 22.2 cm (image);
18.1 x 22.2 cm (sheet)
Inscriptions. Recto: BN stamp l.c. on print. Verso: c.l., *Les Maisons de la rue des / Pretres St Séverin, Vue / de la rue de la Parcheminerie*; u.l., *1639*
Series T 1639 MH38591N
BN T42415
(reproduction: CNMHS)

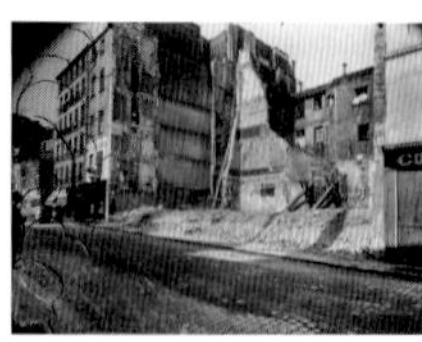

7.82 page 155
Demolition of buildings along the rue des Prêtres-Saint-Séverin, opposite the presbytery of the church, August 1914
Unmounted gelatin silver chloride print
17.7 x 22.1 cm (image);
18.1 x 22.5 cm (sheet)
Inscriptions. Recto BN stamp l.c. on print. Verso: c.l., *Un coin de la rue des/ Prêtres St Séverin / autrefois 4, 6, 8*; u.l., *1638*
Series T 1638 MH38580N
BN T42414
(reproduction: CNMHS)

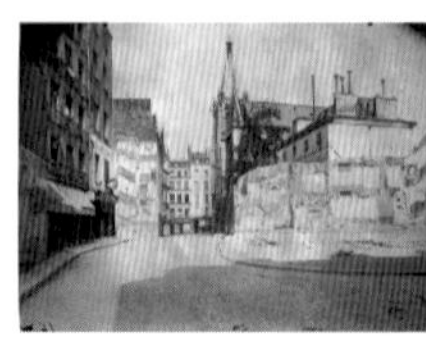

7.83 page 156
After the demolitions at the intersection of the rue Boutebrie, the rue de la Parcheminerie, and the rue des Prêtres-Saint-Séverin, toward the presbytery and the church, August 1914
Unmounted gelatin silver chloride print
18 x 24.4 cm (image and sheet)
Inscriptions. Recto: BN Stamp l.c. on print. Verso: c.l., *La rue des Pretres St Séverin de la rue / de la Parcheminerie*; u.l., *1634*
Series T 1634 MH38582N
BN T42410

vii. **Final views,** 1920–1923 (7.90–7.96)

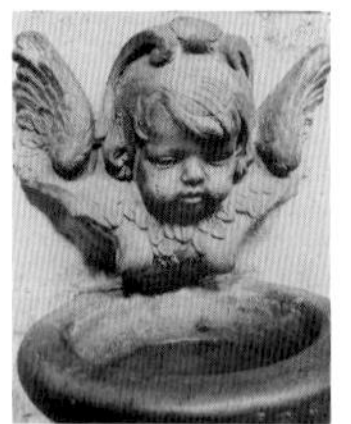

7.90
Holy water font, near the Portal of Saint-Martin, 1920
23.7 x 17.9 cm (negative)
Series AP 6201
APMAP MH87332N
(reproduction: CNMHS)

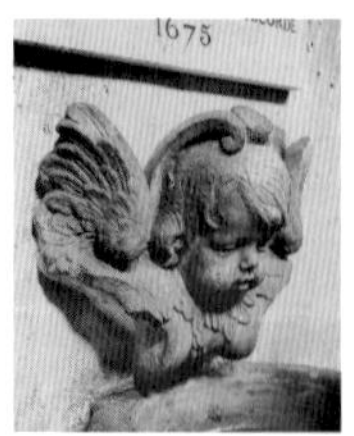

7.91
Holy water font, near the Portal of Saint-Martin, 1920
23.7 x 17.9 cm (negative)
Series AP 6202
APMAP MH87333N
(reproduction: CNMHS)

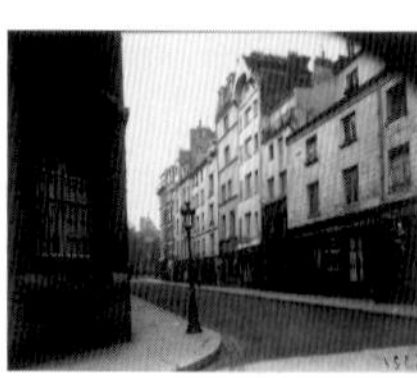

7.92 page 161
Rue Boutebrie, from the intersection of the rue la Parcheminerie and the rue des Prêtres-Saint-Séverin toward the Musée de Cluny, March 1922
17.5 x 21.7 cm (sheet);
18 x 21.7 cm (sheet)
Inscriptions. Verso: u.l., *6321*
Series AP 6321
MC Ph 4602 (page 33 in the album *Vieux Paris, Coins Pittoresques, Vieux Montmartre*)

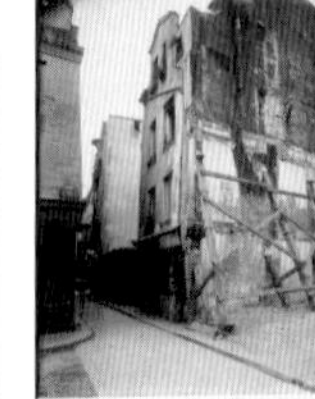

7.93 page 162
Demolition of the building at the corner of the rue de la Parcheminerie and the rue des Prêtres-Saint-Séverin, 1922
21.7 x 17.7 cm (image);
22.8 x 18 cm (sheet)
Inscriptions. Verso: u.c., *Cour Rue Parcheminerie / et Boutebrie*; u.r., *6371*
Series AP 6371 MH87286N
MC Ph 3781 (page 8 in the album *Vieux Paris, Coins Pittoresques*)

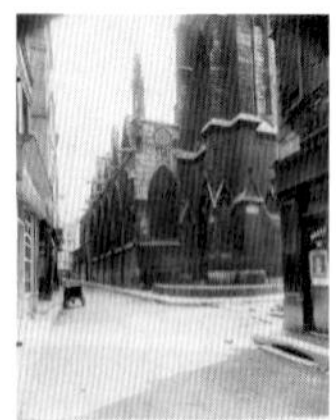

7.94 page 163
Rue Saint-Séverin at the intersection with the rue des Prêtres-Saint-Séverin, toward the rue Saint-Jacques, June 1923
Unmounted mat albumen silver print
22.3 x 17.6 cm (image);
22.4 x 17.9 cm (sheet)
Inscriptions. Verso: u.l., *Rue St Severin*; u.r., *6446*; Atget stamp l.c.,; r. of stamp, *17 bis*
Series AP 6446 MH87035N
MC Ph 3834 (page 9 in the album *Vieux Paris, Coins Pittoresques*).

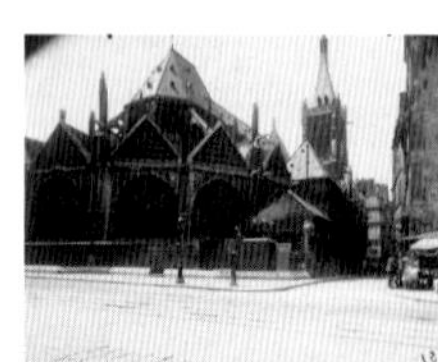

7.95 page 164
Corner of the rue Galande and the rue Saint-Jacques, toward the church and the rue Saint-Séverin, June 1923
Unmounted mat albumen silver print
17.6 x 22.4 cm (image);
17.9 x 22.4 cm (sheet)
Inscriptions. Verso: c.l., *St Severin*; u.l, *6451*; Atget stamp l.c.; below stamp, *17 bis*
Series AP 6451 MH87032N
MC Ph 3837 (page 12 in the album *Vieux Paris, Coins Pittoresques*)

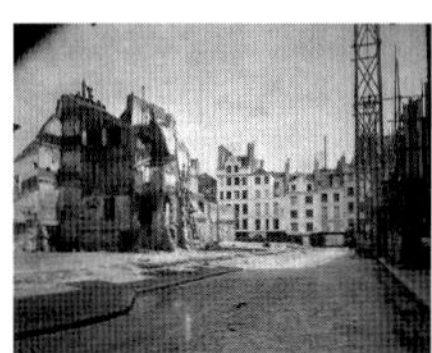

7.84 page 157
After the demolitions at the intersection of the rue Boutebrie, the rue de la Parcheminerie, and the rue des Prêtres-Saint-Séverin, toward the rue Saint-Jacques, August 1914
Unmounted gelatin silver chloride print
17.6 x 22.5 cm (image and sheet)
Inscriptions. Recto: BN stamp l.c. on print. Verso: c.l., *Ancienne rue de la / Parcheminerie, après la démolition / de la rue des Prêtres St Séverin / aout 1914 (5e arr)*; c.r., *Ancienne rue de la Parcheminerie*; u.l., *1635*
Series T 1635 MH38583N
BN T42411

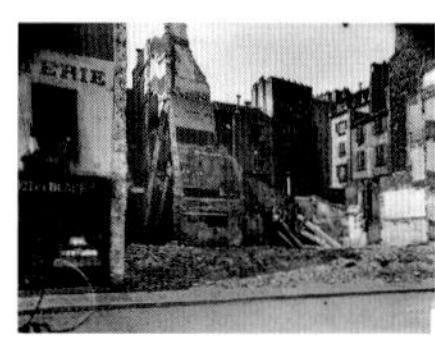

7.85
Demolition of buildings along the rue des Prêtres-Saint-Séverin, opposite the presbytery of the church, August 1914
Unmounted gelatin silver chloride print
17.9 x 22 cm (image);
18 x 22 cm (sheet)
Inscriptions. Recto: BN stamp l.c. on print. Verso: c.l., *Un coin de la rue des / Prètres St Séverin / autrefois 6, 8, 10*; u.l., *1636*
Series T 1636 MH38587N
BN T42412
(reproduction: CNMHS)

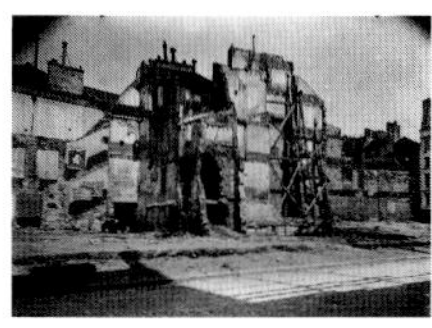

7.86
Demolitions, rue de la Parcheminerie, toward the rue Saint-Jacques, August 1914
Unmounted gelatin silver chloride print
17.6 x 22.4 cm (image and sheet)
Inscriptions. Recto: BN stamp l.c. on print. Verso: c.l., *Un coin de la rue de / la Parcheminerie après La démolition / Aout 1914 (5e arr)*; u.l., *1637*
Series T 1637 MH38592N
BN T42413
(reproduction: CNMHS)

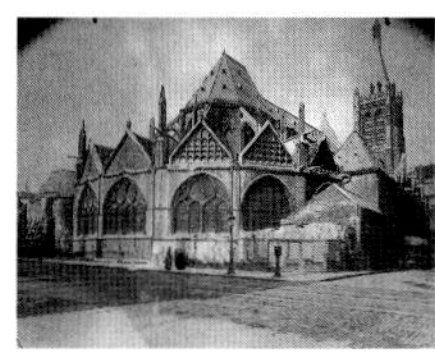

7.87
After the demolitions, from the corner of the rue Galande and the rue Saint-Jacques toward the church and the rue Saint-Séverin, August 1914
Unmounted gelatin silver chloride print
17.6 x 22.6 cm (image);
18 x 22.6 cm (sheet)
Inscriptions. Recto: BN stamp l.c. on print. Verso: c.l., *St Séverin, après la / demolition des Vieilles / maisons (Aout 1914)*; u.l., *1641*
Series T 1641 MH38586N
BN T42417

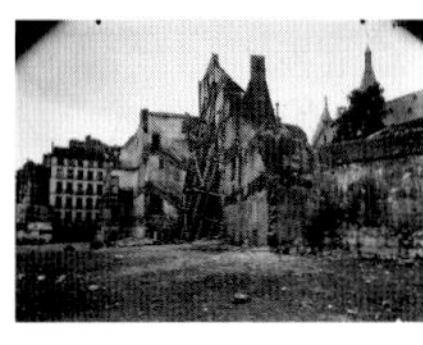

7.88 page 158
After the demolition of the buildings along the rue de la Parcheminerie, from the rue Saint-Jacques toward the rue des Prêtres-Saint-Séverin and the church, August 1914
Unmounted gelatin silver chloride print
17.7 x 22.4 cm (image and sheet)
Inscriptions. Recto: BN stamp l.c. on print. Verso: c.l., *Ce qui reste de la rue / de la Parcheminerie / en Aout 1914*; u.l., *1642*
Series T 1642 MH38584N
BN T42418
(reproduction: CNMHS)

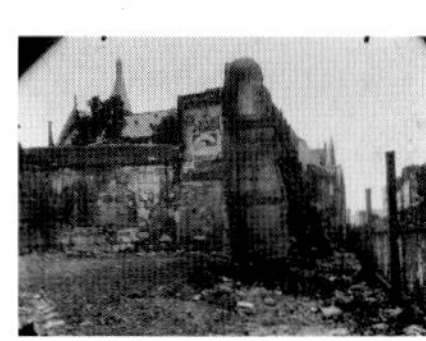

7.89 page 159
Demolition site, view along the rue Saint-Jacques, August 1914
Unmounted gelatin silver chloride print
17.6 x 22.2 cm (image and sheet)
Inscriptions. Recto: BN stamp l.c. on print. Verso: c.l., *Le choeur de L'Eglise S^{t} / Severin en Aout 1914*; u.l., *1643*
Series T 1643 MH38581N
BN T42419
(reproduction: CNMHS)

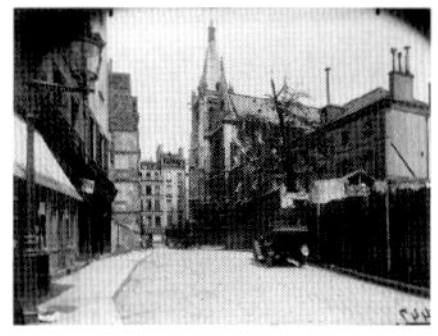

7.96 page 165
Rue des Prêtres-Saint-Séverin, toward the presbytery and the church, June 1923
Unmounted mat albumen silver print
17.5 x 23 cm (image and sheet)
Inscriptions. Verso: l.l., *Rue des Pretres St Severin*; u.l., *6447*; Atget stamp c.; below stamp, *17 bis*
Series AP 6447 MH87034N
MC Ph 3835 (page 10 in the album *Vieux Paris, Coins Pittoresques*)

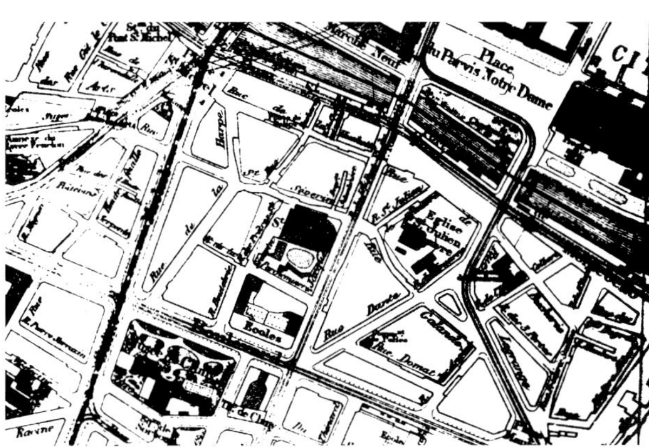

Detail of 1920 map, showing the Church of Saint-Séverin

Notes

Chapter 1: Observing Eugène Atget

1. These views are reproduced in John Szarkowski and Maria Morris Hambourg, *The Work of Atget: Volume II. The Art of Old Paris* (New York: The Museum of Modern Art, 1982), pl. 34 and fig. 30.

2. For reproductions of Atget's reflection in glass doors, see Szarkowski and Hambourg, *Old Paris*, pls. 58 and 63–65.

3. As discussed in chapter 3, the reconstruction of the order in which Atget made these two negatives derives from his normal practice, the overall view followed by the detail. On the same visit, Atget made two views of the base of the staircase; these are negatives numbered 4957 and 4959, also from the series *L'Art dans le vieux Paris*.

4. Atget first photographed the convent in 1900, negatives 3906–09 from his series *L'Art dans le vieux Paris*. In 1914, he made a further sixteen views; these are numbered 1586–96 from the series *Topographie du vieux Paris*, and negatives 6133–37 from the series *L'Art dans le vieux Paris*. The Institut catholique de Paris is located at 70 rue de Vaugirard.

Chapter 2: Atget's Life As a Commercial Photographer

1. Abbott's collection, comprising approximately 1,300 glass-plate negatives, 8,500 prints (representing approximately 5,000 negatives), 118 reference albums, Atget's *Répertoire*, and the album *L'Art dans le vieux Paris*, was purchased by the Museum of Modern Art in 1968.

2. Abbott's typewritten transcription of Calmettes' now lost letter is published in Szarkowski and Hambourg, *Old Paris*, 32–33. The quotations in this paragraph are excerpted from the English translation in Berenice Abbott, *The World of Atget* (New York: Horizon, 1964), xi–xiii.

3. For Abbott's writings on Atget, which draw substantially on Calmettes' information, see among others, "Eugène Atget," *Creative Art* 5, no. 3 (1929): 651–56; "Eugène Atget," *The Complete Photographer* 6, no. 6 (1941): 335–39; and *The World of Atget*. Photographs from Abbott's collection provided the images for *Atget: Photographe de Paris* (Paris: Henri Jonquières; New York: E. Weyhe, 1930), and Arthur D. Trottenberg, ed., *A Vision of Paris: The Photographs of Eugène Atget, The Words of Marcel Proust* (New York: Macmillan, 1963). In addition to selling individual photographs, including both original Atget prints and reprints, in 1956 Abbott published the portfolio *Twenty Photographs by Eugène Atget 1856–1927*, comprising twenty gold-toned gelatin silver prints in a limited edition of 100. For Abbott's promotion of Atget, see Maria Morris Hambourg, "Eugène Atget, 1857–1927: The Structure of the Work" (Ph.D. diss., Columbia University, 1980), 14–17, 21, 24–25, and 30–31, and Hank O'Neal, *Berenice Abbott, American Photographer* (New York: McGraw-Hill, 1982), 11 ff.

4. The most important researchers have been Jean Leroy, Maria Morris Hambourg, and Molly Nesbit. Leroy's research began in 1957 and was gradually published in a number of articles, notably "Who was Eugène Atget?" *Camera* 41, no. 12 (1962): 6–8, before appearing in *Atget, magicien du vieux Paris et son époque* (Paris: Pierre Jean Balbo éditeur, 1975); a second, revised edition was published in 1992. In addition to Hambourg's 1980 dissertation, she also co-authored with John Szarkowski a four-volume set of publications, *The Work of Atget* (New York: The Museum of Modern Art, 1981–1985). The individual volumes are *Volume 1: Old France* (1981); *Volume 2: The Art of Old Paris* (1982); *Volume 3: The Ancien Regime* (1983); and *Volume 4: Modern Times* (1985). See also her "Atget, Precursor of Modern Documentary Photography," in David Featherstone, ed., *Observations: Essays on Documentary Photography: Untitled*, no. 35 (Carmel, California: The Friends of Photography, 1984): 24–39. Nesbit's thesis was "Atget's Book, *L'Art dans le vieux Paris*: Tradition and the Individual Photographic Talent" (master's thesis, Yale University, 1976). Her dissertation "Atget's Seven Albums, in Practice" (Ph.D. diss., Yale University, 1983) was published as *Atget's Seven Albums* (New Haven and London: Yale University Press, 1992). See also her "The Use of History," *Art in America* 74, no. 2 (1986): 72–83, and "'In the absence of the parisienne. . . .'" in Beatriz Colomina, ed. *Sexuality & Space*, (New York: Princeton Architectural Press, 1992): 307–25. In addition, the work of Atget has become known through a number of exhibitions and related publications drawn from the collection of the Musée Carnavalet. See Molly Nesbit and Françoise Reynaud, *Eugène Atget 1857–1927. Intérieurs parisiens* (Paris: Musée Carnavalet / Mois de la Photo, 1982), re-edited as *Intérieurs parisiens: un album du Musée Carnavalet* (Paris: Paris-Musées / Éditions Carré, 1992); Françoise Reynaud and Sophie Grossiord, *Atget, Géniaux, Vert: Petits métiers et types parisiens vers 1900* (Paris: Musée Carnavalet / Mois de la Photo, 1984); and Françoise Reynaud, *Les voitures d'Atget au Musée Carnavalet* (Paris: Paris-Musées/ Éditions Carré, 1992).

5. Various documents are published in Hambourg, "Eugène Atget," 395–467; Nesbit, "Seven Albums," 355–67. A summary of transcribed interviews in the Atget archives at the Museum of Modern Art is listed in Szarkowski and Hambourg, *Old Paris*, 40–41.

6. Full biographical information on Atget are found in Hambourg, "Eugène Atget," Leroy, *Atget*, 37–102, and her "A Biography of Eugène Atget," in Szarkowski and Hambourg, *Old Paris*, 9–39.

7. Hambourg, "Eugène Atget," 57–61 and 158–178; and Nesbit, *Seven Albums*, 28–41.

8. On these developments, see Anthony Sutcliffe, *The Autumn of Central Paris: the Defeat of Town Planning, 1850–1970* (London: Edward Arnold, 1970): 179–212.

9. On Atget's relationship with institutions and amateurs of *le vieux Paris*, see Hambourg, "Eugène Atget," 195–204, and Nesbit, *Seven Albums*, 62–75. On Atget's relationship with Detaille and Sardou, see Hambourg, "Eugène Atget," 60–61 and 198, and Nesbit, *Seven Albums*, 29–31 and 63.

10. Since this study deals solely with Atget's photographs in Paris, a discussion of his concurrent photography of the surrounding royal parks and villages in the Ile-de-France region has been omitted. This comprised approximately 3,500 negatives. On these other series, see Hambourg, "Eugène Atget," 158–178 and 190–204; Szarkowski and Hambourg,

Old France and *Ancien regime*; and *Catalogue de photographies anciennes: Fonds Atget, Hauts-de-Seine* (Département des Hauts-de-Seine, Centre de documentation du Musée de l'Ile-de-France, Château de Sceaux, 1991). On Atget's complex classification and numbering system, see Barbara Michaels, "An Introduction to the Dating and Organization of Eugène Atget's Photographs," *Art Bulletin* 61, no. 3 (1979): 460–68; and especially Hambourg's extended discussion in "Eugène Atget," 103–57.

11. Atget developed this series continuously until 1927, and it eventually comprised approximately 2,225 photographs, which were numbered, with gaps, from 3500 to 6721. According to Hambourg ("Eugène Atget," 182, 184, and 189), Atget referred to this series as *Vieux Paris* before 1905 and after 1921 but between these dates as *L'Art dans le vieux Paris*.

12. This series eventually comprised approximately 900 photographs. It was divided into three separate sections, each of which was separately numbered; see Hambourg, "Eugène Atget," 178–81 and 204–19. On the *petits métiers*, see Reynaud and Grossiord, *Atget, Géniaux, Vert*, and Guillaume Le Gall, *Atget, Paris pittoresque* (Paris: Éditions Hazan, 1998).

13. The series included 1,630 negatives, numbered from 10 to 1676, with a break between 1325 and 1360. Atget added nine images in 1919 (numbers 1687–1695). In preparing his captions, Atget relied extensively upon the second edition of Felix, Marquis de Rochegude's 1903 *Guide pratique à travers le vieux Paris: Maisons historiques ou curieuses, anciens hôtels, pouvant être visités en trent-trois itinéraires détaillés*; see Nesbit, "Seven Albums," 274–77, and *Seven Albums*, 106 and 227, note 3. This series is exhaustively treated in Hambourg, "Eugène Atget," 234–314. Related to this series was the briefer commission *Topographie des Tuileries* (Topography of the Tuileries), which Atget also carried out for the Bibliothèque historique de la Ville de Paris in 1910–1911. This was a systematic survey of the garden's sculpture, independently numbered from 100 to 348; see Hambourg, "Eugène Atget," 290–93, and Nesbit, *Seven Albums*, 68–71.

14. On Marville's documentation of Paris, see Marie de Thézy, *Marville, Paris* (Paris: Éditions Hazan, 1994), and *Charles Marville, Photographs of Paris, 1852–1878*, exhibition catalogue (New York: Alliance Française, 1981).

15. For two examples of Atget's working concurrently on more than one series, see the discussions of the passage des Singes in Chapter 3, and the Hôtel de Ranes, 21 rue Visconti, in the catalogue.

16. All of Atget's prints were contact-printed by means of the sun. Since the color and contrast of albumen prints are directly related to the intensity of ultraviolet radiation, printing in the summer was clearly preferable. As well, the sensitivity of albumen paper is greatly reduced in temperatures below 5° C. See James Reilly, *The Albumen & Salted Paper Book: The History and Practice of Photographic Printing, 1840–1895* (Rochester: Light Impressions, 1980), 70–74. Atget's 1903 correspondence with the Victoria and Albert Museum reveals that he was printing images in February; see Hambourg, "Eugène Atget," 72 and 411–12.

17. See "Records of Atget's Sales to the Paris Institutions, 1898–1928," in Nesbit, *Seven Albums*, 260–70.

18. These two different types of albums are described in Hambourg, "Eugène Atget," 108–09 and 123–29. See also Nesbit, *Seven Albums*, 82–83. In Atget's letter to Léon of 22 November 1920, he refers to sending him "vingt-cinq albums représentant mille cinquante trois clichés" (Leroy, *Atget* [1992], 31).
19. In 1904, Atget sold a paper-bound album on the church of Saint-Gervais-Saint-Protais to the Musée Carnavalet. On this album, see Guillaume Le Gall, "Eugène Atget: L'Album Saint-Gervais-et-Protais" (master's thesis, Université Paris X Nanterre, 1995).
20. Atget first sold the photographs as a set of sixty mounted prints to the Bibliothèque historique de la Ville de Paris on July 6, 1910, then as a paper-bound album with a printed cover to the Musée Carnavalet on August 27, and finally as a leather-bound album to the Bibliothèque nationale on January 6, 1911; see Nesbit, *Seven Albums*, 119. See also Nesbit and Reynaud, *Intérieurs parisiens*.
21. These albums are exhaustively treated in Nesbit, *Seven Albums*.
22. The sales figures in this paragraph are drawn from the information in "Records of Atget's Sales to the Paris Institutions, 1898–1928," in Nesbit, *Seven Albums*, 260–70.
23. The principal source of information concerning Atget's clients and his business practices derives from his notebook, known as the *Répertoire*, now in the collection of the Museum of Modern Art. This notebook provides information on individual clients' interests, their addresses, and indicates suitable times to visit them. See Hambourg, "Eugène Atget," 74–79, and Nesbit, *Seven Albums*, 20–27 and 271–84.
24. Nesbit, *Seven Albums*, 28–79.
25. The will is reproduced in facsimile in Leroy, *Atget* (1992), 48.
26. The entire correspondence is reproduced in facsimile in Leroy, *Atget* (1992), 30–37. The translations are my own.
27. See Hambourg, "Eugène Atget," 335–36, and Szarkowski and Hambourg, *Ancien Regime*, 31, note 51.
28. Only the list of negatives survives; it is published in Nesbit, "Seven Albums," 365–67.
29. It is not clear whether these negatives were sold or given to the government; see Hambourg and Szarkowski, *Old France*, 152.

Chapter 3: Atget at Work

1. That Atget has so prominently positioned himself, when he could have partially or entirely hidden his presence behind one of the window mullions, further supports the interpretation that this was conceived in part as a self-portrait.
2. Berenice Abbott, "Eugène Atget," *The Complete Photographer* 6, no. 6 (1941), 338.
3. On Atget's camera and technique, see Hambourg, "Eugène Atget," 66–67 and pl. 11–18, where she reproduces a contemporary advertisement for the type of camera probably used by Atget.
4. Abbott, *The World of Atget*, xxviii.
5. The camera must also have allowed Atget some degree of lateral movement, since the vignetting is not always symmetrical.
6. Abbott, "Eugène Atget," *The Complete Photographer*, 338.
7. It remains uncertain whether, in exposing his negatives, Atget used a cable release or removed the lens cover, and his practice may have varied with different lighting condi-

tions. In *The Complete Photographer*, pp. 338–39, Abbott wrote that "Atget made a practice of closing down to a very small aperture, he told me, and giving long exposures." In all likelihood, for interiors, he probably made his exposures by removing the lens cover, a supposition supported by interior views that reveal his camera: See, for example his photograph of one of the fireplaces in the Hôtel Matignon, at 57 rue de Varenne (Szarkowski and Hambourg, *Old Paris*, pl. 34), or "Intérieur de Mme D Petite rentière Bd du Port Royal," (Nesbit and Reynaud, *Intérieurs parisiens*, pl. 6).

8. During 1898 and 1899, Atget normally made single views of sites, although he occasionally devoted several views to one. For example, in early October 1899, Atget took four views of the partially demolished *hôtel* at 17 rue Laffitte (titled "Palais de la Reine Hortense" and numbered 3755–58 in the series *L'Art dans le vieux Paris*). By June 1900, when he made seven views of the Church of Saint-Germain de Charonne (numbers 3848–54 from the series *L'Art dans le vieux Paris*), Atget was routinely devoting two, and often several, views to each site.

9. These are reproduced in Szarkowski and Hambourg, *Old Paris*, pl. 50–51.

10. For examples, see catalogue entries 1.11 and 1.12; 1.13 and 1.14; 2.4 and 2.5; 3.11 and 3.12; 4.7 and 4.8; 4.9 and 4.10; 7.50 and 7.51; 7.78 and 7.79; 7.83 and 7.84; and 7.88 and 7.89. The earliest example that I have found of this practice comprises two views of the facade of the Church of Saint-Gervais-et-Protais taken in 1899 (numbers 3634 and 3635 from the series *L'Art dans le vieux Paris*).

11. The rue des Prêtres-Saint-Germain-L'Auxerrois now terminates at the rue de l'Arbre Sec.

12. On Baldus, see Barry Bergdoll, "A Matter of Time: Architects and Photographers in Second Empire France," in *The Photographs of Édouard Baldus* (New York: The Metropolitan Museum of Art; Montreal: Canadian Centre for Architecture, 1994), 99–119.

13. Once one photograph from a site has been identified, it is a relatively straightforward matter to reassemble all of the related images by examining photographs with contiguous numbers, and by cross-checking other topographically related series Atget was developing at the same time. This process is facilitated by the topographical arrangement of Atget's photographs in the Musée Carnavalet, the Bibliothèque historique de la Ville de Paris, and the Bibliothèque nationale. The passage des Singes runs between 6 rue des Guillemites and 43 rue Vieille-du-Temple. This group of photographs is also discussed in Hambourg, "Eugène Atget," 262–64.

14. This reconstructed sequence is supported by the location of the adjacent negatives. The proceeding negative (1088 from the series *Topographie du Vieux Paris*) was made along the rue Vieille-du-Temple, and the two succeeding ones (1094–1095) were made along the rue des Guillemites.

15. This photograph forms plate 33 in his album *Métiers, boutiques et étages de Paris*; see Nesbit, *Seven Albums*, 252 and 374.

16. Lacking written documentation, estimations concerning Atget's daily output derive entirely from the evidence of surviving numbered negatives. It can never be known, to consider one possibility, how many negatives, after being developed, Atget deemed unsuccessful or redundant, and may have destroyed. Hambourg has suggested that Atget may

have carried twelve plates on day excursions from Paris, based upon the groups of consecutively numbered photographs that Atget made at the same location; see "Eugène Atget," 246–47.

Chapter 4: Seven Parisian Sites

1. During Atget's lifetime, the Musée Carnavalet collected not only photographs of the city of Paris but also ones of the Ile-de-France region. The Musée de l'Ile de France, occupying the Château de Sceaux, was created in 1930; in 1937, the Musée Carnavalet transferred all of its non-Parisian holdings to this museum. See *Fonds Atget*, 8–13.

2. The creation of the Voie Georges Pompidou has completely changed the sections of the port du Louvre and port de la Mégisserie adjacent to the Pont-Neuf on the Right Bank, and the widening of the rue de la Parcheminerie, the rue Saint-Jacques, and rue des Prêtres-Saint-Séverin has altered the neighborhood around the Church of Saint-Séverin.

3. Marquis de Rochegude, *Guide pratique à travers le vieux Paris*, 83.

4. While it is possible to reconstruct the sequence of images that Atget made of the entrance door, and within the courtyard and the vestibule, it is not possible to know in what order he covered these three areas of the *hôtel*.

5. These comprise negatives 966, 967, and 1020–1045 from the series *Topographie du vieux Paris* (although numbers 1032 and 1033 have not been located) and number 5748 from the series *L'Art dans le vieux Paris*.

6. In his 1903 *Guide pratique à travers le vieux Paris*, Rochegude stated that Racine had died in the Hôtel de Ranes in 1699, an error that was corrected in later editions.

7. Atget had previously photographed along the opposite sides of these streets. He recorded the south side of the rue du Parc-Royal in 1907 (negatives 61–63 from the series *Topographie du vieux Paris*) just prior to the demolition of buildings between the rue de Sévigné and the rue Payenne. He may have also omitted the *hôtel* at 4 rue du Parc-Royal from his 1911 survey since he had previously photographed it in 1900 and 1907 (negatives 4250 and 5444 from the series *L'Art dans le vieux Paris*). Earlier, in 1898, 1900, 1903, and 1905, he had extensively documented both the Bibliothèque historique de la Ville de Paris and the Musée Carnavalet, both situated along the east side of the rue de Sévigné (negatives 3530, 3533, 3550, 3560–65, 4080, 4838–39, and 5037–40 from the series *L'Art dans le vieux Paris*).

8. That this day's work ended with negative 1159 (cat. 3.20) is confirmed by the succeeding negative numbers, beginning with number 1160, which comprise views made along the rue des Tournelles on an overcast day.

9. The sequence of photographs comprises negatives 1138–1159 from the series *Topographie du vieux Paris*, except for number 1146 "Terre Plein au Pont-Neuf" (see cat 5.7), and number 1147 "Vieille boutique 8 rue Volta, 3e arr."

10. As part of the photographs taken on the sunny afternoon, Atget made three views along the rue de Furstenberg (negatives 988–990 from the series *Topographie du vieux Paris*), and possibly one view along the rue de l'Abbaye (negative 995); and as part of the work on the overcast day, he made two additional views along the rue de l'Échaudé (negatives 996 and 997).

11. While Atget photographed the bridges, quays, and ports along the river Seine during

his entire career, he intensively photographed them between 1911 and 1913 as part of his series *Paris pittoresque*. Beginning with the quai de Montebello, he systematically worked in a westerly direction along the Left Bank as far as the Pont Royal, adding photographs in small increments of between two and eight images. Having reached the Pont Royal, he crossed the river and worked along the Right Bank as far as the Pont de Sully, but in a less systematic manner. In 1913, he added four images of the Port de l'Hôtel de Ville and seventeen views of the quays along both sides of the river between the Pont Royal and the pont des Invalides. Atget may have originally intended this group of photographs to form a similar album to the six that he sold to the Bibliothèque Nationale between 1911 and 1915, but was prevented from completing the project because of the war; see Hambourg, "Eugène Atget," 216, note 1.

12. The sequence of views around the quai du Vert-Galant were made under two different lighting conditions. The first three views (negatives 273–75 from the series *Paris pittoresque*, together with possibly negative 1146 [cat. 5.7] from the series *Topographie du vieux Paris*) were taken on an overcast day, while the final four (numbers 280–83 from the series *Paris pittoresque*) were made on a sunny afternoon.

13. In reaching this figure, only the photographs of the church and the streets immediately bordering it have been included.

Chapter 5: Conclusion

1. Some researchers have been aware of Atget's method of working, even if in their own writings they have concentrated upon other aspects of his practice. While, to cite one example, Hambourg and Szarkowski present Atget's photographs in the plate section of *The Work of Atget* as individual images, they frequently discuss the larger context in their invaluable "Notes to the Plates" in each of the four volumes. See also, Hambourg, "Eugène Atget," 187, 239, and 249–61. The only study that specifically addresses the issue of sequencing in Atget's work is Ulrich Keller's stimulating article, "The Twilight of the Masterpiece: Photography's Problematic Adaptation to the Art Space," *CMP Bulletin* 6, no. 1 (1987): 2–12.

2. Abbott, *The World of Atget*, ix.

Selected Bibliography

Abbott, Berenice. "Eugène Atget." *Creative Art* 5, no. 3 (1929): 651–56.

———. "Eugène Atget, Forerunner of Modern Photography." *U.S. Camera* 1, no. 2 (Autumn 1940): 20–23, 48–49, 76; and 1, no. 13 (Winter 1940): 68–71.

———. "Eugène Atget." *The Complete Photographer* 6, no. 6 (1941): 335–39.

———. *The World of Atget*. New York: Horizon, 1964.

Atget: Photographe de Paris. Introduction by Pierre Mac Orlan. Paris: Henri Jonquières, 1930; New York: E. Weyhe, 1930. Also published as *Eugène Atget: Lichtbilder*. Introduction by Camille Recht. Leipzig: Henri Jonquières, 1930.

Beaumont-Maillet, Laure. *Atget Paris*. Paris: Éditions Hazan, 1992.

Bergdoll, Barry. "A Matter of Time: Architects and Photographers in Second Empire France," in *The Photographs of Édouard Baldus*, 99–119. New York: The Metropolitan Museum of Art; Montreal: Canadian Centre for Architecture, 1994.

Borcoman, James. *Eugène Atget, 1857–1927*. Ottawa: National Gallery of Canada, 1984.

Buisine, Alain. *Eugène Atget ou la mélancholie en photographie*. Nîmes: Éditions Jacqueline Chambon, 1994.

Catalogue de photographies anciennes: Fonds Atget, Hauts-de-Seine. Départment des Hauts-de-Seine, Centre de documentation du Musée de l'Ile-de-France, Château de Sceaux, 1991.

Christ, Yuan. *Saint-Germain-des-Prés 1900, vu par Atget*. Paris: Comité de la Quinzaine, 1951.

———. *Le Paris d'Atget*. Paris: Balland, 1971.

Eugène Atget: A Selection of Photographs from the Collection of the Musée Carnavalet, Paris. Introduction by Françoise Reynaud. Translated by Gill Bennett. Paris: Centre national de la photographie. New York: Pantheon Books, 1985.

Fraser, John. "Atget and the City." *Cambridge Quarterly* 3 (1968): 199–233.

Hambourg, Maria Morris. "Eugène Atget, 1857–1927: The Structure of the Work." Ph.D. diss., Columbia University, 1980.

———. "Atget, Precursor of Modern Documentary Photography," in *Observations: Essays on Documentary Photography: Untitled*, no. 35, edited by David Featherstone, 24–39. Carmel, Calif.: The Friends of Photography, 1984.

Hambourg, Maria Morris and Marie de Thézy. *Charles Marville, Photographs of Paris, 1852–1878*. Exhibiton catalogue. New York: Alliance Française, 1981.

Hillairet, Jacques. *Dictionnaire historique des rues de Paris.* 8th ed., 2 vols. Paris: Les Éditions de Minuit, 1985.

Johnson, William. "Eugène Atget: A Chronological Bibliography." *Exposure* 15, no. 2 (May 1977): 13–15.

Keller, Ulrich. "The Twilight of the Masterpiece: Photography's Problematic Adaptation to the Art Space." *CMP Bulletin* 6, no. 1 (1987): 2–12.

Kozloff, Max. "Abandoned and Seductive: Atget's Streets," in *The Privileged Eye: Essays on Photography.* Albuquerque: University of New Mexico Press, 1987: 279–304.

Krauss, Rosalind. "Photography's Discursive Spaces: Landscape/View." *Art Journal* 41 (1982): 311–19.

Le Gall, Guillaume. "Eugène Atget: L'Album Saint-Gervais-et-Protais." Master's thesis, Université Paris X Nanterre, 1995.

———. *Atget, Paris pittoresque.* Paris: Éditions Hazan, 1998.

Leroy, Jean. "Who Was Eugène Atget?" *Camera* 41, no. 12 (December 1962): 6–8. Reprinted in *Camera* 57, no. 3 (March 1978): 40–42.

———. "Atget et son temps, 1857–1927." *Terre des images* 5–6, no. 3 (1964): 357–72.

———. *Atget, magicien du vieux Paris et son époque*, 2nd ed. Paris: Paris Audiovisuel / Pierre Jean Balbo, 1992.

Michaels, Barbara. "An Introduction to the Dating and Organization of Eugène Atget's Photographs." *Art Bulletin* 61, no. 3 (1979): 460–68.

Nesbit, Molly. "Atget's Book *L'art dans le vieux Paris*: Tradition and the Individual Photographic Talent." Master's thesis, Yale University, 1976.

———. "Atget's Seven Albums, in Practice." Ph.D. diss., Yale University, 1983.

———. "La seconde nature d'Atget." Colloque Atget. Actes du colloque, Collège, de France, 14–15 June 1985. *Photographies.* Numèro hors-serie (March 1986): 20–29.

———. "The Use of History." *Art in America* 74, no. 2 (1986): 72–83.

———. *Atget's Seven Albums.* New Haven and London: Yale University Press, 1992.

———. "'In the absence of the parisienne. . . .'" in *Sexuality & Space*, edited by Beatriz Colomina, 307–25. New York: Princeton Architectural Press, 1992.

———. "Photography and History: Eugène Atget," in *A New History of Photography*, edited by Michel Frizot, 398–409. Translated by Susan Bennett, et al. Cologne: Könemann, 1998.

Nesbit, Molly and Françoise Reynaud. *Eugène Atget 1857–1927. Intérieurs parisiens.* Exhibition catalogue. Paris: Musée Carnavalet / Mois de la Photo, 1982. Re-edited as *Intérieurs parisiens: un album du Musée Carnavalet.* Paris: Paris-Musées / Éditions Carré, 1992.

Puttnies, Hans Georg. *Atget.* Exhibition catalogue. Cologne: Galerie Rudolf Kicken, 1980.

Reilly, James. *The Albumen & Salted Paper Book: The History and Practice of Photographic Printing, 1840–1895*. Rochester: Light Impressions, 1980.

Reynaud, Françoise. "Richesse des collections publiques françaises." Colloque Atget. Actes du colloque, Collège de France, 14–15 June 1985. *Photographies*. Numéro hors-série (March 1986): 93–99.

———. *Les voitures d'Atget au Musée Carnavalet*. Paris: Paris-Musées/Éditions Carré, 1992.

Reynaud, Françoise and Sophie Grossiord. *Atget, Géniaux, Vert: Petits métiers et types parisiens vers 1900*. Exhibition catalogue. Paris: Musée Carnavalet / Mois de la Photo, 1984.

Rochegude, Félix, marquis de. *Guide pratique à travers le vieux Paris: Maisons historiques ou curieuses, anciens hôtels, pouvant être visités en trent-trois itinéraires détaillés*. Paris: Hachette, 1903.

Solomon-Godeau, Abigail. "Canon Fodder: Authoring Eugène Atget," in *Photography at the Dock: Essays on Photographic History, Institutions, and Practices*. Minneapolis: University of Minnesota Press, 1991: 28–51.

Sutcliffe, Anthony. *The Autumn of Central Paris: The Defeat of Town Planning, 1850–1970*. London: Edward Arnold, 1970.

Szarkowski, John. "Atget." *Album* no. 3 (April 1970): 4–12.

———. "Atget's Trees." In *One Hundred Years of Photographic History: Essays in Honor of Beaumont Newhall*, edited by Van Deren Coke, 161–68. Albuquerque: University of New Mexico Press, 1975.

Szarkowski, John and Maria Morris Hambourg. *The Work of Atget*. Vol. 1, *Old France*; Vol. 2, *The Art of Old Paris*; Vol. 3, *The Ancien Regime*; Vol. 4, *Modern Times*. New York: The Museum of Modern Art, 1981–1985.

Szegedy-Maszak, Andrew. *Atget's Churches*. Exhibition catalogue. Middletown, Conn.: Davison Art Center, Wesleyan University, 1992.

Thézy, Marie de. "Marville et la naissance du Paris d'Haussmann." Colloque Atget. Actes du colloque, Collège de France, 14–15 June 1985. *Photographies*. Numéro hors-série (March 1986): 46–51.

———. *Marville Paris*. Paris: Éditions Hazan, 1994.

A Vision of Paris: The Photographs of Eugène Atget, The Words of Marcel Proust, edited by Arthur D. Trottenberg. New York: Macmillan, 1963.

Maps and Plans

Hotel de Beauvais, plan of the ground floor (page 175)
Engraving by J. Marot in J. F. Blondel, *L'Architecture française* (Paris: Jombert, 1752–1756)

Rue Visconti (page 175)
Intersection of the rue de l'Abbaye, the rue Cardinale, the rue de l'Échaudé, the Passage de la Petite-Boucherie, and the rue Bourbon-le-Château, (page 187)
Detail from the map in Alexis Martin, *Les étapes d'un touriste in France: Paris promenades dans les vingt arrondissements, sixième arrondissement* (Paris: A Hennuyer, 1900)

Rue François Miron (page 175)
Rue du Parc-Royal, the Rue de Sévigné, the Rue de Jarente, and the Rue de Turenne (page 177)
Detail from the map in Alexis Martin, *Les étapes d'un touriste in France: Paris promenades dans les vingt arrondissements, quatrième arrondissement* (Paris: A Hennuyer, 1900)

Quays along the river Seine (page 178)
Detail of the map in Alexis Martin, *Les étapes d'un touriste in France: Paris promenades dans les vingt arrondissements, premier arrondissement* (Paris: A Hennuyer, 1900)

Place Bernard Halpern (page 180)
Neighborhood of the Church of Saint-Séverin in 1900 (page 181)
Details from the map in Alexis Martin, *Les étapes d'un touriste in France: Paris promenades dans les vingt arrondissements, cinquième arrondissement* (Paris: A Hennuyer, 1900)

Church of Saint-Séverin, plan (page 183)
Engraving in Marquis de Rochegude and Maurice Dumolin, *Guide practique à travers le vieux Paris: nouvelle édition entièrement refondue avec 69 croquis* (Paris: Librairie ancienne Edouard Champion, n.d.)

Neighborhood of the church of Saint-Séverin in 1920 (page 187)
Detail from the map in *Atlas Municipal des vingt arrondissements de la Ville de Paris. Edition révisée en 1919 par les Soins de M. J.-M. Petit, Géomètre en chef avec le concours des géomètres du Plan de Paris, sous l'administration de M. A. Autrand, Préfet de la Seine, de la direction de M. Malherbe, directeur général des travaux de Paris et du département de la Seine, M. P. Doumerc, directeur de l'extension de Paris, M. L. Bonnier, inspecteur général des services techniques d'architecture de d'esthétique de al Préfecture de la Seine*, 1920.

Photographic Credits

Archives photographiques de la direction du Patrimoine au fort de Saint-Cyr
Eugène Atget © Arch. phot. / CNMHS, Paris
Catalogue: 7.90, 7.91

Bibliothèque historique de la Ville de Paris
© Reproduction: Centre de restauration et de conservation des photographies de la Ville de Paris (CRCP), photographer Daniel Lifermann: p. 44 t. l., 47–51, 54 b. l., 57 b. l. / catalogue: 1.10, 2.2, 2.3, 2.6, 3.9, 7.85, 7.86, 7.88

Bibliothèque nationale de France
© Bibliothèque nationale de France
p. 91, 153, 156, 157 / catalogue 7.87

Caisse nationale des monuments historiques et des sites
Eugène Atget © Arch. phot. / CNMHS, Paris
p. 154, 155, 158, 159 / catalogue 7.85, 7.86

Private collection
© Paris-Musées, photographer Karin Maucotel: p. ii

Musée Carnavalet
© Photothèque des musées de la Ville de Paris, photographers Irène Andréani, Rémi Briant, Lyliane Degrâces, Phillippe Joffre, Philippe Ladet, Daniel Lifermann and Patrick Pierrain: p. ii, 2–7, 16, 18–22, 25, 27–35, 39–43, 44 t. r. and b. r., 45, 53, 54 t. r. and b. r., 55, 56, 57 t. r. and b. r., 58–65, 67–87, 89, 90, 95–105, 107–113, 115–121, 123, 125–139, 141–151, 161–165 / catalogue: 1.1, 1.4, 1.6, 1.8, 1.16, 1.17, 3.10, 3.19, 3.20, 4.4, 4.5, 7.3, 7.4, 7.8, 7.9, 7.10, 7.12, 7.17, 7.19, 7.20, 7.34, 7.38, 7.39, 7.40, 7.41, 7.45, 7.48, 7.49, 7.50, 7.56, 7.58, 7.66, 7.68

Original Book Design
Atalante / Paris